TEACHING ABROAD

**Edited by
Edrice Marguerite Howard
and Carol Weeg**

The Institute gratefully acknowledges special grant support
from the United States Information Agency, which made
publication of this book possible.

 *INSTITUTE OF INTERNATIONAL EDUCATION
809 UNITED NATIONS PLAZA, NEW YORK, N.Y. 10017*

Production Editor: Ellen L. Goodman
Copy Editor: Lynn Anderson
Indexer: Anne K. Wolf
Production Assistant: Lisa C. Rhoades
Cover Art: Christoph Blumrich

Fourth Edition.
Copyright © 1988 Institute of International Education
All rights reserved.
Printed in the United States of America.
ISBN: 87206-142-6

CONTENTS

PART 2: Study Opportunities Abroad for Teachers

HOW TO USE THIS BOOK

BACKGROUND INFORMATION

Today increasing numbers of U.S. educators and educational administrators are interested in teaching and working in other countries. In response to their need for information on the availability of suitable positions and how to locate them, plus guidance on living and working in another country, IIE has prepared this new, expanded, and revised edition of *Teaching Abroad*. The information contained in this book can help educators plan and prepare for what may be one of the most rewarding experiences of a lifetime.

Part 1 describes employment opportunities abroad on every educational level—from prekindergarten and primary grades to university, senior scholar, and professional education. Areas of teaching represented include general academic subjects, physical education, special education, adult/continuing education, vocational/technical fields, and English as a second language.

Administrative openings exist on all levels, as well. Although most of the administrative opportunities listed are not categorized by type of position or level, specific openings have been mentioned wherever an organization provided this information.

Both full-time and part-time positions are listed at a variety of institutions—U.S.-owned and -operated, international, and foreign; public and private; religious and lay institutions. In addition, Part 1 lists post-for-post exchange programs, lecturing and research opportunities for senior scholars, unpaid volunteer positions, and government programs for U.S. nationals. There are possibilities for recent graduates seeking their first job experience, for seasoned professionals, and for retirees interested in a rewarding experience in a different culture.

Part 2 describes nearly 200 study programs of interest to teachers and administrators. They represent the gamut of professional courses, language study on all levels, courses in teaching foreign languages, and background courses in the civilization and culture of the host country.

Additions and Suggestions

We are always pleased to receive information on schools or job opportunities not listed in this edition, as well as suggestions for improving the book. Write to: Edrice Marguerite Howard, Editor, IIE Publications, 809 United Nations Plaza, New York, NY 10017. Please enclose background information on the institution or organization when you write to us.

Using the Book

IIE tries to make the information contained in this book as accurate and useful as possible. Bear in mind, however, that information-gathering in publishing takes place long before a book appears, and that work and study opportunities and requirements can change dramatically from year to year—and even from day to day. For this reason, it's a good idea to use this book as a *general resource* for locating positions of interest. We strongly suggest that interested teachers and administrators contact specific schools or organizations for more detailed information.

To derive maximum benefit from *Teaching Abroad,* be sure to read this section, "HOW TO USE THIS BOOK," carefully. It explains how the entries are organized and the various terms used in the program listings.

The special chapter entitled "PLANNING FOR TEACHING ABROAD" should also be reviewed thoroughly. It describes what to consider in locating a position, how to apply for one, and various aspects of living abroad. Following that is a brief discussion of tax planning for U.S. citizens who work abroad.

PART 1: TEACHING AND ADMINISTRATIVE OPPORTUNITIES ABROAD

The information in Part 1 is based on a survey conducted in August 1987. Questionnaires were sent to all the schools, organizations, and government offices listed in the 1984 edition of the book, as well as to a comprehensive list of other U.S. and foreign government agencies, private organizations that sponsor teacher exchange programs, American and international schools abroad, and foreign schools, colleges, and institutes.

Most respondents returned completed questionnaires accompanied by brochures, catalogs, or other printed materials describing their schools and organizations, giving us a fairly comprehensive picture of their programs. In other cases, only a few items of information were provided by the respondents. For this reason, the listings vary a great deal in length and completeness. In all cases, however, they represent the most accurate and complete description of each organization and program that we have been able to put together from the information provided.

Arrangement of the Listings

The listings are arranged first by the geographical region in which they are located: Africa South of the Sahara, Asia and Oceania, Europe, the Middle East and North Africa, and the Western Hemisphere. Each region is subdivided alphabetically by country and then by city.

In addition to the specific country and city listings, there is a "Worldwide" chapter at the beginning of the book for organizations or schools that operate in more than one region of the world. Similarly, there may be "More Than One Country" listings at the beginning of a chapter and "More Than One City" listings at the front of a country section. Remember to consult these general worldwide, regional, and country sections in addition to listings for specific cities.

Entry Number and Organization Name

Each entry begins with a number used to identify it within the listing sequence and in the indexes at the back of the book.

The name of the organization described in the entry is next. The organizations listed include individual schools, educational organizations, U.S. and foreign governmental bodies, employment agencies, and voluntary and religious organizations.

Program Title

If a listed organization, such as the U.S. Information Agency, offers more than one teaching opportunity, the specific program discussed in the listing will be indicated by the title immediately below the organization name.

General Information Paragraph

The opening paragraph of each entry gives general background information about the organization described, such as the type of school, program, or organization; academic level; the year it was founded; current enrollment (in 1987); the percentage of faculty who are U.S. nationals; and any requirements that would apply to *all* applicants.

The statement "Faculty are recruited locally" indicates that the school does not announce openings in the U.S., but only locally. U.S. citizens would generally be considered for these openings *if they were already living in the country* and saw the announcement or advertisement. In some cases, schools require that applicants already possess work permits; unless they are completely unable to find native staff to fill their needs, they will not attempt to obtain work permits for foreign applicants.

Language of Instruction

This includes the primary language and any other languages of instruction.

Opportunities

Listed are the average number of positions per year for teachers of general curriculum, teachers of English as a second/foreign language (referred to as ESL throughout the book), and educational administrators, and whether those positions are full- or part-time. If applicable, subject areas for general teachers are given.

Requirements

Listed separately for general teachers, ESL teachers, and administrators, requirements include those related to university degrees, teaching or administrative experience, teaching or administrative certification, international experience, and proficiency in a language other than English. Any requirements concerning age, sex, marital status, or religious affiliation not covered in the opening paragraph will also be noted here.

Duration

Average length of contract and renewal options are noted.

Salary

Listed separately for teachers and administrators, the salary is stated with the period of time it covers (calendar year, academic year, etc.). A range in salaries is often based on academic degrees and experience. Where no salary information is given, the survey respondent did not complete this section. In any case, it is always advisable to contact the school or organization for complete current information.

Benefits

Benefits listed may include round-trip transportation from the U.S., housing or housing allowance, paid home leave, insurance, retirement or pension plans, and tuition for dependent children. "Other benefits" may refer to any of the following: settling-in allowance, free classes for the applicant, food allowance, paid utilities, paid trips to conferences, etc. Contact the school or organization for complete information.

Academic Calendar

The opening and closing months of the regular school year are listed here.

Orientation

The duration and location of a pre-assignment orientation, if any, is given here.

Application Deadline

Deadline for submission of application and supportive materials is indicated. A number of responding schools and institutes stated that all applicants must be interviewed, usually at U.S. recruiting fairs.

Contact

Complete contact information for the school, organization, or program described in the listing is given here: the name or title of the individual, full address, phone numbers including country and city codes for use when dialing from the U.S., telex and telefax numbers, and cable addresses, if available.

Where a ministry or embassy indicates that there is no need for U.S. teachers or educational administrators, the ministry/embassy's address is given *only* for the purpose of obtaining general information on education in that country.

PART 2: STUDY OPPORTUNITIES ABROAD FOR TEACHERS

The information in Part 2 is based on a survey conducted in May 1987. Questionnaires were sent to all sponsors of programs listed in the 1987 editions of IIE's study-abroad guides (*Vacation Study Abroad, Academic Year Abroad,* and *Study in the United Kingdom and Ireland*), to organizations that informed IIE of new programs after publication of that edition, and to all U.S. colleges and universities listed in *Accredited Institutions of Postsecondary Education 1986-87,* published by the American Council on Education for the Council on Postsecondary Accreditation.

In addition, this year IIE sought to reach all non-U.S. universities and language schools through the purchase of comprehensive mailing lists of these institutions.

The programs selected for inclusion in this book are those which the sponsoring institution designated as being designed for, open to, or of special interest to teachers and/or educational administrators.

Overall Organization of the Program Listings

As in Part 1, the listing are geographical by the region in which they take place, subdivided alphabetically by country and then by city. Within each city subsection, the arrangement is alphabetical by the name of the sponsoring institution.

Program Sponsor and Name

Each entry begins with a number used to identify the program within the listing sequence and in the indexes at the back of the book. The name of the sponsoring institution is next, followed by the program title.

Location

This line identifies the countries or cities in which resident study takes place. Some programs include incidental travel to other places, which is noted in the "Highlights" section of the entry, but the programs are listed under the country and city where the major portion of resident study takes place.

Dates

Enrollment is generally for the full period indicated here, unless variations are given. Be sure to contact the program sponsor for current information.

Subjects

Courses of study available through the program are listed here, along with information on concentrations and specializations. Consult INDEX II: Fields of Study for assistance in locating programs in your field of interest.

Credit

The availability of academic credit—or a certificate, diploma, or degree—is indicated after this heading. Undergraduate credits are listed first, then graduate credits.

On the graduate level, be especially careful to clarify the awarding of academic credit in advance. Some programs accept graduate students only as auditors.

Eligibility

All the programs in this book have been selected because they include courses designed for or of interest to educators, but some of them may be open to college undergraduates, graduate students ("graduates"), adult or continuing education students ("adults"), and professionals in other fields, as well as teachers.

Other eligibility requirements and course prerequisites are mentioned last in this section and usually require clarification by the sponsor, since space considerations do not permit us to list them fully.

Instruction

The first item provided here is the language in which courses are taught. Where more than one language is listed, consult the program sponsor for exact information. Foreign language courses are usually taught in the language being studied, while other courses may be taught in English. For lecture courses taught exclusively in a foreign language, be sure to determine in advance whether your level of fluency is sufficient to understand the course content.

Entries then indicate the type of courses students attend: courses specifically arranged for the program group (in which most of the participants will be U.S. nationals), special courses for foreigners at a foreign institution (where Americans mingle with other foreign students), or regular courses from the general curriculum of a foreign institution (in these classes, U.S. students can expect to sit next to native students).

The term "foreign faculty" generally refers to instructors native to the host country, while "U.S. faculty" usually means faculty of the sponsoring institution.

Highlights

This section includes information on the year the program was established, orientation, program-related and miscellaneous travel, and the availability of a postsession review. The postsession review, or re-entry session, is designed to help the student analyze, digest, and utilize his or her experiences abroad.

The "program evaluations" mentioned here may vary from comments of former participants to a full academic review by a faculty committee; they are a valuable resource to use in evaluating programs. The phrase "Contact with previous participants available" indicates that, if requested to do so, the sponsor will provide contact with a former student by mail, phone, or in person. This can be extremely helpful both in selecting a program and in preparing for a rewarding experience abroad.

Costs

In this section, we have asked sponsors to provide a fairly complete picture of the main expenses involved in their programs. Where possible, they have given a "package amount" for the full program, followed by a list of the items it includes.

A cost amount followed by "(1987)" indicates that fees for the 1988 program had not yet been set at the time information was submitted for this book; consult the sponsor for current information. The word "about" preceding the amount indicates the sponsor has estimated 1988 program fees; again, contact the sponsor directly for current information.

Housing

Most programs provide housing for members of the group. Entries indicate the type of housing available. Organizations that do not provide living facilities will generally assist in locating available housing in the area.

Deadline

In most cases, deadlines are for the receipt of completed applications with all necessary supporting material: transcripts, recommendations, deposits, etc. Find out well in advance what application material is needed. Occasionally programs will admit students after the deadline if space is still available.

Contact

The primary contact for information and applications is the individual, department, or organization listed first; full addresses, phone numbers, and telex numbers are provided, if available.

IMPORTANT NOTICE

The Institute of International Education does not attempt to review or evaluate the institutions, organizations, and programs listed in this book. Inclusion of a program or organization does not imply IIE recommendation, nor does omission imply IIE disapproval. Applications and additional information must be requested directly from the school or program sponsor, NOT from IIE.

PLANNING FOR TEACHING ABROAD

There are many rewards, both personal and professional, for those who take teaching positions overseas. Many do so to broaden their knowledge of particular subjects, deepen their understanding of other cultures, learn or perfect foreign languages, or gain new perspectives on teaching methods; others simply see overseas teaching as an adventure. What one gains depends on personal goals, expectations, and commitment.

Most teachers who spend time abroad do so for limited assignments of one to three years. It is difficult to measure the benefits that U.S. education receives once these teachers return home. It is inevitable, however, that an international dimension will be brought into the U.S. classroom as a result of this overseas experience. Thus future students, as well as teachers themselves, will benefit from a greater international understanding of the world in which we live.

RESEARCHING THE OPTIONS

Teaching abroad may entail a dramatic change of lifestyle, and there are numerous factors to consider before accepting an assignment. In addition to the obvious professional considerations of finding a position suited to one's academic qualifications, level of experience, and salary requirements, there are also personality, language, geographical, and other factors to examine.

Individual Adaptibility

Each individual must realistically assess his or her ability to adapt to new situations, environments, people, and cultures. Those who adapt readily to unfamiliar circumstances may thrive on the rugged adventure of life in a developing country, for instance, whereas a more timid personality might be well advised to choose a less challenging assignment.

Be careful not to underestimate the amount of adjustment required to live in a foreign milieu for an extended period, particularly if your expectations of a foreign country are based on vacation experiences. Coping with a brief stay in a first-class foreign hotel is one thing; facing day-to-day life in another country for a year or more is another thing entirely.

Language Proficiency

A major difference between traveling and working abroad is the need for language proficiency. Limited knowledge of French, for example, may be sufficient for a week's vacation in Paris but grossly inadequate for a year-long stay in Madagascar.

Most institutions prefer that faculty possess some familiarity with the native language, even if the language of instruction is English. Language classes prior to leaving the United States will help you over the intial period of adjustment; enrolling in a language school or class during your stay abroad can be helpful both in learning the language and in making social contacts.

Geographic Location

Geographic setting may be as important as professional characteristics in determining whether a situation is appropriate for you. Large cities may offer excellent cultural opportunities but tend to be expensive and impersonal. Small towns offer more contact with local residents and a traditional way of life, but some people may find the provincial lifestyle too limiting.

Proximity to friends and activities of interest should also be considered, because social contacts can be vitally important in helping a person overcome the periods of loneliness and disorientation nearly everyone encounters when coping with a strange environment for an extended period of time.

Climate is another important consideration. If you wilt in extreme heat and humidity, for instance, you will certainly want to avoid the tropics. Don't forget to examine such factors as mean temperatures, elevation above sea level, annual rainfall, average humidity, and prevailing seasonal weather conditions. The government tourist office of the country you are considering will usually be happy to provide such information.

The Third World

Teaching in the Third World can be especially meaningful for a variety of reasons. The fact that nearly three-quarters of the world's population live in these nations is bound to have a significant effect on the course of history. From an economic standpoint, it is worth noting that U.S. trade with Third World countries now approaches 40 percent of all U.S. imports and exports. In today's economically interdependent world, knowledge of

Third World nations may prove to be a valuable career asset.

In addition, the cultures of the Third World countries pose a sharp contrast to that of the United States. They effectively challenge our customary assumptions about our own society and values and provide a unique perspective on our larger world role.

One legacy of colonialism in the Third World is that the language of instruction is often English, Spanish, or French rather than the native tongue. This generalization does not apply, however, to countries like China, which has an extensive scientific and technical literature of its own.

Maintaining Ties with the Home School

Another consideration is whether to sever ties with one's U.S. school or institution. Since many positions are short-term (1–2 years), one option is to take an unpaid leave of absence. For assignments shorter than a year, an alternative may be to take a sabbatical for that period of time. Either option would allow teachers to resume their current teaching positions upon their return. Prospective overseas teachers can look to their present schools and their unions or professional organizations for details on these or other alternatives.

Disabled Teachers

Many educational institutions provide facilities for the handicapped. The extent to which disabled faculty can be accommodated, however, depends on the nature of their disabilities and the subject to be taught. Specific needs should be discussed with the school or organization well in advance of departure from the United States.

Information for the handicapped traveler is available from the U.S. branch of Mobility International (MIUSA), which publishes a newsletter and several booklets. For full details, write to MIUSA, P.O. Box 3551, Eugene, OR 97403.

APPLICATION PROCEDURES

As a general rule, applicants should write directly to the school, institution, organization, or government agency concerned at least eight to ten months prior to the beginning of the academic year for which they are seeking a position. At the same time, gather together all supporting materials that may be needed—references, school transcripts, publications, and proof of teaching experience—so that your completed application can be returned with all required documentation shortly after you receive it.

The Employment Interview

After reviewing all documentation, schools may require a personal interview. Personnel officers of some overseas institutions make seasonal trips to the United States specifically to recruit staff and conduct these interviews. In other instances, a U.S. agency may be engaged to handle the interview process. In cases where schools hire only faculty who already reside in their country, applicants may be interviewed at the school itself.

EVALUATING AND CLARIFYING THE JOB OFFER

The importance of clarifying all the conditions and arrangements involved in an assignment *before a job offer is accepted* cannot be underestimated. There are wide variations in working conditions, salary levels, and benefits offered to teachers abroad. Never assume that there will be any similarity between conditions in the United States and those in another country, or that you will be in a better position to discuss these details thousands of miles away from your teachers' union, family, friends, and other support systems.

Working Conditions

In reviewing an offer of employment, be sure that the contract specifies the total number of classroom or actual teaching hours per week, subjects to be taught, adding classes to the teaching load, and any extracurricular requirements.

If another teacher leaves the staff, for instance, can his classes be assigned to you until a replacement is found? If so, will you be paid for the additional work? Will you be expected to take charge of the students' English Club or coach the baseball team, after hours, on a purely voluntary basis? Does the offer of free housing in fact refer to a single room in a student dormitory, where you will be "on call" several nights a week?

It is important to understand that in most cases the school or organization tendering the job offer is dealing in good faith, but conditions viewed as unreasonable in the United States may be the norm elsewhere. While you may be perfectly agreeable to any or all of the above situations, it is still better to have the contract terms spelled out in advance.

Salary and Other Benefits

Although the job offer will almost certainly specify a salary level, there are other benefits that should also be worked out to the teacher's and employer's mutual satisfaction: health and life insurance, educational opportunities, tax advantages, round-trip transportation from the United States, home leave and vacation privileges, housing, and the availability and cost of local medical services.

An educator who expects to be accompanied by a spouse or children must be especially careful to clarify arrangements relating to them. A school may routinely provide staff housing for single teachers, for example, but it may not have facilities for married couples or for families. Round-trip transportation and discounted tuition may be available for two dependent children, but not for three or four.

A flexible individual will probably have little difficulty accepting most of the terms offered by an institution abroad. All the same, knowing what to expect enables you to prepare for the assignment better and helps avoid unpleasant surprises later on.

LIVING ABROAD

As educators, you will hardly need to be reminded to read up on your host country before you depart. Books, periodicals, plays, films, and museum exhibits can provide valuable specific and general background information, as will the country's embassy, consulate, or tourist office.

If your school or organization offers a pre-assignment orientation either in the U.S. or abroad, make every effort to attend. You will learn more not only about your academic milieu, but also about your cultural environment. It's also a good chance to become acquainted with other members of the faculty, probably your most important source of social contacts and local orientation during your stay there.

It's a good idea to read up on your own country before you leave, too. People encountered abroad are frequently curious about the United States, and you can expect to be hit with a barrage of questions about U.S. history, economics, culture, government policies, and current events. To be forewarned is to be forearmed!

Registering at the U.S. Embassy or Consulate

If you expect to reside abroad for more than a few months, it's a good idea to register with the nearest U.S. embassy or consulate. In the event of political unrest, natural disasters, or other emergency situations, the consulate will then be able to contact you in order to provide advice and assistance.

While at the consulate, it will surely be worthwhile to inquire about the locations of other U.S. government facilities in your area. There may be USIS centers, libraries, and other facilities that provide a variety of services to U.S. citizens abroad, including information on local cultural, educational, and social resources.

Government Employment Regulations

Many foreign countries have strict laws regarding paid employment by foreign nationals. This is especially true in times of economic hardship when competition for jobs may be very stiff among the country's citizenry and there is a fear that foreign nationals will assume positions that could be filled by local nationals. It is imperative, therefore, to investigate as soon as possible the regulations concerning work visas or permits in the country of interest.

Often, an individual must possess evidence that employment has been secured before a permit will be issued. Overseas sponsors may make all these arrangements. If not, you should contact the foreign embassy for the particulars of the laws and application procedures.

Passports and Visas

Each U.S. citizen departing from the United States must, in most cases, carry a valid U.S. passport. If a foreign government does not require a U.S. passport, it may require documentary evidence of U.S. citizenship.

If you need a passport, you may apply in person to a passport agent at U.S. Department of State agencies in Boston, Chicago, Honolulu, Houston, Los Angeles, Miami, New Orleans, New York City, Philadelphia, San Francisco, Seattle, Stamford (Connecticut), or Washington, D.C. Passports are also issued through selected post offices, or by clerks of any federal court or state court of records. Proof of U.S. citizenship (birth certificate, naturalization certificate, or previous U.S. passport), two recent photographs (2" x 2"), and current identification with a personal signature and photograph or physical description (such as a driver's license) are required.

A passport valid for ten years costs $35 plus a required $7 execution fee. For dependent children, a five-year passport for citizens under age 18 is $20 plus a required $7 execution fee. You must appear in person if you are applying for the first time, are renewing a passport issued over eight years ago, or were younger than 18 when your last passport was issued. Apply early: processing an application takes *four to six weeks*—longer during the peak travel season.

Visa requirements and arrangements should be checked with the overseas institution or organization to which you are applying. Information on visa requirements may be obtained from foreign embassies in the United States or from *Visa Requirements of Foreign Governments* (Publication M-264) available at any passport agency or by writing to the Office of Passport Services, Room 386, 1425 K Street NW, Washington, DC 20524.

Laws and Customs

Familiarize yourself with the laws and customs of your host country before you leave the United States. It is a mistake to assume that behavior and actions acceptable in the U.S. are appropriate everywhere, or that other countries will excuse inappropriate or illegal acts simply because you are a foreigner. At the very least, inappropriate behavior will tend to alienate you from the local populace. Illegal acts, on the other hand, may result in the loss of your job, deportation from the country, or imprisonment, with very little that the local U.S. consulate can do to help.

Civil rights issues are not the same in many other countries as they are in the U.S. American notions regarding freedom of speech and expression have no parallel in many countries, especially when they contravene long-established customs.

Narcotics laws are strictly enforced overseas, particularly when the offenders are foreigners. Harsh sentences, including life imprisonment or death, are not unknown, even in countries where natives may break such laws with impunity.

Warnings aside, there are few pleasures to compare with the experience of forming friendships with people who have spent their entire lives in a different milieu and who can communicate whole new perspectives on the most ordinary of life's experiences.

Medical Insurance and Other Health Concerns

The importance of having adequate insurance in another country cannot be overestimated. If the school or organization that hires you does not provide insurance, check your U.S. medical and accident insurance policies to be sure they are valid while overseas.

While it is easy to stay healthy abroad, in certain countries this requires taking some elementary precautions. Some countries, particularly those in tropical regions, have bacterial, fungal, and parasitical diseases which can be difficult to cure. Do not hesitate to ask about these during orientation sessions, and take the advice seriously.

Foreign governments also have their own immunization requirements. Check current regulations with your local public health department.

If you require prescription medicines, even intermittently, be aware that foreign drugs are not necessarily closely related to those standard in the United States. Drugs may be marketed under different names and may not be available in the strengths you desire. Try to bring an adequate supply of any medication you need. Label all bottles clearly and carry copies of the prescriptions to avoid problems with Customs. In the case of narcotic medicines, it may not be prudent to carry additional supplies because of possible Customs difficulties. Reasonable amounts of nonprescription drugs, such as aspirin and stomach remedies, can come in handy in some of the more remote regions of the world.

Finally, if you wear prescription eyeglasses or contact lenses, bring an extra pair and your prescription. This is particularly important with contact lenses, because the specific type of lens you wear may not be available abroad.

Transportation

Many job opportunities include transportation to and from the school. In others, faculty make their own arrangements. If this is the case for you, a good place to begin researching your travel options is the government tourist office of the country you in which you will be teaching.

Once abroad, if you plan to drive a car, most countries will accept your U.S. driver's license. However, it may be necessary to supplement it with an International Driver's License, which provides a multilingual translation of the information on your U.S. license and is available from your local AAA office.

Railroads are often an economical and convenient way to travel. In many countries, rail passes offer unlimited train travel at considerable savings to those who travel extensively. Rail passes are available from many travel agencies and, in some cases, must be purchased in the United States before your departure.

STUDY ABROAD

Although living abroad is a learning experience in itself, you may want to avail yourself of the opportunity to learn or perfect your knowledge of the language and culture of your host country, to continue studies toward an advanced degree or diploma, or to develop a completely new skill or activity. In most countries, there are courses available at language schools, adult education centers, graduate schools, continuing education programs of universities, sporting clubs, and professional organizations, to name a few possibilities.

Part 2 of this book lists nearly 200 study opportunities abroad for educators. Many additional study programs are described in the other IIE study-abroad books, *Vacation Study Abroad*, *Academic Year Abroad*, and *Study in the United Kingdom and Ireland*. For current prices and ordering information, write to: Publications Service, Institute of International Education, 809 United Nations Plaza, New York, NY 10017.

If you cannot find study opportunities listed for the area in which you will be living, check with the director or personnel officer of your host school, who may be able to direct you to a source of information on local educational resources. Information may also be available from the ministry of education of your host country or from the U.S. embassy, consulate, or USIS center.

ADDITIONAL INFORMATION

Additional information is available by visiting the IIE Information Center, which maintains an extensive reference collection on teaching and studying abroad. The Center is open to the public from 10:00 AM to 4:00 PM daily except weekends and holidays; on Wednesdays the Center remains open until 7:00 PM.

Please note that the materials in the reference collection are NOT available by mail or phone, but only upon a personal visit to the Center at 809 United Nations Plaza (First Avenue between 45th and 46th streets) in New York City.

TAX PLANNING FOR U.S. EDUCATORS ABROAD

by Ernest R. Larkins
Associate Professor of Accounting
Georgia State University

In addition to many professional and personal benefits, teaching abroad can provide considerable tax benefits. In this chapter, we will review the most important tax rules affecting U.S. educators abroad and provide some general guidelines for utilizing the major exclusions and deductions.

Because of their infinite variety, individual situations are not addressed here. Educators planning to work in another country are advised to discuss their specific circumstances with an experienced tax accountant or attorney well in advance of departure.

Similarly, only the federal income tax laws will be discussed. State laws, although close to the federal law in many cases, can vary substantially. For state tax information, consult *State Tax Guide: All States (1988)* (available from Commerce Clearing House, 4025 W. Peterson Ave., Chicago, IL 60646).

EXCLUSION FOR WORKING ABROAD

U.S. citizens and residents are subject to U.S. taxation on their worldwide income. However, Section 911 of the Internal Revenue Code contains two exclusions (that is, income not subject to taxation)—one for foreign earned income and the other for foreign housing costs. The former is limited to an annual amount of $70,000. This exclusion is determined on a daily basis. Consequently, if an individual only qualifies during 30 percent of 1988, the exclusion is only $21,000.

Foreign earned income is all income earned from personal services rendered outside the United States, including salaries, professional fees, overseas allowances, and reimbursements. It does not include investment income, such as dividends or interest. Neither does it include amounts paid to an employee of the U.S. government. Employees of the U.S. State Department schools abroad, for example, are not eligible for these exclusions.

The second exclusion under Section 911 is for a "housing cost amount," which is the educator's housing expenses minus a base amount ($7,469 in 1988). For example, housing expenses of $10,469 would allow an individual to exclude $3,000 ($10,469 minus $7,469) of his salary in addition to excluding the $70,000 mentioned above. Housing expenses include rent or lease payments, the fair rental value of housing provided by an employer, utilities other than telephone expenses, insurance,

nonrefundable fees paid to obtain a lease, rental payments for furniture and accessories, repair and maintenance expenses, and payments for residential parking. Housing expenses do not include the cost of a house or home improvements, the cost of furniture or accessories, payments for domestic labor, interest, taxes, or television subscription fees. In nations with a low cost of living, this exclusion may prove small, while in high-cost areas like Tokyo it can be quite large.

To be eligible for the Section 911 exclusions, a person must have a "tax home" in a foreign country and must meet either foreign residency or foreign presence requirements. Specifically, the individual must be (1) a foreign resident for a period that includes an entire tax year or (2) a person who is physically present abroad for at least 330 days during any period of 12 consecutive months. These requirements are discussed below.

Foreign Tax Home

To claim the Section 911 benefits, an individual must demonstrate that his tax home is located in a foreign country. The term "tax home," as used in Section 911, means the general area of a person's regular place of business. If the educator has two or more businesses, such as a foreign teaching position and a position in the United States, the location of the tax home depends on the amount of time spent abroad, although other factors may also be important.

As a general rule of thumb, foreign stays of less than one year are not long enough to establish the required foreign tax home. Consequently, the Section 911 exclusions normally are not available on temporary assignments. If the visit abroad lasts at least two years, on the other hand, the person is usually considered to have a foreign tax home. Stays abroad between one and two years depend on several complex factors. An individual can usually ensure that he has a foreign tax home by selling his home in the United States, or cancelling his lease, and taking his family abroad.

Foreign Residency Test

In addition to having a foreign tax home, the educator must meet the requirements of either the residency test or the presence test. Only U.S. citizens are eligible for the Section 911 exclusions under the residency test. To qualify, an individual must establish that he has been a resident of a foreign country for an uninterrupted period that includes an entire taxable year.

The courts have held that a person's intention to become a foreign resident must be supported by his actions. In general, anyone desiring to establish foreign residency should break as many ties with the United States as possible and establish new ties in the foreign country. These actions should be documented and placed in a permanent file.

Foreign residency must be established for an uninterrupted period that includes an entire taxable year. By "uninterrupted," the Internal Revenue Code does not mean that trips to the United States, whether business or pleasure, are entirely forbidden. If the trips are too often or too long, however, the educator's residence in the foreign country may be questioned. Trips longer than one month, for example, may result in the loss of foreign residency.

The uninterrupted period of residency must include an entire taxable year. The courts have interpreted this rule literally; that is, the period of residence must be from January 1 through December 31 in at least one taxable year. In one court case, the taxpayer arrived in Australia and established residency on January 3, 1966, and departed during 1967. Consequently, the residency test was not met for either year. If the taxpayer had become a resident of Australia on January 1, 1966, he would have qualified during his entire stay abroad.

Foreign Presence Test

Proving residence in a foreign country may be difficult. For this reason, most U.S. citizens choose the relative certainty of the foreign presence test. To meet this test, the individual must be present in a foreign country for 330 days in a 12-month period. The 330 days need not be consecutive, but only full days count toward the total. Also, the 12-month period does not have to include an entire taxable year, as required by the residence test. So an educator who goes abroad on November 1, 1988, and returns to the United States on October 1, 1989, should qualify.

The 330 days do not have to be accumulated in the country where the individual is living. A person who spends a few weeks in each of several foreign countries, for example, can meet this test. Similarly, an individual who has accumulated 316 days of foreign presence when his overseas assignment expires should consider vacationing for two additional weeks before returning to the United States in order to meet the 330-day requirement.

Educators and Spouses May Qualify

Professors, teachers, and school administrators may qualify for the Section 911 exclusions. It does not matter whether the educator is employed by a U.S. school (as in a teacher exchange program) or by a foreign institution. Neither does it matter whether the employment is full-time or only part-time. Recipients of U.S government fellowships, such as the Fulbright grants, may have

difficulty qualifying. Case law suggests that many grantees *might* not be able to establish the required foreign tax home; present law is uncertain on this point.

Nonteaching spouses who accompany educators abroad can also qualify for the Section 911 exclusions, if they have foreign earnings. For example, if a university professor makes $60,000 teaching overseas and his wife accompanies him abroad where she makes $25,000 as an administrative coordinator, the Section 911 exclusions are available separately to each person. The entire $85,000 would escape U.S. taxation.

Further information about the Section 911 exclusions can be found in IRS Publication 54, *Tax Guide for U.S. Citizens and Resident Aliens Abroad.*

AN ALTERNATIVE TO THE EXCLUSION

If the taxpayer's stay abroad is only temporary so that there is no foreign tax home, the Section 911 exclusions are not available. Instead, the individual may qualify for the foreign tax credit and a travel expense deduction.

Foreign Tax Credit

The foreign tax credit enables the taxpayer to avoid paying both U.S. and foreign taxes on the same income. To illustrate, assume that a U.S. citizen has foreign earnings of $50,000. The foreign tax on this income is $10,000, and the U.S. tax on the income, before the credit, is $15,000. If the foreign tax credit is elected, this individual will pay $10,000 to the foreign country, but only $5,000 ($15,000 less the $10,000 foreign tax) to the United States.

For a more detailed discussion, see IRS Publication 514, *Foreign Tax Credit for U.S. Citizens and Resident Aliens.*

Travel Expense Deductions

Persons traveling away from home on business may deduct travel expenses that are not reimbursed. Anyone who does not have a foreign tax home while abroad can qualify. Travel expenses include the cost of traveling to the foreign location and back, transportation costs while abroad, 80 percent of expenses for meals, and lodging expenses. These items are miscellaneous itemized deductions and can be deducted only to the extent they exceed two percent of adjusted gross income.

Additional information can be found in IRS Publication 463, *Travel, Entertainment, and Gift Expenses.*

Strategy

Generally speaking, U.S. citizens working abroad in a low-tax country are better off electing the Section 911 exclusions. Individuals working in high-tax countries usually come out ahead by electing the foreign tax credit and the travel expense deduction. If the high-tax country has a tax treaty with the U.S., however, foreign income taxes may be drastically reduced or totally eliminated. In these cases, the Section 911 exclusions are preferable.

TAX TREATIES AND EXEMPTIONS FROM FOREIGN TAXES

Tax treaties are agreements between two countries in which each modifies its own tax laws in return for similar benefits from the other country. At present, the United States has income tax treaties in effect with 36 countries: Australia, Austria, Barbados, Belgium, Canada, China, Cyprus, Denmark, Egypt, Finland, France, Germany, Greece, Hungary, Iceland, Ireland, Italy, Jamaica, Japan, Korea, Luxembourg, Malta, Morocco, the Netherlands, the Netherlands Antilles, New Zealand, Norway, Pakistan, the Philippines, Poland, Romania, Sweden, Switzerland, Trinidad and Tobago, the USSR, and the United Kingdom.

Treaty Exemption Specifically for Educators

Most of our income tax treaties contain a provision to exempt the earnings of U.S. educators while teaching or conducting research abroad. Notable exceptions include Australia, Canada, and New Zealand. Thus, educators in these countries must pay foreign taxes, unless they qualify under the more general treaty provision discussed in the next section.

Educator exemption articles in U.S. treaties are available only to "professors and teachers." U.S. business executives who accept temporary teaching positions abroad only to return later to their regular jobs in the United States have been held ineligible. Individuals who have been trained to teach and who plan careers as teachers normally are treated as professors or teachers, even though the teaching assignment abroad may be their first real classroom experience.

Most of our older treaties pertain only to teaching abroad. Accordingly, whether an educator is eligible for the treaty exemption often hinges on whether his presence in the foreign country is "for the purpose of teaching." The IRS has interpreted this phrase to mean that teaching must be the *primary* purpose. As long as a substantial amount of time is devoted to teaching activities, the treaty exemption applies to the full salary, even though some research may be conducted. Furthermore, the term "teaching" has been defined broadly by the IRS:

> The normal duties of a teacher embrace not only the formal classroom work involving regularly scheduled lectures, demonstrations or other student-participation activities but also the less formal methods of imparting ideas in seminars or other informal groups and in efforts undertaken jointly in a laboratory.

Some treaties, such as the one with Sweden, state that the educator's purpose must be "solely" for teaching and/or research. Thus, a teacher who vacations extensively in Sweden may not be able to claim exemption under the educator treaty clause. Likewise, individuals who plan to consult in one of the countries with the "solely" stipulation may lose the treaty benefits.

Treaties restrict the time an educator can spend in a country. In many cases, the foreign stay may not exceed two years. The newer treaties, however, state that the individual's presence must not be *expected* to exceed two years. In these countries, the exemption apparently is not lost if expectations change and the educator remains in the country for, say, three years.

The exemption for research activities is not available in many countries if the research is primarily for the benefit of private persons and not for the public good. For example, research intended to perfect a design or discover a process for commercial exploitation is not an activity that qualifies for the educator exemption. As a practical matter, a professor who expects to conduct research abroad that does not clearly benefit the public should request that the contract be written solely for teaching purposes. Some allocation of the total compensation could be made to separate income from teaching (eligible for exemption) and income from research (not eligible for exemption).

Commercial Traveler Provision

A professor or teacher may be unable to satisfy the requirements as an educator, but may be able to qualify for exemption under a different treaty provision—the commercial traveler clause. The educator's spouse may be able to qualify for this general treaty exemption, as well.

To qualify, an individual generally must limit his time in the foreign country to no more than 183 days during any given year. It is possible for a person to qualify for this treaty exemption and also to exclude the earnings from income in the United States by splitting his stay in the foreign country between two taxable years. For example, as long as the individual does not arrive in the treaty country prior to July 2 and departs from the treaty country by July 2 (July 1 in leap years) of the following year, no more than 183 days will have been spent in the country during either year. The treaty exemption is available even though the person may have been in the country for a continuous period of 366 days. Moreover, this time spread conveniently overlaps the academic year of most foreign teaching institutions.

If at least 330 full days during this period were spent in the country, the person would meet the foreign presence test and, accordingly, might be eligible for the Section 911 exclusions. Thus, to avoid tax in both the United States and the foreign country, an individual's presence in the country cannot be greater than both 366 days in total and 183 days in either of the two taxable years, but it must not be less than 330 days in total. Careful planning and record-keeping are crucial to the success of such fence-straddling.

The commercial traveler exemption usually presumes employment by a U.S. enterprise. Employees of U.S. educational institutions should be able to satisfy these requirements. But professors and teachers contracting directly with foreign institutions will not be able to use this exemption except in rare cases.

Some U.S. tax treaties impose additional limits on the use of the personal traveler exemption. In Korea, for example, a person does not qualify for the exemption if he earns more than $3,000, while in Jamaica the limit is $5,000. Most people would reject compensation at these low levels. For such persons, the personal traveler exemption is an alternative only if the treaty does not limit annual salary, such as in the United Kingdom and France.

General information on income tax treaties is available in IRS Publication 901, *U.S. Tax Treaties*.

WHAT TO DO WITH YOUR U.S. RESIDENCE

Home owners who move abroad must decide whether to sell or to lease their U.S. residence. For those who decide to sell, income tax must be paid on any resulting capital gain, unless a replacement residence is acquired and occupied within two years. This two-year period is suspended for up to two additional years during any time the person has a home outside the United States. This means that an individual working abroad for two years has up to four years to replace the old residence. The new residence can be acquired in the United States or in a foreign country.

Home owners who lease their U.S. residence and reoccupy it upon their return are faced with a different set of rules. The Internal Revenue Code allows a deduction for passive activities (rental of real estate, for example) only to the extent of income from passive activities. There are two exceptions for the rental of a residence. First, the mortgage interest is always deductible on a principle and second residence. Second, up to $25,000 of losses from the rental of real estate is deductible against nonpassive income if the owner "actively participates" in the activity of renting. This active participation standard can be met if the owner (1) makes management decisions such as approving tenants and lease terms and (2) authorizes repairs and capital improvements. An agent can carry out the day-to-day activities.

To illustrate this passive loss rule, assume that Mrs. Saunders accepts a position overseas that will last three years. She leases her U.S. home through an agent during her time abroad. The first year her net rental loss is $5,000, including $2,000 of mortgage interest. If Mrs. Saunders actively participates in the rental activity, the entire $5,000 is deductible and, of course, may be used to offset other income that she may have, such as dividends. If she does not actively participate, only the $2,000 interest expense is deductible.

For additional information, see the article by Ernest R. Larkins, Mary Jill Lockwood Martin, and Deborah Anderson Hughes entitled "Making the Right Tax Moves When Moving Abroad" in *U.S. Taxation of International Operations (1988)*, pp. 13,521–38 (available from Prentice-Hall, Book Order Department, 200 Old Tappan Road, Old Tappan, NJ 07675).

RETIREMENT CONSIDERATIONS

Among the many questions often asked by those considering employment abroad are "Will I still be covered by Social Security?" and "Can I deduct my IRA contribution?"

Individual Retirement Accounts

U.S. citizens working abroad are entitled to make contributions of up to $2,000 to an individual retirement account (IRA). The contribution is entirely deductible, however, only if (1) the individual is not a participant in an employer-maintained retirement plan or (2) the adjusted gross income (AGI) is below certain limits. For example, married couples can deduct their entire contribution to an IRA if their AGI is no more than $40,000. A partial deduction is allowed if AGI is no more than $50,000.

The Section 911 exclusions may not be used to reduce AGI in order to qualify for the full IRA deduction. For example, a married couple with foreign earnings of $90,000, of which $70,000 is excluded under Section 911, cannot deduct an IRA contribution. A nondeductible contribution, however, would be allowed.

Those claiming the Section 911 exclusions should be careful not to make *any* IRA contribution if the exclusions totally wipe out their foreign earnings, such as when foreign earnings do not exceed $70,000. Contributions, deductible or otherwise, are not permitted unless there are some *taxable* earnings. Failure to heed this rule can result in an "excess contributions" penalty.

Social Security Coverage

U.S. citizens working abroad are not subject to Social Security withholding if they work for a foreign employer. However, they may have to make similar payments to a foreign government. U.S. employers of persons working abroad, on the other hand, must continue to withhold Social Security.

Anyone who discovers that they must pay Social Security to both the United States and the foreign country should check to see whether the two countries have a totalization agreement between them. These agreements, among other things, are intended to eliminate double taxation problems. The United States has concluded totalization agreements with several countries, including Canada, the United Kingdom, and the Federal Republic of Germany.

CONCLUSION

The tax laws affecting U.S. educators working abroad are many and complex. A more detailed discussion of the subject appeared in the article "Professors Who Teach Outside the United States: Tax Planning and Policy Analysis," by Ernest R. Larkins, in the Fall 1987 issue of *The Journal of the American Taxation Association*, Volume 9, Number 1, pages 48–74.

Because of the complexity of the laws and of each individual's circumstances, it is essential to seek the guidance of a experienced tax accountant or attorney before embarking on a foreign assignment. Otherwise, opportunities will be missed, and pitfalls will prove difficult to sidestep.

TEACHING ABROAD

PART 1

Teaching and Administrative Opportunities Abroad

WORLDWIDE

1 AFS INTERNATIONAL/INTERCULTURAL PROGRAMS
AFS International Teachers Programs.
This program recruits teachers of general subjects and ESL for
Argentina, Chile, China, Costa Rica, Peru, Thailand, and the USSR.
Requirements: Educational requirements vary. Language proficiency in
the host country's primary language is usually required.
Duration: 7 weeks–1 year.
Salary: Varies from none to a small monthly salary.
Benefits: Teachers live with local families, or accommodations are
provided in hotels or dormitories and an allowance is given to cover
meals and daily expenses.
Academic Calendar: Varies.
Orientation: For all participants.
Application Deadline: Varies.
Contact: AFS International/Intercultural Programs, 313 E. 43rd St.,
New York, NY 10017. *Phone:* (800) AFS-INFO.

2 EUROPEAN COUNCIL OF INTERNATIONAL SCHOOLS
(ECIS)
This association, founded in 1965, serves private primary and secondary
international schools worldwide. ECIS matches teachers and
administrators seeking jobs with schools seeking staff. Membership in
ECIS is required in order to use its services.
Language of Instruction: English; sometimes French.
Opportunities: *General:* About 250 full-time positions for teachers,
mostly at the primary level, teachers of special education, and teachers
of gifted children. *ESL:* About 15 full-time positions. *Administrators:*
About 50–60 full-time positions.
Requirements for General Teachers: Bachelor's degree in subject
taught is required; master's degree is sometimes preferred. 2 years of
recent teaching experience is required. Teaching certificate is frequently
required. International experience is sometimes preferred.
Requirements for ESL Teachers: Bachelor's degree in TESL/TEFL is
preferred; master's degree is sometimes preferred. 2 years of recent
teaching experience is required. Teaching certificate is frequently
required. International experience is sometimes preferred.
Requirements for Administrators: Bachelor's degree is required;
master's degree is frequently preferred. 5 years of administrative
experience is usually required. International experience is preferred or
required. Knowledge of British curriculum and international
baccalaureate exams is helpful.
Duration: 2 years; usually renewable.
Salary: Varies.
Benefits: Round-trip transportation from U.S. for appointee and
dependents is usually provided. Housing provision varies. Paid home
leave is sometimes provided. Health insurance varies. Other benefits
may be provided.
Academic Calendar: August/September–June.
Application Deadline: Usually Easter.
Contact: Deborah Jordan, Staffing Services Officer, European Council
of International Schools, 21B Lavant St., Petersfield, Hants GU32 3EL,
England. *Phone:* (44-730) 68244. *Telex:* 265871 (ref ECL 001).

3 EXPERIMENT IN INTERNATIONAL LIVING
Summer Abroad Leadership.
This organization, founded in 1932, recruits foreign language teachers to
lead small groups of students through a planned summer curriculum in
over 20 countries.

Requirements: Knowledge of the language and culture of another
country. Experience with U.S. teenagers. Minimum age of 24.
Contact: Luella Sauro, Admissions Officer, Outbound Educational
Travel, Experiment in International Living, Kipling Rd., Brattleboro,
VT 05301-0676. *Phone:* (800) 345-2929/(802) 257-7751. *Telex:* 6817462
EXPER UW. *Cable:* EXPERIMENT BRATTLEBORO VERMONT.

4 INTERNATIONAL SCHOOLS SERVICES
Founded in 1955, ISS serves private primary and secondary
international and American schools worldwide except Australia and
Canada. ISS matches teachers and administrators seeking jobs with
schools seeking staff; membership in the organization is required.
Language of Instruction: English.
Opportunities: *General:* 550 full-time positions for teachers of all
subjects and special education. *ESL:* 30 full-time positions.
Administrators: 75 full-time positions.
Requirements for General Teachers: Bachelor's degree is required. 2
years of current teaching experience is required. Teaching certificate is
preferred. Math, science, and business candidates with no teaching
experience who are fully certified will be accepted. International
experience is preferred.
Requirements for ESL Teachers: Bachelor's degree is required. 2 years
of current teaching experience is required.
Requirements for Administrators: Bachelor's and master's degrees are
required. Administrative experience is required. International experience
is preferred.
Duration: 2 years; renewable for 1–2 years.
Salary: Varies.
Benefits: Round-trip transportation from U.S. for appointee and
dependents. Housing or housing allowance for appointee and
dependents. Paid home leave for about 25% of schools. Health, life, and
disability insurance. Retirement plan. Tuition for dependent children.
Other benefits are provided.
Academic Calendar: September–June.
Orientation: For some schools.
Application Deadline: Jan. 1.
Contact: Mary Rabbitt, Director, Educational Staffing, International
Schools Services, 13 Roszel Rd., Box 5910, Princeton, NJ 08543. *Phone:*
(609) 452-0990. *Telex:* 843 308 SCHOLSERV PRIN. *Cable:*
SCHOOLSERV PRINCETON.

5 MENNONITE CENTRAL COMMITTEE
This Christian organization, founded in 1921, serves private primary,
secondary, and postsecondary vocational/technical schools, and
nonformal educational programs. Applicants must be active members of
a Christian church.
Opportunities: *General:* 16 full-time positions for teachers in Egypt,
Zambia, Zimbabwe, and China. *ESL:* 14 full-time positions.
Administrators: None.
Requirements for General Teachers: Bachelor's degree in mathematics
or sciences is required in Africa. 1–2 years of teaching or practical
experience is preferred.
Requirements for ESL Teachers: Bachelor's or master's degree is
preferred. Teaching or practical experience is required.
Duration: 2–3 years; renewable.
Salary: All expenses are paid plus a stipend of $43 per month.
Benefits: Round-trip transportation from U.S. for appointee and
dependents. Housing for appointee and dependents. Health and life
insurance. Pension plan. Other benefits are provided.

Academic Calendar: Varies.
Orientation: 10–15 days.
Contact: Ruth Keidel, Personnel Administrator, Mennonite Central Committee, 21 S. 12th St., Akron, PA 17501. *Phone:* (717) 859-1151.

6 NATIONAL SCIENCE FOUNDATION, DIVISION OF INTERNATIONAL PROGRAMS

The NSF Division of International Programs promotes U.S. participation in international science and engineering activities that would benefit U.S. research and training efforts.
Opportunities: 4 types of activities receive support: cooperative research projects designed and conducted jointly by principal investigators from the U.S. and a foreign country; long- and medium-term research visits at foreign centers of excellence; research-oriented seminars or workshops to exchange information, review the current status of a specific field of science or engineering, and plan cooperative research; and short-term scientific visits for planning cooperative activities.
Requirements: Doctoral degree in science or engineering is required. Professional experience equivalent to 5 years of postdoctoral scientific work is required. Written proposal must be submitted to the NSF.
Application Deadline: Varies.
Contact: Division of International Programs, National Science Foundation, Washington, DC 20550.

7 ROTARY FOUNDATION
Rotary Grants for University Teachers Program.

Opportunities: 15 competitive grants for teachers of academic and applied studies valuable to developing countries.
Requirements: University rank of assistant professor, its equivalent, or higher. 3 years of university teaching or a research post for 3 years prior to the year in which the grant is to be used is required. Applicants may not be Rotarians, Rotary employees, or related to Rotary employees. The host country must have a Rotary club; preference is given to applicants with firm invitations to teach in developing nations.
Duration: Recipients have 2 years to complete their work abroad, spending a minimum of 6 months at their host universities. At least half of their working time will be spent teaching.
Salary: $10,000; grants may be spent at the discretion of recipients. Recipients may receive other stipends.
Application Deadline: April 15.
Contact: The Rotary Foundation, One Rotary Center, 1560 Sherman Ave., Evanston, IL 60201. *Phone:* (312) 866-3333. *Telex:* 724-465. *Cable:* INTEROTARY.

8 U.S. INFORMATION AGENCY
Fulbright Scholar Program.

This USIA program serves public and private universities, postsecondary vocational/technical schools, and teacher colleges in over 120 countries.
Opportunities: *General:* Over 900 grants for full-time university lecturers and researchers in all fields. *ESL:* Full-time positions. *Administrators:* Full-time positions in the United Kingdom, West Germany, and Japan.
Requirements for General Teachers: Doctor's degree is usually required. Teaching experience is required. Language proficiency in the country's primary language is usually preferred in Latin America and Francophone Africa.
Requirements for ESL Teachers: Doctor's degree in TEFL or applied linguistics is usually required. Teaching experience is required. Language proficiency in the country's primary language is usually preferred in Latin America and Francophone Africa.
Requirements for Administrators: Doctor's degree is usually required. Language proficiency in the country's primary language is usually preferred in Latin America and Francophone Africa.
Duration: 3 months–1 academic year; extensions are sometimes possible.
Salary: Stipend varies.
Benefits: Transportation is usually provided for grantee. For grants of more than 1 year, transportation may be provided for 1 dependent. Health insurance.
Academic Calendar: Varies.
Application Deadline: June 15 for Australasia, India, and Latin America; Sept. 15 for Africa, Asia, Europe, the Middle East, and lecturing awards to Mexico, Venezuela, and the Caribbean.
Contact: Council for International Exchange of Scholars, 11 Dupont Circle NW, Suite 300, Washington, DC 20036. *Phone:* (202) 939-5401.

9 U.S. INFORMATION AGENCY
Fulbright Teacher Exchange Program.

USIA recruits teachers for public and private school exchanges at all levels around the world. The program also provides opportunities for teachers to participate in summer seminars 3–8 weeks in length. U.S. citizenship is required.
Opportunities: *General:* 250 full-time positions for teachers of all subjects worldwide. *ESL:* Full-time positions. *Administrators:* Full-time positions in Canada or the United Kingdom.
Requirements for General Teachers: Bachelor's degree is required. 3 years of teaching experience is required. Proficiency in the local language is sometimes preferred or required. Teacher's school must agree to accept a foreign teacher.
Requirements for ESL Teachers: Bachelor's degree is required. 3 years of teaching experience is required. International experience is preferred. Proficiency in the local language is sometimes preferred or required. Teacher's school must agree to accept a foreign teacher.
Requirements for Administrators: Bachelor's degree is required; master's degree is preferred. Administrative experience is required. International experience is preferred. Administrator's school must agree to accept a foreign administrator or teacher.
Duration: 1 year; sometimes renewable.
Salary: *Teachers:* Generally retain salary from home school. *Administrators:* Generally retain salary from home school.
Benefits: Round-trip transportation from U.S. is sometimes provided for appointee. Exchange partners may exchange housing or assist each other in locating housing. Health and accident insurance.
Academic Calendar: Varies.
Orientation: Usually 2 days in Washington (DC), San Francisco, or abroad.
Application Deadline: Oct. 15.
Contact: Teacher Exchange Branch, E/ASX, U.S. Information Agency, 301 Fourth St. SW, Washington, DC 20547. *Phone:* (202) 485-2555/6.

10 U.S. PEACE CORPS
Teacher Recruiting Program.

The Peace Corps was founded in 1961 to aid developing countries worldwide and to promote cross-cultural awareness and understanding. In the host country, Peace Corps volunteers work for a government department, agency, or organization, are supervised by host nationals, speak the native language, and are subject to local laws.
Opportunities: *General:* About 1,000 full-time positions for elementary, secondary, vocational/technical, postsecondary, and adult education teachers; all fields are needed, especially science, mathematics, special education, and vocational/technical subjects. *ESL:* Many positions are available. *Administrators:* None.
Requirements for General Teachers: Bachelor's degree is required. Teaching experience is preferred. Formal or informal experience is preferred. U.S. citizenship is required.
Requirements for ESL Teachers: Bachelor's degree in ESL, TEFL, or linguistics is required. Master's degree in linguistics is required for university positions. Teaching experience is preferred. Previous international experience is preferred.
Duration: 2 years; renewable for 2 years or possible transfer to another country.
Salary: Living allowance for food, clothing, housing, utilities, vacation, transportation, and incidentals. A $200 readjustment allowance for each month of service is paid about 6 weeks after termination; 1/3 of this allowance is available prior to departure from host country.
Benefits: Round-trip transportation from U.S. for appointee. Medical care. Life insurance.
Academic Calendar: Varies.
Orientation: About 3 months in U.S. and abroad.
Application Deadline: Open.
Contact: Peace Corps Recruitment, 806 Connecticut Ave. NW, Washington, DC 20526. *Phone:* (800) 424-8580, Ext. 93.

11 UNIVERSITY OF MARYLAND UNIVERSITY COLLEGE
Overseas Programs.

The University recruits teachers for its overseas programs in Europe and Asia for members of U.S. military communities.
Opportunities: *General:* 90 full-time positions for teachers of standard undergraduate academic disciplines except education, counseling, and foreign languages. *ESL:* None. *Administrators:* None.

Requirements for General Teachers: Master's degree in subject taught is required; master's degree in second discipline is preferred; doctor's degree is preferred. More than 1 year of teaching experience is preferred. International experience is preferred. Appointee must be willing to relocate every 2–4 months.

Duration: 1 year; renewable for 4 years.

Salary: $16,500–$28,000 per academic year.

Benefits: Round-trip transportation from U.S. for appointee and dependents. University assists in locating housing. Health insurance. TIAA/CREF. Other benefits are provided.

Academic Calendar: August–May, summer session optional.

Orientation: 7 days in Heidelberg, West Germany, or Tokyo, Japan.

Application Deadline: Rolling.

Contact: Ralph E. Millis, Assistant to the Chancellor, Overseas Programs, University of Maryland University College, University Blvd. at Adelphi Rd., College Park, MD 20742-1642. *Phone:* (301) 985-7070.

12 YMCA INTERNATIONAL
International Camp Counselor Program/Abroad.

This program of the YMCA recruits counselors for youth camps and voluntary work camps in 26 countries.

Opportunities: About 110 positions.

Requirements: Leadership experience with groups of children. Language proficiency in the country's primary language is often required.

Duration: Several weeks–several months.

Salary: None.

Benefits: Counselors pay application fee and transportation. Room and board provided. Health and accident insurance. Pocket money and domestic transportation is sometimes provided.

Academic Calendar: Summer for most camps; December–March for Southern Hemisphere.

Application Deadline: Jan. 1 for most camps; Oct. 1 for Southern Hemisphere.

Contact: International Camp Counselor Program/Abroad, YMCA of Greater New York, 356 W. 34th St., Third Floor, New York, NY 10001. *Phone:* (212) 563-3441. *Telex:* ISS 620675. *Cable:* FORSTUDENT.

AFRICA, SOUTH OF THE SAHARA

BURKINA FASO

MORE THAN ONE CITY

13 EMBASSY OF BURKINA FASO
The Embassy reports a need for U.S. ESL teachers, educational administrators, and curriculum developers on the university and other postsecondary levels. Some secondary school teachers are also needed.
Language of Instruction: *Primary:* French. *Other:* English, German, Spanish, and Arabic.
Requirements for General Teachers: Doctor's degree is preferred. Teaching experience is required. International experience is preferred. Language proficiency in French on the intermediate level is preferred.
Requirements for ESL Teachers: Bachelor's or master's degree in applied linguistics or English is required; doctor's degree is preferred. Teaching experience is required. International experience is preferred. Language proficiency in French on the intermediate level is preferred.
Requirements for Administrators: Doctor's degree is preferred. Teaching experience is required. International experience is preferred. Language proficiency in French on the intermediate level is preferred.
Duration: 1–2 years; renewable.
Benefits: Housing is provided. Health care.
Academic Calendar: October–July.
Application Deadline: April 15.
Contact: Embassy of Burkina Faso, 2340 Massachusetts Ave. NW, Washington, DC 20008. *Or:* Ministry of Higher Education and Scientific Research, University of Ouagadougou, B.P. 7021, Ouagadougou, Burkina Faso.

BURUNDI

BUJUMBURA

14 U.S. INFORMATION AGENCY
English Teaching Program.
USIA recruits teachers and educational administrators for the English Teaching Program, a public adult/continuing education program at the USIS American Cultural Center in Bujumbura.
Opportunities: *General:* None. *ESL:* 1 full-time position, 6–8 part-time positions for up to 12 hours per week. *Administrators:* 1 full-time position.
Requirements for ESL Teachers: Master's degree in TESL/TEFL is preferred. Teaching experience is preferred. Experience in learning a second or third language is required. International experience is preferred. Language proficiency in French on the beginning level is preferred. Part-time teachers are recruited locally.
Requirements for Administrators: Master's degree in TESOL or applied linguistics is required. 4 years of administrative experience is required. International experience is required. Language proficiency in French on the intermediate level is required.
Duration: Full-time positions: 1 year; renewable. Part-time positions: 12 weeks; renewable.

Salary: *Teachers:* $20,000 per calendar year for full-time positions; $10 per hour for part-time positions. *Administrators:* $25,000 per calendar year.
Benefits: For full-time positions: Round-trip transportation from U.S. for appointee only. Housing allowance. Paid home leave if contract is renewed. Health insurance for teaching position. Other benefits are provided.
Academic Calendar: Year-round.
Orientation: 2–3 days in Washington, DC.
Application Deadline: March–April.
Contact: USIA English Teaching Section (E/CE), U.S. Information Agency, Washington, DC 20547.

CAMEROON

YAOUNDE

15 AMERICAN SCHOOL OF YAOUNDE
This private coed K-9 school was founded in 1964. Current enrollment is 175; 54% of the faculty are U.S. nationals.
Language of Instruction: English.
Opportunities: *General:* 5–6 full-time positions for teachers of all subjects. *ESL:* Less than 1 position per year. *Administrators:* Less than 1 position per year for a resource room/counselor.
Requirements for General Teachers: Bachelor's degree in subject taught is required; master's or doctor's degree is preferred. 2 years of teaching experience is required. Teaching certificate is required. International experience is preferred. Language proficiency in French on the beginning level is preferred.
Requirements for ESL Teachers: Bachelor's degree is required; master's or doctor's degree is preferred. 2 years of teaching experience is required. Teaching certificate is required. International experience is preferred. Language proficiency in French is preferred.
Requirements for Administrators: Bachelor's degree is required; master's degree in curriculum supervision is required; doctor's degree in educational administration is preferred. Administrative experience is required. Administrative certificate is required. International experience is preferred. Language proficiency in French on the beginning level is preferred.
Duration: 1–2 years; renewable indefinitely.
Salary: *Teachers:* $22,000–$26,000 per academic year. *Administrators:* $35,000 per academic year.
Benefits: Round-trip transportation from U.S. for appointee and dependents. Housing for appointee and dependents. Paid leave to Paris every 2 years. Health insurance. Tuition for dependent children enrolled at this school. Other benefits are provided.
Academic Calendar: September–June.
Orientation: 1-week on-site.
Application Deadline: Feb. 1.
Contact: Dr. Kathryn Edwards, Director, American School of Yaounde, B.P. 7475, Yaounde, Cameroon. *Phone:* (237) 23 04 21. *Telex:* 8223 KN.

CENTRAL AFRICAN REPUBLIC

BANGUI

16 U.S. INFORMATION SERVICE
USIS recruits faculty for its adult ESL course.
Opportunities: *General:* None. *ESL:* Possibly 3–4 part-time positions. In the future, USIS may employ an English teacher at the local French language university. *Administrators:* Possibly 1 position.
Requirements for Teachers: Bachelor's or master's degree in TESL/TEFL, education, or administration is preferred. 2 years of teaching experience is preferred. International experience is preferred. Language proficiency in French is required.
Requirements for Administrators: Bachelor's or master's degree in TEFL or administration is preferred. 4 years of administrative experience is preferred. International experience is preferred. Language proficiency in French is required. Also requires ability to interest a French-speaking public in English courses.
Duration: 1 year; renewable for 1 year.
Salary: *Teachers:* 8,000 CFA per hour. *Administrators:* About $27,858 per calendar year.
Benefits: USIS assists in locating housing.
Academic Calendar: September–July.
Application Deadline: May.
Contact: Victoria A. Rose, Public Affairs Officer, USIS Martin Luther King Center, B.P. 48, Bangui, Central African Republic. *Phone:* 61-47-66. *Telex:* AMBAUSA 5287RC.

CONGO

BRAZZAVILLE

17 UNIVERSITE MARIEN NGOUABI
This public coed university was founded in 1971. Current enrollment is 12,000; fewer than 5 of the faculty are U.S. nationals. The university participates in the USIA Fulbright Teacher Exchange and an exchange program with Penn State University.
Language of Instruction: *Primary:* French. *Other:* English and Russian.
Opportunities: *General:* 2 full- and part-time positions for teachers of management/economics. *ESL:* 1 full-time Fulbright position. *Administrators:* None.
Requirements for General Teachers: Doctor's degree in humanities or economics/management is required. Teaching experience is required. International experience is preferred. Language proficiency in French on the advanced level is required.
Duration: 1 year; renewable for 1 year.
Benefits: Housing for appointee and dependents.
Academic Calendar: September–June.
Application Deadline: March–April.
Contact: Dr. Hilaire Bouhoyi, Rector, Universite Marien Ngouabi, B.P. 69, Brazzaville, Congo. *Phone:* 81 24 36.

ETHIOPIA

ADDIS ABABA

18 INTERNATIONAL COMMUNITY SCHOOL OF ADDIS ABABA
This private coed primary/secondary school was founded in 1964. Current enrollment is 510; about 45% of the faculty are U.S. nationals.
Language of Instruction: English.
Opportunities: *General:* 25 full-time positions for teachers of all subjects. *ESL:* 2 full-time positions. *Administrators:* 2 full-time positions.
Requirements for General Teachers: Bachelor's degree is required; master's degree is preferred. 2 years of teaching experience is preferred. International experience is preferred.
Requirements for ESL Teachers: Bachelor's degree in English or TEFL is required; master's degree is preferred. 2 years of teaching experience is required. International experience is preferred.

Requirements for Administrators: Master's degree in educational administration is required; doctor's degree is preferred. 5 years of administrative experience is required. International experience is preferred.
Duration: 2 years; renewable.
Salary: *Teachers:* $9,000–$18,000 per calendar year. *Administrators:* Negotiable.
Benefits: Round-trip transportation from U.S. for appointee and dependents. Housing for appointee and dependents. Health insurance. Tuition for dependent children enrolled at this school. Other benefits are provided.
Academic Calendar: August–June.
Orientation: 2 weeks on-site.
Application Deadline: Dec. 1, or through a recruiting conference.
Contact: Dr. Anthony Horton, Director, International Community School of Addis Ababa, Box 70282, Addis Ababa, Ethiopia. *Phone:* (25-1) 200870/201062. *Or:* Director, International Community School of Addis Ababa, Department of State/Addis Ababa, Washington, DC 20520.

ASMARA

19 ASMARA UNIVERSITY
This is a public coed university. Current enrollment is 1,800; 0.5% of the faculty are U.S. nationals.
Language of Instruction: English.
Opportunities: *General:* About 15 full-time positions. *ESL:* Less than 1 position per year. *Administrators:* None.
Requirements for General Teachers: Master's degree in biology, chemistry, physics, mathematics, geology, management, economics, or accounting is required; doctor's degree is preferred. Teaching experience is preferred. International experience is preferred. Language proficiency in any major European language is preferred.
Requirements for ESL Teachers: Master's degree in biology, chemistry, physics, mathematics, geology, management, economics, or accounting is required; doctor's degree is preferred. Teaching experience is preferred. International experience is preferred. Language proficiency in any major European language is preferred.
Duration: 2 years; renewable.
Salary: $600–$1,050 per month.
Benefits: Round-trip transportation from U.S. for appointee, spouse, and dependents under age 18. Housing for appointee and dependents. Paid home leave every 2 years.
Academic Calendar: September–June.
Application Deadline: August.
Contact: Personnel Officer, Asmara University, P.O. Box 1220, Asmara, Ethiopia. *Phone:* (251-4) 113600. *Telex:* 42091. *Cable:* ASMUNIV.

GABON

LIBREVILLE

20 AMERICAN INTERNATIONAL SCHOOL OF LIBREVILLE
This private coed primary school was founded in 1975. Current enrollment is 55; 60% of the faculty are U.S. nationals.
Language of Instruction: *Primary:* English. *Other:* French.
Opportunities: *General:* 3 full-time positions. *ESL:* 1 part-time position. *Administrators:* 1 full-time position.
Requirements for General Teachers: Bachelor's degree is required; master's degree in education is preferred. 5 years of teaching experience is preferred. Teaching certificate is required. International experience is preferred. Language proficiency in French on the advanced level is preferred.
Requirements for ESL Teachers: Bachelor's degree is required; master's degree in TESL is preferred. 5 years of teaching experience is preferred. Teaching certificate is required. International experience is preferred. Language proficiency in French on the advanced level is preferred.
Requirements for Administrators: Bachelor's degree is required; master's degree in educational administration is preferred. 5 years of administrative experience is preferred. Administrative certificate is required. International experience is preferred. Language proficiency in

French on the advanced level is preferred. Applicants must have teaching spouse.
Duration: 1 year; renewable for 1 year.
Salary: *Teachers:* 4,400,000–7,600,000 CFA per academic year. *Administrators:* $23,000 per academic year.
Benefits: For Administrators Only: Round-trip transportation from U.S. for appointee and dependents. Housing for appointee and dependents. Paid home leave every 2 years. Health insurance.
Academic Calendar: September–June.
Application Deadline: February.
Contact: Thomas G. Hunt, Director, American International School of Libreville, B.P. 4000, Libreville, Gabon. *Phone:* (241) 731449. *Telex:* 9815250 GO. *Cable:* AMEMBAS LBV.

GHANA

MORE THAN ONE CITY

21 CONSULATE OF GHANA
The Consulate reports that there is no need for U.S. teachers or educational administrators at this time.
For General Information, Contact: Mr. Ofori Tannor, Consul, Consulate of Ghana, 19 E. 47th St., New York, NY 10017. *Phone:* (212) 832-1300.

22 U.S. PEACE CORPS
Virginia Teachers in International Education (VTIE).
In 1988 the Peace Corps established a pilot program to provide experienced public school teachers on all levels with the opportunity to serve as teacher trainers for the Peace Corps in Ghana. The teachers will train other Peace Corps volunteers to teach various subjects in Ghanaian schools.

Through the cooperation of the Virginia State Board of Education, participating teachers receive a 1-year sabbatical from their home schools, with no loss of tenure or benefits.

Although the pilot program is limited to Virginia teachers, the Peace Corps hopes to expand the program eventually to all 50 states, as well as to other overseas locations. Participants should be single or married U.S. citizens without dependent children.
Opportunities: *General:* About 10 full-time positions for teqchers in all fields and all levels from pre-K to postsecondary. *ESL:* Positions are available. *Administrators:* None.
Requirements for General Teachers: U.S. bachelor's degree (or higher degree, as appropriate) is required. Current teaching position in a Virginia public school, college, or university is required. Teaching experience is required; 10 years of experience is preferred. International experience and foreign language proficiency are preferred.
Requirements for ESL Teachers: Bachelor's degree (or higher degree, as appropriate) in ESL, TEFL, or linguistics is required. Current teaching position in a Virginia public school, college, or university is required. Teaching experience is required; 10 years of experience is preferred. International experience and foreign language proficiency are preferred.
Duration: 1 year; not renewable.
Salary: Living allowance for food, clothing, housing, utilities, vacation, transportation, and incidentals. A $200 readjustment allowance for each month of service is paid about 6 weeks after termination; 1/3 of this allowance is available prior to departure from host country.
Benefits: Round-trip transportation from U.S. for appointee only. Medical care. Life insurance.
Academic Calendar: September–May.
Orientation: About 2 months in U.S. and Ghana.
Application Deadline: Open.
Contact: Peace Corps, 806 Connecticut Ave. NW, Washington, DC 20526. *Phone:* (800) 424-8580, Ext. 284.

ACCRA

23 GHANA INTERNATIONAL SCHOOL
This private coed primary/secondary school was founded in 1957. Current enrollment is 820; 5% of the faculty are U.S. nationals. Teachers are recruited locally.
Language of Instruction: *Primary:* English. *Other:* French.

Opportunities: *General:* Full- and part-time positions. *ESL:* None. *Administrators:* Full-time positions.
Academic Calendar: September–July.
Contact: Judith S. Sawyerr, Principal, Ghana International School, Box 2856, Accra, Ghana. *Phone:* 777163.

GUINEA

CONAKRY

24 INTERNATIONAL SCHOOL OF CONAKRY
This private coed primary school was founded in 1974. Current enrollment is 55; 20% of the faculty are U.S. nationals.
Language of Instruction: *Primary:* English. *Other:* French.
Opportunities: *General:* None. *ESL:* 2 full-time positions. *Administrators:* 1 full-time position.
Requirements for Teachers: Bachelor's degree in elementary education or TESL/TEFL is required. Teaching experience is preferred. International experience is preferred. Language proficiency in French is required.
Requirements for Administrators: Master's degree in educational administration or elementary education is required. 2 years of administrative experience is required. International experience is required. Language proficiency in French is preferred.
Duration: 1 year for teachers, 2 years for administrators; renewable.
Salary: *Teachers:* $8,000–$15,000 per academic year. *Administrators:* $27,000 per calendar year.
Benefits: Round-trip transportation from U.S. for appointee and dependents. Housing for appointee and dependents. Paid home leave. Health insurance. Other benefits are provided.
Academic Calendar: September–June.
Application Deadline: May 1.
Contact: Brian Jones, Director, International School of Conakry—Guinea, Department of State/Conakry, Washington, DC 20520-2110.

KENYA

MORE THAN ONE CITY

25 EMBASSY OF THE REPUBLIC OF KENYA
The Embassy reports that there is no need for U.S. teachers or educational administrators except for those recruited through the Peace Corps (see listing 10).
Language of Instruction: *Primary:* English. *Other:* Vernacular languages and Swahili.
Academic Calendar: January–December.
For General Information, Contact: Embassy of the Republic of Kenya, 2249 R St. NW, Washington, DC 20008. *Phone:* (202) 387-6101.

26 WORLDTEACH
This private organization recruits volunteer teachers and educational administrators for public secondary schools.
Language of Instruction: English.
Opportunities: *General:* About 100 full-time positions for teachers of all subjects. *ESL:* 20–40 full-time positions. *Administrators:* About 5–10 full-time positions.
Requirements for General Teachers: Bachelor's degree is required.
Requirements for ESL Teachers: Bachelor's degree is required.
Requirements for Administrators: Bachelor's degree is required.
Duration: 1 year; renewable.
Salary: *Teachers:* $75 per month. *Administrators:* $120–$180 per month.
Benefits: Housing for appointee and dependents.
Academic Calendar: Rolling.
Orientation: 2 days in Boston, 4 weeks in Kenya.
Application Deadline: Rolling.
Contact: WorldTeach, Phillips Brooks House, Harvard University, Cambridge, MA 02138. *Phone:* (617) 495-5527.

MACHAKOS

27 FRIENDS WORLD COLLEGE—EAST AFRICAN CENTER
This private coed university was founded in 1965. Current enrollment is
15–20; 80% of the faculty are U.S. nationals.
Language of Instruction: *Primary:* English. *Other:* Swahili.
Opportunities: *General:* 2 full- and part-time positions. *ESL:* None.
Administrators: 1 full-time position.
Requirements for Teachers: Doctor's degree is preferred. Teaching
experience or field work in Africa is required. International experience is
required. Language proficiency in Swahili on the advanced level is
required.
Requirements for Administrators: Doctor's degree is preferred.
Administrative experience is required. International experience is
required. Language proficiency in Swahili on the advanced level is
required.
Duration: 1 year; renewable indefinitely.
Salary: *Teachers:* $12,000–$15,000 per calendar year. *Administrators:*
$17,000 per calendar year.
Benefits: Round-trip transportation from U.S. for appointee only.
Housing for 1–2 appointees. Health insurance. Other benefits are
provided.
Academic Calendar: September–June.
Orientation: In Huntington, NY.
Application Deadline: Rolling.
Contact: Jane Ann Smith, Academic Vice President, Friends World
College—East African Center, Box 526, Machakos, Kenya. *Phone:*
(254-145) 21610; in U.S. (516) 549-5000.

NAIROBI

28 INTERNATIONAL SCHOOL OF KENYA
This private primary/secondary school was founded in 1976.
Language of Instruction: English.
Opportunities: *General:* 7 full- and part-time positions, 1 special
education position. *ESL:* 1 full- or part-time position. *Administrators:* 1
full-time position.
Requirements for General Teachers: Bachelor's degree in English,
ESL, or subject taught is required; master's degree is preferred. 2 years
of teaching experience is required. Teaching certificate is required.
International experience is preferred. Language proficiency in any
foreign language on the beginning level is preferred.
Requirements for ESL Teachers: Bachelor's degree in English or ESL
is required; master's degree is preferred. 2 years of teaching experience
is preferred. Teaching certificate is required. International experience is
preferred. Language proficiency in any foreign language is preferred.
Requirements for Administrators: Bachelor's degree is required;
master's or doctor's degree in educational administration is preferred. 5
years of administrative experience is required; 5 years of classroom
experience is preferred. International experience is preferred.
Duration: 2 years; renewable.
Salary: *Teachers:* $15,955–$36,854 per academic year. *Administrators:*
$42,000–$60,000 per academic year.
Benefits: Round-trip transportation from U.S. for appointee and
dependents. Housing for appointee and dependents. Paid home leave
every 2 years. Health, life, and disability insurance. TIAA/CREF.
$2,000 settling-in allowance. Retirement plan. Other benefits are
provided.
Academic Calendar: August–May.
Orientation: 4 days in Nairobi.
Application Deadline: Jan. 15.
Contact: Dr. David T. Bratt, Superintendent, International School of
Kenya Ltd., P.O. Box 14103, Nairobi, Kenya. *Phone:* (254-2)
582421/422. *Telex:* U.S. Embassy Nairobi. *Cable:* U.S. Embassy
Nairobi.

THIKA

29 IMANI SCHOOL
This private coed primary/secondary school was founded in 1969.
Current enrollment is 282; 4% of the faculty are U.S. nationals.
Positions are advertised in the British press.
Language of Instruction: English.

Opportunities: *General:* 1 part-time position. *ESL:* None.
Administrators: None.
Duration: 2 years; renewable for 2 years.
Salary: 13,000–20,500 shillings per month.
Benefits: Housing for appointee and dependents. Paid home leave every
2 years. Health insurance. Tuition for dependent children enrolled at
this school. Other benefits are provided.
Academic Calendar: September–August.
Application Deadline: February.
Contact: C. Rutherford, Headmaster, Imani School, Box 750, Thika,
Kenya. *Phone:* (254-151) 21071. *Telex:* 22549 KENCAN.

LESOTHO

MORE THAN ONE CITY

30 MINISTRY OF EDUCATION
The Ministry of Education and Lesotho Mission to the UN report a
need for U.S. teachers of mathematics, science, and English as a
second/foreign language, and educational administrators on all levels.
The government assists in locating positions.
Language of Instruction: *Primary:* English. *Other:* Sesotho.
Academic Calendar: January–December.
Contact: Permanent Secretary, Ministry of Education, Maseru, Lesotho.
For General Information, Contact: Lesotho Mission to the United
Nations, 866 United Nations Plaza, Suite 580, New York, NY 10017.
Phone: (212) 421-7543/4/5.

MASERU

31 MASERU ENGLISH MEDIUM PREPARATORY
This public coed primary school was founded in 1890. Current
enrollment is 480; 13% of the faculty are U.S. nationals.
Language of Instruction: *Primary:* English. *Other:* Sesotho, Afrikaans,
Irish, French, German.
Opportunities: *General:* 3–4 full-time positions. *ESL:* 2 part-time
positions. *Administrators:* None.
Requirements for General Teachers: Bachelor's degree in primary
education is required. 3 years of teaching experience is required.
International experience is preferred. Language proficiency in French is
required for teachers of grades 5–6.
Requirements for ESL Teachers: Bachelor's degree in TEFL is
preferred. 3 years of teaching experience is required. International
experience is preferred.
Duration: 2–3 years; renewable.
Salary: 930–1,521 maloti per month.
Benefits: Round-trip transportation from U.S. for appointee and 3
dependents. Housing for appointee and dependents. Health insurance.
Other benefits are provided.
Academic Calendar: September–July.
Orientation: 1 week on-site.
Application Deadline: March.
Contact: Mrs. A. Ball, Headmistress, Maseru English Medium
Preparatory, P.O. Box 34, Maseru, Lesotho. *Phone:* (266) 322176.

LIBERIA

MONROVIA

32 AMERICAN COOPERATIVE SCHOOL
This private coed primary/secondary school was founded in 1960.
Current enrollment is 250; 95% of the faculty are U.S. nationals.
Language of Instruction: English.
Opportunities: *General:* 4–8 positions for teachers of mathematics,
science, business education on the secondary level. *ESL:* None.
Administrators: None.
Requirements: Bachelor's degree is required; master's degree is
preferred. 2 years of teaching experience is preferred. Teaching
certificate is required.
Duration: 2 years.

All information is subject to change without notice
and must be confirmed directly with the employer.

8

Salary: $16,000–$25,000 per academic year.
Benefits: Round-trip transportation from U.S. for appointee and dependents. Housing for appointee and dependents. Paid home leave every year. Health insurance. TIAA/CREF. Tuition for dependent children enrolled at this school. Other benefits are provided.
Academic Calendar: August–June.
Application Deadline: Varies.
Contact: Dr. Robert Ambrogi, Superintendent, American Cooperative School, c/o U.S. Embassy, P.O. Box 98, Monrovia, Liberia.

MADAGASCAR

MORE THAN ONE CITY

33 EMBASSY OF MADAGASCAR
The Embassy does not report a need for U.S. teachers or educational administrators at this time.
Language of Instruction: *Primary:* Malagasy. *Other:* French and English.
Academic Calendar: September–June.
For General Information, Contact: Embassy of Madagascar, 2347 Massachusetts Ave. NW, Washington, DC 20008. *Phone:* (202) 265-5525.

ANTANANARIVO

34 AMERICAN SCHOOL OF ANTANANARIVO
This private coed primary school was founded in 1969. Current enrollment is 55; 75% of the faculty are U.S. nationals.
Language of Instruction: English.
Opportunities: *General:* 1–2 full-time positions. *ESL:* Part-time positions. *Administrators:* Less than 1 position per year.
Requirements for General Teachers: Bachelor's degree in elementary education is preferred; master's degree in education or specialization is preferred. 2 years of teaching experience is preferred. International experience is required. Language proficiency in French on the beginning level is preferred.
Requirements for ESL Teachers: Bachelor's degree in elementary education or TESL is preferred; master's degree in TESL/TEFL is preferred. 2 years of teaching experience is preferred.
Requirements for Administrators: Master's degree in education or specialization is required. 2 years of administrative experience is preferred. International experience is preferred. Language proficiency in French on the beginning level is preferred.
Duration: 2 years; renewable for 1–2 years.
Salary: *Teachers:* $12,000–$16,000 per academic year. *Administrators:* Negotiable.
Benefits: School assists in locating housing.
Academic Calendar: September–June.
Application Deadline: February.
Contact: David L. Hollinger, Director, American School of Antananarivo, Department of State/Antananarivo, Washington, DC 20520-2040. *Phone:* In Madagascar: 420-39.

MALAWI

ZOMBA

35 UNIVERSITY OF MALAWI
This public coed university was founded in 1964. 3% of the faculty are U.S. nationals. The university has a link with Florida A&M and the University of Maryland.
Language of Instruction: English.
Opportunities: *General:* 2 positions for teachers of engineering, science education, nursing, mathematics, computers. *ESL:* 1 full-time position. *Administrators:* None.
Requirements for General Teachers: Master's degree in subject taught is required; doctor's degree is preferred. 3 years of teaching experience is required.

Requirements for ESL Teachers: Master's degree is required; doctor's degree is preferred.
Duration: 2 years; renewable for 2 years.
Salary: 6,537–20,162 kwacha per academic year.
Benefits: Round-trip transportation from U.S. for appointee, spouse, and dependents under age 18. Housing for appointee and dependents. Paid home leave every 2 years. Health care.
Academic Calendar: September–July.
Orientation: On-site.
Application Deadline: March 31.
Contact: University Registrar, University of Malawi, University Office, P.O. Box 278, Zomba, Malawi. *Phone:* (265-50) 522 622. *Telex:* 4613 POLYTEC. *Cable:* UNIVERSITY, ZOMBA.

NIGERIA

IBADAN

36 INTERNATIONAL SCHOOL
This private coed secondary school was founded in 1963. Current enrollment is 1,100; 4% of the faculty are U.S. nationals.
Language of Instruction: English.
Opportunities: *General:* Full-time positions for teachers of all subjects. *ESL:* Full-time positions. *Administrators:* None.
Requirements for General Teachers: Master's degree is preferred. Teaching experience is required. International experience is preferred.
Requirements for ESL Teachers: Master's degree is preferred. Teaching experience is required. International experience is preferred.
Duration: 2 years; renewable.
Salary: 5,316–13,092 naira per calendar year.
Benefits: Round-trip transportation from U.S. for appointee and dependents. Housing for appointee and dependents. Paid home leave every 2 years. Health care. Other benefits are provided.
Academic Calendar: January–December.
Contact: Rev. Dr. Dapo Ajayi, Principal, International School, University of Ibadan, Ibadan, Oyo State, Nigeria. *Phone:* 400550, Ext. 1302.

37 UNIVERSITY OF IBADAN
This public coed university was founded in 1948. Current enrollment is 12,000; less than 1% of the faculty are U.S. nationals.
Language of Instruction: English.
Opportunities: *General:* 5 full-time positions. *ESL:* None. *Administrators:* None.
Requirements: Bachelor's degree is preferred. Teaching experience is preferred.
Duration: 3 years; renewable indefinitely.
Salary: 7,550–15,720 naira per calendar year.
Benefits: Round-trip transportation from U.S. for appointee and dependents. Housing for appointee and dependents. Other benefits are provided.
Academic Calendar: October–September.
Contact: Mr. K. Okusanya, Assistant Registrar, University of Ibadan, Ibadan, Oyo State, Nigeria. *Phone:* 400550/400614.

JOS

38 HILLCREST SCHOOL
This private coed primary/secondary school was founded in 1942. Current enrollment is 500. The school employs U.S. nationals but does not recruit directly.
Language of Instruction: English.
Contact: Kenneth L. Reiner, Principal, Hillcrest School, Box 652, Jos, Nigeria. *Phone:* 55410.

MAIDUGURI

39 UNIVERSITY OF MAIDUGURI
This public coed university was founded in 1975. Current enrollment is 8,000; 1% of the faculty are U.S. nationals.
Language of Instruction: English.

All information is subject to change without notice
and must be confirmed directly with the employer.

9

Opportunities: *General:* Full-time positions for teachers of medicine, engineering, agriculture, physics, veterinary medicine. *ESL:* 5 full-time positions. *Administrators:* Full-time positions.
Requirements for General Teachers: Doctor's degree in subject taught is required. Teaching experience is required. Publication in international academic journals is required.
Requirements for ESL Teachers: Doctor's degree in English is required. 3 years of teaching experience is preferred.
Requirements for Administrators: Master's degree in educational administration/planning is required. 5 years of administrative experience is required.
Duration: 2 years; renewable.
Salary: *Teachers:* 6,282–15,720 naira per calendar year. *Administrators:* 6,282–15,372 naira per calendar year.
Benefits: Round-trip transportation from U.S. for appointee and dependents. Housing or housing allowance for appointee and dependents. Paid home leave. Health care. Pension plan. Other benefits are provided.
Academic Calendar: October–August.
Application Deadline: None.
Contact: Mr. M.L. Buba, Registrar, University of Maiduguri, P.M.B. 1069, Maiduguri, Nigeria. *Phone:* 232968. *Cable:* University, Maiduguri.

SOKOTO

40 UNIVERSITY OF SOKOTO
This public coed university was founded in 1975. Current enrollment is 3,487; 2% of the faculty are U.S. nationals.
Language of Instruction: English.
Opportunities: *General:* Full-time positions. *ESL:* None. *Administrators:* None.
Requirements: Doctor's degree is required. 10–15 years of teaching experience is required. International experience is required.
Duration: 2 years; renewable for 2 years.
Salary: Contact university for information.
Benefits: Round-trip transportation from U.S. for appointee and dependents. Housing allowance. Paid home leave every 2 years. Health insurance. Other benefits are provided.
Academic Calendar: October–July.
Application Deadline: 3 months prior to start.
Contact: The Registrar, University of Sokoto, P.M.B. 2346, Sokoto, Nigeria. *Phone:* 232134/232058. *Telex:* 73134 UNISOK NG. *Cable:* UNISOKOTO.

SIERRA LEONE

KABALA

41 KABALA RUPP MEMORIAL SCHOOL
This private coed primary school was founded in 1956. Current enrollment is 30; 100% of the faculty are U.S. nationals. Teaching applicants must be members of the Missionary Church, Wesleyan Church, or United Brethren in Christ Church, and must be approved by the sending Mission board.
Language of Instruction: English.
Opportunities: *General:* 3 full- and part-time positions. *ESL:* None. *Administrators:* 1 full-time position.
Requirements for Teachers: Bachelor's degree in education is required; master's degree is preferred. 2 years of teaching experience is required. International experience is preferred. Language proficiency in French on the intermediate level is preferred.
Requirements for Administrators: Bachelor's degree in education is required; master's degree is preferred. 2 years of administrative experience is preferred. International experience is preferred.
Duration: 2–3 years; renewable.
Salary: *Teachers:* $4,800–$12,000 per calendar year. *Administrators:* $10,000–$12,000 per calendar year.
Benefits: Round-trip transportation from U.S. for appointee and dependents. Housing for appointee and dependents. Paid home leave. Health insurance and health care. Pension plan.
Academic Calendar: August–May.

Orientation: On-site.
Contact: Missionary Church members: Department of Overseas, Missionary Church, 3901 South Wayne Avenue, Fort Wayne, IN 46807. *Phone:* (219) 456-4502. *Others:* Janet E. Nickel, Principal, Kabala Rupp Memorial School, Box 28, Kabala, Sierra Leone.

SOMALIA

MOGADISHU

42 AMERICAN SCHOOL OF MOGADISHU
This private coed primary school was founded in 1959. Current enrollment is 188; 60% of the faculty are U.S. nationals.
Language of Instruction: *Primary:* English. *Other:* French.
Opportunities: *General:* 20 full- and part-time positions. *ESL:* 1 full-time position. *Administrators:* 2 full-time positions.
Requirements for General Teachers: Bachelor's degree in education is required; master's degree is preferred. 2 years of teaching experience is required. International experience is preferred.
Requirements for ESL Teachers: Master's degree is preferred. Teaching experience is preferred. International experience is preferred.
Requirements for Administrators: Bachelor's degree in administration is required; master's degree is preferred.
Duration: 1–2 years; renewable.
Salary: *Teachers:* $13,000–$19,000 per academic year. *Administrators:* $20,000–$40,000 per calendar year.
Benefits: Round-trip transportation from U.S. for appointee and dependents. Housing for appointee and dependents. Paid home leave every 2 years. Health insurance. Other benefits are provided.
Academic Calendar: August–June.
Application Deadline: December–February.
Contact: James Swetz, Director, American School of Mogadishu, Department of State/Mogadishu, Washington, DC 20520-2360. *Phone:* In Somalia: 81988/80176. *Telex:* 789 AEMBA MOG. *Cable:* c/o US Embassy.

SOUTH AFRICA

MORE THAN ONE CITY

43 U.S. INFORMATION SERVICE
USIS reports that because of South Africa's labor laws, it is difficult for foreigners to obtain work permits. The law states that permits will be issued only if there are no South Africans available to fill the positions.

Some U.S. nationals have been invited to teach at South African universities for varying lengths of time in fields where expertise is not available among South African citizens. Direct contact with individual universities may result in such employment.
For General Information, Contact: U.S. Information Service, Second Floor, Scott's Building, 10 Plein St., Cape Town, South Africa. *Phone:* (27-21) 419-4822.

JOHANNESBURG

44 AMERICAN INTERNATIONAL SCHOOL OF JOHANNESBURG
This private coed primary/secondary school was founded in 1982. Current enrollment is 175; 50% of the faculty are U.S. nationals.
Language of Instruction: *Primary:* English. *Other:* French and Spanish.
Opportunities: *General:* 8 full- or part-time positions. *ESL:* 2 full-time positions. *Administrators:* 1 full- or part-time position.
Requirements for General Teachers: Bachelor's degree is required; master's degree is preferred. 2 years of teaching experience is preferred.
Requirements for ESL Teachers: Bachelor's degree in TESL is required; master's degree is preferred. Practical experience is preferred. International experience is preferred.
Requirements for Administrators: Master's degree in school administration is required. Administrative experience is required. International experience is preferred.
Duration: 2 years; renewable indefinitely.

All information is subject to change without notice and must be confirmed directly with the employer.

10

Salary: *Teachers:* 13,000–18,000 rand per academic year. *Administrators:* Determined by Board of Directors.
Benefits: Round-trip transportation from U.S. for appointee and dependents. Housing allowance. School assists in locating housing. Other benefits are provided.
Academic Calendar: August–June.
Orientation: 1 week on-site.
Application Deadline: January.
Contact: Mr. H.L. Hanley, Superintendent, American International School of Johannesburg, Private Bag X4, Bryanston, Johannesburg 2021, South Africa. *Phone:* (27-11) 464-1505. *Telex:* 4-31452.

MAFIKENG

45 UNIVERSITY OF BOPHUTHATSWANA

This public coed university was founded in 1979 to serve residents of Bophuthatswana, one of the "homelands" in South Africa. Current enrollment is 2,275.
Language of Instruction: English.
Opportunities: *General:* Full-time positions. *ESL:* Full-time positions. *Administrators:* Full-time positions.
Requirements for General Teachers: Doctor's degree in subject taught is preferred. Teaching experience is preferred. International experience is preferred.
Requirements for ESL Teachers: Master's degree in English is required; doctor's degree is preferred. 5 years of teaching experience is preferred or practical experience is required. International experience is preferred.
Requirements for Administrators: Master's or doctor's degree is required. Administrative experience is preferred. International experience is preferred.
Duration: 3 years; renewable for 3 years.
Salary: *Teachers:* $12,000–$25,000 per calendar year. *Administrators:* $15,000–$28,000 per calendar year.
Benefits: Round-trip transportation from U.S. for appointee and dependents. Housing for appointee and dependents. Paid home leave every 3 years. Health and life insurance. Pension plan. Other benefits are provided.
Academic Calendar: January–December.
Contact: Personnel Department, University of Bophuthatswana, Private Bag X2046, Mafikeng, Bophuthatswana, South Africa. *Phone:* (1401) 21171, Ext. 433. *Telex:* 3072 BP. *Cable:* UNIBO.

SUDAN

KHARTOUM

46 KHARTOUM AMERICAN SCHOOL

This private coed pre-K and primary school was founded in 1961. Current enrollment is 210.
Language of Instruction: *Primary:* English. *Other:* Arabic and French.
Opportunities: *General:* 3 full-time positions. *ESL:* None. *Administrators:* Less than 1 position per year.
Requirements for Teachers: Bachelor's degree is required. 2 years of teaching experience is required. International experience is preferred.
Requirements for Administrators: Master's degree in administration is required. Administrative experience is required. International experience is required.
Duration: 2 years; renewable for 2 years.
Salary: *Teachers:* $12,400–$21,600 per academic year. *Administrators:* $40,000 per calendar year.
Benefits: Round-trip transportation from U.S. for appointee and dependents. Housing for appointee and dependents. Paid home leave every year. Health insurance. Other benefits are provided.
Academic Calendar: August–May.
Contact: Richard T. Eng, Superintendent, Khartoum American School, P.O. Box 699, Khartoum, Sudan. *Phone:* 221386. *Telex:* AmEmbassy 22619 SD.

SWAZILAND
MBABANE

47 SWAZILAND COLLEGE OF TECHNOLOGY

This public coed postsecondary vocational/technical institution was founded in 1968. Current enrollment is 570; none of the faculty are U.S. nationals.
Language of Instruction: English.
Opportunities: *Teachers:* 2–4 positions. *Administrators:* None.
Requirements for General Teachers: Bachelor's or master's degree in engineering is preferred. 2 years of teaching experience is preferred. Work experience in relevant technical field is required. International experience is preferred.
Requirements for ESL Teachers: Bachelor's degree in technical or business English is required. 3 years of teaching experience is required. International experience is preferred.
Duration: 30 months; renewable for 30 months.
Salary: Positions are voluntary.
Benefits: Housing is provided. Health care.
Academic Calendar: July–June.
Application Deadline: None.
Contact: Principal, Swaziland College of Technology, P.O. Box 69, Mbabane, Swaziland. *Phone:* (268) 42681/2/3.

ZAIRE
KINSHASA

48 AMERICAN SCHOOL OF KINSHASA

This private coed primary/secondary school was founded in 1961. Current enrollment is 510; 70% of the faculty are U.S. nationals.
Language of Instruction: *Primary:* English. *Other:* French.
Opportunities: *General:* 5–10 full- and part-time positions. *ESL:* 3 full- and part-time positions. *Administrators:* Less than 1 position per year.
Requirements for General Teachers: Bachelor's degree in subject taught is required; master's degree is preferred. 2–3 years of teaching experience is required. Teaching certificate is required. International experience is preferred.
Requirements for ESL Teachers: Bachelor's degree in TESL is required. 2 years of teaching experience is required. Teaching certificate is required.
Requirements for Administrators: Master's degree in administration is required. Administrative experience is required. International experience is preferred. Language proficiency in French is preferred.
Duration: 2 years; renewable indefinitely.
Salary: *Teachers:* $20,000–$35,000 per academic year. *Administrators:* Teacher scale plus 10% per calendar year.
Benefits: Round-trip transportation from U.S. for appointee and dependents. Housing for appointee and dependents. Paid home leave every year after second year. Health and life insurance.
Academic Calendar: August–June.
Application Deadline: Most applicants are hired through Overseas Placement Fairs.
Contact: Dave Holmer, Superintendent, American School of Kinshasa, APO New York 09662-0006. *Phone:* In Zaire: (243-12) 31506.

ZIMBABWE
MORE THAN ONE CITY

49 MINISTRY OF EDUCATION

The Ministry reports a need for U.S. teachers of physics, chemistry, mathematics, and biology on the secondary level. Teachers are recruited locally.
Language of Instruction: *Primary:* English. *Other:* Shona and Ndebele.
Requirements: Master's degree is required; doctor's degree is preferred. Teaching experience is required. Teaching certificate is required.
Salary: Varies.
Academic Calendar: January–December.
Application Deadline: None.
Contact: Secretary for Education, Ministry of Education, Box 8022, Harare, Zimbabwe. *Phone:* (263-0) 734050.

All information is subject to change without notice and must be confirmed directly with the employer.

11

ASIA AND OCEANIA

MORE THAN ONE COUNTRY

50 FRIENDS WORLD COLLEGE—CHINA PROGRAM
This private coed university was founded in 1965. Current enrollment is 8 in Taiwan and the People's Republic of China; none of the faculty are U.S. nationals.
Language of Instruction: *Primary:* English. *Other:* Chinese.
Opportunities: *General:* Less than 1 part-time position per year. *ESL:* None. *Administrators:* Less than 1 position per year.
Requirements for General Teachers: Doctor's degree in subject taught is preferred. Teaching experience is required. International experience is required. Language proficiency in Chinese on the advanced level is required. A faculty exchange for recipients of sabbatical leave can be considered.
Requirements for Administrators: Doctor's degree is preferred. Administrative experience is required. International experience is required. Language proficiency in Chinese on the advanced level is required.
Duration: 1 year; renewable indefinitely.
Benefits: Round-trip transportation from U.S. for appointee only. Possibly housing for appointee. Health insurance. Other benefits are provided.
Orientation: In Huntington, New York.
Application Deadline: Rolling.
Contact: Dr. Maria Jaschok, Director, Friends World College—China Program, Arena, A4, 2/5, G-Block, Hung Hom Bay Center, 104–108 Baker St., Hung Hom, Kowloon, Hong Kong. *Phone:* (852-3) 337737; in U.S.: (516) 549-5000. *Telex:* 33977 MBC HX. *Cable:* ASIARENA.

51 PRINCETON-IN-ASIA
This foundation sends recent graduates to public and private postsecondary vocational/technical schools and universities in Asia and the Near East as volunteers. Priority is given to Princeton students but other applications are accepted.
Opportunities: *General:* None. *ESL:* 50 full-time positions. *Administrators:* None.
Requirements: Bachelor's degree is required. Practical experience is preferred. Language proficiency in Chinese or Japanese is preferred.
Duration: 1 year; renewable for 1 year.
Salary: Subsistance allowance.
Benefits: Usually half of round-trip transportation from U.S. for appointee only. Housing for appointee only. Health insurance.
Academic Calendar: September–July.
Orientation: At Princeton.
Application Deadline: Dec. 15.
Contact: M.B. Williamson, Executive Director, Princeton-in-Asia, 224 Palmer Hall, Princeton, NJ 08544. *Phone:* (609) 452-3657. *Telex:* 499-1258 TIGER.

AMERICAN SAMOA

52 DEPARTMENT OF EDUCATION
The Department reports an annual need for 5 U.S. secondary school teachers, secondary vocational/technical school teachers, and special education teachers.
Language of Instruction: *Primary:* English. *Other:* Samoan.
Requirements: Bachelor's degree in subject taught is required; master's degree is preferred. 5 years of teaching experience is required.
Duration: 2 years; renewable for 2 years.
Salary: $10,916–$25,061 per academic year.
Benefits: Round-trip transportation from U.S. for appointee and dependents. Housing for appointee and dependents. Paid home leave. Other benefits are provided.
Academic Calendar: August–June.
Orientation: 2 weeks in American Samoa.
Application Deadline: March 1.
Contact: Mr. S.E. Sala, Director of Personnel, Department of Education, General Delivery, Pago Pago, American Samoa 96799. *Phone:* (684) 633-5237.

PAGO PAGO

53 FA'ASAO HIGH SCHOOL
This private female-only secondary school was founded in 1974. Current enrollment is 260; 40% of the faculty are U.S. nationals. It is a volunteer exchange program with St. Joseph's University, Philadelphia; VICS; and Lay Missionaries, Los Angeles. A religious affiliation is required.
Language of Instruction: *Primary:* English. *Other:* Samoan.
Opportunities: *General:* 5 full-time positions. *ESL:* 5 full-time positions. *Administrators:* None.
Requirements for General Teachers: Bachelor's degree is required. 2 years of teaching experience is preferred. Language proficiency in Spanish on the beginning or intermediate level is preferred. Health clearance is required.
Requirements for ESL Teachers: Bachelor's degree is required. 2 years of teaching experience is preferred. Language proficiency in Spanish on the beginning or intermediate level is preferred. Health clearance is required.
Duration: 2 years; renewable.
Salary: $100 per month.
Benefits: Round-trip transportation from U.S. for appointee. Housing for appointee only.
Academic Calendar: September–June.
Orientation: 1 week on-site.
Application Deadline: January.
Contact: Sister Margo Delaney, Principal, Fa'asao High School, P.O. Box 729, Pago Pago, American Samoa 96799. *Phone:* (684) 688-7559/7731.

AUSTRALIA

54 DEPARTMENT OF EMPLOYMENT, EDUCATION AND TRAINING
The Department reports that there is no need for U.S. teachers or educational administators at this time.

State or Territory education departments recruit teachers for government schools. For a listing, contact the Department at the address below and request *Australian State Departments of Education.*

Catholic school systems in each state recruit their own teachers. Contact the Department at the address below and request *Catholic Education Offices.*

For schools that operate outside these sectors, contact the National Council for Independent Schools, P.O. Box 279, Woden, ACT 2606, Australia.

Higher education institutions in Australia advertise staff vacancies in the national newspapers, available at the nearest Australian Embassy. *Australian Institutions of Higher Education* can be ordered from the Australian Government Publishing Service, Mail Order Sales, GPO Box 84, Canberra, ACT 2601, Australia.
Academic Calendar: February–December.
For General Information, Contact: Department of Employment, Education and Training, 64 Northbourne Ave., 14 Mort St., Canberra, NSW, Australia. *Phone:* (61-62) 438111.

BATHURST

55 ALL SAINTS' COLLEGE

This private coed primary/secondary school was founded in 1873. Current enrollment is 500; none of the faculty are U.S. nationals.
Language of Instruction: English.
Opportunities: *General:* 1 full-time position. *ESL:* None. *Administrators:* None.
Requirements: Bachelor's degree in arts, commerce, mathematics, or science is required. 4 years of teaching experience is required. Teaching certificate is required.
Duration: 1–3 years; renewable for 1–3 years.
Salary: AUS $21,207–$30,444 per calendar year.
Benefits: Housing is sometimes provided for appointee and dependents, or school assists in locating housing.
Academic Calendar: February–December.
Application Deadline: June.
Contact: Robert N.J. Bickerdike, Headmaster, All Saints' College, Bathurst, NSW 2795, Australia. *Phone:* (61-63) 313767.

BRISBANE

56 ST. PETERS LUTHERAN COLLEGE

This private coed primary/secondary school was founded in 1945. Current enrollment is 1,250; 3% of the faculty are U.S. nationals.
Language of Instruction: English.
Opportunities: *General:* 2 full-time positions. *ESL:* None. *Administrators:* None.
Requirements: Teaching experience is required.
Salary: AUS $24,000–$30,000 per calendar year.
Benefits: Benefits are provided.
Academic Calendar: January–December.
Orientation: 3 days on-site.
Application Deadline: None.
Contact: Dr. C.R. Dron, Headmaster, St. Peters Lutheran College, 66 Harts Rd., Indooroopilly, Brisbane 4068, Australia. *Phone:* (61-7) 879-7141.

GEELONG

57 GEELONG COLLEGE

This private coed primary/secondary school was founded in 1861. Current enrollment is 1,182; 1% of the faculty are U.S. nationals.
Language of Instruction: English.
Opportunities: *General:* Full-time positions. *ESL:* None. *Administrators:* None.
Requirements: Bachelor's degree is required; master's degree is preferred. Teaching experience is required.
Duration: 1–5 years; renewable for 5 years.
Salary: AUS $23,000–$37,000 per calendar year.
Benefits: School assists in locating housing. Other benefits are provided.
Academic Calendar: February–December.
Contact: Mr. A.P. Sheahan, Principal, The Geelong College, P.O. Box 5, Geelong 3220, Australia. *Phone:* (61-52) 263111.

SYDNEY

58 AUSTRALIAN INTERNATIONAL INDEPENDENT SCHOOL

This private coed secondary school was founded in 1969. Current enrollment is 215; 5% of the faculty are U.S. nationals. The school is interested only in exchanging teachers.
Language of Instruction: English.
Opportunities: *General:* 1 full- or part-time position for teachers of all subjects. *ESL:* None. *Administrators:* None.
Requirements: Bachelor's degree in subject taught is required; master's degree is preferred. Teaching experience is required. Language proficiency in any foreign language is required.
Duration: 1 year; not renewable.
Salary: AUS $20,000–$30,000 per academic year.
Benefits: Housing for appointee and dependents.
Academic Calendar: February–December.
Application Deadline: November.
Contact: Dr. Mark S. Butler, Deputy Principal, Australian International Independent School, 110 Talavera Rd., North Ryde, Sydney, NSW 2113, Australia. *Phone:* (61-2) 8887804.

BANGLADESH

DHAKA

59 AMERICAN INTERNATIONAL SCHOOL/DHAKA

This private coed primary school was founded in 1972. Current enrollment is 400; 50% of the faculty are U.S. nationals.
Language of Instruction: English.
Opportunities: *General:* 10 full- and part-time positions. *ESL:* 4 full- and part-time positions. *Administrators:* Less than 1 position per year.
Requirements for General Teachers: Bachelor's degree in education or related field is preferred. 2 years of teaching experience is required.
Requirements for ESL Teachers: Bachelor's degree in education or related field is preferred. 2 years of teaching experience is required. International experience is preferred.
Requirements for Administrators: Master's degree in administration is preferred. 2 years of administrative experience is preferred. International experience is preferred.
Duration: 2 years; renewable indefinitely.
Salary: *Teachers:* $11,623–$33,060 per academic year. *Administrators:* $30,000–$60,000 per calendar year.
Benefits: Round-trip transportation from U.S. for appointee only. Housing for appointee and dependents. Paid home leave every 2 years. Health insurance. Pension plan. Other benefits are provided.
Academic Calendar: August–June.
Orientation: 1 week on-site.
Application Deadline: February.
Contact: Stephen Kapner, Superintendent, American International School/Dhaka, Department of State, Washington, DC 20520. *Or:* Stephen Kapner, Superintendent, American International School/Dhaka, United Nations Road, Baridhara, Bangladesh. *Phone:* (880-2) 602298.

BURMA

RANGOON

60 INTERNATIONAL HIGH SCHOOL—RANGOON

This private coed secondary school was founded in 1975. Current enrollment is 25; 30% of the faculty are U.S. nationals. Faculty are recruited only from those presently residing in Burma.
Language of Instruction: English.
Opportunities: *Teachers:* Full- and part-time positions. *Administrators:* Full-time positions.
Salary: *Teachers:* From $10.50 per period per day. *Administrators:* $18,000 per calendar year.
Academic Calendar: August–June.
Contact: International High School—Rangoon, Department of State/Rangoon, Washington, DC 20520. *Or:* Georgianna Bell, Principal, International High School—Rangoon, 20A Dubern Rd., Rangoon, Burma. *Phone:* 61626/30209.

CHINA/HONG KONG

MORE THAN ONE CITY

61 EMBASSY OF THE PEOPLE'S REPUBLIC OF CHINA
The Embassy reports a need for full-time teachers of English as a second/foreign language, English literature, and linguistics at the university level.
Language of Instruction: Chinese.
Requirements: Bachelor's degree in any field is required; master's degree in related field is required for expert positions. Teaching experience is required for expert positions. International experience is preferred.
Duration: 1 year; renewable for 1 year.
Benefits: Housing for appointee and dependents. Other benefits are provided.
Academic Calendar: September–July.
Contact: Wang Ruizhong, Third Secretary, Embassy of the People's Republic of China, 2300 Connecticut Ave. NW, Washington, DC 20008. *Phone:* (202) 328-2563.

62 CHINESE AMERICAN EDUCATIONAL EXCHANGE
This organization, founded in 1980, recruits teachers for public medical colleges, postsecondary vocational/technical institutes, professional institutes, and universities in the provinces of Hebei and Shandong and the city of Shanghai.
Language of Instruction: English.
Opportunities: *General:* 15–20 full-time positions for teachers of all subjects. *ESL:* 10 full-time positions. *Administrators:* None; possibly in future.
Requirements for General Teachers: Bachelor's degree in subject taught is required; not applicable for "practical" teaching. Teaching or practical experience is required.
Requirements for ESL Teachers: Bachelor's degree is required; master's or doctor's degree is sometimes preferred. 2 years of teaching or practical experience is required.
Duration: 3 months–1 year; renewable.
Salary: $200–$325 per month.
Benefits: Round-trip transportation from U.S. for experts; half paid for teachers. Housing for appointee and dependents. Health insurance. Education for children. Other benefits are provided.
Academic Calendar: September–July.
Orientation: In U.S.
Contact: Dr. Teresa O'Connor or Dr. Judith Stelboum, Directors, Chinese American Educational Exchange, Rm. A-323, The College of Staten Island, 715 Ocean Terrace, Staten Island, NY 10301. *Phone:* (718) 390-7654.

63 NATIONAL ACADEMY OF SCIENCES, COMMITTEE ON ECONOMICS EDUCATION AND RESEARCH IN CHINA (CEERC)
CEERC recruits teachers for public professional institutes and universities in the People's Republic of China.
Opportunities: *General:* 4 full-time positions for teachers of economics education: macro/micro and international finance. *ESL:* None. *Administrators:* None.
Requirements: Doctor's degree in economics is required. 4 years of teaching experience is required.
Duration: 1 semester; not renewable consecutively.
Salary: Half of appointee's 9-month university salary or equivalent.
Benefits: Round-trip transportation from U.S. for appointee and spouse. Housing for appointee and spouse. Health and pension benefits are equal to half of appointee's 9-month university benefits or equivalent.
Academic Calendar: January–August and June–December.
Application Deadline: Rolling.
Contact: Dr. Todd M. Johnson, Executive Director, CEERC, National Academy of Sciences, Harris 486, 2101 Constitution Ave. NW, Washington, DC 20418. *Phone:* (202) 334-2718. *Telex:* 4900007565 NRC UI.

BEIJING

64 INTERNATIONAL SCHOOL OF BEIJING
This private coed primary school was founded in 1980. Current enrollment is 136; 50% of the faculty are U.S. nationals.
Language of Instruction: English.
Opportunities: *General:* 8 full-time positions. *ESL:* None. *Administrators:* 1 full-time position.
Requirements for Teachers: Bachelor's degree in subject taught is required. 2 years of teaching experience is required. International experience is required.
Requirements for Administrators: Master's degree in administration or related field is required. 2 years of administrative experience is required. International experience is required. Language proficiency in Chinese (Mandarin) is preferred.
Duration: 2 years; renewable for 1 year.
Salary: *Teachers:* $17,000–$26,600 per academic year. *Administrators:* Varies.
Benefits: Round-trip transportation from U.S. for appointee only. Housing for appointee and spouse. Paid home leave every year. Health insurance. Other benefits are provided.
Academic Calendar: September–June.
Orientation: 2 weeks on-site.
Application Deadline: January.
Contact: Scott Chambers, Principal, The International School of Beijing, c/o American Embassy, Beijing, People's Republic of China. *Phone:* (86-1) 523 831, Ext. 445. *Telex:* 22701 AMEMB CN.

GUANGZHOU

65 AMERICAN SCHOOL OF GUANGZHOU
This private coed primary school was founded in 1981. Current enrollment is 25; 60% of the faculty are U.S. nationals.
Language of Instruction: English.
Opportunities: *General:* 4 full- and part-time positions. *ESL:* None. *Administrators:* 1 full-time position.
Requirements for Teachers: Bachelor's degree in elementary education is required. 2 years of teaching experience is preferred. International experience is preferred.
Requirements for Administrators: Master's degree in educational administration is required. Administrative experience is required. International experience is preferred.
Duration: 1–2 years; renewable.
Salary: *Teachers:* $10,000–$21,000 per academic year. *Administrators:* $24,000–$36,000 per academic year.
Benefits: Round-trip transportation from U.S. for administrators only. Housing for appointee and dependents. Paid home leave every year for administrators only. Health insurance. Pension plan.
Academic Calendar: September–June.
Orientation: 1 week on-site.
Application Deadline: April 1.
Contact: William Vodarski, Principal, American School of Guangzhou, AMCONGEN, Box 100, FPO San Francisco 96655-0002. *Or:* American School of Guangzhou, Garden Hotel Office Tower, P Level, 368 Huanshi Rd. East, Guangzhou, People's Republic of China. *Phone:* (86-20) 338999, Ext. 7433.

HONG KONG

66 EDUCATION DEPARTMENT
The Department reports that pre-K, primary, and secondary schools catering to English-speaking children in Hong Kong employ expatriate staff. In addition, the British Council has recently launched a 2-year pilot program of hiring native English speakers from overseas to strengthen English language teaching in Hong Kong.

For a list of English-speaking schools, write to the address below and request *Information Sheet: Education Facilities for English-Speaking Children.*
Contact: Julie Chen, Education Officer, Education Department, Lee Gardens, 33–37 Hysan Ave., Causeway Bay, Hong Kong. *Phone:* (852-5) 8392233. *For pilot program information:* British Council, 255 Hennessy Rd., Wan Chai, Hong Kong.

All information is subject to change without notice and must be confirmed directly with the employer.

15

67 HONG KONG INTERNATIONAL SCHOOL
This private coed primary/secondary school was founded in 1966.
Language of Instruction: English.
Opportunities: *General:* Full- and part-time positions. *ESL:* None. *Administrators:* Full-time positions.
Requirements for Administrators: Bachelor's degree in education is preferred. 5 years of administrative experience is required. Membership in a Christian church is required.
Duration: 3 years; renewable for 2–3 years.
Salary: *Teachers:* $15,720–$41,660 per academic year. *Administrators:* $57,000–$74,300 per academic year.
Benefits: Round-trip transportation from U.S. for appointee and dependents. Housing for appointee and dependents. Paid home leave every 2 years. Health and disability insurance. Retirement plan. Other benefits are provided.
Academic Calendar: August–June.
Orientation: 10 days on-site.
Application Deadline: February.
Contact: Mr. David F. Rittman, Headmaster, Hong Kong International School, 6 & 23 South Bay Close, Repulse Bay, Hong Kong. *Phone:* (852-5) 8122305. *Fax:* (852-5) 8127037. *Cable:* HKISCHOOL.

SHANGHAI

68 SHANGHAI AMERICAN SCHOOL
This private coed primary school was founded in 1980. Current enrollment is 44; 75% of the faculty are U.S. nationals.
Language of Instruction: English.
Opportunities: *General:* 4 full-time positions. *ESL:* None. *Administrators:* 1 full-time position.
Requirements for Teachers: Bachelor's degree in education is required. Teaching experience is preferred or practical experience is required.
Requirements for Administrators: Bachelor's degree in education, administration, or business is preferred. Administrative experience is preferred. Language proficiency in Chinese is preferred.
Duration: 1 year; renewable.
Salary: *Teachers:* $1,400–$1,900 per month. *Administrators:* $1,600–$2,000 per month.
Academic Calendar: September–June.
Application Deadline: June.
Contact: Marla Leung, Administrator, Shanghai American School, c/o American Consulate General—Shanghai, U.S. Department of State, Washington, DC 20520. *Or:* Shanghai American School, 1469 Huai Hai Zhong Lu, Shanghai, People's Republic of China. *Phone:* (86-21) 379-880, Ext. 218.

TAIWAN

69 MORRISON CHRISTIAN ACADEMY
This is a private coed primary/secondary school. Current enrollment is 610; 85% of the faculty are U.S. nationals. Most of the faculty come from church-affiliated missions.
Language of Instruction: English.
Opportunities: *Teachers:* 10–18 positions for teachers of all subjects. *Administrators:* None.
Requirements: Bachelor's degree in subject taught is required; master's degree is preferred. 3 years of teaching experience is preferred. International experience is preferred.
Duration: 3 years; renewable.
Benefits: Round-trip transportation from U.S. for appointee and dependents.
Academic Calendar: August–May.
Orientation: On-site.
Application Deadline: Rolling.
Contact: Arthur L. Westcott, Superintendent, Morrison Christian Academy, P.O. Box 27-24, Taichung 40098, Taiwan.

70 TAIPEI AMERICAN SCHOOL
This private primary/secondary school was founded in 1949. Total enrollment is 1,620; 85% of the faculty are U.S. nationals.
Language of Instruction: *Primary:* English. *Other:* Chinese, French, German, Spanish, and Dutch.
Opportunities: *General:* 25–35 full-time positions for teachers of all subjects and special education. *ESL:* 1–2 full-time positions. *Administrators:* Less than 1 position per year.

Requirements for General Teachers: Bachelor's degree is required; master's degree is preferred. 2 years of full-time primary or secondary teaching experience is required. Teaching certificate is required. International experience is preferred.
Requirements for ESL Teachers: Bachelor's degree is required; master's degree is preferred. 2 years of full-time primary or secondary teaching experience is required. Teaching certificate is required. International experience is preferred.
Requirements for Administrators: Master's degree is required; doctor's degree is preferred. 3 years of administrative experience is required. Administrative certificate is required.
Duration: 2 years; renewable indefinitely.
Salary: *Teachers:* $24,873–$42,476 per calendar year. *Administrators:* $37,513–$55,547 per calendar year.
Benefits: Round trip transportation from the U.S. for appointee and dependents. Housing for appointee only. Paid home leave every 2 years. Health, life, and disability insurance. Retirement plan. Tuition for children enrolled at this school. Other benefits are provided.
Academic Calendar: August–June.
Orientation: 7 days on-site.
Application Deadline: Jan. 1.
Contact: Director of Personnel, Taipei American School, 731 Wen Lin Rd., Sec. 1, Taipei 11141, Taiwan. *Phone:* (886-2) 831-2111.

71 TAMKANG UNIVERSITY, GRADUATE INSTITUTE OF AMERICAN STUDIES
This private coed university was founded in 1971. Current enrollment is 10,000; 50% of the GIAS faculty are U.S. nationals.
Language of Instruction: *Primary:* English. *Other:* Chinese.
Opportunities: *General:* 4–5 full- and part-time positions for teachers of political science, economics, sociology, history, and law. *ESL:* None. *Administrators:* None.
Requirements: Doctor's degree in subject taught is required. Teaching experience is preferred. Language proficiency in Chinese on the beginning level is preferred.
Duration: 1–2 years; renewable.
Salary: Negotiable.
Benefits: One-way transportation from U.S. for appointee only. Housing is sometimes provided, or university assists in locating housing.
Academic Calendar: September–June.
Application Deadline: None.
Contact: Chen Yea-hung, President, Tamkang University, Main Campus, 151 Ying Chuan Rd., Tamsui, Taipei Hsien 25137, Taiwan. *Or:* Thomas B. Lee, Director, Graduate Institute of American Studies, Tamkang University, City Campus, Kinhua St., Taipei 10606, Taiwan. *Phone:* (886-2) 393-2517.

72 YMCA OVERSEAS SERVICE CORPS
This association recruits ESL teachers for adults and children at its associations throughout Taiwan.
Requirements: Bachelor's degree is required. Teaching experience and/or TESL training is preferred.
Duration: 1 year; renewable for 1 year.
Salary: NT $14,000 per month.
Benefits: Transportation to U.S. on completion of assignment. Housing for appointee. Meals provided. Reimbursement for half of Mandarin study tuition. Health insurance. Other benefits are provided.
Academic Calendar: July–July or October–October.
Application Deadline: Jan. 15 or April 15.
Contact: USA/OSCY Taiwan, International Division, YMCA of the USA, 101 N. Wacker Dr., Chicago, IL 60606. *Phone:* (312) 977-0031. *Or:* National Council of YMCAs of the Republic of China, 35 Shaohsing N. St., 9F-1, Taipei 10043, Taiwan. *Phone:* (886-2) 396-3961.

FIJI

MORE THAN ONE CITY

73 MINISTRY OF EDUCATION
The Ministry reports that there is no need for U.S. teachers or educational administrators at this time.
For General Information, Contact: Ministry of Education, Marela House, Suva, Fiji.

74 U.S. PEACE CORPS IN FIJI
The U.S. Peace Corps in Fiji reports a need for U.S. teachers.
Opportunities: *General:* 20 positions for secondary school teachers, primarily of mathematics and physics. Positions also for postsecondary vocational/technical teachers. *ESL:* None. *Administrators:* None.
Requirements: Bachelor's degree in subject taught is required; master's degree is preferred. 2–3 years of teaching experience is preferred. For some teaching of accounting/bookkeeping, practical experience is preferred. Language proficiency in any foreign language is preferred.
Duration: 2 years; renewable for 1 year.
Salary: Monthly allowance is provided.
Benefits: Round-trip transportation from U.S. for appointee and dependents. Housing for appointee and dependents. Health insurance. Education for dependent children.
Orientation: 1 week in the U.S., 8–10 weeks in Fiji.
Contact: Recruitment Office, U.S. Peace Corps, 806 Connecticut Ave. NW, Washington, DC 20526.

GUAM

TALOFOFO

75 NOTRE DAME HIGH SCHOOL
This private Catholic female-only secondary school was founded in 1967. Current enrollment is 273; 90% of the faculty are U.S. nationals.
Language of Instruction: English.
Opportunities: *General:* Full- and part-time positions for teachers of all subjects. *ESL:* None. *Administrators:* Full-time positions. Requirements for *Teachers:* Bachelor's degree in subject taught is required; master's degree is preferred. Teaching experience is preferred.
Requirements for Administrators: Bachelor's degree in administration is required; master's degree in administration is preferred. 2 years of administrative experience is required.
Duration: 1 year; renewable for 1 year.
Salary: *Teachers:* $9,000–$12,700 per academic year. *Administrators:* $16,000–$18,000 per academic year.
Benefits: Benefits are provided.
Academic Calendar: August–June.
Orientation: 2 days on-site.
Application Deadline: July 15.
Contact: Sister Jean Ann Crisostomo, Principal, Notre Dame High School, San Miguel St., Talofofo, Guam 96930. *Phone:* (671) 789-1676/1745.

HONG KONG (see CHINA/HONG KONG)

INDIA

AHMADABAD

76 GUJARAT VIDYAPITH
This public coed university was founded in 1920. None of the faculty are U.S. nationals.
Language of Instruction: *Primary:* Gujarati. *Other:* Hindi.
Opportunities: *General:* 1 full-time position for a teacher of peace studies. *ESL:* None. *Administrators:* None.
Requirements: Master's degree in subject taught is required; doctor's degree is preferred. 10 years of teaching experience is required.
Duration: 4–5 months.
Salary: 3,000 rupees per month.
Benefits: Housing for appointee only.
Academic Calendar: July–October and December–April.
Application Deadline: Open.

Contact: Prof. Ramlal Parikh, Vice-Chancellor, Gujarat Vidyapith, Ahmadabad 380014, India. *Phone:* (91-272) 447292/446148. *Telex:* 121-254 GUVI IN.

BANGALORE

77 FRIENDS WORLD COLLEGE—SOUTH ASIAN CENTER
This private coed university was founded in 1965. Current enrollment is 10; none of the faculty are U.S. nationals.
Language of Instruction: English.
Opportunities: *General:* 1 full- or part-time position. *ESL:* None. *Administrators:* Less than 1 position per year. Requirements for *Teachers:* Doctor's degree is preferred. Teaching experience is required. International experience is required. Faculty exchanges for recipients of sabbatical leave can be considered.
Requirements for Administrators: Doctor's degree is preferred. Administrative experience is required. International experience is required.
Duration: 1 year; renewable indefinitely.
Salary: *Teachers:* $12,000–$15,000 per calendar year. *Administrators:* $17,000 per calendar year.
Benefits: Round-trip transportation from U.S. for appointee only. Possibly housing for appointee. Health insurance. Other benefits are provided.
Academic Calendar: September–June.
Orientation: In Huntington, New York.
Application Deadline: Open.
Contact: E.P. Menon, Director, Friends World College—South Asian Center, No. 57, First Floor, Chabria Layout, Kumara Krupa Rd., Bangalore 560001, India. *Phone:* (91-812) 71877; in U.S. (516) 549-5000.

KODAIKANAL

78 KODAIKANAL INTERNATIONAL SCHOOL
This private coed primary/secondary school was founded in 1901. Current enrollment is 450; 25% of the faculty are U.S. nationals.
Language of Instruction: English.
Opportunities: *General:* 10–15 full-time positions for teachers of all subjects. *ESL:* 1 full-time position. *Administrators:* 1 full-time position.
Requirements for General Teachers: Bachelor's degree is required; master's degree is preferred for teachers of upper secondary school. 2 years of teaching experience is required. International experience is preferred.
Requirements for ESL Teachers: Bachelor's degree in ESL is preferred. Teaching experience is preferred. International experience is preferred.
Requirements for Administrators: Master's degree in education is required. 10 years of administrative experience is required. International experience is preferred.
Duration; 3 years: renewable for 3 years.
Salary: *Teachers:* 15,000–30,000 rupees per calendar year. *Administrators:* 25,000–40,000 rupees per calendar year.
Benefits: Round-trip transportation from U.S. for appointee and dependents. Housing for appointee and dependents. Other benefits are provided.
Academic Calendar: July–May.
Orientation: 1 week on-site.
Application Deadline: None.
Contact: Dr. Paul Wiebe, Principal, Kodaikanal International School, Post Box No. 25, Kodaikanal 624 101, Tamil Nadu, India. *Phone:* (91-4542) 278. *Cable:* HIGHCLERC.

MADRAS

79 UNIVERSITY OF MADRAS
This is a public coed university. None of the faculty are U.S. nationals.
Opportunities: *General:* Less than 1 position per year. *ESL:* Less than 1 position per year. *Administrators:* None.
Requirements for General Teachers: Doctor's degree is required. Teaching experience is required. International experience is required.
Duration: Varies.
Salary: $4,000–$6,000 per year.

Benefits: Housing allowance. University assists in locating housing. Other benefits are provided.
Academic Calendar: July–April.
Application Deadline: None.
Contact: Registrar, University of Madras, Chepauk, Madras-5, Tamil Nadu 600005, India. *Phone:* (91-44) 568778.

NEW DELHI

80 AMERICAN EMBASSY SCHOOL
This private coed secondary school, adult/continuing and special education program was founded in 1952. 60% of the faculty are U.S. nationals.
Language of Instruction: English.
Opportunities: *General:* 6–8 full- and part-time positions. *ESL:* 1–2 full- and part-time positions. *Administrators:* 1–2 full-time positions.
Requirements for General Teachers: Bachelor's degree is required; master's degree is preferred. Teaching experience is required. International experience is preferred.
Requirements for ESL Teachers: Bachelor's degree is required; master's degree is preferred. Teaching experience is preferred.
Requirements for Administrators: Master's degree is required; doctor's degree is preferred. Administrative experience is required.
Duration: 2 years; renewable for 1–2 years.
Salary: *Teachers:* $18,336–$27,431 per academic year. *Administrators:* $35,000 per academic year.
Benefits: Round-trip transportation from U.S. for appointee and dependents. Housing for appointee and dependents. Paid home leave every 2 years. Health insurance. Retirement plan. Tuition for children enrolled at this school. Other benefits are provided.
Academic Calendar: August–May.
Orientation: 2 days on-site.
Application Deadline: Dec. 15.
Contact: Mr. James R. Pepperling Jr., Director, American Embassy School, Chandragupta Marg, Chankyapuri, New Delhi 110021, India. *Phone:* (91-11) 605949. *Telex:* 031-65764 AESA IN.

INDONESIA

MORE THAN ONE CITY

81 EMBASSY OF THE REPUBLIC OF INDONESIA
The Embassy reports that there is no need for U.S. teachers or educational administrators at this time.
For General Information, Contact: Dr. Jakub Isman, Education and Cultural Attache, Embassy of the Republic of Indonesia, 2020 Massachusetts Ave. NW, Washington, DC 20036. *Phone:* (202) 775-5275.

82 MINISTRY OF EDUCATION AND CULTURE
The Ministry reports that there is no need for U.S. teachers or educational administrators at this time.
Language of Instruction: Bahasa Indonesia.
Academic Calendar: July–May.
For General Information, Contact: W.P. Napitupulu, Director General, Ministry of Education and Culture, Jalan Proklamasi 17A, Jakarta 10320, Indonesia. *Phone:* (62-21) 332635/326294. *Cable:* DIKLUSEPORA.

BANDUNG

83 BANDUNG ALLIANCE SCHOOL
This is a coed primary school. Current enrollment is 40; 82% of the faculty are U.S. nationals.
Language of Instruction: *Primary:* English. *Other:* Indonesian.
Opportunities: *General:* 6 full-time positions. *ESL:* None.
Administrators: 1 full-time position. Requirements for *Teachers:* Bachelor's and master's degrees in elementary education are required. Teaching experience is required.
Requirements for Administrators: Bachelor's and master's degrees in elementary education are required. Administrative experience is

required. International experience is preferred. Language proficiency in Indonesian is preferred.
Duration: 4 years; renewable indefinitely.
Benefits: Round-trip transportation from U.S. for appointee and dependents. Housing for appointee and dependents. Health insurance.
Academic Calendar: August–July.
Orientation: In the U.S.
Contact: Don Young, Overseas Personnel, The Christian and Missionary Alliance, 350 N. Highland Ave., Nyack, NY 10960-0992. *Phone:* (914) 353-0750. *Telex:* 6818052. *Cable:* PAROUSIA NYACK/NEWYORKSTATE. *Or:* Susan Mealhow, Principal, Bandung Alliance School, Jalan Gunung Agung 14, Bandung, Java 40142, Indonesia. *Phone:* (62-22) 81844. *Telex:* 796-61573. *Cable:* PAROUSIA JAKARTA.

84 BANDUNG INTERNATIONAL SCHOOL
This private coed primary/secondary school was founded in 1972. Current enrollment is 121; 10% of the faculty are U.S. nationals.
Language of Instruction: English.
Opportunities: *General:* 2 full-time positions. *ESL:* None.
Administrators: None.
Requirements: Bachelor's degree in English or mathematics/science is required. Teaching experience is required. International experience is preferred.
Duration: 2 years; renewable for 1–2 years.
Salary: *Teachers:* $14,000–$21,000 per calendar year.
Benefits: Round-trip transportation from U.S. for appointee and dependents. Housing for appointee and dependents. Other benefits are provided.
Academic Calendar: September–July.
Application Deadline: Jan. 30.
Contact: Gavin Allen, Principal, Bandung International School, Kotak Pos 132, Bandung 40164, Indonesia. *Phone:* (62-22) 85615.

JAKARTA

85 JAKARTA INTERNATIONAL SCHOOL
This private coed primary/secondary school and special education program was founded in 1951. Current enrollment is 2,015; 64% of the faculty are U.S. nationals.
Language of Instruction: *Primary:* English. *Other:* Dutch, French, German, Spanish, and Indonesian.
Opportunities: *General:* 20–25 full- and part-time positions for teachers of all subjects and primary school teachers for learning disabilities. *ESL:* 6–7 full- and part-time positions. *Administrators:* Full-time positions.
Requirements for General Teachers: Bachelor's degree is required; master's degree is preferred. Teaching experience is preferred. International experience is preferred.
Requirements for ESL Teachers: Bachelor's degree is required; master's degree in TESL/TEFL is preferred. Teaching experience is required. International experience is preferred.
Requirements for Administrators: Bachelor's degree is required; master's degree is preferred. 2 years of administrative experience is required. International experience is preferred.
Duration: 2 years; renewable.
Salary: *Teachers:* $18,000–$23,000 per academic year. *Administrators:* $28,000–$40,000 per calendar year.
Benefits: Round-trip transportation from U.S. for appointee and dependents. Housing for appointee and dependents. Health, life, and disability insurance. Retirement plan. Tuition for children enrolled at this school. Other benefits are provided.
Academic Calendar: August–June.
Orientation: 2 weeks on-site.
Application Deadline: Jan. 1.
Contact: John F. Magagna, Headmaster, Jakarta International School, P.O. Box 79/JKS, Jakarta Selatan, Indonesia. *Phone:* (62-21) 762-555. *Telex:* 47949 INTSCH IA.

86 PERHIMPUNAN PERSAHABATAN INDONESIA-AMERIKA (INDONESIA-AMERICA FRIENDSHIP SOCIETY)
This private coed adult/continuing education language institute was founded in 1958. Current enrollment is 16,000; 6–7 of the faculty are U.S. nationals. The Society does not hire directly; the current supervisor is on a grant from the U.S. Information Agency.

All information is subject to change without notice
and must be confirmed directly with the employer.

Language of Instruction: *Primary:* Bahasa Indonesia. *Other:* English.
Contact: Gloria C. Kismadi, Deputy Director for Education and Culture, Perhimpunan Persahabatan Indonesia-Amerika, Jalan Pramuka 30, Jakarta Timur 13120, Indonesia. *Phone:* (62-21) 881241/8580536.

JAMBI

87 UNIVERSITAS JAMBI

This coed university was founded in 1963. Current enrollment is 5,800; 0.5% of the faculty are U.S. nationals. This is an exchange program with the University of Kentucky.
Language of Instruction: Indonesian.
Opportunities: *General:* None. *ESL:* 1 full-time position. *Administrators:* None.
Requirements: Master's degree is preferred. 2–3 years of teaching experience is preferred. International experience is preferred. Language proficiency in Indonesian on the beginning level is preferred.
Duration: 1 year; renewable for 1 year.
Salary: 230,000 rupiah per month.
Benefits: Housing for appointee and dependents or housing allowance.
Academic Calendar: August–July.
Application Deadline: None.
Contact: Drh. Md. Toha, MSC, Vice Rector 1, Universitas Jambi, Jalan Prof. Sri Sudewi Maschun Sofyan, Sh Telanaipura, Jambi 36122, Indonesia. *Phone:* (62-741) 23198.

MEDAN

88 MEDAN INTERNATIONAL SCHOOL

This private coed primary school was founded in 1967. Current enrollment is 40; 20% of the faculty are U.S. nationals. Faculty are only recruited locally.
Language of Instruction: *Primary:* English. *Other:* Indonesian and French.
Opportunities: *General:* Full-time positions. *ESL:* None. *Administrators:* None.
Requirements: Bachelor's degree is required. 3 years of teaching experience is required. International experience is preferred.
Duration: 1 year; renewable.
Salary: $13,595–$21,915 per academic year.
Academic Calendar: September–June.
Contact: Mrs. A.D.J. Plant, Principal, Medan International School, P.O. Box 191, Medan, Sumatra, Indonesia. *Phone:* (62-61) 27099.

SURABAYA

89 PETRA CHRISTIAN UNIVERSITY

This private coed university was founded in 1961. Current enrollment is 2,800; 7% of the faculty are U.S. nationals.
Language of Instruction: *Primary:* Indonesian. *Other:* English.
Opportunities: *General:* 1 part-time position for a teacher of literature. *ESL:* 1 part-time position for a teacher of English language skills. *Administrators:* None.
Requirements for General Teachers: Master's degree in literature is required. 1 year of teaching experience is required.
Requirements for ESL Teachers: Bachelor's degree in ESL is required. 1 year of teaching experience is required.
Duration: 2 years; renewable for 2 years.
Salary: $2,000–$4,000 per calendar year.
Benefits: Housing for appointee and dependents. Paid home leave every year. Other benefits are provided.
Academic Calendar: August–June.
Orientation: On-site.
Application Deadline: Dec. 31.
Contact: Dr. Daniel Z. Pribadi, Assistant Rector for Academic Affairs, Petra Christian University, Jalan Siwalankerto 121–131, Surabaya 60002, Indonesia. *Phone:* (62-31) 813040.

90 SURABAYA INTERNATIONAL SCHOOL

This private coed pre-K and primary/secondary school was founded in 1971. Current enrollment is 130; 50% of the faculty are U.S. nationals.
Language of Instruction: English.

Opportunities: *General:* Full-time positions. *ESL:* None. *Administrators:* Full-time positions. Requirements for *Teachers:* Bachelor's degree in education is required; master's degree is preferred. 2 years of teaching experience is preferred. International experience is preferred.
Requirements for Administrators: Master's degree in educational administration is required. 2 years of administrative experience is required. International experience is required.
Duration: 2 years; renewable.
Salary: *Teachers:* $15,000–$20,000 per academic year. *Administrators:* $40,000 per academic year.
Benefits: Round-trip transportation from U.S. for appointee and dependents. Housing for appointee and dependents. Paid home leave every 2 years. Health insurance. Other benefits are provided.
Academic Calendar: August–June.
Application Deadline: Applicants are interviewed at recruitment centers in February. Mail applications are not considered.
Contact: Don O. Hill, Principal, Surabaya International School, Jalan Kupang Indah IX/17, Tromol Pos 2/SBDK, Surabaya 60225, Indonesia. *Phone:* (62-31) 69324.

JAPAN

MORE THAN ONE CITY

91 JAPAN EXCHANGE AND TEACHING PROGRAM (JET)

JET recruits ESL teachers for public and private secondary schools, colleges, and private companies throughout Japan.
Opportunities: 500 positions.
Requirements: Bachelor's degree is required. Language proficiency in Japanese on the beginning level is preferred. Candidates should be under 35 years of age.
Duration: 1 year; renewable for 1 year.
Salary: From $2,000 per month.
Benefits: Round-trip transportation from U.S. for appointee only. Program assists in locating housing. Paid home leave. Accident insurance.
Academic Calendar: April–March.
Orientation: 1 day at Japanese Embassy or Consulate, 1 week in Tokyo.
Application Deadline: Dec. 20.
Contact: JET Program Office, Embassy of Japan, 2520 Massachusetts Ave. NW, Washington, DC 20008. *Phone:* (202) 939-6700.

FUKUOKA

92 FUKUOKA INTERNATIONAL SCHOOL

This coed primary/secondary school was founded in 1972. Current enrollment is 40; 93% of the faculty are U.S. nationals. Faculty are recruited from those presently residing in Japan.
Language of Instruction: *Primary:* English. *Other:* Japanese.
Opportunities: *General:* Full- and part-time positions. *ESL:* None. *Administrators:* None.
Requirements for Teachers: Bachelor's degree in elementary education is required; master's degree is preferred. 2 years of teaching experience is required. International experience is preferred.
Duration: 1 year; renewable.
Salary: Varies.
Benefits: School assists in locating housing. Paid home leave every 2 years. Health insurance. Other benefits are provided.
Academic Calendar: September–June.
Application Deadline: Open.
Contact: Administrator, Fukuoka International School, 1-28 Maidashi 4-chome, Higashi-ku, Fukuoka 812, Japan. *Phone:* (81-92) 641-0326.

HIROSHIMA

93 HIROSHIMA INTERNATIONAL SCHOOL

This private coed primary school was founded in 1962. Current enrollment is 600; 23% of the faculty are U.S. nationals.

The school runs a series of language programs, including English as a second language, for 500 Japanese children on all primary/secondary levels, language classes and counseling services for about 50 Japanese

All information is subject to change without notice
and must be confirmed directly with the employer.

19

children who have lived overseas for 1–4 years and speak English, and Japanese language instruction for about 50 foreign adults.

The school serves as the center of the foreign community, publishes a monthly magazine, and runs a community club and international library.
Language of Instruction: *Primary:* English. *Other:* Japanese.
Opportunities: *General:* 1–3 positions on the primary level. *ESL:* 1–5 positions on the secondary level.
Requirements for General Teachers: Bachelor's degree in liberal arts is required; master's or doctor's degree is preferred. 3 years of teaching experience or related practical experience is required. International experience is preferred. Language proficiency in Japanese on the beginning level is preferred.
Requirements for ESL Teachers: Bachelor's, master's, or doctor's degree in linguistics, applied linguistics, or English is preferred. 3 years of teaching experience is required. International experience is preferred. Language proficiency in Japanese on the beginning level is preferred.
Duration: 1–2 years; renewable.
Salary: $30,000–$55,000 per academic year.
Benefits: Round-trip transportation from U.S. for appointee and dependents. Tuition for children enrolled at this school. Other benefits are provided.
Academic Calendar: August–June.
Orientation: 2–3 weeks on-site.
Application Deadline: November–January.
Contact: Dr. Walter Enloe, Principal, Hiroshima International School, 3-49-1, Kurakake, Asa Kita-ku, Hiroshima 739-17, Japan. *Phone:* (81-82) 843-4111.

KOBE

94 MARIST BROTHERS INTERNATIONAL SCHOOL
This private coed primary/secondary school was founded in 1951. Current enrollment is 266; 50% of the faculty are U.S. nationals.
Language of Instruction: English.
Opportunities: *General:* 4 full-time positions. *ESL:* 1 full-time position. *Administrators:* Full-time positions.
Requirements for General Teachers: Bachelor's degree is required; master's degree is preferred. 2 years of teaching experience is preferred.
Requirements for ESL Teachers: Master's degree in TESL is required. 3 years of teaching experience is required.
Requirements for Administrators: Master's degree in education is required. 3 years of administrative experience is required.
Duration: 2 years; renewable for 2 years.
Salary: *Teachers:* $16,897–$34,482 per calendar year. *Administrators:* $25,000–$50,000 per calendar year.
Benefits: Round-trip transportation from U.S. for appointee only. Housing allowance. School assists in locating housing. Other benefits are provided.
Academic Calendar: September–June.
Application Deadline: January–February.
Contact: Br. Luke A. Pearson, Principal, Marist Brothers International School, 2-1, 1-chome Chimori-cho Suma-ku, Kobe 654, Japan. *Phone:* (81-78) 732-6266.

KYOTO

95 FRIENDS WORLD COLLEGE—EAST ASIAN CENTER
This private coed university was founded in 1965. Current enrollment is 10; 50% of the faculty are U.S. nationals.
Language of Instruction: *Primary:* English. *Other:* Japanese.
Opportunities: *General:* 1 full- or part-time position. *ESL:* None. *Administrators:* None.
Requirements: Doctor's degree in subject taught is required. Teaching experience is required. International experience is required. A faculty exchange for recipients of sabbatical leave can be considered.
Duration: 1 year; renewable indefinitely.
Salary: $12,000–$15,000 per calendar year.
Benefits: Round-trip transportation from U.S. for appointee only. Possibly housing for appointee. Health insurance. Other benefits are provided.
Academic Calendar: September–June.
Orientation: In Huntington, New York.
Application Deadline: Rolling.

Contact: Seiko Furuhashi, Director, Friends World College—East Asian Center, 38 Yanaginoshita-cho, Higashikujo, Minami-ku, Kyoto 601, Japan. *Phone:* (81-75) 672-6160; in U.S.: (516) 549-5000. *Cable:* FRIENDSWORLD KYOTO.

96 KYOTO INTERNATIONAL SCHOOL
This is a private coed primary/secondary school. Current enrollment is 72; 75% of the faculty are U.S. nationals.
Language of Instruction: *Primary:* English. *Other:* Japanese.
Opportunities: *General:* 5–6 full- and part-time positions. *ESL:* None. *Administrators:* None.
Requirements: Bachelor's degree is required. 2 years of teaching experience is required. Teaching certificate is required. International experience is preferred. Applicants must be able to teach 2 or 3 grade levels in 1 class.
Duration: 2 years; renewable.
Salary: 2,712,000–3,603,600 yen per year.
Benefits: Transportation from U.S. for appointee. Housing allowance. Paid home leave every 2 years. Health insurance. Other benefits are provided.
Academic Calendar: September–June.
Application Deadline: February.
Contact: Ms. M.B. Gehl, Kyoto International School, 29-1 Kami Miyanomae-cho, Shishigatani, Sakyo-ku, Kyoto 606, Japan.

NAGOYA

97 INTERFACE
This is a private English school for children. Current enrollment is 500; 100% of the faculty are U.S. nationals.
Language of Instruction: English.
Opportunities: *General:* None. *ESL:* 5 full-time positions for teachers on the primary, secondary, and adult education levels. Administrative: None.
Requirements: Bachelor's or master's degree in linguistics, Japanese, TESOL, education, or related fields is required. Teaching experience is preferred. Teaching certificate if required. International experience is preferred. Language proficiency in Japanese on any level is preferred.
Duration: 1 year; renewable.
Salary: 180,000–200,000 yen per month.
Benefits: Housing allowance. 5 weeks of paid vacation each year. Health insurance. Other benefits are provided.
Academic Calendar: April–March.
Orientation: 2 days on-site.
Application Deadline: Open.
Contact: Ken Nakamura, Interface, Fortress Yotsuya 2F, 1-1 Yotsuya-Dori, Chikusa-ku, Nagoya 464, Japan. *Phone:* (81-52) 781-2001.

98 NAGOYA INTERNATIONAL SCHOOL
This private coed primary/secondary school was founded in 1964. Current enrollment is 220; 65% of the faculty are U.S. nationals.
Language of Instruction: English.
Opportunities: *General:* 3–5 full-time positions for teachers of all subjects. *ESL:* Less than 1 position per year. *Administrators:* Less than 1 position per year.
Requirements for General Teachers: Bachelor's degree in elementary education or subject taught is required; master's degree is preferred. 2 years of teaching experience is required. International experience is preferred.
Requirements for ESL Teachers: Bachelor's degree in TESL is required; master's degree is preferred. 2 years of teaching experience is required. Secondary school teaching certificate is required. International experience is preferred. Language proficiency in Japanese is helpful.
Requirements for Administrators: Doctor's degree is preferred. 2 years of school administrative experience is required. Administrative certificate is required.
Duration: 2 years; renewable indefinitely.
Salary: *Teachers:* About $18,000–$21,000 per academic year. *Administrators:* About $25,000–$30,000 per academic year.
Benefits: Round-trip transportation from U.S. for appointee and dependents. Housing for appointee and dependents. Home leave partially paid every 2 years. Health insurance.
Academic Calendar: September–June.

All information is subject to change without notice and must be confirmed directly with the employer.

20

Orientation: 1 week on-site.
Application Deadline: Dec. 15.
Contact: Dr. Don Bergman, Headmaster, Nagoya International School, 2686 Minamihara, Nakashidami, Moriyama-ku, Nagoya 463, Japan. *Phone:* (81-52) 736 2025.

ODAWARA

99 LANGUAGE INSTITUTE OF JAPAN
This private coed language institute was founded in 1967. Current enrollment is 600; 90% of the faculty are U.S. nationals. The school offers English language courses on all levels, including total language immersion courses for professionals.
Language of Instruction: English.
Opportunities: *General:* None. *ESL:* 4–5 positions. *Administrators:* None.
Requirements: Bachelor's degree in TEFL or related field is required; master's degree is preferred. 2–3 years of teaching experience is preferred. International experience is preferred. Language proficiency in any foreign language on the intermediate level is preferred.
Duration: 2–3 years; renewable for 3 years.
Salary: 320,000 yen per month.
Benefits: Round-trip transportation from U.S. Health insurance. Other benefits are provided.
Academic Calendar: July–June.
Orientation: 1–2 weeks in Japan.
Application Deadline: Jan. 10.
Contact: Director, Language Institute of Japan (LIOJ), 4-14-1 Shiroyama, Odawara, Kanagawa 250, Japan. *Phone:* (81-465) 23-1677.

TOKYO

100 INTERNATIONAL SCHOOL OF THE SACRED HEART
This private female only primary/secondary school was founded in 1908. Current enrollment is 637; 32% of the faculty are U.S. nationals.
Language of Instruction: *Primary:* English. *Other:* Japanese and French.
Opportunities: *General:* 10 full- and part-time positions. *ESL:* 1 full-time position. *Administrators:* 1 full-time position.
Requirements for General Teachers: Bachelor's degree in subject taught is required; master's degree is preferred. 2 years of teaching experience is required.
Requirements for ESL Teachers: Bachelor's degree in applied linguistics is required; master's degree is preferred. 2 years of teaching experience is required. International experience is preferred.
Requirements for Administrators: Bachelor's degree is required; master's degree is preferred. 8–10 years of administrative experience is required.
Duration: 2 years; renewable for 1 year.
Salary: *Teachers:* 4,300,000–4,500,000 yen per calendar year. *Administrators:* Varies.
Benefits: Round-trip transportation from U.S. for appointee and dependents. Housing allowance. Home leave partially paid every year. Health insurance.
Academic Calendar: September–June.
Orientation: 1 week on-site.
Application Deadline: February.
Contact: Sr. Ruth Sheehy, Headmistress, International School of the Sacred Heart, 4-3-1 Hiroo, Shibuya-ku, Tokyo 150, Japan. *Phone:* (81-3) 400-3951.

101 NICHIBEI KAIWA GAKUIN
This private coed postsecondary vocational/technical school and adult/continuing education program was founded in 1945. 70% of the faculty are U.S. nationals.
Language of Instruction: *Primary:* English. *Other:* Japanese.
Opportunities: *General:* None. *ESL:* 2 full- and part-time positions. *Administrators:* None.
Requirements: Master's degree in ESL is required; doctor's degree in linguistics or education is preferred. 2 years of teaching experience is required. International experience is preferred. Language proficiency in Japanese on the intermediate level is preferred.
Duration: 2 years; renewable indefinitely.
Salary: 5,000,000–8,000,000 yen per calendar year.

Benefits: School assists in locating housing. Health insurance. Pension plan. Other benefits are provided.
Academic Calendar: April–September and October–March.
Orientation: 1–2 weeks on-site.
Application Deadline: Jan. 15 for spring; Aug. 15 for fall.
Contact: Takashi Suzuki, Administrative Director, Nichibei Kaiwa Gakuin, 21 Yotsuya 1-chome, Shinjuku-ku, Tokyo 160, Japan. *Phone:* (81-3) 359-9621.

102 ST. MARY'S INTERNATIONAL SCHOOL
This private male-only primary/secondary school was founded in 1954. Current enrollment is 900; 80% of the faculty are U.S. nationals.
Language of Instruction: *Primary:* English. *Other:* Japanese, French, and Spanish.
Opportunities: *General:* 10 full-time positions. *ESL:* 2 full-time positions. *Administrators:* 1–2 full-time positions.
Requirements for General Teachers: Bachelor's degree in education is required; master's degree is required for secondary school. 3 years of teaching experience is required. International experience is preferred.
Requirements for ESL Teachers: Bachelor's degree in English/education is required. Teaching experience is preferred. International experience is preferred.
Requirements for Administrators: Master's degree in education/administration is required. 3 years of administrative experience is required. International experience is preferred.
Duration: 2 years; renewable indefinitely.
Salary: *Teachers:* $35,000–$50,000 per calendar year. *Administrators:* $50,000 per calendar year.
Benefits: Round-trip transportation from U.S. for appointee and dependents. School assists in locating housing. Health insurance. TIAA.
Academic Calendar: September–June.
Orientation: 2 days on-site.
Application Deadline: Feb. 1.
Contact: B. Andrew Boisvert, Headmaster, St. Mary's International School, 6-19 Seta 1-chome, Setagaya-ku, Tokyo 158, Japan. *Phone:* (81-3) 709-3411. FAX: (81-3) 707-1950. *Cable:* INTERSCHOOLTOK.

103 TOKYO YMCA COLLEGE OF ENGLISH
This private coed postsecondary vocational/technical school was founded in 1890. Current enrollment is 1,286; 20% of the faculty are U.S. nationals.
Language of Instruction: *Primary:* Japanese. *Other:* English.
Opportunities: *General:* None. *ESL:* Positions may be available. Administrative: None.
Requirements: Bachelor's degree in TESL, TEFL, linguistics, applied linguistics, or English is required; master's degree is preferred. 2 years of teaching experience is required. International experience is preferred.
Duration: 2–3 years; renewable.
Salary: 240,000–300,000 yen per month.
Benefits: Round-trip transportation from U.S. for appointee only. Health insurance.
Academic Calendar: April–March.
Orientation: 1 week on-site.
Application Deadline: January.
Contact: Vice-President, Tokyo YMCA College of English, 7 Mitoshiro-cho, Kanda, Chiyoda-ku, Tokyo 101, Japan.

YOKOHAMA

104 ST. JOSEPH INTERNATIONAL SCHOOL
This private coed primary/secondary school was founded in 1901. Current enrollment is 305; 53% of the faculty are U.S. nationals.
Language of Instruction: English.
Opportunities: *General:* Full- and part-time positions. *ESL:* 1 full-time position. *Administrators:* 2 full- or part-time positions.
Requirements for General Teachers: Bachelor's degree is required. 2 years of teaching experience is preferred. Language proficiency in Japanese is preferred.
Requirements for ESL Teachers: Bachelor's degree in English is required. Teaching experience is preferred. Language proficiency in Japanese is preferred.
Requirements for Administrators: Bachelor's degree in administration is preferred. Administrative experience is preferred. International experience is preferred. Language proficiency in Japanese is preferred.

Duration: 1 year; renewable.
Salary: *Teachers:* 3,800,000–6,150,000 yen per academic year.
Benefits: Round-trip transportation from U.S. for appointee only. Housing allowance. School assists in locating housing. Paid home leave every 2 years. Health insurance.
Academic Calendar: September–June.
Orientation: 1 week on-site.
Application Deadline: None.
Contact: Fr. James J. Mueller, Principal, St. Joseph International School, 85 Yamate-cho, Naka-ku, Yokohama 231, Japan. *Phone:* (81-45) 641-0065. *Fax:* (81-45) 641-6572.

KOREA

SEOUL

105 EWHA WOMEN'S UNIVERSITY, INTERNATIONAL EDUCATION INSTITUTE

This is a private female-only university; the IEI is coed. Current enrollment is 17,000; 9 of the faculty are U.S. nationals. The university exchanges teachers with a variety of U.S. colleges and universities.
Language of Instruction: *Primary:* Korean. *Other:* English.
Opportunities: *General:* None. *ESL:* 4 full-time positions. *Administrators:* None.
Requirements: Master's degree in English language and literature is required; doctor's degree is preferred. Teaching experience is preferred. International experience is preferred. Language proficiency in Korean on the advanced level is preferred.
Duration: 7 years; renewable for 7 years.
Benefits: University assists in locating housing. Other benefits are provided.
Academic Calendar: March–February.
Contact: Dr. Byong-Suh Kim, Director, International Education Institute, Ewha Women's University, 11-1, Daehyun-Dong, Sudaemun-Ku, Seoul 120, Korea. *Phone:* (82-2) 362-6151, Ext. 744 or 362-6078. *Cable:* EWHASIA.

106 SEOUL ACADEMY

This private coed primary school and special education program was founded in 1983. Current enrollment is 275; 60% of the faculty are U.S. nationals.
Language of Instruction: *Primary:* English. *Other:* Korean, Hindi, Tagalog, and Arabic.
Opportunities: *General:* Full- and part-time positions. *ESL:* Full- and part-time positions. *Administrators:* Full-time positions.
Requirements for General Teachers: Bachelor's degree in education or subject taught is preferred. Teaching or practical experience is preferred. International experience is preferred. Language proficiency in any foreign language on the advanced level is preferred.
Requirements for ESL Teachers: Bachelor's degree is preferred. Teaching or practical experience is preferred. International experience is preferred. Language proficiency in Korean is required.
Requirements for Administrators: Master's degree in education or academic field is required. Administrative experience is required. Language proficiency in Korean on the advanced level is preferred.
Duration: 1 year; renewable indefinitely.
Salary: *Teachers:* From $13,000 per academic year. *Administrators:* From $15,000 per academic year.
Academic Calendar: August–June.
Application Deadline: February.
Contact: Mr. T. O'Connor, Director, Seoul Academy, Young Dong, P.O. Box 85, Seoul, Korea. *Phone:* (82-2) 554-1690.

107 SEOUL FOREIGN SCHOOL

This private coed primary/secondary school was founded in 1912. Current enrollment is 707; more than 90% of the faculty are U.S. nationals.
Language of Instruction: English.
Opportunities: *General:* 10–30 full-time positions for teachers of all subjects. *ESL:* Less than 1 position per year. *Administrators:* Less than 1 position per year.
Requirements for General Teachers: Bachelor's degree in subject taught is required; master's degree is preferred. 2 years of teaching

experience is required. International experience is preferred. Christian faith is required.
Requirements for ESL Teachers: Bachelor's degree is required; master's degree in TESL is preferred. Teaching experience is required. International experience is preferred.
Requirements for Administrators: Bachelor's degree is required; master's degree in educational administration is preferred. 2 years of teaching experience and 1 year of administrative experience are required. International experience is preferred.
Duration: 2 years; renewable indefinitely.
Salary: *Teachers:* $16,500–$29,000 per calendar year. *Administrators:* $26,000–$50,000 per calendar year.
Benefits: Round-trip transportation from U.S. for appointee and dependents. Housing for appointee and dependents. Paid home leave every 2 years. Health insurance. Pension plan. Tuition for children enrolled at this school. Other benefits are provided.
Academic Calendar: August–June.
Orientation: 10 days on-site.
Application Deadline: None.
Contact: Richard F. Underwood, Headmaster, Seoul Foreign School, 55 Yonhi-dong, Seoul 120, Korea. *Phone:* (82-2) 323-4784.

108 SEOUL INTERNATIONAL SCHOOL

This private coed primary/secondary school was founded in 1973. Current enrollment is 620; 93% of the faculty are U.S. nationals.
Language of Instruction: English.
Opportunities: *General:* 20 full-time positions for teachers of all subjects and special education. *ESL:* 2–3 full-time positions. *Administrators:* 2–3 full-time positions.
Requirements for General Teachers: Bachelor's degree is required; master's degree is preferred for secondary school. 2 years of teaching experience is preferred or practical experience is required. International experience is preferred.
Requirements for ESL Teachers: Bachelor's degree in ESL is required; master's degree is preferred. 2 years of teaching experience is preferred or practical experience is required. International experience is preferred.
Requirements for Administrators: Bachelor's degree in counseling, curriculum, or special education is required; master's degree in supervision and administration is required. 2 years of administrative experience is required. International experience is preferred.
Duration: 2 years; renewable for 2 years.
Salary: *Teachers:* $10,000–$16,500 per academic year. *Administrators:* From $15,000 per academic year.
Benefits: Round-trip transportation from U.S. for appointee; half paid for dependents. Housing for appointee and dependents. Paid home leave every 2 years. Health insurance. Pension plan. Other benefits are provided.
Academic Calendar: August–June.
Orientation: 1 week on-site.
Application Deadline: February.
Contact: Edward B. Adams, Headmaster, Seoul International School, Kangdong P.O. Box 61, Seoul 134, Korea. *Phone:* (82-2) 233-4551/2.

109 SOOK MYUNG WOMEN'S UNIVERSITY

This is a private female-only university. Current enrollment is 6,264; 0.65% of the faculty are U.S. nationals.
Language of Instruction: *Primary:* Korean. *Other:* English and French.
Opportunities: *General:* 1 full- or part-time position. *ESL:* 1 full- or part-time position. *Administrators:* None.
Requirements for General Teachers: Master's or doctor's degree in English language and literature is required. 1 year of teaching experience is preferred. International experience is preferred. Language proficiency in Korean on the beginning level is preferred.
Requirements for ESL Teachers: Master's degree in English is required; doctor's degree is preferred. 1 year of teaching experience is required. International experience is preferred. Language proficiency in Korean is preferred.
Duration: 1 semester–1 year; renewable for 1 year.
Academic Calendar: March–August and September–February.
Application Deadline: 2 months before semester begins.
Contact: Sook Myung Women's University, 12-1 Chung Pa Dong 2-ka Yongsan-Ku, Seoul 140, Korea. *Phone:* (82-2) 713-9391.

MALDIVES

MORE THAN ONE CITY

110 MINISTRY OF EDUCATION

The Ministry reports a need for U.S. teachers of general subjects, ESL teachers, and educational administrators.
Language of Instruction: *Primary:* Dhivehi. *Other:* English.
Opportunities: Positions on primary, secondary, vocational/technical, and professional levels.
Requirements for General Teachers: Bachelor's degree is required; master's degree is preferred. 3 years of teaching experience is required. International experience is preferred.
Requirements for ESL Teachers: Bachelor's degree in linguistics is required. 3 years of teaching experience is required. International experience is preferred.
Duration: 3 years; renewable.
Benefits: Housing for appointee and dependents. Paid home leave. Medical care. Other benefits are provided.
Academic Calendar: February–December.
Application Deadline: August.
Contact: Ministry of Education, Ghazee Building, 20-05 Male', Republic of Maldives.

FEDERATED STATES OF MICRONESIA

POHNPEI (PONAPE)

110A COMMUNITY COLLEGE OF MICRONESIA

This public coed postsecondary vocational/technical school was founded in 1970. Current enrollment is 271; 50% of the faculty are U.S. nationals.
Language of Instruction: *Primary:* English.
Opportunities: *General:* 15 full- and part-time positions for teachers of science and mathematics, business, education, and social studies. *ESL:* 10 full- and part-time positions. *Administrators:* 3 full-time positions.
Requirements for General Teachers: Bachelor's degree in science and mathematics or business is required; master's or doctor's degree in science and mathematics, business, or education is preferred. 3 years of teaching experience is preferred. International experience is preferred.
Requirements for ESL Teachers: Bachelor's degree in English, TESL, or linguistics is required; master's or doctor's degree is preferred. 3 years of teaching experience is preferred. International experience is preferred.
Requirements for Administrators: Bachelor's or master's degree in administration is preferred. 3 years of administrative experience is preferred. International experience is preferred.
Duration 2 years; renewable for 2 years.
Salary: $13,000–$20,000 per academic year.
Benefits: Round-trip transportation from U.S. for appointee and dependents. Housing for appointee and dependents or housing allowance. School assists in locating housing. Health insurance. Other benefits are provided.
Academic Calendar: August–May.
Application Deadline: None.
Contact: President, Community College of Micronesia, Box 159, Kolonia, Ponape 96941, FSM. *Phone:* (691) 320-2479/2480.

NEPAL

MORE THAN ONE CITY

111 MINISTRY OF EDUCATION AND CULTURE

The Ministry reports a need for volunteers as teachers of mathematics and ESL, guidance counselors, and curriculum developers at the primary/secondary level.

There is no formal employment program for hiring U.S. faculty. General information on faculty recruitment is listed below.
Language of Instruction: *Primary:* Nepali. *Other:* English.

Requirements for General Teachers: Bachelor's degree in education is required; master's or doctor's degree is preferred. 5 years of teaching experience is preferred. International experience is preferred.
Requirements for ESL Teachers: Bachelor's, master's, or doctor's degree in applied linguistics is preferred. 5 years of teaching experience is preferred. International experience is preferred.
Duration: 3 years; renewable for 2 years.
Salary: Volunteers are preferred.
Benefits: Housing for appointee.
Academic Calendar: March–December.
Orientation: 1 month in Nepal.
Contact: Chief, Curriculum Text-Book and Supervision Development Centre, Ministry of Education and Culture, Harihar Bhawan, Pulchowk, Lalitpur, Nepal. *Phone:* 5-21621.

KATHMANDU

112 ST. XAVIER'S SCHOOL, JAWALAKHEL

This private male-only primary/secondary school was founded in 1951. Current enrollment is 740; 10% of the faculty are U.S. nationals.
Language of Instruction: *Primary:* English. *Other:* Nepali.
Opportunities: 3–5 volunteer teachers and administrators.
Requirements for General Teachers: Bachelor's degree is required. Teaching experience is preferred. International experience is preferred.
Requirements for ESL Teachers: Bachelor's degree is required. Teaching experience is preferred. International experience is preferred.
Duration: 2 years.
Academic Calendar: February–December.
Application Deadline: July.
Contact: Jesuit International Volunteers, Box 25478, Washington, DC 20007. *Or:* Rev. G. William Robins, S.J., Director, Nepal Jesuit Society, St. Xavier's School, Jawalakhel, G.P.O. Box 50, Kathmandu, Nepal. *Phone:* 521-050/150.

PAKISTAN

MURREE HILLS

113 MURREE CHRISTIAN SCHOOL

This private coed primary/secondary school was founded in 1956. Current enrollment is 160; 35% of the faculty are U.S. nationals. Applicants should be affiliated with a mission.
Language of Instruction: English.
Opportunities: *General:* 10 full-time positions. *ESL:* 1 part-time position. *Administrators:* 2 full-time positions.
Requirements for General Teachers: Bachelor's degree in English, mathematics, French, or history is required; master's degree is preferred. 2 years of teaching experience is preferred.
Requirements for ESL Teachers: Bachelor's degree in English is required; master's degree is preferred. 2 years of teaching experience is required.
Requirements for Administrators: Bachelor's degree in education or business is preferred. 5 years of administrative experience is required. International experience is preferred.
Duration: 2 years.
Salary: Paid by mission.
Benefits: Housing for appointee and dependents.
Academic Calendar: August–July.
Application Deadline: Rolling.
Contact: Mr. Stewart W. Georgia, Principal, Murree Christian School, P.O. Jhika Gali, Murree Hills, Pakistan. *Phone:* (92-593) 2321.

PALAU

KOROR

114 MICRONESIAN OCCUPATIONAL COLLEGE

This public coed postsecondary vocational/technical school and adult/continuing education program was founded in 1969. 6% of the faculty are U.S. nationals.
Language of Instruction: English.

All information is subject to change without notice and must be confirmed directly with the employer.

Opportunities: *General:* 2 full- and part-time positions for teachers of natural science, math, and computers. *ESL:* 2 full- and part-time positions. *Administrators:* 1 full-time position.
Requirements for General Teachers: Bachelor's degree in vocational courses is required; master's degree in liberal arts is preferred. 2 years of teaching or practical experience is preferred. International experience is preferred.
Requirements for ESL Teachers: Bachelor's degree in English or related field is required; master's degree in TOEFL is preferred. Teaching or practical experience is preferred. International experience is preferred.
Requirements for Administrators: Bachelor's degree in education or business is required; master's degree in education, vocational education, or business administration is preferred. Administrative experience is preferred. International experience is preferred.
Duration: 1–2 years; renewable.
Salary: *Teachers:* $9,000–$14,000 per calendar year. *Administrators:* $12,000–$25,000 per calendar year.
Benefits: Round-trip transportation from U.S. for appointee, spouse, and dependents under age 18. Housing for appointee and dependents. Paid home leave every 2 years. Health and life insurance. Other benefits are provided.
Academic Calendar: August–May.
Application Deadline: None.
Contact: Mr. Mario Katosang, Dean of Instruction, Micronesian Occupational College, P.O. Box 9, Koror 96940, Republic of Palau. *Phone:* 470/1.

PAPUA NEW GUINEA

BOROKO

115 GORDON INTERNATIONAL SCHOOL
This private coed primary school was founded in 1969. Current enrollment is 460; 5% of the faculty are U.S. nationals.
Language of Instruction: English.
Opportunities: *General:* 3 full-time positions for teachers of all subjects, especially computers and outdoor education. *ESL:* 1 part-time position. *Administrators:* None.
Requirements for General Teachers: Bachelor's degree in education is preferred. 4 years of teaching experience is preferred. International experience is preferred. Language proficiency in French on the beginning level is preferred.
Requirements for ESL Teachers: Bachelor's degree in ESL or education is required. International experience is preferred. Language proficiency in French is preferred.
Duration: 3 years; renewable indefinitely.
Salary: 15,000–20,000 kina per calendar year. *Administrators:* 15,000–30,000 kina per calendar year.
Benefits: Round-trip transportation from U.S. for appointee and dependents. Housing for appointee and dependents. Paid home leave every year. Other benefits are provided.
Academic Calendar: February–December.
Orientation: 3 days on-site.
Application Deadline: None.
Contact: G. Mamai, Secretary, Gordon International School, P.O. Box 1825, Boroko, Papua New Guinea. *Phone:* (675) 254517. *Telex:* NE 23052.

MOUNT HAGEN

116 HAGEN INTERNATIONAL PRIMARY SCHOOL
This private coed primary school was founded in 1975. Current enrollment is 260; 3% of the faculty are U.S. nationals.
Language of Instruction: English.
Opportunities: *General:* 3–6 full-time positions. *ESL:* None. *Administrators:* Less than 1 position per year.
Requirements for Teachers: Equivalent of Australian primary teachers' diploma is required. 3 years of teaching experience is required.
Requirements for Administrators: Administrative experience is preferred.
Duration: 3 years; renewable.

Salary: *Teachers:* 12,000–21,000 kina per calendar year. *Administrators:* 17,000–25,000 kina per calendar year.
Benefits: Round-trip transportation from U.S. for appointee and dependents. Housing for appointee and dependents. Paid home leave every 2 years. Health insurance. Other benefits are provided.
Academic Calendar: February–December.
Orientation: 1 week in Port Moresby.
Application Deadline: Open.
Contact: N. Crawford, Principal, Hagen International Primary School, P.O. Box 945, Mt. Hagen, W.H.P., Papua New Guinea. *Phone:* (675) 521964.

PORT MORESBY

117 UNIVERSITY OF PAPUA NEW GUINEA
This public coed professional college and university was founded in 1969. Current enrollment is 3,000; 2–5% of the faculty are U.S. nationals.
Language of Instruction: English.
Opportunities: *General:* 5 full-time positions for teachers of all subjects. *ESL:* None. *Administrators:* 2–3 full-time positions.
Requirements for Teachers: Master's degree is required; doctor's degree is preferred. Teaching experience is preferred. International experience in a developing country is preferred. Language proficiency in English and knowledge of Oxford spelling is required.
Requirements for Administrators: Bachelor's degree is required; master's or doctor's degree is preferred. Administrative experience is required. International experience in a developing country is preferred. Language proficiency in Melanesian pidgin and Hiri Motu is preferred.
Duration: 3 years; renewable for 3 years.
Salary: *Teachers:* 19,000–26,000 kina per calendar year. *Administrators:* 19,000–26,000 kina per calendar year.
Benefits: Round-trip transportation from U.S. for appointee and dependents. Housing for appointee and dependents. Paid home leave every 18 months.
Academic Calendar: February–November.
Application Deadline: Rolling.
Contact: T.I. Tioti, Registrar, University of Papua New Guinea, Box 320, University Post Office, Port Moresby, Papua New Guinea. *Phone:* (675) 245200. *Fax:* (675) 245187. *Telex:* NE 22366.

PHILIPPINES

ILOILO CITY

118 CENTRAL PHILIPPINE UNIVERSITY
This private coed primary/secondary school, professional college, and university was founded in 1905. Current enrollment is 9,900; 1% of the faculty are U.S. nationals. Faculty are affiliated with a Christian mission society or the United Board for Christian Higher Education in Asia.
Language of Instruction: *Primary:* English. *Other:* Filipino.
Opportunities: *General:* 2 part-time positions. *ESL:* None. *Administrators:* None.
Requirements: Teaching experience is preferred. International experience is preferred.
Duration: 1 year; renewable.
Contact: Elma S. Herradura, Vice President for Academic Affairs, Central Philippine University, Iloilo City 5901, Philippines. *Phone:* (63-33) 73471/3.

QUEZON CITY

119 ATENEO DE MANILA UNIVERSITY
This private coed primary/secondary school, professional college, and university was founded in 1858. 3% of the faculty are U.S. nationals. Faculty are permanent residents of the Philippines.
Language of Instruction: *Primary:* English. *Other:* Filipino.
Opportunities: *General:* Full-time positions. *ESL:* Full-time positions. *Administrators:* Full-time positions.
Contact: Concepcion L. Rosales, Assistant Dean, Ateneo de Manila University, P.O. Box 154, Quezon City, Philippines. *Phone:* (63-2) 998-721, Ext. 108.

All information is subject to change without notice and must be confirmed directly with the employer.

24

SOLOMON ISLANDS

120 MINISTRY OF EDUCATION, TRAINING, AND CULTURAL AFFAIRS
The Ministry reports that teaching opportunities are available only through the Peace Corps Volunteer Program. Volunteer secondary school teachers are needed for English, mathematics, science, mechanics, woodwork, small engine, and home economics.
Language of Instruction: English.
Requirements for General Teachers: Bachelor's degree is preferred.
Academic Calendar: January–November.
Contact: Peace Corps, 806 Connecticut Ave. NW, Washington, DC 20526. *Phone:* (202) 254-6886.
For General Information, Contact: Ministry of Education, Training, and Cultural Affairs, P.O. Box G28, Honiara, Solomon Islands. *Phone:* 23900. *Cable:* EDUCATION HONIARA.

SRI LANKA

BATTARAMULLA

121 OVERSEAS CHILDREN'S SCHOOL
This private coed primary/secondary school was founded in 1957. Current enrollment is 494; 6% of the faculty are U.S. nationals.
Language of Instruction: English.
Opportunities: *General:* Full-time positions. *ESL:* None. *Administrators:* Full-time positions.
Requirements for Teachers: Bachelor's degree is required; master's degree is preferred. 2 years of teaching experience is required. International experience is preferred.
Requirements for Administrators: Bachelor's degree is required; master's degree is preferred. 5 years of administrative experience is required. International experience is required.
Duration: 2–3 years; renewable for 1–2 years.
Salary: *Teachers:* $6,000–$21,000 per academic year. *Administrators:* $11,000–$42,000 per academic year.
Benefits: Round-trip transportation from U.S. for appointee, spouse, and up to 2 dependent children. Housing for appointee and dependents. Health insurance. Tuition for children enrolled at this school. Other benefits are provided.
Academic Calendar: September–June.
Application Deadline: Rolling.
Contact: D.J. MacKinnon, Headmaster, Overseas Children's School, Pelawatte, P.O. Box 9, Battaramulla, Sri Lanka. *Phone:* (94-1) 564920.

COLOMBO

122 UNIVERSITY OF COLOMBO
This public coed university was founded in 1942. None of the faculty are U.S. nationals. This is an exchange program with American University in Washington, DC.
Language of Instruction: *Primary:* Sinhala. *Other:* English.
Opportunities: *General:* 1 part-time position. *ESL:* None. *Administrators:* None.
Requirements: Master's degree in business administration and doctor's degree in internal relations are required. Teaching experience is required. International experience is preferred.
Duration: 3–12 months; may be renewable.
Benefits: Housing for appointee and dependents.
Academic Calendar: October–September.
Contact: H.M.N. Warakaulle, Registrar, University of Colombo, 94, Cumaratunga Munidasa Mawatha, Colombo 3, Sri Lanka. *Phone:* (94-1) 583818. *Telex:* 21979 Sri Lanka CF.

TAIWAN (see CHINA/HONG KONG)

THAILAND

MORE THAN ONE CITY

123 MINISTRY OF EDUCATION
The Ministry reports that there is no need for U.S. teachers or educational administrators at this time.
Language of Instruction: Thai.
For General Information, Contact: Chief of Information and Documentation Section, External Relations Division, Ministry of Education, Rajdamnoen Ave., Bangkok 10300, Thailand. *Phone:* (66-2) 282-2866.

BANGKOK

124 INTERNATIONAL SCHOOL BANGKOK
This private coed primary/secondary school was founded in 1951. Current enrollment is 1,365; 75% of the faculty are U.S. nationals.
Language of Instruction: English.
Opportunities: *General:* 25 full-time positions for teachers of all subjects. *ESL:* 1 full-time position. *Administrators:* 1 full-time position.
Requirements for General Teachers: Bachelor's degree in education is required; master's degree in education or subject taught is preferred. 2 years of teaching experience is required. International experience is preferred.
Requirements for ESL Teachers: Bachelor's degree in education or English is required; master's degree in TESL is preferred. Teaching experience is required. International experience is preferred. Language proficiency in any foreign language on the beginning level is preferred.
Requirements for Administrators: Bachelor's degree in education or academic field is required; master's degree in educational administration is preferred. 3 years of administrative experience is required. International experience is preferred.
Duration: 2 years; renewable for 10 years.
Salary: *Teachers:* $23,000–$28,000 per academic year. *Administrators:* $33,000–$62,000 per calendar year.
Benefits: Round-trip transportation from U.S. for appointee and dependents. Housing allowance. School assists in locating housing. Health, disability, and life insurance. Retirement plan. Tuition for children enrolled at the school. Other benefits are provided.
Academic Calendar: August–June.
Orientation: 2 days on-site.
Application Deadline: February.
Contact: Milton D. Jones, Superintendent, International School Bangkok, P.O. Box 1513, Nana Post Office, Bangkok 10112, Thailand. *Phone:* (66-2) 253-0109. *Cable:* ISBAN.

125 KASETSART UNIVERSITY
This public coed university was founded in 1943. Current enrollment is 11,118; 6% of the faculty are U.S. nationals.
Language of Instruction: *Primary:* Thai. *Other:* English.
Opportunities: *General:* None. *ESL:* 7 full-time positions. *Administrators:* None.
Requirements: Master's degree in TESL, English, literature, or linguistics is required; doctor's degree is preferred. Teaching experience is preferred. International experience is preferred.
Duration: 1 years; renewable for 1 year.
Salary: 10,365 baht per month.
Benefits: Housing allowance is provided. University assists in locating housing. Health insurance. Pension plan.
Academic Calendar: June–March.
Contact: Head, Department of Languages, Faculty of Humanities, Kasetsart University, 50 Paholyothin Road, Bangkhen, Bangkok 10900, Thailand. *Phone:* (66-2) 579-3624. *Cable:* UNIKASE 10900 THAILAND.

126 SRINAKHARINWIROT UNIVERSITY
This public coed university was founded in 1974. Current enrollment is 23,000; less than 1% of the faculty are U.S. nationals.
Language of Instruction: *Primary:* Thai. *Other:* English.

Opportunities: *General:* None. *ESL:* 10 full-time positions. *Administrators:* None.
Requirements: Doctor's degree in linguistics, literature, or English is required. 3 years of teaching experience is preferred. International experience is preferred.
Duration: 1 year; renewable for 1 year.
Salary: 10,365 baht per month.
Benefits: Housing allowance. University assists in locating housing. Other benefits are provided.
Academic Calendar: June–March.
Application Deadline: Rolling.
Contact: Dr. Witaya Jeradechakul, Vice President for International Relations, Srinakharinwirot University, Sukhumvit Soi 23, Bangkok 10110, Thailand. *Phone:* (66-2) 258-4006. *Telex:* 72270 UNISHRINTH.

NONTHABURI

127 SUKHOTHAI THAMMATHIRAT OPEN UNIVERSITY
This public coed university was founded in 1978. Current enrollment is 156,962; none of the faculty are U.S. nationals.
Language of Instruction: *Primary:* Thai. *Other:* English.
Opportunities: *General:* None. *ESL:* 1–2 full-time positions. *Administrators:* None.
Requirements: Master's degree is required. 3–5 years of teaching experience is required. International experience is preferred. Language proficiency in Thai on the beginning level is preferred.
Duration: 1 year; renewable for 1–2 years.
Salary: 16,225 baht per month.
Benefits: Housing allowance is provided. University assists in locating housing. Other benefits are provided.
Academic Calendar: July–June.

Contact: Dr. Pratya Vesarach, Vice-Rector for Development, Sukhothai Thammathirat Open University, 9/9 Moo 9 Chaengwatana Rd., Tambol Bangpood, Pakkred, Nonthaburi 11120, Thailand. *Phone:* (66-573) 0030-3. *Telex:* 72353 UNISUKO. *Cable:* UNISUKO TH.

WESTERN SAMOA

MORE THAN ONE CITY

128 DEPARTMENT OF EDUCATION
The Department reports a need for U.S. teachers, technical instructors, lecturers, researchers, and curriculum developers on all educational levels. Recruitment is also done through the Peace Corps Volunteer Program.
Language of Instruction: *Primary:* Samoan. *Other:* English.
Opportunities: 10–30 positions through the Peace Corps Volunteer Program.
Requirements for General Teachers: Bachelor's degree is required; master's degree is preferred. 5 years of teaching experience is required.
Requirements for ESL Teachers: Bachelor's or master's degree in English is required. 5 years of teaching experience is preferred, or technical and vocational experience is accepted.
Duration: 2 years; renewable.
Academic Calendar: January/February–December.
Contact: Ministry of Foreign Affairs, Apia, Western Samoa. *Or:* The Secretary, Public Service Commission, Apia, Western Samoa. *Or:* Peace Corps, 806 Connecticut Ave. NW, Washington, DC 20526. *Phone:* (202) 254-6886.

EUROPE

MORE THAN ONE COUNTRY

129 BOSTON UNIVERSITY
This private coed university was founded in 1839. The university recruits professors to teach in graduate degree programs in 54 Boston University locations throughout Europe.
Language of Instruction: English.
Opportunities: *General:* 32 full- and part-time positions for teachers of business administration, computer information systems, counseling, human services, international relations, mechanical engineering, and early childhood. *ESL:* None. *Administrators:* None.
Requirements: Doctor's degree in subject taught is required. Teaching experience at the graduate level is required. International experience is preferred.
Duration: 1 year; renewable.
Salary: Varies.
Benefits: Round-trip transportation from U.S. for appointee, spouse, and 2 dependent children. Housing for appointee and dependents. Health and life insurance. TIAA/CREF. Half tuition for 2 children. Other benefits are provided.
Academic Calendar: September–August.
Application Deadline: November.
Contact: Mary Sabanek Farrell, Assistant to the Vice President for Overseas Programs, Boston University, 143 Bay State Rd., Boston, MA 02215. *Phone:* (617) 353-3028.

130 SCHILLER INTERNATIONAL UNIVERSITY
This private coed university, founded in 1964, has campuses in France, Spain, West Germany, and the United Kingdom. Current enrollment is 1,400. Faculty are recruited from those presently residing in Europe.
Language of Instruction: *Primary:* English. *Other:* French, German, Spanish.
Opportunities: *General:* Full- and part-time positions. *ESL:* None. *Administrators:* Full- and part-time positions.
For General Information, Contact: Sandra Russeff, Director, U.S. Office, Schiller International University, 1425 LaSalle Ave., Minneapolis, MN 55402. *Phone:* (612) 871-6988.

AUSTRIA

MORE THAN ONE CITY

131 BUNDESMINISTERIUM FUER UNTERRICHT, KUNST UND SPORT (MINISTRY OF EDUCATION, ART AND SPORT)
The Ministry reports that there is no need for U.S. teachers or educational administrators at this time.
Language of Instruction: German.
Academic Calendar: September–June.
For General Information, Contact: Bundesministerium fuer Unterricht, Kunst und Sport, Minoritenplatz 5, A-1014 Vienna, Austria.

132 AUSTRIAN-AMERICAN EDUCATIONAL COMMISSION (FULBRIGHT COMMISSION)
The Commission recruits teaching assistants for English teachers in public secondary and secondary vocational/technical schools.

Requirements: Bachelor's degree is required. Language proficiency in German is required. Applicants must be under age 30.
Duration: 1 year; may be renewable.
Salary: 12,706 schillings per month.
Benefits: Health and accident insurance.
Academic Calendar: October–May.
Application Deadline: March 1.
Contact: Dr. Gunther Fruhwirth, Executive Secretary, Austrian-American Educational Commission, Schmidgasse 14, A-1082 Vienna, Austria.

KLAGENFURT

133 UNIVERSITAET KLAGENFURT, INSTITUT FUER INFORMATIK
This public coed university was founded in 1970. Current enrollment is 4,000; few of the faculty are U.S. nationals.
Language of Instruction: *Primary:* German. *Other:* English.
Opportunities: *General:* 1–2 full- and part-time positions for teachers of computer science, information science, business administration, economics. *ESL:* None at the institute, but positions may be available at the university. *Administrators:* None.
Requirements: Doctor's degree in computer science or related field is required. Teaching experience is required. Language proficiency in German on the intermediate level is preferred.
Duration: 1 semester–1 year; shorter periods are possible.
Salary: Varies.
Benefits: University assists in locating housing. Health insurance.
Academic Calendar: October–June.
Contact: Roland Mittermeir, Professor and Chairman, Universitaet Klagenfurt, Institut fuer Informatik, Universitaetsstrasse 65–67, A-9022 Klagenfurt, Austria. *Phone:* (43-4222) 463-5317/575.

VIENNA

134 AMERICAN INTERNATIONAL SCHOOL
This private coed primary/secondary school was founded in 1959. Current enrollment is 679; 71% of the faculty are U.S. nationals.
Language of Instruction: *Primary:* English. *Other:* German, French, and Latin.
Opportunities: *General:* 7–10 full- and part-time positions for teachers of all subjects and special education. *ESL:* Less than 1 position per year. *Administrators:* Less than 1 position per year.
Requirements for General Teachers: Bachelor's degree in subject taught is required; master's or doctor's degree is preferred. 2 years of teaching experience is required. International experience is preferred. Language proficiency in German on the intermediate level is preferred.
Requirements for ESL Teachers: Bachelor's degree is required; master's degree is preferred. 2 years of teaching experience is required. International experience is preferred. Language proficiency in German on the intermediate level is preferred.
Requirements for Administrators: Master's degree in administration is required. 5 years of administrative experience is required. International experience is preferred. Language proficiency in German on the intermediate level is preferred.
Duration: 2 years; renewable for 2 years.
Salary: *Teachers:* 270,142–550,000 schillings per calendar year. *Administrators:* 500,000–800,000 schillings per calendar year.

All information is subject to change without notice
and must be confirmed directly with the employer.

27

Benefits: Round-trip transportation from U.S. for appointee and dependents. School assists in locating housing. Paid home leave every 3 years. Health and life insurance. Pension plan.
Academic Calendar: August–June.
Orientation: 1 day on-site.
Contact: Dr. J. Geoffrey Pierson, Director, American International School, Salmannsdorferstrasse 47, A-1190 Vienna, Austria. *Phone:* (43-222) 44 27 63.

WEISSENBACH

135 DOUBLE REED CENTER EICHENDORFF'S RUH
This private coed professional college and adult/continuing education program was founded in 1987. It offers summer seminars on instrument making and workshop facilities. None of the faculty are U.S. nationals.
Language of Instruction: *Primary:* English. *Other:* German, French, and Spanish.
Academic Calendar: Classes begin in June.
Application Deadline: May.
Contact: Walter Hermann Sallagar, Double Reed Center Eichendorff's Ruh, A-2564 Weissenbach/Tr., Austria. *Phone:* (43-2674) 88265.

BELGIUM

MORE THAN ONE CITY

136 COMMISSION FOR EDUCATIONAL EXCHANGE BETWEEN THE U.S.A., BELGIUM, AND LUXEMBOURG (FULBRIGHT COMMISSION)
The Commission reports that teaching opportunities for U.S. nationals in public schools in Belgium and Luxembourg are very limited.

For information on secondary school teacher exchanges, contact the Teacher Exchange Branch, U.S. Information Agency, 301 Fourth St. SW, Washington, DC 20547. For information on opportunities for university lecturers, contact the Council for International Exchange of Scholars (see listing 2).

Some private English-language schools in Belgium regularly employ U.S. teachers; applicants should contact directly any school in which they are interested. Positions may be available through International Schools Services (see listing 5).

The U.S. Government operates schools in Brussels for children of U.S. government and NATO employees. For information, contact the Office of Educational Administration and Recruitment, U.S. Department of Defense, Washington, DC 20301.

Any foreigner residing in Belgium for more than 3 months must have a Belgian visa. Foreign teachers need work permits obtained for them by the employer, a process that takes a minimum of 2 months. Instruction is generally in English; however, beginning French or Dutch is required.
For General Information, Contact: Commission for Educational Exchange between the U.S.A., Belgium, and Luxembourg, Rue de Marteau 21, Hamerstraat, 1040 Brussels, Belgium. *Phone:* (32-2) 218 47 80.

ANTWERP

137 E.E.C. INTERNATIONAL SCHOOL
This private coed primary/secondary school was founded in 1979. Current enrollment is 300; 20% of the faculty are U.S. nationals.
Language of Instruction: English.
Opportunities: *General:* 3 full- and part-time positions for teachers of all subjects and remedial/language difficulties/dyslexia. *ESL:* 1 full- or part-time position. *Administrators:* 2 full- and part-time positions.
Requirements for General Teachers: Bachelor's degree is required; master's or doctor's degree is preferred. Teaching or practical experience is preferred. International experience is preferred. Language proficiency in Dutch or French on the intermediate level is preferred.
Requirements for ESL Teachers: Bachelor's degree in ESL is preferred. Teaching experience is preferred. International experience is preferred. Language proficiency in Dutch or French is preferred.
Requirements for Administrators: Bachelor's, master's, or doctor's degree is preferred. Administrative experience is preferred. International

experience is preferred. Language proficiency in Dutch or French on the intermediate or advanced level is preferred.
Duration: 10 months; renewable for 11 months and then indefinitely.
Salary: *Teachers:* $100–$180 net per month. *Administrators:* $150–$200 net per month.
Benefits: School assists in locating housing. Health insurance. Pension plan.
Academic Calendar: September–June.
Application Deadline: Rolling.
Contact: M.C. Catt, Assistant Head, E.E.C. International School, Jacob Jordaensstraat 75–87, 2018 Antwerp, Belgium. *Phone:* (32-3) 218 81 82/237 27 18. *Telex:* 34044 EUROUN.

BRUSSELS

138 EUROPEAN UNIVERSITY
This private coed university and adult/continuing education program was founded in 1977. Current enrollment is 1,500; 20% of the faculty are U.S. nationals. European University also has campuses in Antwerp, Belgium; Montreux, Switzerland; Monaco; and Jakarta, Indonesia.
Language of Instruction: *Primary:* English. *Other:* French.
Opportunities: *General:* 3 full- and part-time positions for teachers of business administration. *ESL:* None. *Administrators:* None.
Requirements: Master's degree in business administration is required; doctor's degree in related field is preferred. 2 years of teaching experience is required. International experience is preferred. Language proficiency in French on the beginning level is preferred.
Duration: 1 year; renewable.
Salary: $22,000 per calendar year.
Benefits: University assists in locating housing. Health insurance.
Academic Calendar: October–August.
Application Deadline: June.
Contact: Dominique Jozeau, Dean of the Faculty, European University, 116–120 rue de Livourne, 1050 Brussels, Belgium. *Phone:* (32-2) 648 67 81.

139 VESALIUS COLLEGE (VRIJE UNIVERSITEIT BRUSSEL)
This private coed university was founded in 1987. Current enrollment is 50; 35% of the faculty are U.S. nationals.
Language of Instruction: English.
Opportunities: *General:* 15 part-time positions for teachers of all subjects. *ESL:* None. *Administrators:* Less than 1 position per year.
Requirements for Teachers: Doctor's degree in subject taught is required. Teaching experience is preferred.
Requirements for Administrators: Doctor's degree in any subject is required. Administrative experience is preferred. Language proficiency in Dutch and French on the advanced level is required.
Duration: 1 semester–1 year; renewable indefinitely.
Salary: *Teachers:* 51,200 Belgian francs per credit hour per semester.
Benefits: Possibly transportation to and from U.S. University assists in locating housing. Possibly paid home leave. Health insurance.
Academic Calendar: September–May.
Application Deadline: 1 year prior to start.
Contact: Raoul Van Esbroeck, Assistant Dean for Student Affairs, Vesalius College, Vrije Universiteit Brussel, Pleinlaan 2, 1050 Brussels, Belgium. *Phone:* (32-2) 641 21 11/641 28 21. *Telex:* 61 0 51.

LEUVEN

140 KATHOLIEKE UNIVERSITEIT LEUVEN
This private coed university was founded in 1426. Current enrollment is 23,748; 0.7% of the faculty are U.S. nationals.
Language of Instruction: *Primary:* Dutch. *Other:* English.
Opportunities: *General:* Part-time positions as guest professors. *ESL:* None. *Administrators:* None.
Requirements: Teaching experience is required. International experience is required. International recognition in a specific field of study is required.
Duration: 2 weeks–2 years.
Salary: 97,000–114,000 francs per month.
Benefits: Round-trip transportation from U.S. for appointee only. University assists in locating housing. Other benefits are provided.
Academic Calendar: October–July.

All information is subject to change without notice
and must be confirmed directly with the employer.

28

Contact: A. Bellefroid, Study and Planning, Katholieke Universiteit Leuven, Naamsestraat 22, 3000 Leuven, Belgium. *Phone:* (32-16) 28 38 11/ 28 40 92.

LOUVAIN-LA-NEUVE

141 UNIVERSITE CATHOLIQUE DE LOUVAIN
This private coed university was founded in 1425. Current enrollment is 18,090; 0.23% of the faculty are U.S. nationals.
Language of Instruction: *Primary:* French. *Other:* English.
Opportunities: *General:* 1 full-time position. *ESL:* None. *Administrators:* None.
Requirements: Doctor's degree is required.
Duration: 1 year; not renewable.
Benefits: Round-trip transportation from U.S. for appointee. Housing allowance. University assists in locating housing. Health and accident insurance.
Academic Calendar: September–June.
Contact: Prof. P. Macq, Rector, Universite Catholique de Louvain, 1 Place de l'Universite, 1348 Louvain-la-Neuve, Belgium. *Phone:* (32-10) 47 21 11/47 38 05. *Telex:* 59516 UCL AC.

BULGARIA

SOFIA

142 ANGLO-AMERICAN SCHOOL
This private coed primary school was founded in 1967. Current enrollment is 84; 100% of the faculty are U.S. nationals.
Language of Instruction: English.
Opportunities: *General:* Positions available. *ESL:* Positions available. *Administrators:* Positions available.
Requirements for General Teachers: Bachelor's degree is required. 2 years of teaching experience is required. International experience is preferred.
Requirements for ESL Teachers: Bachelor's degree in TESL/TEFL is required. 2 years of teaching experience is required. International experience is preferred.
Requirements for Administrators: Master's degree in education is required.
Duration: 2 years; renewable.
Salary: *Teachers:* $16,000–$22,000. *Administrators:* $28,000.
Benefits: Round-trip transportation from U.S. for appointee and dependents. Housing for appointee and dependents. Health and life insurance.
Academic Calendar: September–June.
Application Deadline: Jan. 1.
Contact: Director, Anglo-American School, Department of State/Sofia, Washington, DC 20520-5740. *Or:* Anglo-American School, 8 Studen Kladonez, Sofia, Bulgaria.

CZECHOSLOVAKIA

MORE THAN ONE CITY

143 AMERICAN EMBASSY PRESS AND CULTURE SECTION
English Teaching Seminars.
The Embassy organizes 2-week summer ESL seminars for Czechoslovak teachers, in cooperation with the British Council and the Czech and Slovak Ministries of Education.
Opportunities: ESL positions.
Requirements: Bachelor's degree is required. Teaching experience is required.
Academic Calendar: Summer.
Contact: Office of Education Programs, U.S. Information Agency, Washington, DC 20547. *Or:* American Embassy Press and Culture Section, AM CON GEN (PRG), APO New York 09213. *Phone:* In Czechoslovakia: (42-2) 536-641.

144 U.S. INFORMATION AGENCY
Fulbright Scholar Program.
The U.S. Embassy Press and Culture Section reports that there are opportunities on the university level for U.S. ESL and general teachers and scholars.
Opportunities: *General:* Up to 10 positions for teachers and scholars in any field. *ESL:* 2 positions on the university level. *Administrators:* None.
Requirements: Czech or Slavic language proficiency is preferred. Previous teaching experience is required.
Duration: 10 months; not renewable.
Salary: $20,080–$22,620.
Benefits: Housing for appointee.
Application Deadline: Sept. 15.
Contact: Council for International Exchange of Scholars, 11 Dupont Circle NW, Suite 300, Washington, DC 20036. *Phone:* (202) 939-5401.

PRAGUE

145 INTERNATIONAL SCHOOL OF PRAGUE
This private coed primary school was founded in 1948. Current enrollment is 113; 90% of the faculty are U.S. nationals.
Language of Instruction: *Primary:* English. *Other:* German and French.
Opportunities: *General:* 10 positions. *ESL:* 1 position. *Administrators:* None.
Requirements for General Teachers: Bachelor's degree in elementary education is required. 5 years of teaching experience is required. International experience is preferred. Teaching couples are preferred.
Requirements for ESL Teachers: Bachelor's degree in linguistics is required. 2 years of teaching experience is preferred. International experience is preferred.
Duration: 2 years; renewable annually.
Salary: $10,962–$22,953.
Benefits: Round-trip transportation from U.S. for appointee and dependents. Housing for appointee and dependents. Paid home leave. Health insurance. TIAA/CREF. Baggage allowance of $800 at beginning and end of contract.
Academic Calendar: August–June.
Orientation: 1 week on-site.
Application Deadline: Feb. 1.
Contact: Alan Conkey, Director, International School of Prague, Department of State/Prague, Washington, DC 20520.

DENMARK

MORE THAN ONE CITY

146 MINISTRY OF EDUCATION AND RESEARCH
The Ministry reports that there is no need for U.S. teachers or educational administrators in public primary and secondary schools at this time.
For General Information, Contact: Ellen Hansen, Secretary General, Ministry of Education and Research, Frederiksholms Kanal 21, 1220 Copenhagen, Denmark. *Phone:* (45-1) 92 50 00. *Telex:* 16243 EDUC DK. *Telefax:* (45-1) 92 55 47.

COPENHAGEN

147 COPENHAGEN INTERNATIONAL SCHOOL
This private coed secondary school was founded in 1963. Current enrollment is 120; 45% of the faculty are U.S. nationals.
Language of Instruction: English.
Opportunities: *General:* 3 full- and part-time positions for teachers of mathematics, science, and history. *ESL:* Less than 1 position per year. *Administrators:* Less than 1 position per year.
Requirements for General Teachers: Bachelor's degree in subject taught is required. 2 years of teaching experience is required. International experience is preferred. Language proficiency in any foreign language on the intermediate level is preferred.
Requirements for ESL Teachers: Bachelor's degree in TEFL is preferred. Teaching experience is preferred. International experience is preferred. Language proficiency in any foreign language on the advanced level is preferred.

Requirements for Administrators: Master's degree in administration or academic field is required. Administrative experience is required. International experience is required. Language proficiency in any foreign language on the intermediate level is preferred.
Duration: 2 years; renewable indefinitely.
Salary: *Teachers:* $28,000–$42,000 per calendar year. *Administrators:* $30,000–$50,000 per calendar year.
Benefits: Round-trip transportation from U.S. for appointee and dependents. School assists in locating housing. Other benefits are provided.
Academic Calendar: August–June.
Application Deadline: April 1.
Contact: James Keson, Headmaster, Copenhagen International School, Gammel Kongevej 15, 1610 Copenhagen, Denmark. *Phone:* (45-1) 21 46 33.

ELSINORE

148 INTERNATIONAL PEOPLE'S COLLEGE
This public coed adult/continuing education college was founded in 1921. Current enrollment is 69; none of the faculty are U.S. nationals.
Language of Instruction: English.
Opportunities: *General:* Part-time positions. *ESL:* 1 part-time position. *Administrators:* None.
Academic Calendar: August–December and January–May.
Contact: Mr. Jorgen Milwertz, Extension Consultant, The International People's College, 1 Montebello Alle, 3000 Elsinore, Denmark. *Phone:* (45-2) 21 33 61.

ESBJERG

149 ESBJERG INTERNATIONAL SCHOOL
This private coed primary/secondary school was founded in 1982. Current enrollment is 18; none of the faculty are U.S. nationals, but the school would consider appropriate applicants.
Language of Instruction: English.
Contact: Ole Jerg, Headmaster, Esbjerg International School, Gjesinglund Alle, 6715 Esbjerg, Denmark. *Phone:* (45-5) 12 02 89.

FINLAND

MORE THAN ONE CITY

150 MINISTRY OF EDUCATION
The Ministry reports a need for U.S. teachers of ESL, biotechnology, and other new fields in professional colleges, adult/continuing education programs, and universities.
Language of Instruction: *Primary:* Finnish and Swedish. *Other:* English.
Requirements for General Teachers: Master's degree in subject taught is required; doctor's degree is preferred. Teaching experience is required. International experience is preferred. Language proficiency in Finnish or Swedish is preferred.
Requirements for ESL Teachers: Master's degree is required. Teaching experience is required. International experience is preferred. Language proficiency in Finnish or Swedish is preferred.
Salary: 7,000–12,000 markkas per month in a university.
Academic Calendar: August–July.
Contact: Finland-U.S. Educational Exchange Commission, Mechelininkatu 10A, 00100 Helsinki, Finland. *Phone:* (358-0) 449 415.

TAMPERE

151 TAMPERE UNIVERSITY OF TECHNOLOGY
This public coed university was founded in 1965. Current enrollment is 3,382; 1% of the faculty are U.S. nationals. Occasionally the university has a direct exchange of professors.
Language of Instruction: *Primary:* Finnish. *Other:* English.
Opportunities: *General:* Less than 1 position per year for teachers of electronics and computer technology. *ESL:* Less than 1 position per year. *Administrators:* None.

Requirements: Doctor's degree in subject taught is preferred.
Duration: 1 year; renewable.
Salary: $3,000 per month.
Academic Calendar: September–May.
Contact: Eila Hirvonen, Department Secretary, Tampere University of Technology, P.O. Box 527, 33101 Tampere, Finland. *Phone:* (358-31) 162 111. *Telex:* 22313 TTKTR SF. *Telefax:* (358-31) 162 907.

VAASA

152 UNIVERSITY OF VAASA
This public coed university was founded in 1968. Current enrollment is 1,900; none of the faculty are U.S. nationals.
Language of Instruction: *Primary:* Finnish. *Other:* Swedish.
Opportunities: *General:* Less than 1 position per year. *ESL:* Less than 1 position per year. *Administrators:* None.
Requirements for ESL Teachers: Master's degree in English language or literature is required. Teaching experience is preferred. International experience is preferred. Language proficiency in Finnish or Swedish on the advanced level is required.
Duration: 1 year; renewable indefinitely.
Salary: 7,000 markka per month.
Benefits: University assists in locating housing. Health and life insurance. Pension plan.
Academic Calendar: August–July.
Contact: Taru Lommi, Assistant, University of Vaasa, Raastuvankatu 31, SF-65100 Vaasa, Finland. *Phone:* (358-61) 122 511.

FRANCE

MORE THAN ONE CITY

153 FRENCH EMBASSY CULTURAL SERVICE
The Embassy reports that only French citizens may teach at French primary and secondary schools or hold permanent positions in public universities.

There are opportunities for U.S. nationals to teach in French lycees through the USIA Fulbright Teacher Exchange Program (see listing 155) and the French Government Teaching Assistantship Program (see listing 154).

On the postsecondary level, only French citizens may hold permanent positions in public universities. On a temporary basis, however, universities may hire foreign specialists as visiting professors ("Professeurs Associes"), as "Maitres de Conferences Associes," "Assistants," and "Lecteurs." Inquiries and applications for these positions should be directed to the head of the relevant department of the university in which the applicant is interested.

Post-for-post direct teaching exchanges between U.S. and French universities in all fields are available through the Franco-American Commission for Education Exchange (see listing 156).
Language of Instruction: French.
Academic Calendar: September–June.
For General Information, Contact: French Embassy, Cultural Service, 4101 Reservoir Rd. NW, Washington, DC 20001-2178.

154 MINISTRY OF EDUCATION
French Government Teaching Assistantships in English.
Opportunities: *General:* None. *ESL:* 40 positions for teachers on the secondary level. *Administrators:* None.
Requirements: Bachelor's degree in French or English is preferred. Language proficiency in French on the advanced level is required. Unmarried applicants under age 30 are preferred.
Duration: 8 months; not renewable.
Salary: From 3,700 francs per month.
Benefits: Housing may be provided.
Academic Calendar: October–June.
Orientation: 3 days in France.
Application Deadline: May–Oct. 31.
Contact: U.S. Student Programs, Institute of International Education, 809 United Nations Plaza, New York, NY 10017. *Phone:* (212) 984-5330.

155 FRANCO-AMERICAN COMMISSION FOR EDUCATIONAL EXCHANGE (FULBRIGHT COMMISSION)
USIA Fulbright Teacher Exchange Program.
Opportunities: 15 positions for teachers of English as a second/foreign language and American civilization in public junior and senior secondary schools.
Requirements: Bachelor's degree in French is required; master's degree is preferred. 3 years of teaching experience is required. International experience is preferred. Language proficiency in French on the advanced level is required. Teacher's home school must be willing to accept French teacher.
Duration: 1 year; may be renewable for 1 year.
Salary: Teacher retains salary from home school.
Benefits: Round-trip transportation from U.S. for appointee only. Housing exchange with French teacher. Health and accident insurance.
Academic Calendar: September–June.
Orientation: 4 days in Washington (DC) or San Francisco, 2 days in Paris.
Application Deadline: Oct. 15.
Contact: Patricia Schaefer, Chief, Teacher Exchange Branch, E/ASX, U.S. Information Agency, 301 Fourth St. SW, Washington, DC 20547. *Phone:* (202) 485-2555.

156 FRANCO-AMERICAN COMMISSION FOR EDUCATIONAL EXCHANGE (FULBRIGHT COMMISSION)
University Teaching Exchanges.
The Commission has established an informational service on post-to-post teaching exchanges between U.S. and French universities and assists in the negotiation of exchange agreements between specific institutions.
Opportunities: University-level positions in all fields.
Requirements: Specific requirements depend upon agreement between home and French institution. Current college/university position is required; U.S. institution must agree to faculty exchange. Language proficiency in French is required.
Academic Calendar: September–June.
Contact: Mr. Roland Husson, Director, or Ms. Genevieve Ramos Acker, Deputy Director, Franco-American Commission for Educational Exchange, 9 rue Chardin, F-75016 Paris, France. *Phone:* (33-1) 45 20 46 54.

AVEYRON

157 ROUDYBUSH FOREIGN SERVICE SCHOOL
This private coed postsecondary foreign service school, founded in 1852, prepares candidates for careers in diplomatic and consular services, international banking, journalism, and importing/exporting. Current enrollment is 30; 33% of the faculty are U.S. nationals.
Language of Instruction: *Primary:* English and French. *Other:* Spanish and Portuguese.
Opportunities: *General:* 1 full-time position. *ESL:* Less than 1 position per year. *Administrators:* None.
Requirements for General Teachers: Master's degree is preferred. 2 years of teaching experience is preferred.
Requirements for ESL Teachers: Bachelor's degree is preferred. Teaching experience is preferred. Language proficiency in French, Spanish, or Portuguese is preferred.
Duration: 1 year; renewable.
Salary: Negotiable.
Benefits: School assists in locating housing.
Academic Calendar: October–June.
Contact: Dr. Franklin Roudybush, Director, Roudybush Foreign Service School, Sauveterre de Rouergue, 12800 Aveyron, France. *Phone:* (33-65) 72 09 18.

NICE

158 AMERICAN INTERNATIONAL SCHOOL ON THE COTE D'AZUR
This private coed primary/secondary school was founded in 1977. Current enrollment is 220; 40% of the faculty are U.S. nationals.
Language of Instruction: *Primary:* English. *Other:* French.
Opportunities: *General:* 2 full-time positions. *ESL:* Less than 1 position per year. *Administrators:* Less than 1 position per year.

Requirements for General Teachers: Bachelor's degree is required. Teaching experience is preferred. International experience is preferred. Language proficiency in French is preferred.
Requirements for ESL Teachers: Bachelor's degree in English or ESL is required. Teaching or practical experience is required. International experience is preferred.
Duration: 1 year; renewable indefinitely.
Salary: *Teachers:* $17,000–$24,000 per calendar year. *Administrators:* $20,000–$43,000 per calendar year.
Benefits: Round-trip transportation from U.S. for appointee only. School assists in locating housing. Other benefits are provided.
Academic Calendar: September–June.
Application Deadline: March.
Contact: David Russell, The American International School on the Cote d'Azur, 15 avenue Claude Debussy, 06200 Nice, France. *Phone:* (33-93) 21 04 00. *Telex:* 970-809 F-AIS.

PARIS

159 ECOLE EUROPEENNE DES AFFAIRES (EUROPEAN SCHOOL OF MANAGEMENT)
This private coed postsecondary vocational/technical school and adult/continuing education program was founded in 1973. Current enrollment is 100; 2% of the faculty are U.S. nationals. The school also has branches in Oxford, England; Berlin, Germany; and Madrid, Spain.
Language of Instruction: *Primary:* French. *Other:* English, German, and Spanish.
Opportunities: *General:* 2 full- and part-time positions. *ESL:* Positions available. *Administrators:* 2 full-time positions.
Requirements for General Teachers: Master's degree is required; doctor's degree is preferred. 3 years of teaching experience is required. International experience is preferred.
Requirements for Administrators: Master's degree is required; doctor's degree is preferred. Administrative experience is required. International experience is preferred. Language proficiency in French on the intermediate level is preferred.
Duration: 2 years; renewable for 2 years.
Benefits: School assists in locating housing. Other benefits are provided.
Academic Calendar: September–July.
Application Deadline: June.
Contact: Henri Jolles, Director, Ecole Europeenne des Affaires, 108 boulevard Malesherbes, 75017 Paris, France. *Phone:* (33-1) 47 54 65 00. *Telex:* EAPFRAN 640611. *Telefax:* (33-1) 42 67 46 19.

160 INTERNATIONAL SCHOOL OF PARIS
This private coed primary/secondary school was founded in 1964. Current enrollment is 335; 20% of the faculty are U.S. nationals.
Language of Instruction: *Primary:* English. *Other:* French.
Opportunities: *General:* Full-time positions for teachers of all subjects and special education. *ESL:* Less than 1 position per year. *Administrators:* Full-time positions.
Requirements for General Teachers: Bachelor's degree is required; master's or doctor's degree is preferred for secondary level. 2–3 years of teaching experience is required. International experience is preferred. Language proficiency in French on the intermediate level is preferred.
Requirements for ESL Teachers: Bachelor's degree is preferred. 2–3 years of teaching experience is required. International experience is preferred. Language proficiency in French on the intermediate level is preferred.
Requirements for Administrators: Bachelor's degree is required. 5 years of administrative experience is required. International experience is preferred. Language proficiency in French on the intermediate level is preferred.
Duration: 1 year; renewable.
Salary: *Teachers:* $18,335–$27,000 per calendar year. *Administrators:* $33,350–$50,000 per calendar year.
Benefits: School assists in locating housing. Health insurance. Pension plan.
Academic Calendar: September–June.
Orientation: 1–4 weeks on-site.
Application Deadline: May 15.
Contact: Robin Stuart, Director, International School of Paris, 96 bis rue du Ranelagh, 75016 Paris, France. *Phone:* (33-1) 42 24 43 40.

ST. CLOUD

161 AMERICAN SCHOOL OF PARIS
This private coed primary/secondary school was founded in 1947. Current enrollment is 700; 75% of the faculty are U.S. nationals.
Language of Instruction: *Primary:* English. *Other:* French.
Opportunities: *General:* 5 full-time positions. *ESL:* Less than 1 position per year. *Administrators:* 1 full-time position.
Requirements for General Teachers: Bachelor's degree in subject taught is required. 2 years of teaching experience is required. International experience is preferred. Language proficiency in French on the intermediate level is preferred.
Requirements for ESL Teachers: Bachelor's degree in ESL is required. 2 years of teaching experience is required. International experience is required. Language proficiency in French on the intermediate level is preferred.
Requirements for Administrators: Master's degree in administration is required. 2 years of administrative experience is required. International experience is preferred. Language proficiency in French on the advanced level is preferred.
Duration: 1 year; renewable for 1 year.
Salary: *Teachers:* $25,000–$48,000 per calendar year. *Administrators:* $49,000–$60,000 per calendar year.
Benefits: Round-trip transportation from U.S. for appointee and dependents. Health and life insurance. Retirement plan.
Academic Calendar: September–June.
Orientation: 2 days on-site.
Application Deadline: April 1.
Contact: Jim Moriarty, Acting Headmaster, The American School of Paris, 41 rue Pasteur, 92210 St. Cloud, France. *Phone:* (33-1) 46 02 54 43.

TALENCE

162 UNIVERSITE DE BORDEAUX I
This is a public coed university.
Language of Instruction: French.
Opportunities: *General:* 4–5 part-time positions for teachers of the sciences or economics. *ESL:* 1–2 part-time positions. *Administrators:* None.
Requirements for General Teachers: Doctor's degree is required. Teaching experience is required. Language proficiency in French is preferred.
Requirements for ESL Teachers: Master's degree is required.
Duration: 1–12 months.
Benefits: University assists in locating housing.
Academic Calendar: September–July.
Contact: The President, Universite de Bordeaux I, 351 cours de la Liberation, 33405 Talence, France. *Phone:* (33-56) 80 84 50.

VERSAILLES

163 EUROPEAN UNIVERSITY AT VERSAILLES
This private coed university was founded in 1973. Current enrollment is 80; 40% of the faculty are U.S. nationals.
Language of Instruction: *Primary:* English and French. *Other:* German, Italian, and Spanish.
Opportunities: *General:* Full- and part-time positions for teachers of business courses. *ESL:* 2 positions. *Administrators:* 1 part-time position.
Requirements for General Teachers: Bachelor's degree in commerce, economics, or languages is required; MBA or master's degree in related field is preferred. 2 years of teaching or relevant practical experience is preferred. Language proficiency in French on the beginning level is preferred.
Requirements for ESL Teachers: Master's degree is required. 1 year of teaching experience is preferred. International experience is preferred. Language proficiency in French is preferred.
Requirements for Administrators: Bachelor's degree in management is required; MBA is preferred. 2 years of administrative experience is required. Language proficiency in French is preferred.
Duration: 9 months; renewable.
Salary: *Teachers:* 200–500 francs per hour. *Administrators:* Negotiable.
Benefits: University assists in locating housing. Health and life insurance. Other benefits are provided.

Academic Calendar: October–September.
Orientation: In Paris and Versailles.
Application Deadline: June 31 or Jan. 31.
Contact: Francois Xavier Jean, Director of Admissions, European University at Versailles, 35 rue des Chantiers, 78000 Versailles, France. *Phone:* (33-1) 30 21 11 77.

GERMAN DEMOCRATIC REPUBLIC

MORE THAN ONE CITY

164 BUREAU FOR FOREIGN PROJECTS
The Bureau reports that there is no need for U.S. teachers or administrators at this time.
Language of Instruction: *Primary:* German. *Other:* Russian.
Academic Calendar: September–July.
For General Information, Contact: Buero fuer Auslandsprojekte, Mommsenstrasse 13, DDR-8027 Dresden, German Democratic Republic.

FEDERAL REPUBLIC OF GERMANY

MORE THAN ONE CITY

165 COMMISSION FOR EDUCATIONAL EXCHANGE BETWEEN THE U.S.A. AND THE FEDERAL REPUBLIC OF GERMANY (FULBRIGHT COMMISSION)
Fulbright Lecturing Awards.
The Commission fills about 20 positions per year for general and ESL teachers on university, professional, and vocational levels. Applicants are encouraged to identify a host institution in Germany; otherwise the Fulbright Commission will assist in placement negotiation.
Language of Instruction: *Primary:* German. *Other:* English, French.
Opportunities: *General:* About 20 positions. *ESL:* Positions available. *Administrators:* None.
Requirements for General Teachers: Doctor's degree in field of assignment is required. Several years of university teaching experience is required. International experience is preferred. Language proficiency in German is preferred.
Requirements for ESL Teachers: Bachelor's, master's, and doctor's degrees in linguistics, applied linguistics, American studies, or German are required. Several years of university teaching experience is required. Language proficiency in German is preferred.
Duration: 4–10 months; not renewable.
Salary: Up to 4,600 marks per month.
Benefits: Round-trip transportation from U.S. for appointee only. Health and accident insurance.
Orientation: 3 days in Bonn.
Application Deadline: Sept. 30.
Contact: Dr. Frederick Ohles, Program Officer, Council for International Exchange of Scholars, 11 Dupont Circle NW, Washington, DC 20036.

166 COMMISSION FOR EDUCATIONAL EXCHANGE BETWEEN THE U.S.A. AND THE FEDERAL REPUBLIC OF GERMANY (FULBRIGHT COMMISSION)
USIA Fulbright Teacher Exchange Program.
Language of Instruction: *Primary:* German. *Other:* English, French.
Opportunities: About 25 positions per year for general and ESL teachers on primary, secondary, and vocational levels.
Requirements for General Teachers: Bachelor's degree in field of assignment is required; master's or doctor's degree is preferred. 3 years of teaching experience is required. International experience is preferred. Language proficiency in German on the advanced level is required.
Requirements for ESL Teachers: Bachelor's, master's, or doctor's degree in linguistics, applied linguistics, or English is preferred. 3 years of teaching experience is required. Language proficiency in German on the advanced level is required.
Duration: 1 year; not renewable.
Salary: Teacher retains salary from home school; small supplement is available.

Benefits: Round-trip transportation from U.S. for appointee only. Housing is included if exchange partners agree. Health and accident insurance.
Orientation: 4 days in Bonn.
Application Deadline: Oct. 15.
Contact: Teacher Exchange Branch, E/ASX, U.S. Information Agency, 301 Fourth St. SW, Washington, DC 20547. *Phone:* (202) 485-2555/6.

167 PAEDAGOGISCHER AUSTAUSCHDIENST (PAD)
German Teaching Assistantship Program.
Jointly administered by the PAD and the Fulbright Commission, the program assigns U.S. students of German to German secondary schools as teaching assistants in English, American studies, and American literature.
Language of Instruction: *Primary:* German. *Other:* English, French.
Opportunities: About 30 positions per year.
Requirements: Bachelor's or master's degree, preferably in linguistics, applied linguistics, English, or German is required. Teaching experience is preferred. Language proficiency in German is required. Applicants must be under age 30.
Duration: 1 year; not renewable.
Salary: About 1,000 marks per month.
Benefits: Round-trip transportation from U.S. for appointee only. Schools assist in locating housing. Health and accident insurance.
Academic Calendar: August–June.
Orientation: 4 days in Bonn.
Application Deadline: Oct. 31.
Contact: U.S. Student Programs, Institute of International Education, 809 United Nations Plaza, New York, NY 10017. *Phone:* (212) 984-5330.

BERLIN

168 JOHN F. KENNEDY SCHOOL
Founded in 1960, this public coed primary/secondary school is bilingual and bicultural. Current enrollment is about 1,400; 50% of the faculty are U.S. nationals.
Language of Instruction: German and English.
Opportunities: *Teachers:* 10–15 positions for teachers of mathematics, science, and English composition on the secondary level. *Administrators:* none.
Requirements: Bachelor's degree in subject taught is required; master's degree is required for secondary level. 2 years of teaching experience is required. Teaching certificate is required. Language proficiency in German on the advanced level is preferred.
Duration: 2 years; renewable for 3 years.
Salary: Varies.
Benefits: Round-trip transportation from U.S. for appointee and dependents. Paid home leave every 2 years. Health insurance. Other benefits are provided.
Academic Calendar: August–July.
Orientation: 3 weeks on-site.
Application Deadline: Jan. 30.
Contact: Managing Principal, John F. Kennedy School, Teltowerdamm 87, 1000 Berlin 37, Federal Republic of Germany. *Phone:* (49-30) 807 27 01.

BIELEFELD

169 UNIVERSITAT BIELEFELD
This public coed university was founded in 1967. Current enrollment is 13,000; less than 1% of the faculty are U.S. nationals.
Language of Instruction: German.
Opportunities: *General:* Less than 1 position per year. *ESL:* None. *Administrators:* None.
Contact: Dr. W. Aufderlandwehr, Director of International Students Office, Universitat Bielefeld, Universitatsstrasse 25, Postfach 8640, 4800 Bielefeld 1, Federal Republic of Germany. *Phone:* (49-521) 106-4088. *Telex:* 932 362 UNIBI.

HAMBURG

170 INTERNATIONAL SCHOOL—HAMBURG
This private coed primary/secondary school was founded in 1957. Current enrollment is 530; 20% of the faculty are U.S. nationals.
Language of Instruction: English.
Opportunities: *Teachers:* 5 positions. *Administrators:* None.
Requirements for General Teachers: Bachelor's degree is required; master's degree is preferred. Teaching experience is required. International experience is preferred. Language proficiency in German on the intermediate level is preferred.
Requirements for ESL Teachers: Bachelor's degree in linguistics is required; master's degree is preferred. 2 years of teaching experience is required. International experience is required. Language proficiency in German on the intermediate level is preferred.
Duration: 2 years; renewable.
Salary: 50,000 marks.
Benefits: Round-trip transportation from U.S. for appointee and dependents. Health insurance. Tuition for children enrolled at this school.
Academic Calendar: September–June.
Application Deadline: April 15.
Contact: Headmaster, International School—Hamburg, Holmbrook 20, 2000 Hamburg 52, Federal Republic of Germany.

KANDERN

171 BLACK FOREST ACADEMY
This private coed primary/secondary school was founded in 1961. Current enrollment is 230; 50% of the faculty are U.S. nationals. Applicants must be sponsored by a Christian mission.
Language of Instruction: *Primary:* English. *Other:* German and French.
Opportunities: *General:* 4 full-time positions. *ESL:* 1 full- or part-time position. *Administrators:* 1 full-time position.
Requirements for General Teachers: Bachelor's degree in subject taught is required; master's degree is preferred. 2 years of teaching experience is required. International experience is preferred. Language proficiency in German is preferred.
Requirements for ESL Teachers: Bachelor's degree is required; master's degree is preferred. 2 years of teaching experience is preferred. Language proficiency in German is preferred.
Requirements for Administrators: Master's degree is required. 4 years of administrative experience is required. International experience is preferred. Language proficiency in German on the intermediate level is required.
Duration: 3 years; renewable.
Salary: Sponsoring mission pays salary.
Benefits: Academy assists in locating housing.
Academic Calendar: September–June.
Orientation: On-site.
Contact: Henry J. Toews, Administrative Director, Black Forest Academy, Postfach 1109, 7842 Kandern, Federal Republic of Germany. *Phone:* (49-7626) 7740.

MUNICH

172 FERGUSON INSTITUT
This private coed adult/continuing education program was founded in 1977. Current enrollment is several hundred; 30% of the faculty are U.S. nationals.
Language of Instruction: *Primary:* English. *Other:* French, German, Italian, and Spanish.
Opportunities: *General:* None. *ESL:* About 2 full- and part-time positions for teachers of technical/management English. *Administrators:* None.
Requirements: Bachelor's degree in English, German, or economics is required; master's degree is preferred. 1 year of teaching experience is required. International experience is preferred. Language proficiency in German on the intermediate level is preferred. Economic/technical background is required.
Duration: 1 year; renewable.
Salary: Up to 3,000–4,000 marks per month depending on number of hours per week.
Benefits: Institute may assist in locating housing.

Academic Calendar: September–July.
Contact: Mrs. Forest, Director, Ferguson Institut, Rotkreuzplatz 2a, 8000 Munich 19, Federal Republic of Germany. *Phone:* (49-89) 16 40 44. *Telex:* 52 13 587.

OBERURSEL

173 FRANKFURT INTERNATIONAL SCHOOL
This private coed primary/secondary school was founded in 1961. Current enrollment is 1,015; 47% of the faculty are U.S. nationals.
Language of Instruction: *Primary:* English. *Other:* German and French.
Opportunities: *General:* 7 full-time positions. *ESL:* 1 full-time position. *Administrators:* Less than 1 position per year.
Requirements for General Teachers: Bachelor's degree is required. 2 years of teaching experience is required. International experience is preferred. Language proficiency in German is preferred.
Requirements for ESL Teachers: Bachelor's degree is required. 2 years of teaching experience is preferred. International experience is preferred. Language proficiency in German is preferred.
Requirements for Administrators: Doctor's degree is preferred. Previous administrative experience is preferred. International experience is preferred. Language proficiency in German is preferred.
Duration: 2 years; renewable indefinitely.
Salary: *Teachers:* 42,710–83,194 marks per academic year. *Administrators:* 80,000–150,000 marks per academic year.
Benefits: Round-trip transportation from U.S. for appointee and dependents. School assists in locating housing. Health insurance. Pension plan. Tuition for children enrolled at this school. Other benefits are provided.
Academic Calendar: August–June.
Orientation: 1 week on-site.
Application Deadline: April.
Contact: Dr. Peter D. Gibbons, Headmaster, The Frankfurt International School, An der Waldlust 15, 6370 Oberursel, Federal Republic of Germany. *Phone:* (49-6171) 20920.

WUPPERTAL

174 BERGISCHE UNIVERSITAET—GESAMTHOCHSCHULE WUPPERTAL
This public coed university was founded in 1972.
Language of Instruction: German.
Opportunities: *General:* 3 full-time positions. *ESL:* None. *Administrators:* None.
Requirements: Doctor's degree is required. Teaching experience is preferred. Language proficiency in German is required.
Contact: M. Rumker, Bergische Universitat—Gesamthochschule, Gauss-Strasse 20, Postfach 100127, 5600 Wuppertal 1, Federal Republic of Germany. *Phone:* (49-202) 439-1. *Telex:* 8 592 262 GHW.

GREECE

MORE THAN ONE CITY

175 CONSULATE GENERAL 0F GREECE
The Consulate reports that there is no need for U.S. teachers or educational administrators in Greek public schools at this time. For information on obtaining employment at individual private institutions, write directly to the school.
Language of Instruction: Greek.
Academic Calendar: September–June.
For General Information, Contact: Consulate General of Greece, 69 E. 79th St., New York, NY 10021.

ATHENS

176 AMERICAN COMMUNITY SCHOOLS OF ATHENS
This private coed primary/secondary school was founded in 1946. Current enrollment is 1,360; 80% of the faculty are U.S. nationals.
Language of Instruction: *Primary:* English. *Other:* Greek, French, German, Spanish, and Arabic.

Opportunities: *Teachers:* 15 positions for teachers of elementary education, English, social studies, mathematics, science, and physical education on the secondary level; mechanical drawing/industrial arts on the secondary vocational/technical level; and remedial and learning disability specialists. *Administrators:* None.
Requirements: Bachelor's degree in subject taught is required. 2 years of teaching experience is required. Teaching certificate is required.
Duration: 3 years; renewable.
Salary: 1,912,000–3,488,000 drachmas.
Benefits: Round-trip transportation from U.S. for appointee and dependents. Paid home leave. Health insurance. Retirement plan. Other benefits are provided.
Academic Calendar: September–June.
Orientation: 3 days on-site.
Application Deadline: March.
Contact: Superintendent of Schools, American Community Schools of Athens, 129 Aghias Paraskevis St., 152 34 Halandri, Athens, Greece. *Or:* Personnel, American Community Schools, APO New York 09253.

177 ATHENS COLLEGE
This private coed primary/secondary school and adult/continuing education program was founded in 1925. Current enrollment is 3,500; 5–10% of the faculty are U.S. nationals.
Language of Instruction: *Primary:* Greek. *Other:* English.
Opportunities: *General:* None. *ESL:* 1–2 full- and part-time positions. *Administrators:* Less than 1 position per year.
Requirements for Teachers: Bachelor's degree in English is required; master's degree in English, ESL, or education is preferred. Teaching experience is required. International experience is preferred. Language proficiency in Greek on the intermediate level is preferred.
Requirements for Administrators: Bachelor's degree is required; master's degree is preferred. Administrative experience is required. International experience is preferred. Language proficiency in Greek on the intermediate level is required.
Duration: 1–3 years; renewable.
Salary: *Teachers:* 1,400,000–2,100,000 drachmas per calendar year. *Administrators:* Negotiable.
Benefits: School assists in locating housing. Health insurance. Pension plan. Other benefits are provided.
Academic Calendar: September–June.
Orientation: Informal on-site.
Application Deadline: January.
Contact: Walter McCann, President, Athens College, P.O. Box 65005, Psychico 154 10, Athens, Greece. *Phone:* (30-1) 671-2771.

178 HELLENIC AMERICAN UNION
English Studies Program.
Opportunities: *General:* None. *ESL:* 2–3 part-time positions. *Administrators:* 1 position.
Requirements: Bachelor's or master's degree in TESL is required. 2–3 years of teaching experience is required.
Duration: 1 year; renewable.
Salary: 800 drachmas per hour.
Benefits: Health insurance. Other benefits are provided.
Application Deadline: May 1.
Contact: Executive Director, Hellenic American Union, 22 Massalias St., GR-106 80 Athens, Greece. *Phone:* (30-1) 360-7305.

THESSALONIKI

179 ANATOLIA COLLEGE
This private coed secondary school was founded in 1886. Current enrollment is 1,200; 20% of the faculty are U.S. nationals.
Language of Instruction: *Primary:* Greek. *Other:* English.
Opportunities: *General:* None. *ESL:* 2–3 full-time positions. *Administrators:* Less than 1 position per year.
Requirements for Teachers: Bachelor's degree in English is required; master's degree in applied linguistics is preferred. Teaching experience is required. Teaching certificate is required. International experience is preferred. Language proficiency in Greek is preferred.
Requirements for Administrators: Bachelor's degree is required; master's degree is preferred. 2 years of administrative experience is required. International experience is preferred. Language proficiency in Greek on the intermediate or advanced level is preferred.

All information is subject to change without notice
and must be confirmed directly with the employer.

34

Duration: 3 years; renewable for 3 years.
Salary: *Teachers:* $11,000–$21,000 per calendar year. *Administrators:* $15,000–$25,000 per calendar year.
Benefits: Round-trip transportation from U.S. for appointee and dependents. Housing for appointee and dependents. Paid home leave every 3 years. Health insurance. Retirement plan. Tuition for children enrolled at this school. Other benefits are provided.
Academic Calendar: September–June.
Orientation: On-site.
Application Deadline: Open.
Contact: Michael R. Bash, Chairman, English Department, Anatolia College, P.O. Box 10143, 541 10 Thessaloniki, Greece. *Phone:* (30-31) 301-071/2/3. *Telex:* 863 410 452.

HUNGARY

MORE THAN ONE CITY

180 EMBASSY OF THE HUNGARIAN PEOPLE'S REPUBLIC
The Embassy reports that there is no need for U.S. teachers or educational administrators at this time.
Language of Instruction: Hungarian.
For General Information, Contact: Dr. Karoly Lakatos, Second Secretary, Embassy of the Hungarian People's Republic, 3910 Shoemaker St. NW, Washington, DC 20008. *Phone:* (202) 362-6737.

BUDAPEST

181 AMERICAN INTERNATIONAL SCHOOL OF BUDAPEST
This private coed pre-K and primary school was founded in 1973. Current enrollment is 103; 66% of the faculty are U.S. nationals.
Language of Instruction: English.
Opportunities: *General:* 2 full- and part-time positions. *ESL:* 1 part-time position. *Administrators:* Less than 1 position per year.
Requirements for General Teachers: Bachelor's degree is required; master's degree is preferred. Teaching experience is required. International experience is preferred.
Requirements for ESL Teachers: Bachelor's degree is required; master's degree in ESL is preferred. Teaching experience is preferred. International experience is preferred.
Requirements for Administrators: Master's degree in school administration is required. Administrative experience is required. International experience is preferred.
Duration: 2 years; renewable for 2 years.
Salary: *Teachers:* $12,000–$19,000 per academic year. *Administrators:* Varies.
Benefits: Round-trip transportation from U.S. for appointee and dependents. Housing for appointee and dependents. Paid home leave every 2 years. Health insurance.
Academic Calendar: September–June.
Orientation: 3 days on-site.
Contact: John K. Johnson, Director, American International School of Budapest, AMCONGEN (BUD), APO New York 09213. *Phone:* In Hungary: (36-1) 312-955.

ICELAND

MORE THAN ONE CITY

182 ICELAND-U.S. EDUCATIONAL COMMISSION
USIA Fulbright Scholar Program.
The Commission reports positions at public universities for senior lecturers and researchers in various fields, under the Fulbright Scholar Program.
Language of Instruction: *Primary:* Icelandic. *Other:* English, Danish, French, and German.
Opportunities: 2–3 positions per year.
Requirements: Doctor's degree in relevant field is required. U.S. citizenship is required.
Duration: 1 semester–1 year.

Salary: About $2,000 per month.
Benefits: Round-trip transportation from U.S. for appointee only. Universities assist in locating housing. Health insurance.
Academic Calendar: September–May.
Orientation: 3 days in Reykjavik.
Contact: Council for International Exchange of Scholars, 11 Dupont Circle NW, Suite 300, Washington, DC 20036. *Phone:* (202) 939-5401.
For General Information, Contact: Robert Berman, Executive Director, Iceland-United States Educational Commission, Box 752, 121 Reykjavik, Iceland. *Phone:* (354-1) 20830.

183 ICELAND-U.S. EDUCATIONAL COMMISSION
USIA Fulbright Teacher Exchange Program.
The Commission reports that, under the Fulbright Teacher Exchange Program, positions are available for teachers of science/mathematics at public secondary schools.
Language of Instruction: *Primary:* Icelandic. *Other:* English, Danish, French, and German.
Opportunities: 1 position per year.
Requirements: Bachelor's degree is required. 3 years of teaching experience is required. International experience is preferred. Teacher's school must agree to accept a foreign teacher. U.S. citizenship is required.
Duration: 1 year; sometimes renewable for 1 year.
Salary: About $1,500 per month.
Benefits: Round-trip transportation from U.S. for appointee only. School assists in locating housing. Health insurance.
Academic Calendar: September–May.
Orientation: 3 days in Reykjavik.
Contact: USIA Fulbright Teacher Exchange Program, E/ASX, U.S. Information Agency, 301 Fourth St. SW, Washington, DC 20547. *Phone:* (202) 485-2555.
For General Information, Contact: Robert Berman, Executive Director, Iceland-United States Educational Commission, Box 752, 121 Reykjavik, Iceland. *Phone:* (354-1) 20830.

IRELAND

MORE THAN ONE CITY

184 DEPARTMENT OF EDUCATION
The Department reports that there is no need for U.S. teachers or educational administrators at this time.
Language of Instruction: *Primary:* English. *Other:* Irish.
Academic Calendar: September–July.
For General Information, Contact: Department of Education, Marlborough St., Dublin 1, Ireland. *Phone:* (353-1) 717101.

ITALY

MORE THAN ONE CITY

185 U.S. INFORMATION SERVICE
USIS reports that it is generally very difficult for citizens of countries outside the European Economic Community to obtain jobs as teachers or educational administrators in Italy. Public primary and secondary schools employ only Italians. Private schools occasionally hire Americans.
For General Information, Contact: Gloria I. Kreisher, English Teaching Officer, U.S. Information Service, Embassy of the U.S.A., Via Boncompagni 2, 00187 Rome, Italy. *Phone:* (39-6) 46741.

BAGNO A RIPOLI

186 AMERICAN INTERNATIONAL SCHOOL OF FLORENCE
This private coed primary/secondary school was founded in 1952. Current enrollment is 150; 75% of the faculty are U.S. nationals. Teachers are recruited locally.
Language of Instruction: *Primary:* English. *Other:* Italian.

All information is subject to change without notice and must be confirmed directly with the employer.

35

Opportunities: *General:* 2–3 full-time positions. *ESL:* None. *Administrators:* Less than 1 position per year.
Requirements for Teachers: Bachelor's degree in subject taught is required. Teaching or relevant practical experience is preferred. International experience is preferred.
Requirements for Administrators: Master's degree in administration is required. Administrative experience is required. International experience is required. Language proficiency in Italian is preferred.
Duration: 1 year; renewable.
Salary: *Teachers:* 1,400,000–1,900,000 lire per month. *Administrators:* 4,000,000 lire per month.
Benefits: Round-trip transportation from U.S. for administrators and dependents. School assists in locating housing. Health insurance.
Academic Calendar: September–June.
Application Deadline: Open.
Contact: Roger Frost, Headmaster, American International School of Florence, Via del Carota 23/25, 50012 Bagno a Ripoli, Italy. *Phone:* (39-55) 64 00 33.

BOLOGNA

187 JOHNS HOPKINS UNIVERSITY, SCHOOL OF ADVANCED INTERNATIONAL STUDIES
Bologna Center.
This coed university center was founded in 1955. Current enrollment is 140; 30% of the faculty are U.S. nationals.
Language of Instruction: *Primary:* English. *Other:* Italian, French, and German.
Opportunities: *General:* 9 full- and part-time positions for teachers of international relations, economics, or international affairs. *ESL:* None. *Administrators:* 10 full- and part-time positions.
Requirements for Teachers: Doctor's degree in international relations, economics, or international affairs is required. 5–15 years of teaching experience is required. International experience is required. Language proficiency in a European languages is required.
Requirements for Administrators: Bachelor's degree is required; master's degree in international relations, economics, or international affairs is preferred. 7–10 years of administrative experience is required. International experience is preferred. Language proficiency in Italian on the advanced level is required.
Duration: 3 years; renewable.
Salary: *Teachers:* $25,000–$40,000 per calendar year. *Administrators:* $25,000–$40,000 per academic year.
Benefits: Round-trip transportation from U.S. for appointee and dependents. Other benefits are provided.
Academic Calendar: October–May.
Contact: Dr. Stephen Low, Director, Bologna Center, Johns Hopkins University, School of Advanced International Studies, Via Belmeloro 11, 40126 Bologna, Italy. *Phone:* (39-51) 232 185. *Telex:* 511339. *Cable:* CENTRO JHU.

FLORENCE

188 ABC CENTRO DI LINGUA E CULTURA ITALIANA
This private coed adult school of language and culture was founded in 1981. Current enrollment is 100; 10% of the faculty are U.S. nationals.
Language of Instruction: *Primary:* Italian. *Other:* English, French, German, and Spanish.
Opportunities: *General:* None. *ESL:* 2 part-time positions. *Administrators:* None.
Requirements: Bachelor's degree is preferred. Teaching experience is preferred. Language proficiency in Italian is preferred.
Duration: 3 months; renewable indefinitely.
Benefits: School assists in locating housing.
Academic Calendar: Year-round.
Application Deadline: None.
Contact: Dr. Marco Giannini, ABC Centro di Lingua e Cultura Italiana, Borgo Pinti 38, 50121 Florence, Italy. *Phone:* (39-55) 24 79 220. *Telex:* 574022 ATT: ABC SCHOOL.

188A STUDIO ART CENTERS INTERNATIONAL (SACI)
This private university-level art school was founded in 1975. Current enrollment is 115; 80% of the faculty are U.S. nationals.
Language of Instruction: English.

Opportunities: *General:* 8 part-time positions for university-level teachers of studio arts. *ESL:* None. *Administrators:* None.
Requirements: Bachelor's and master's degrees in studio arts are required. Teaching experience is required. International experience is preferred. Language proficiency in Italian is preferred.
Duration: Academic year; renewable indefinitely.
Salary: $2,500 per course per semester.
Academic Calendar: September–May.
Orientation: 2 weeks on-site.
Application Deadline: 6 months before semester begins.
Contact: J. Maidoff, Director, Studio Art Centers International, Via dei Ginori 40, 50123 Florence, Italy. *Phone:* (39-55) 26 39 48.

GENOA

189 AMERICAN INTERNATIONAL SCHOOL IN GENOA
This private coed pre-K and primary school was founded in 1966. Current enrollment is 75.
Language of Instruction: *Primary:* English. *Other:* Italian.
Opportunities: *Teachers:* 4 full-time positions for teachers with ESL/EFL experience and an interest in computer-related instruction. *Administrators:* None.
Requirements: Bachelor's degree is required. 2 years of teaching experience is required.
Duration: 2 years; renewable.
Salary: 16,000,000–17,450,000 lire per year.
Benefits: Round-trip transportation from U.S. for appointee only. Life and disability insurance. Other benefits are provided.
Academic Calendar: September–June.
Application Deadline: Feb. 1.
Contact: Michael D. Popinchalk, Director, American International School in Genoa, Via Quarto 13/C, 16148 Genoa, Italy. *Phone:* (39-10) 386 528.

ROME

190 INTERNATIONAL ACADEMY
This is a private coed primary/secondary school. Current enrollment is 90.
Language of Instruction: *Primary:* English. *Other:* French and Italian.
Opportunities: *General:* 1 full- or part-time position for a teacher of all subjects and special education. *ESL:* Full- and part-time positions. *Administrators:* 1 full- or part-time position.
Requirements for General Teachers: Master's degree is required. 2 years of teaching experience is required. International experience is preferred.
Requirements for ESL Teachers: Bachelor's degree in education is required. 2 years of teaching experience is required.
Requirements for Administrators: Master's degree is required. Administrative experience is required. Language proficiency in Italian is preferred.
Duration: 2–3 years; renewable.
Salary: *Teachers:* 1,000,000–1,400,00 lire per academic year.
Benefits: Health insurance. Pension plan. Other benefits are provided.
Orientation: 1 month on-site.
Application Deadline: None.
Contact: Mrs. J.B. Bulgarini, Headmistress, International Academy, Via di Grottarossa 295, 00189 Rome, Italy. *Phone:* (39-6) 36 66 071/2.

191 NOTRE DAME INTERNATIONAL SCHOOL
This private coed primary school and male-only secondary school was founded in 1952. Current enrollment is 175; 90% of the faculty are U.S. nationals.
Language of Instruction: English.
Opportunities: *General:* 3–4 full-time positions for teachers of all subjects. *ESL:* Recruited locally. *Administrators:* 1–2 full-time positions.
Requirements for Teachers: Bachelor's degree in subject taught is required; master's degree is preferred. 2 years of teaching experience is preferred.
Requirements for Administrators: Bachelor's degree is required; master's degree in administration is preferred. 2 years of administrative experience is preferred.
Duration: 1 year; renewable.

Salary: *Teachers:* 15,575,000–28,000,000 lire per academic year.
Administrators: 25,000,000–45,000,000 lire per calendar year.
Benefits: Round-trip transportation from U.S. for appointee only.
Housing for appointee only. Health insurance.
Academic Calendar: September–June.
Application Deadline: March 1.
Contact: Brother Joseph Umile, Headmaster, Notre Dame International
School, Via Aurelia 796, 00165 Rome, Italy. *Phone:* (39-6) 621 6057.

TRIESTE

192 INTERNATIONAL SCHOOL OF TRIESTE
This private coed primary/secondary school was founded in 1964.
Current enrollment is 150; 25% of the faculty are U.S. nationals.
Language of Instruction: *Primary:* English. *Other:* Italian, French, and
German.
Opportunities: *General:* 3–5 full- and part-time positions. *ESL:* 1 full-
or part-time position. *Administrators:* 1 full- or part-time position.
Requirements for General Teachers: Bachelor's degree in education is
required; master's degree is preferred. 2 years of teaching experience is
required. International experience is preferred. Language proficiency in
Italian is preferred.
Requirements for ESL Teachers: Bachelor's degree in TEFL is
preferred. 2 years of teaching experience is required. International
experience is preferred. Language proficiency in Italian is preferred.
Requirements for Administrators: Master's degree in administration is
required. 3 years of administrative experience is required. International
experience is preferred. Language proficiency in Italian is preferred.
Duration: 2 years; renewable indefinitely.
Salary: *Teachers:* $13,000–$15,000 per calendar year. *Administrators:*
$20,000–$25,000 per calendar year.
Benefits: Round-trip transportation from U.S. for appointee only.
School assists in locating housing. Health insurance. Other benefits are
provided.
Academic Calendar: September–June.
Application Deadline: May.
Contact: Peter Metzger, Director, International School of Trieste, Via
Conconello 16 (Opicina), 34016 Trieste, Italy. *Phone:* (39-40) 211 452.

LUXEMBOURG

MORE THAN ONE CITY

193 MINISTERE DE L'EDUCATION NATIONALE ET DE LA JEUNESSE
The Ministry reports that there is no need for U.S. teachers or
educational administrators at this time.
Academic Calendar: September–July.
Language of Instruction: *Primary:* German. *Other:* French.
For General Information, Contact: Head of Eurydice Unit, Ministere
de l'Education Nationale et de la Jeunesse, 6 Boulevard Royal, L-2910
Luxembourg, Luxembourg. *Phone:* (352) 46802 551. *Telex:* 3311 MENJ
LU.

LUXEMBOURG

194 AMERICAN INTERNATIONAL SCHOOL OF LUXEMBOURG
This private coed primary/secondary school was founded in 1963.
Current enrollment is 325; 46% of the faculty are U.S. nationals.
Language of Instruction: English.
Opportunities: *General:* 2–3 full- and part-time positions for teachers of
all subjects. *ESL:* None. *Administrators:* None.
Requirements: Bachelor's degree is required; master's degree is
preferred. 2 years of teaching experience is required. International
experience is preferred. Language proficiency in French or German on
the beginning or intermediate level is preferred.
Duration: 2 years; renewable indefinitely.
Salary: $18,000–$34,000 per calendar year.
Benefits: Round-trip transportation from U.S. for appointee, spouse,
and up to 2 children. Housing allowance. School assists in locating
housing. Health insurance. Pension plan. Other benefits are provided.

Academic Calendar: September–June.
Orientation: 2 days on-site.
Application Deadline: Open.
Contact: Dr. Harry C. Barteau, Director, American International
School of Luxembourg, 188 ave. de la Faiencerie, L-1511 Luxembourg,
Luxembourg. *Phone:* (352) 47 00 20.

MALTA

MORE THAN ONE CITY

195 U.S. INFORMATION AGENCY
Fulbright Scholar Program.
The USIS office in Valletta reports opportunities for senior faculty in the
fields of management and architecture/urban development, under the
Fulbright Scholar Program. This is a exchange program.
Opportunities: 2 positions per year.
Requirements: Doctor's degree is required. 5–10 years of teaching
experience is required. International experience is preferred.
Duration: 9 months; not renewable.
Salary: Fixed stipend.
Benefits: Round-trip transportation from U.S. for appointee and
dependents. Housing for appointee and dependents. Low cost local
medical care.
Academic Calendar: September–June.
Orientation: In Washington (DC).
Contact: Council for International Exchange of Scholars, 11 Dupont
Circle NW, Suite 300, Washington, DC 20036. *Phone:* (202) 939-5401.

ST. ANDREWS

196 VERDALA INTERNATIONAL SCHOOL
This private coed primary/secondary school was founded in 1977.
Current enrollment is 94; 25% of the faculty are U.S. nationals.
Language of Instruction: English.
Opportunities: *General:* Less than 1 position per year. *ESL:* None.
Administrators: Less than 1 position per year.
Requirements for Teachers: Bachelor's degree in subject taught is
required. 2 years of teaching experience is required. International
experience is preferred.
Requirements for Administrators: Bachelor's degree is required; ·
master's degree is preferred. Administrative experience is required.
International experience is required.
Duration: 1 year; renewable.
Salary: *Teachers:* $13,500–$18,000 per calendar year. *Administrators:*
$19,000–$21,000 per calendar year.
Benefits: Round-trip transportation from U.S. for appointee only.
Housing for appointee and dependents if spouse supervises boarding.
Health insurance. Tuition for children enrolled at this school.
Academic Calendar: September–June.
Application Deadline: May 15.
Contact: Lawrence Simpson, Acting Headmaster, Verdala International
School, Fort Pembroke, St. Andrews, Malta. *Phone:* 821413/4. *Telex:*
548 MANDIA MW.

MONACO

MONACO

197 EUROPEAN UNIVERSITY
This is a private coed university. 10% of the faculty are U.S. nationals.
Language of Instruction: *Primary:* English. *Other:* Spanish, German,
and French.
Opportunities: *General:* 10–20 part-time positions for teachers of
business, economics, marketing, computer, and management. *ESL:* 1
part-time position. *Administrators:* 1 part-time position.
Requirements for General Teachers: Master's degree in economics or
business science is required; doctor's degree is preferred. Teaching
experience is required. International experience is preferred. Language
proficiency in French is preferred.

Requirements for ESL Teachers: Master's degree in English or humanities is required. Teaching experience is required. International experience is preferred.

Requirements for Administrators: Master's degree in economics or business sciences is preferred. Administrative experience is required. International experience is preferred. Language proficiency in French is preferred.

Duration: 1 year; renewable.

Salary: *Teachers:* 100–150 French francs per hour. *Administrators:* Negotiable.

Benefits: University assists in locating housing. Health insurance. Pension plan. Other benefits are provided.

Academic Calendar: September–August.

Application Deadline: None.

Contact: Mr. Saleh, Academic Dean, European University, Stade Louis II, Avenue du Prince Hereditaire Albert II, MC-98000 Monaco. *Phone:* (33-93) 25 17 87.

NETHERLANDS

MORE THAN ONE CITY

198 **NETHERLANDS AMERICA COMMISSION FOR EDUCATIONAL EXCHANGE (FULBRIGHT COMMISSION)**
USIA Fulbright Teacher Exchange Program.
The Commission reports post-for-post exchange opportunities at secondary schools and teacher colleges through the Fulbright Teacher Exchange Program.

Language of Instruction: English; fluency in Dutch not required.

Opportunities: *General:* 8–10 positions per year. *ESL:* None. *Administrators:* None.

Requirements: Current teaching position at U.S. institution and leave of absence with pay are required. The U.S. school must be willing to accept a Dutch teacher.

Salary: Paid by home institution; maintenance allowances may be given.

Benefits: Transportation allowance for appointee only.

Academic Calendar: August–June.

Contact: Teacher Exchange Branch, E/ASX, U.S. Information Agency, 301 Fourth St. SW, Washington, DC 20547. *Phone:* (202) 485-2555/6.

For General Information, Contact: Joanna Wind, Executive Director, Netherlands America Commission for Educational Exchange, Nieuwe Spiegelstraat 26, 1017 DG Amsterdam, Netherlands.

AMSTERDAM

199 **INTERNATIONAL SCHOOL OF AMSTERDAM**
This private coed primary/secondary school was founded in 1964. Current enrollment is 425; 33% of the faculty are U.S. nationals.

Language of Instruction: English.

Opportunities: *General:* 3–4 full-time positions for secondary school teachers. *ESL:* Less than 1 position per year. *Administrators:* Less than 1 position per year.

Requirements for General Teachers: Bachelor's degree in subject taught or education is required. 2 years of teaching experience is required. International experience is preferred.

Requirements for ESL Teachers: Bachelor's degree in linguistics is required. Teaching experience is required.

Requirements for Administrators: Master's degree is preferred. 5 years of administrative experience is required. International experience is preferred.

Duration: 2 years; renewable indefinitely.

Salary: *Teachers:* $22,500–$35,000 per calendar year. *Administrators:* $37,500–$45,000 per calendar year.

Benefits: Round-trip transportation from U.S. for appointee only. Paid home leave every 2 years. Health and disability insurance. Tuition for children enrolled at this school. Additional benefits are provided.

Academic Calendar: August–June.

Orientation: 3 days on-site.

Application Deadline: None.

Contact: Dr. Brian S. Wilks, Director, International School of Amsterdam, P.O. Box 7983, 1008 AD Amsterdam, Netherlands. *Phone:* (31-20) 422235.

NORWAY

MORE THAN ONE CITY

200 **ROYAL MINISTRY OF CHURCH AND EDUCATION and ROYAL MINISTRY OF CULTURAL AND SCIENTIFIC AFFAIRS**
The Ministry reports that it is difficult for foreigners to obtain teaching positions in Norway. Since 1975 there has been a ban on immigration; in most cases, work permits needed to enter Norway have been denied. In addition, foreign teachers must pass an examination in Norwegian language and civilization, administered by the National Council for Teacher Training.

All vacancies in Norwegian schools are advertised in the quarterly publication *Norsk Lysingsblad*, available from P.O. Box 177, 8501 Narvik, Norway (125 kroner per copy). Foreign teachers and university faculty should apply directly to the institution in which they are interested.

Information about temporary and part-time positions is available from various adult educational organizations in Norway, including Studentersamfundets Friundervisning (Nedre Vollgt. 20, Oslo 1, Norway) and Arbeidernes Opplysningsforbund (Storgt. 23, Oslo 1, Norway).

Language of Instruction: *Primary:* Norwegian. *Other:* Sami in parts of the northern region.

Academic Calendar: August–June.

For General Information, Contact: Brynhild Sirevag, Senior Executive Officer, The Royal Ministry of Church and Education, P.O. Box 8119 Dep., N-0032 Oslo 1, Norway. *Phone:* (47-2) 119090. *Telex:* 77241 nsbdp n. *Telefax:* (47-2) 116005.

POLAND

MORE THAN ONE CITY

201 **EMBASSY OF THE POLISH PEOPLE'S REPUBLIC**
The Embassy reports that there is no need for U.S. teachers or educational administrators at this time.

Language of Instruction: Polish.

Academic Calendar: October–June.

For General Information, Contact: Embassy of the Polish People's Republic, 2640 16th St. NW, Washington, DC 20009.

WARSAW

202 **UNIVERSITY OF WARSAW, INSTITUTE OF ENGLISH STUDIES**
USIA Fulbright Teacher Exchange Program.
This public coed university was founded in 1816. Current enrollment is 12,000; 4% of the faculty are U.S. nationals. The Institute recruits American professors through the Fulbright Program and through direct exchanges with Indiana University, Kent State University, Kansas University, and State University of New York at Stony Brook.

Language of Instruction: English.

Opportunities: *General:* 2 full-time positions for teachers of American literature and American culture. *ESL:* 1 full-time position. *Administrators:* None.

Requirements for General Teachers: Doctor's degree in American literature is required. Teaching experience is required. Language proficiency in Polish on the beginning level is preferred.

Requirements for ESL Teachers: Doctor's degree in linguistics is required. Language proficiency in Polish is preferred.

Duration: 1 year; renewable for 1 year.

Salary: *Teachers:* 150% of the salary for the corresponding post in the U.S.

Benefits: Housing for appointee and dependents. Health insurance and health care. Free education for children. Other benefits are provided.

Academic Calendar: October–September.

Orientation: 2 weeks in Cracow.

Contact: Fulbright Teacher Exchange Program, E/ASX, U.S. Information Agency, 301 Fourth St. SW, Washington, DC 20547. *Phone:* (202) 485-2555.

PORTUGAL

MORE THAN ONE CITY

203 MINISTRY OF EDUCATION AND CULTURE
The Ministry reports a need for U.S. university teachers and for teachers of pre-K and elementary education at teacher colleges.
Language of Instruction: *Universities:* English. *Teacher Colleges:* Portuguese; some English and French.
Requirements for General Teachers: Master's degree in subject taught is required; doctor's degree is preferred. Teaching experience is preferred. International experience is preferred for teacher colleges. Language proficiency in Portuguese or Spanish is preferred for teacher colleges.
Duration: 4 months at universities, 11 months at teacher colleges; renewable.
Salary: *Universities:* Contact Luso-American Educational Commission for information. *Teacher Colleges:* $714 per month.
Benefits: Teacher Colleges: Housing for appointee and dependents. Other benefits are provided.
Academic Calendar: October–July.
Contact: For university positions: Luso-American Educational Commission, Avenida Eias Garcia, 59-5, P-1000 Lisbon, Portugal. *Phone:* (351-1) 767976. *Cable:* FULCOM-LISBOA. For positions in teacher colleges: Ministerio da Educacao e Cultura, Instituto Politecnico de Santarem, Escola Superior de Educacao, Av. Madre Andaluz, P-2000 Santarem, Portugal. *Phone:* (351-43) 28418/22626. *Telex:* 43003.

EVORA

204 UNIVERSIDADE DE EVORA
This public coed university was founded in 1973. Current enrollment is 3,000; none of the faculty are U.S. nationals.
Language of Instruction: Portuguese.
Opportunities: *General:* Full-time positions for visiting professors. *ESL:* 1 full-time position. *Administrators:* None.
Requirements for General Teachers: Doctor's degree is required. Current teaching experience is required. Language proficiency in Portuguese on the intermediate level is required.
Requirements for ESL Teachers: Bachelor's degree is required; master's degree is preferred. Teaching experience is preferred. International experience is preferred. Language proficiency in Portuguese is preferred.
Duration: 1 year; renewable indefinitely.
Salary: $700–$1,400 per month.
Benefits: Round-trip transportation from U.S. for visiting professors only. University may assist in locating housing. Health care. Other benefits are provided.
Academic Calendar: October–September.
Application Deadline: None.
Contact: Rector, Universidade de Evora, Apartado 94, P-7001 Evora Codex, Portugal. *Phone:* (351-66) 25572/3/4. *Telex:* 18771. For ESL positions: Departamento de Linguas e Literatura, Universidade de Evora, Apartado 94, P-7001 Evora Codex, Portugal.

LINDA-A-VELHA

205 AMERICAN INTERNATIONAL SCHOOL—LISBON
This private coed primary/secondary school was founded in 1956. Current enrollment is 283; 85% of the faculty are U.S. nationals.
Language of Instruction: *Primary:* English. *Other:* Portuguese and French.
Opportunities: *General:* 10 full- and part-time positions for teachers of all subjects and special education. *ESL:* 3 full-time positions. *Administrators:* None.
Requirements for General Teachers: Bachelor's degree is required; master's degree is preferred. 3 years of teaching experience or relevant practical experience is preferred.

Requirements for ESL Teachers: Bachelor's degree is required; master's degree is preferred. 3 years of teaching experience is required.
Duration: 2 years; renewable for 1 year.
Salary: 91,900–135,200 escudos per month.
Benefits: Round-trip transportation from U.S. for appointee and dependents. Housing allowance. School assists in locating housing. Paid home leave if contract is renewed. Health insurance. Additional benefits are provided.
Academic Calendar: September–June.
Orientation: 1–2 days on-site.
Application Deadline: March.
Contact: Dr. Dorrit M. Smith, Director, American International School—Lisbon, Quinta da Casa Branca, Carnaxide, 2795 Linda-a-Velha, Portugal. *Phone:* (351-1) 2187549. *Telex:* 13453 EAP P.

LISBON

206 DENTAL SCHOOL OF LISBON
Language of Instruction: *Primary:* Portuguese. *Other:* English.
Opportunities: *General:* 2–4 positions for teachers of oral hygiene, laboratory dental technicians, and dental education. *ESL:* None. *Administrators:* 1 position.
Requirements for Teachers: Doctor's degree is required. Teaching experience is required. Language proficiency in Portuguese or Spanish is preferred.
Requirements for Administrators: Bachelor's degree is required. Administrative experience is preferred. Language proficiency in Portuguese or Spanish is preferred.
Benefits: Round-trip transportation from U.S. is sometimes provided. Housing for appointee only. Paid home leave. Other benefits are provided.
Academic Calendar: September–July.
Contact: Armando Simoes dos Santos, Director, Dental School, Cidade Universitaria, 1600 Lisboa, Portugal. *Phone:* (351-1) 73 69 49. *Telex:* 62028.

207 UNIVERSIDADE NOVA DE LISBOA
This public coed university was founded in 1973. Current enrollment is 5,000.
Language of Instruction: *Primary:* Portuguese. *Other:* English.
Opportunities: *General:* 3–4 positions for teachers in the university's MBA program. *ESL:* None. *Administrators:* None.
Requirements: Doctor's degree in business administration is required. 10 years of teaching experience is required. Experience in teaching at executive seminars is required. International experience is preferred. Language proficiency in Portuguese on the intermediate level is preferred.
Duration: 3 months–1 year; renewable for 3 years.
Salary: $10,000–$15,000 per 3-month term.
Benefits: Round-trip transportation from U.S. for appointee only. Housing allowance. University assists in locating housing. Other benefits are provided.
Academic Calendar: October–July.
Application Deadline: March 31.
Contact: Carlos Jorge Barral, Director, MBA Program, Faculdade de Economia, Universidade Nova de Lisboa, Rue Marques de Fronteira 20, P-1000 Lisboa, Portugal. *Phone:* (351-1) 52 01 27. *Telex:* 42 522 MBA FEP.

MONTE DE CAPARICA

208 UNIVERSIDADE NOVA DE LISBOA
The public university was founded in 1973. Current enrollment is 5,000.
Language of Instruction: *Primary:* Portuguese. *Other:* English.
Opportunities: *General:* 1 full-time position for teacher of industrial engineering. *ESL:* None. *Administrators:* None.
Requirements: Doctor's degree in industrial engineering is preferred. 3 years of teaching experience or relevant practical experience is preferred. Language proficiency in Portuguese on the intermediate level is preferred.
Duration: From 6 months; renewable.
Salary: 128,500–156,600 escudos.
Benefits: University assists in locating housing. Paid home leave.
Academic Calendar: October–September.

All information is subject to change without notice and must be confirmed directly with the employer.

39

Orientation: On-site.
Application Deadline: Jan. 1.
Contact: Virgilio A.P. Machado, Associate Professor, Faculdade de Ciencias e Tecnologia, Universidade Nova de Lisboa, Quinta de Torre, 2825 Monte de Caparica, Portugal. *Phone:* (351-1) 295-4464. *Telex:* 14542 FCTUNL P.

ROMANIA

MORE THAN ONE CITY

209 U.S. INFORMATION AGENCY
Fulbright Scholar Program.
USIA reports openings for university faculty under the Fulbright Scholar Program. Up to 7 research awards for 3–10 months are also available.
Opportunities: *General:* Up to 6 positions for teachers of American literature. *ESL:* University-level positions available. *Administrators:* None.
Requirements for General Teachers: Doctor's degree in subject taught is required. Teaching experience is required. International experience is preferred. Language proficiency in Romanian is preferred.
Requirements for ESL Teachers: Master's degree in applied linguistics is required; doctor's degree is preferred. Teaching experience is required. Language proficiency in Romanian is preferred.
Duration: 10–20 months; not renewable.
Salary: $16,000–$24,000.
Benefits: Round-trip transportation from U.S. for appointee only. Housing for appointee. Dependent children may attend American School in Bucharest.
Orientation: 3 days in Washington (DC).
Application Deadline: Sept. 15.
Contact: Council for International Exchange of Scholars, 11 Dupont Circle NW, Suite 300, Washington, DC 20036. *Phone:* (202) 939-5401.

BUCHAREST

210 AMERICAN SCHOOL OF BUCHAREST
This private coed pre-K and primary school was founded in 1962. Current enrollment is 116; 80% of the faculty are U.S. nationals.
Language of Instruction: *Primary:* English. *Other:* French.
Opportunities: *General:* 3 full-time positions. *ESL:* Less than 1 position per year. *Administrators:* 1 full-time position.
Requirements for General Teachers: Bachelor's degree in elementary education is required. 2 years of teaching experience is required. International experience is preferred. Teaching couples are preferred.
Requirements for ESL Teachers: Bachelor's degree in TESL is preferred. Teaching experience is required. International experience is preferred.
Requirements for Administrators: Master's degree in educational administration is preferred. Administrative experience is required. International experience is preferred.
Duration: 2 years; renewable.
Salary: *Teachers:* $14,000–$21,000 per academic year. *Administrators:* $30,000–$35,000 per calendar year.
Benefits: Round-trip transportation from U.S. for appointee only. Housing for appointee and dependents. Paid home leave every 2 years. Retirement plan. Other benefits are provided.
Academic Calendar: August–June.
Orientation: 3 days on-site.
Contact: Albert Chudler, Director, American School of Bucharest, Department of State/Bucharest, Washington, DC 20520. *Phone:* In Romania: (40-0) 33-21-20.

SPAIN

MORE THAN ONE CITY

211 MINISTERIO DE EDUCACION Y CIENCIA (MINISTRY OF EDUCATION AND SCIENCE)
The Ministry reports a need for U.S. teachers at commercial language academies and on the primary/secondary level at private international schools.

Language of Instruction: *Primary:* Spanish and regional languages. *Other:* English, French, and German.
Academic Calendar: September–May/June.
Contact: Ministerio de Educacion y Ciencia, c/Alcala 34, 28014 Madrid, Spain.

212 COMMISSION FOR EDUCATIONAL EXCHANGE BETWEEN THE U.S.A. AND SPAIN (FULBRIGHT COMMISSION)
USIA Fulbright Scholar Program.
Opportunities: *General:* 4–5 full-time positions for teachers of American literature and political science at the university level. *ESL:* None. *Administrators:* 1 full-time university position.
Requirements for Teachers: Doctor's degree in subject taught is preferred. Teaching experience is required. Language proficiency in Spanish on the intermediate or advanced level is required.
Duration: 3–5 months; not renewable.
Salary: *Teachers:* About $1,500 per month.
Benefits: Round-trip transportation from U.S. for appointee only. Housing may be provided. Health insurance. Other benefits are provided.
Academic Calendar: October–June.
Orientation: 3 days in Madrid for October start.
Contact: Council for International Exchange of Scholars, 11 Dupont Circle NW, Suite 300, Washington, DC 20036. *Phone:* (202) 939-5401.

BILBAO

213 UNIVERSITY OF DEUSTO
This private coed university was founded in 1886. Current enrollment is 12,000; 10% of the faculty are U.S. nationals.
Language of Instruction: *Primary:* Spanish. *Other:* Basque and English.
Contact: Don Manual Breva-Claramonte, Vice-Dean, University of Deusto, Apartado 1, 48080 Bilbao, Spain. *Phone:* (34-94) 445 3100. *Cable:* UNIVERSIDAD.

ESPLUGUES DE LLOBREGAT

214 AMERICAN SCHOOL OF BARCELONA
This private coed pre-K and primary/secondary school was founded in 1962. Current enrollment is 300; 50% of the faculty are U.S. nationals. The school exchanges teachers with Carmel (California) schools.
Language of Instruction: *Primary:* English. *Other:* Spanish and Catalan.
Opportunities: *General:* 3 full-time positions. *ESL:* 1 full-time position. *Administrators:* Full-time positions.
Requirements for General Teachers: Bachelor's degree in elementary education is required; master's degree is preferred for secondary school. 2 years of teaching or relevant practical experience is preferred. International experience is preferred. Language proficiency in Spanish on the intermediate level is preferred.
Requirements for ESL Teachers: Master's degree in English is required. 2 years of teaching or relevant practical experience is preferred. International experience is preferred. Language proficiency in Spanish on the intermediate level is preferred.
Requirements for Administrators: Master's degree in curriculum/supervision is preferred. 2 years of administrative experience is required. International experience is preferred. Language proficiency in Spanish on the intermediate level is preferred.
Duration: 2 years; renewable for 2 years.
Salary: *Teachers:* $12,000–$15,000 per academic year. *Administrators:* $15,000–$17,500 per academic year.
Benefits: School assists in locating housing. Health and life insurance. Retirement plan.
Academic Calendar: September–June.
Orientation: 1 day on-site.
Application Deadline: None.
Contact: Elsa Lamb, Director, American School of Barcelona, Balmes 7, Esplugues de Llobregat (Barcelona), Spain. *Phone:* (34-3) 371 4016/5012.

All information is subject to change without notice
and must be confirmed directly with the employer.

MADRID

215 AMERICAN SCHOOL OF MADRID
This private coed primary/secondary school was founded in 1961. Current enrollment is 585; 63% of the faculty are U.S. nationals.
Language of Instruction: English.
Opportunities: *General:* Full- and part-time positions. *ESL:* Less than 1 position per year. *Administrators:* Less than 1 position per year.
Requirements for General Teachers: Bachelor's degree is required; master's degree is preferred for department chairmen. 2 years of teaching experience is required. Language proficiency in Spanish is preferred.
Requirements for ESL Teachers: Bachelor's degree is required. 2 years of teaching experience is required. Language proficiency in Spanish on the intermediate or advanced level is required.
Requirements for Administrators: Bachelor's degree is required; master's degree is preferred. 10 years of administrative experience is required. Language proficiency in Spanish is preferred.
Duration: 1 year; renewable.
Salary: *Teachers:* $19,925–$22,054 per calendar year. *Administrators:* From $45,000 per calendar year.
Benefits: Round-trip transportation from U.S. for appointee and dependents. School assists in locating housing. Life and accident insurance. Pension plan. Other benefits are provided.
Academic Calendar: September–June.
Application Deadline: January.
Contact: Dr. Max R. Tudor, Superintendent, American School of Madrid, Apartado 80, 28080 Madrid, Spain. *Phone:* (34-1) 207 0641. *Telex:* 49621 EAM E. *Cable:* AMSCHOL.

216 INTERNATIONAL COLLEGE SPAIN
This private coed primary/secondary school was founded in 1980. Current enrollment is 290; 15% of the faculty are U.S. nationals.
Language of Instruction: *Primary:* English. *Other:* Spanish, Swedish, French, Dutch, and Farsi.
Opportunities: *General:* 1–2 full-time positions for teachers of all subjects. *ESL:* 1 full- or part-time position. *Administrators:* Less than 1 position per year.
Requirements for General Teachers: Bachelor's degree in subject taught is required; master's degree in education is preferred. 1 year of teaching experience is required. International experience is preferred. Language proficiency in Spanish on the beginning level is preferred.
Requirements for ESL Teachers: Bachelor's degree in English is required. 3 years of teaching experience is preferred. EFL teaching certificate is required. International experience is required. Language proficiency in Spanish on the beginning level is preferred.
Requirements for Administrators: Bachelor's degree is required; master's degree is preferred. 5 years of administrative experience is required. International experience is preferred. Language proficiency in Spanish on the beginning level is preferred.
Duration: 1 year; renewable indefinitely.
Salary: *Teachers:* $9,025–$16,625 per calendar year. *Administrators:* $13,125–$20,125 per calendar year.
Benefits: Round-trip transportation from U.S. for appointee and dependents. Health insurance. Other benefits are provided.
Academic Calendar: September–June.
Orientation: On-site.
Application Deadline: March/April.
Contact: Bernard Briquet, Director, International College Spain, Calle Vereda Norte 3, 28109 La Moraleja, Madrid, Spain. *Phone:* (34-1) 650 2398/9.

PALMA DE MALLORCA

217 BALEARES INTERNATIONAL SCHOOL
This private coed primary/secondary school was founded in 1957. Current enrollment is 220; 5% of the faculty are U.S. nationals. Faculty are primarily recruited locally.
Language of Instruction: *Primary:* English. *Other:* Spanish, French, and German.
Opportunities: *Teachers:* Less than 1 position per year. *Administrators:* None.

Requirements: Bachelor's degree in education or subject taught is required; master's degree is preferred. 2 years of teaching experience is preferred. Language proficiency in Spanish is preferred.
Duration: 7 years; renewable indefinitely.
Salary: Based on Spanish government scales; about half of U.S. salary in middle range.
Benefits: Round-trip transportation from U.S. for appointee only. Housing allowance. Paid home leave every 2 years. Health insurance. Tuition for children enrolled at this school. Other benefits are provided.
Academic Calendar: September–June.
Orientation: 3 days on-site.
Application Deadline: Open.
Contact: The Director, Baleares International School, Calle Cabo Mateu Coch 17, 07015 Palma de Mallorca, Spain. *Phone:* (34-71) 40 31 61/40 32 02. *Telex:* 69206 XPTS E.

SOTOGRANDE

218 INTERNATIONAL SCHOOL AT SOTOGRANDE
This private coed primary/secondary school was founded in 1978. Current enrollment is 230; 7% of the faculty are U.S. nationals. The school has a British currriculum and does not recruit faculty in the U.S.
Language of Instruction: *Primary:* English. *Other:* Spanish.
Opportunities: *Teachers:* Full-time positions. *Administrators:* None.
Contact: Mr. P.J. Hinton, Bursar, The International School at Sotogrande, Cortijo Paniagua S/N, 11310 Sotogrande (Cadiz), Spain. *Phone:* (34-56) 79 29 02. *Telex:* 78013 SOTOG E.

SWEDEN

MORE THAN ONE CITY

219 SWEDISH NATIONAL BOARD OF EDUCATION
The Board reports that there is no need for U.S. teachers or educational administrators at this time.
Language of Instruction: *Primary:* Swedish. *Other:* English, French, and German.
Academic Calendar: August–June.
For General Information, Contact: Swedish National Board of Education, S-106 42 Stockholm, Sweden. *Phone:* (46-8) 783 20 00.

220 COMMISSION FOR EDUCATIONAL EXCHANGE BETWEEN THE U.S.A. AND SWEDEN (FULBRIGHT COMMISSION)
The Commission reports that it no longer brings U.S. teachers to Sweden. However, foreigners proficient in Swedish and with adequate qualifications can obtain positions as temporary staff teachers.

A list of teaching positions available in Sweden is available from: Lararlistan, The National Labor Market Board, S-171 99 Solna, Sweden.

Teachers may also write directly to the few English-speaking schools located in Sweden. However, an offer of employment does not guarantee a work permit. Apply to the Swedish Embassy or at the nearest Swedish Consulate for a work permit.
Contact: Commission for Educational Exchange between the U.S.A. and Sweden (Fulbright Commission), Norrmalmstorg 1, 111 46 Stockholm, Sweden. *Phone:* (46-8) 10 64 50/10 65 15. *Cable:* FULBRIGHTCOM.

LUND

221 LUND UNIVERSITY
This coed university was founded in 1668. Current enrollment is 23,000; none of the faculty are U.S. nationals.
Language of Instruction: *Primary:* Swedish. *Other:* English.
Opportunities: *Teachers:* Positions available. *Administrators:* None.
Academic Calendar: August–June.
Contact: Lund University, Information Office, Box 117, 22100 Lund, Sweden. *Phone:* (46-46) 10 90 00.

All information is subject to change without notice and must be confirmed directly with the employer.

41

SWITZERLAND

MORE THAN ONE CITY

222 ASSOCIATION SUISSE DES PROFESSEURS D'UNIVERSITE

The Association reports that the only foreign citizens allowed to teach in the Swiss public school system are those placed through the USIA Fulbright Teacher Exchange Program (see listing 9). A very limited number of foreign teachers may find positions in Swiss private schools, provided that a work permit can be obtained.
Language of Instruction: German and French.
Academic Calendar: October–July.
For General Information, Contact: Association Suisse des Professeurs d'Universite, Sophienstrasse 2, CH-8032 Zurich, Switzerland.

BOTTMINGEN

223 INTERNATIONAL SCHOOL OF BASEL

This private coed pre-K and primary school was founded in 1979. Current enrollment is 120; 25% of the faculty are U.S. nationals.
Language of Instruction: *Primary:* English. *Other:* German.
Opportunities: *General:* 2 full-time positions. *ESL:* 1 full- or part-time position. *Administrators:* None.
Requirements for General Teachers: Teaching experiecne is required. International experience is preferred.
Requirements for ESL Teachers: Teaching experience is required. International experience is preferred. Language proficiency in German is required.
Duration: 1 year; renewable indefinitely.
Salary: 35,000–45,000 francs per calendar year.
Benefits: Accident insurance. Pension plan.
Academic Calendar: August–June.
Contact: Geoffrey Tomlinson, Headmaster, International School of Basel, P.O. Box 319, CH-4103 Bottmingen, Switzerland. *Phone:* (41-61) 47 84 83.

CRANS-SUR-SIERRE

224 INTERNATIONAL SCHOOL LE CHAPERON ROUGE

This private coed primary/secondary school was founded in 1955. Current enrollment is 65; 2 of the faculty are U.S. nationals.
Language of Instruction: *Primary:* English. *Other:* French, German, Italian.
Opportunities: *Teachers:* 1–2 full-time positions for teachers of entire curriculum except foreign languages, music, and sports. Teachers of intensive courses in English, French, German, and Italian are also needed. *Administrators:* None.
Requirements: Teaching or relevant practical experience is preferred. International experience is preferred. Language proficiency in French is preferred. Female teachers are preferred.
Duration: 1 year; renewable for several years.
Salary: Varies.
Benefits: Housing for appointee only. Other benefits are provided.
Academic Calendar: September–June.
Contact: Prosper Bagnoud, Head, International School le Chaperon Rouge, CH-3963 Crans-sur-Sierre, Switzerland. *Phone:* (41-27) 41 25 00. *Cable:* CHAPERONROUGE CRANS.

GENEVA

225 UNIVERSITY OF GENEVA

This public coed university was founded in 1559. Current enrollment is about 11,000.
Language of Instruction: French.
Opportunities: *Teachers:* Full-time positions. *Administrators:* None.
Contact: University of Geneva, 24 rue General Dufour, CH-1211 Geneva, Switzerland. *Phone:* (41-22) 20 93 33. *Telex:* 423801.

GUMLIGEN

226 INTERNATIONAL SCHOOL OF BERNE

This private coed primary/secondary school was founded in 1961. Current enrollment is 145; 45% of the faculty are U.S. nationals.
Language of Instruction: *Primary:* English. *Other:* German and French.
Opportunities: *Teachers:* 3 positions. *Administrators:* None.
Requirements: Bachelor's degree is required; master's degree is preferred. 2 years of teaching experience is required. International experience is preferred.
Duration: 1 year; renewable.
Salary: About $21,500.
Benefits: Transportation to Switzerland is provided for appointee. Health insurance. Pension plan.
Academic Calendar: September–June.
Application Deadline: Open.
Contact: Mr. John Kidner, Headmaster, International School of Berne, Mattenstrasse 3, CH-3073 Gumligen, Switzerland.

KILCHBERG

227 AMERICAN INTERNATIONAL SCHOOL OF ZURICH

This is a private coed secondary school. Current enrollment is 260; 40% of the faculty are U.S. nationals.
Language of Instruction: English.
Opportunities: *General:* 1 full- or part-time position for teachers of science, mathematics, English, and computer science. *ESL:* Less than 1 position per year. *Administrators:* Less than 1 position per year.
Requirements for Teachers: Bachelor's degree in subject taught is required; master's degree is preferred. 5 years of teaching experience is required. International experience is preferred.
Requirements for Administrators: Master's degree is preferred. 5 years of administrative experience is preferred. International experience is preferred. Language proficiency in German on the intermediate level is preferred.
Duration: 1 year; renewable.
Benefits: Health insurance, pension plan.
Academic Calendar: September–June.
Application Deadline: March 1.
Contact: Tom Ulmet, Director of Education, American International School of Zurich, Nidelbadstrasse 49, 8802 Kilchberg, Switzerland. *Phone:* (41-1) 715 27 95.

LEYSIN

228 AMERICAN COLLEGE OF SWITZERLAND

This private coed university was founded in 1963. Current enrollment is 300.
Opportunities: *General:* 18 full-time positions for teachers of business, economics, international studies, political science, and library arts. *ESL:* 2 full-time positions. *Administrators:* 7 full-time positions.
Requirements for General Teachers: Master's degree in subject taught is required; doctor's degree is preferred. 3 years of teaching experience is required. International experience is required. Language proficiency in French on the intermediate level is preferred.
Requirements for ESL Teachers: Master's degree in TEFL is required; doctor's degree is preferred. 3 years of teaching experience is required. International experience is required. Language proficiency in French on the intermediate level is preferred.
Requirements for Administrators: Master's degree is required; doctor's degree is preferred. 3 years of administrative experience is required. International experience is required. Language proficiency in French on the advanced level is preferred.
Duration: 1 years; renewable indefinitely.
Salary: *Teachers:* 45,000–70,000 francs per calendar year. *Administrators:* 50,000–80,000 francs per calendar year.
Benefits: University assists in locating housing. Other benefits are provided.
Academic Calendar: August–May.
Application Deadline: February.
Contact: Daniel Queudot, President, The American College of Switzerland, CH-1854 Leysin, Switzerland. *Phone:* (41-25) 34 22 23. *Telex:* 453 227.

All information is subject to change without notice and must be confirmed directly with the employer.

229 HOSTA HOTEL AND TOURISM SCHOOL

This private coed hotel and tourism professional school was founded in 1959. Current enrollment is 190; 20% of the faculty are U.S. nationals.
Language of Instruction: English.
Opportunities: *General:* 4 full-time positions for hotel and tourism specialists. *ESL:* None. *Administrators:* None.
Requirements: Bachelor's degree in hotel and restaurant administration is required; master's degree is preferred. Teaching experience is preferred, or practical experience in hotel/restaurant field is required. International experience is preferred.
Duration: 1 year; renewable.
Salary: 40,000–50,000 francs per calendar year.
Benefits: School assists in locating housing. Health insurance. Pension plan.
Academic Calendar: August–May.
Application Deadline: None.
Contact: D.C. Nott, Academic Dean, Hosta Hotel and Tourism School, 1854 Leysin, Switzerland. *Phone:* (41-25) 34 26 11. *Telex:* 456 152 CRTO CH.

LUGANO

230 FRANKLIN COLLEGE

This private coed college was founded in 1970. Current enrollment is 180; 48% of the faculty are U.S. nationals. The college exchanges faculty with Pace University, George Washington University, the College Consortium for International Studies (CCIS), and Claremont McKenna College.
Language of Instruction: *Primary:* English. *Other:* French, German, and Italian.
Opportunities: *General:* 3 full- and part-time positions. *ESL:* 1 part-time position. *Administrators:* 1 full- and 1 part-time position.
Requirements for General Teachers: Master's degree in business or computer science is required; doctor's degree in history, economics, literature, language, or psychology is preferred. Teaching experience is required. International experience is preferred. Language proficiency in any European language is preferred.
Requirements for ESL Teachers: Master's degree in liberal arts or business is required; doctor's degree in ESL is preferred. Teaching experience is preferred, or relevant practical experience is required. International experience is preferred. Language proficiency in Italian is preferred.
Requirements for Administrators: Bachelor's, master's, or doctor's degree is preferred. Administrative experience is preferred. International experience is preferred. Language proficiency in Italian, French, or German on the intermediate or advanced level is preferred.
Duration: 1 year; renewable for 1 year.
Salary: *Teachers:* $50,000–$60,000 per calendar year. *Administrators:* $60,000–$70,000 per calendar year.
Benefits: Round-trip transportation from U.S. for appointee only. College assists in locating housing. Health and accident insurance. Pension plan.
Academic Calendar: August–May.
Application Deadline: January or summer.
Contact: Dr. Maud S. Walther, Dean of the College, Franklin College, Via Ponte Tresa 29, CH-6924 Sorengo-Lugano, Switzerland. *Phone:* (41-91) 55 01 01.

ZUGERBERG

231 INSTITUT MONTANA

This private boys' boarding and coed day primary/secondary school was founded in 1952. Current enrollment is 40; 25% of the faculty are U.S. nationals.
Language of Instruction: *Primary:* English. *Other:* French and German.
Opportunities: *General:* 1–2 positions for teachers of English, mathematics, social studies, and science on the primary level; same plus French, German, music, and art on the secondary level. *ESL:* Less than 1 position per year. *Administrators:* None.
Requirements for General Teachers: Bachelor's degree in subject taught is required; master's degree is preferred. 1–2 years of teaching experience is preferred. Candidates must be single.

Requirements for ESL Teachers: Bachelor's degree in linguistics or applied linguistics is required; master's degree is preferred. Teaching experience is preferred.
Duration: 2 years; renewable.
Salary: 1,500 francs per month.
Benefits: Housing for appointee only. Health and accident insurance. Other benefits are provided.
Academic Calendar: September–June.
Application Deadline: Early spring.
Contact: Peter H. Oehrlein, Dean of the American School, Institut Montana, CH-6316 Zugerberg (Zug), Switzerland.

UNION OF SOVIET SOCIALIST REPUBLICS

MOSCOW

232 ANGLO-AMERICAN SCHOOL OF MOSCOW

This private coed primary school was founded in 1949. Current enrollment is 250; 45% of the faculty are U.S. nationals.
Language of Instruction: English.
Opportunities: *General:* 6 full- and part-time positions. *ESL:* 1 full-time position. *Administrators:* 1 full-time position.
Requirements for General Teachers: Bachelor's degree in liberal arts is required; master's degree is preferred. 2 years of teaching experience is required.
Requirements for ESL Teachers: Bachelor's degree is required. Specialized training in TESL/TEFL is required. 2 years of teaching experience is required. International experience is preferred.
Requirements for Administrators: Bachelor's degree is required.
Duration: 2 years; renewable.
Salary: *Teachers:* $13,710–$23,900 per academic year. *Administrators:* $20,000–$40,000 per calendar year.
Benefits: Round-trip transportation from U.S. for appointee and up to 3 dependents. Housing for appointee and dependents. Paid home leave every 2 years. Health insurance. Other benefits are provided.
Academic Calendar: September–June.
Orientation: 7–10 days on-site.
Application Deadline: Feb. 1.
Contact: Vera Nordal, Director, Anglo-American School of Moscow, U.S. Embassy Moscow, APO New York 09862. *Phone:* In USSR: 131-8700. *Telex:* 413-160 USGSO-SU.

UNITED KINGDOM

MORE THAN ONE CITY

233 BRITISH COUNCIL

The British Council reports that there is no need for U.S. teachers or educational administrators at this time.
For General Information, Contact: Brian Evans, Deputy Director, The British Council, 65 Davies Street, London W1Y 2AA, England. *Phone:* (44-1) 499-8011.

234 BRITISH INFORMATION SERVICES

At present, opportunities are scarce for foreign teachers in Britain. Foreign employees must possess a work permit issued by the British Department of Employment, and work permits are issued only for teachers of mathematics and/or the natural sciences.

Vacancies for teaching positions are advertised in *The Times Educational Supplement, The Times Higher Education Supplement, The Teacher,* and *The Scottish Educational Journal.*

In Britain, each local Education Authority appoints teachers to the public schools for which they are responsible. Applications should be directed to the appropriate Authority (see *The Education Authorities Directory and Annual*). British Information Services will only supply 2 Authority addresses by mail.

Applications for employment at independent (private) schools should be made directly to the school. A placement service is provided by the European Council of International Schools (see listing 3).

There is an annual post-to-post exchange of teachers under the USIA Fulbright Teacher Exchange Program (see listing 9).

Academic Calendar: October–June.
Contact: British Information Services, 845 Third Ave., New York, NY 10022. *Phone:* (212) 752-8400.

235 CENTRAL BUREAU
USIA Fulbright Teacher Exchange Program.
The Bureau is a cooperating partner with the U.S. Information Agency in the administration of the U.K./U.S. Teacher Exchange Program. The program recruits teachers and lecturers at all levels from nursery school to university. Applicant's home school must be willing to accept a British teacher.
Duration: 1 semester–1 year.
Salary: Teacher retains salary from home school.
Application Deadline: Oct. 15.
Contact: Teacher Exchange Branch, E/ASX, U.S. Information Agency, 301 Fourth St. SW, Washington, DC 20547. *Phone:* (202) 485-2555/6.

ABERDEEN

236 AMERICAN SCHOOL IN ABERDEEN EDUCATIONAL TRUST
This private coed primary/secondary school was founded in 1972. Current enrollment is 210; 80% of the faculty are U.S. nationals.
Language of Instruction: *Primary:* English. *Other:* Spanish and French.
Opportunities: *Teachers:* 5 positions. *Administrators:* None.
Requirements: Bachelor's degree in education is required; master's or doctor's degree is preferred. 2 years of teaching experience is required. International experience is preferred.
Duration: 2 years; renewable annually.
Benefits: Round-trip transportation from U.S. for appointee and dependents. Housing allowance. Paid home leave. Health and life insurance. Other benefits are provided.
Academic Calendar: August–June.
Orientation: 1 week on-site.
Application Deadline: Feb. 1.
Contact: Everett G. Gould, Superintendent/Headmaster, American School in Aberdeen Educational Trust Ltd., Craigton Road, Cults, Aberdeen AB1 9QD, Scotland. *Phone:* (44-224) 868927/861068.

ABERYSTWYTH

237 COLLEGE OF LIBRARIANSHIP WALES
This public coed university was founded in 1964. Current enrollment is 370; none of the faculty are U.S. nationals.
Language of Instruction: *Primary:* English. *Other:* Welsh.
Opportunities: *General:* 1 part-time position for a teacher of library and information science for the summer school. *ESL:* None. *Administrators:* None.
Requirements: Master's degree in library or information science is required; doctor's degree is preferred. Teaching experience is required. International experience is preferred.
Duration: 8 weeks; not renewable.
Benefits: Round-trip transportation from U.S. for appointee only. Housing for appointee only. Other benefits are provided.
Academic Calendar: July–August.
Contact: Frank N. Hogg, Principal, College of Librarianship Wales, Llanbadarn Fawr, Aberystwyth SY23 3AS, Wales, United Kingdom. *Phone:* (44-970) 3181. *Telex:* 35391 CLW G.

ARUNDEL

238 NEW ENGLAND COLLEGE
This private coed university was founded in 1971. Current enrollment is 240; 25% of the faculty are U.S. nationals.
Language of Instruction: English.
Opportunities: *General:* 4–5 full- and part-time positions. *ESL:* None. *Administrators:* 4–5 full-time positions for admissions and student affairs.

Requirements for Teachers: Master's degree is required; doctor's degree is preferred. Teaching experience is preferred. International experience is preferred. British work permit is required.
Requirements for Administrators: Master's degree is required; doctor's degree is preferred. Administrative experience is preferred. International experience is preferred. British work permit is required.
Duration: 1 year; renewable indefinitely.
Salary: *Teachers:* £10,000–£20,000 per academic year. *Administrators:* £8,000–£21,000 per calendar year.
Benefits: Round-trip transportation from U.S. for appointee and dependents. Housing for student affairs personnel. Otherwise, college assists in locating housing. Health and life insurance. Pension plan. Tuition for children enrolled at this school.
Academic Calendar: August–May.
Application Deadline: Open.
Contact: Eric C. Nummela, Director, British Campus, New England College, Arundel, West Sussex BN18 0DA, England. *Phone:* (44-903) 882259. *Telex:* 877450 NECARN G.

BUSHEY

239 INTERNATIONAL UNIVERSITY HIGH SCHOOL
This private coed secondary school was founded in 1978. Current enrollment is 50; 50% of the faculty are U.S. nationals.
Language of Instruction: English.
Opportunities: *General:* 4 full- or part-time positions. *ESL:* 1 full- or part-time position. *Administrators:* 1 full-time position.
Requirements for General Teachers: Bachelor's degree is required; master's degree is preferred. 2 years of teaching experience is required. International experience is preferred.
Requirements for ESL Teachers: Bachelor's or master's degree is preferred.
Requirements for Administrators: Master's degree in administration or curriculum is required. Administrative experience is required. International experience is preferred.
Duration: 1 year; renewable for 1 year.
Salary: *Teachers:* £7,500 plus housing, or £13,000 without housing per academic year.
Benefits: Round-trip transportation from U.S. for appointee only.
Academic Calendar: September–June.
Orientation: 1 week on-site.
Application Deadline: January.
Contact: William F. Russell, Headmaster, International University High School, The Avenue, Bushey, Herts. WD2 2LN, United Kingdom. *Phone:* (44-923) 249067. *Telex:* 223869 IUE-G.

CHATHAM

240 MID-KENT COLLEGE OF HIGHER AND FURTHER EDUCATION
This public coed postsecondary vocational/technical school, professional college, and adult/continuing program was founded in 1900. Current enrollment is 12,000; 0.3% of the faculty are U.S. nationals.
Language of Instruction: English.
Opportunities: *General:* Occasional exchanges have been arranged through national exchange organizations. *ESL:* None. *Administrators:* None.
Requirements: Bachelor's degree is preferred. Teaching experience is preferred.
Duration: 1 year.
Salary: £8,000–£12,000 per calendar year.
Academic Calendar: September–July.
Contact: Dr. M.R. Lane, Vice Principal, Mid-Kent College of Higher and Further Education, Horsted, Maidstone Rd., Chatham, Kent ME5 9UQ, United Kingdom. *Phone:* (44-634) 44470.

COBHAM

241 AMERICAN COMMUNITY SCHOOL (LONDON)
This private coed primary/secondary school was founded in 1967. Current enrollment is 1,650; 65% of the faculty are U.S. nationals. To obtain a work permit, applicants must be under age 53 and not heads of single-parent families.

All information is subject to change without notice and must be confirmed directly with the employer.

44

Language of Instruction: *Primary:* English. *Other:* Dutch.
Opportunities: *General:* 20 full-time positions for teachers of all subjects and special education. *ESL:* 2 full-time positions. *Administrators:* 2 full-time positions.
Requirements for General Teachers: Bachelor's degree is required. 2 years of recent teaching experience is required. International experience is preferred.
Requirements for ESL Teachers: Bachelor's degree is required. Teaching experience is required. International experience is preferred.
Requirements for Administrators: Bachelor's degree is required. 2 years of administrative experience is required.
Duration: 1 year; renewable.
Salary: *Teachers:* £11,000–£15,000 per academic year. *Administrators:* £15,000–£35,000 per calendar year.
Benefits: Transportation from U.S. for appointee only. School assists in locating housing. Health insurance. Other benefits are provided.
Academic Calendar: August–June.
Orientation: 1 week on-site.
Application Deadline: February.
Contact: Mrs. M. Eretzian, Personnel Manager, The American Community Schools (London), Portsmouth Rd., Cobham, Surrey KT11 1BL, United Kingdom. *Phone:* (44-932) 67251. *Telex:* 886645 ACS G.

FAIR OAK

242 ALLINGTON MANOR INTERNATIONAL SPECIAL SCHOOL
This private coed primary/secondary special education school was founded in 1977. Current enrollment is 25. Students enrolled in this program have IQs ranging from 80 to 135 on the WISC test.
Language of Instruction: English.
Opportunities: *General:* 3 positions for teachers of all subjects (special/remedial education). *ESL:* None. *Administrators:* None.
Requirements: Bachelor's degree is preferred. 2 years of teaching experience is preferred. Special emphasis on experience with emotional and behavioral problems in children. Experience and dedication are more important than academic credentials.
Duration: 1–3 years; renewable.
Benefits: Housing for appointee. Health insurance.
Academic Calendar: January–July, March–September, or April–December.
Orientation: On-site.
Application Deadline: Open.
Contact: Dr. L.F. Lowenstein, Director, Allington Manor International Special School, Allington Manor, Fair Oak, Hants. SO5 7DE, United Kingdom. *Phone:* (44-703) 692621.

KINGSTON UPON THAMES

243 MARYMOUNT INTERNATIONAL SCHOOL
This private female-only secondary school was founded in 1955. Current enrollment is 200; 4% of the faculty are U.S. nationals. Teachers are recruited locally; U.S. administrators are Sisters of the Sacred Heart of Mary.
Language of Instruction: English.
Contact: Christine Knight, P.R. Officer, Marymount International School, George Road, Kingston upon Thames, Surrey KT2 7PE, United Kingdom. *Phone:* (41-1) 949-0571.

LONDON

244 AMERICAN COLLEGE IN LONDON
This private coed university was founded in 1970. Current enrollment is 1,000; 45% of the faculty are U.S. nationals.
Language of Instruction: English.
Opportunities: *General:* 3–4 positions for teachers of business administration, fashion merchandising, design, and interior design. *ESL:* None. *Administrators:* None.
Requirements: Bachelor's degree in subject taught is required; master's degree is preferred. 3–5 years of teaching experience is preferred. International experience is preferred. The philosophy of the college is to hire professionals rather than professional educators.
Duration: Varies.

Salary: From £15,000 per year.
Benefits: Round-trip transportation from U.S. for appointee only. Health insurance.
Academic Calendar: September–May.
Application Deadline: Open.
Contact: The President, American College in London, 100 Marylebone Lane, London W1M 5FP, United Kingdom.

245 AMERICAN SCHOOL IN LONDON
This private coed primary/secondary school was founded in 1951. Current enrollment is 1,200; 84% of the faculty are U.S. nationals.
Language of Instruction: English.
Opportunities: *General:* Less than 1 position per year. *ESL:* None. *Administrators:* None.
Requirements: Bachelor's degree is required; master's degree is preferred. 2 years of teaching experience is required.
Duration: 2 years; renewable.
Salary: £13,700–£20,545 per year.
Benefits: Round-trip transportation from U.S. for appointee and dependents. Health, life, and disability insurance. Tuition for children enrolled at this school. Other benefits are provided.
Academic Calendar: September–June.
Application Deadline: Feb. 1.
Contact: Headmaster, American School in London, 2–8 Loudoun Road, London NW8 0NP, United Kingdom. *Phone:* (44-1) 722 0101.

246 HAMPSTEAD INTERNATIONAL SCHOOL
This private coed pre-K and primary school was founded in 1967. Current enrollment is 150; 80% of the faculty are U.S. nationals.
Language of Instruction: English.
Opportunities: *General:* 3–4 full-time positions for teachers of all subjects and special education. *ESL:* 2 full-time positions. *Administrators:* Less than 1 position per year.
Requirements for General Teachers: Bachelor's degree in subject taught or education is required; master's degree is preferred. 2 years of teaching experience is required. International experience is preferred. Language proficiency in any foreign language is preferred.
Requirements for ESL Teachers: Teaching experience is required. International experience is required. Language proficiency in any foreign language is required.
Requirements for Administrators: Bachelor's degree is required; master's or doctor's degree in education or administration is preferred. Administrative experience is required. International experience is required. Language proficiency in any foreign language is preferred. Teaching ability is required.
Duration: 1 year; renewable indefinitely.
Salary: *Teachers:* £9,600–£16,900 per calendar year. *Administrators:* Varies.
Benefits: School assists in locating housing. Health insurance. Pension plan. Other benefits are provided.
Academic Calendar: September–June.
Application Deadline: April.
Contact: Mrs. E. Murphy, Principal, Hampstead International School, 16 Netherhall Gardens, London NW3 5TJ, England. *Phone:* (44-1) 794-0018.

247 MIDDLESEX POLYTECHNIC
This public coed university was founded in 1973. Current enrollment is 9,000; 1% of the faculty are U.S. nationals.
Language of Instruction: English.
Opportunities: *General:* Full-time positions for teachers of law, accounting, computer science, and microelectronics. *ESL:* None. *Administrators:* None.
Requirements: Bachelor's degree in subject taught is required; master's or doctor's degree is preferred. Teaching or relevant practical experience is required.
Duration: 1 year; may be renewable.
Benefits: Health insurance.
Academic Calendar: September–July.
Contact: Mr. Robert Bragg, Head of Personnel, Middlesex Polytechnic, Queensway, Enfield, Middlesex EN3 4SF, United Kingdom. *Phone:* (44-1) 804-8131. *Telex:* 8954762.

248 SOUTHBANK—THE AMERICAN INTERNATIONAL SCHOOL

This private coed secondary school was founded in 1979. Current enrollment is 130; 35% of the faculty are U.S. nationals. Faculty are recruited locally.
Language of Instruction: English.
Opportunities: *General:* 2–3 full- and part-time positions. *ESL:* 3 full-time positions. *Administrators:* Less than 1 position per year.
Contact: Milton Toubkin, Headmaster, Southbank—The American International School, 55 Eccleston Square, London SW1V 1PH, United Kingdom. *Phone:* (44-1) 834 4684. *Telex:* 265871 MONREF G, QUOTE IB0 006.

OXFORD

249 ST. CLARE'S OXFORD

This private coed sixth-form college was founded in 1953. Current enrollment is 179; 5% of the faculty are U.S. nationals.
Language of Instruction: English.
Opportunities: *General:* 2–3 full-time positions. *ESL:* 1 part-time position. *Administrators:* None.
Academic Calendar: September–May.
Contact: Mrs. M. Skarland, Principal, St. Clare's Oxford, 139 Banbury Rd., Oxford OX2 7AI, United Kingdom. *Phone:* (44-865) 52031. *Telex:* 837379. *Cable:* OXCENT.

READING

250 UNIVERSITY OF READING

This coed university was founded in 1926. Current enrollment is 5,800; 1% of the faculty are U.S. nationals. Positions for U.S. teachers and educational administrators are rare.
Language of Instruction: English.
Opportunities: Less than 1 position per year.
Contact: R.M.G. Clark, Senior Assistant Registrar, University of Reading, Whiteknights, Reading RG6 2RT, United Kingdom. *Phone:* (44-734) 875123. *Telex:* 847813 RULIB G.

REPTON

251 REPTON SCHOOL

This is a private secondary school that occasionally employs U.S. teachers.
Language of Instruction: English.
Opportunities: *Teachers:* Less than 1 position per year.
Contact: G.E. Jones, Headmaster, Repton School, The Hall, Repton, Derby DE6 6FH, United Kingdom. *Phone:* (44-283) 702375.

RICHMOND

252 RICHMOND COLLEGE

This private liberal arts college, founded in 1972, is U.S.-accredited and patterned on the U.S. educational system. Current enrollment is 1,000. Because of the difficulty in obtaining work permits for foreign citizens, the college only recruits locally. However, U.S. faculty accompanying groups of students from their home institution may teach specific courses agreed on between the college and the home institution.
Language of Instruction: English.
Salary: Teacher retains salary from home school.
Contact: Robert Leestamper, Deputy to the President, Richmond College, Queens Road, Richmond, Surrey TW10 6JP, United Kingdom. *Phone:* (44-1) 940 9762. *Telex:* 25357 ISSLON G.

SAFFRON WALDEN

253 FRIENDS SCHOOL

This private coed secondary school was founded in 1702. Current enrollment is 300; 1% of the faculty are U.S. nationals. The school recruits staff locally.
Language of Instruction: *Primary:* English. *Other:* French and German.

Opportunities: *General:* Positions may become available. *ESL:* None. *Administrators:* None.
Requirements: Master's degree in subject taught is required. Teaching experience is preferred.
Duration: 1 year; renewable.
Benefits: Round-trip transportation from U.S. for appointee only. Housing for appointee only.
Academic Calendar: September–July.
Contact: John Woods, Headmaster, Friends School, Saffron Walden, Essex CR11 3EB, United Kingdom. *Phone:* (44-199) 25351.

SIBFORD FERRIS

254 SIBFORD SCHOOL

This private coed secondary school was founded in 1842. Current enrollment is 330; 5% of the faculty are U.S. nationals.
Language of Instruction: English.
Opportunities: *General:* Full-time positions. *ESL:* None. *Administrators:* None.
Requirements: Bachelor's degree is required. Teaching experience is required.
Salary: Current government rate.
Benefits: Housing is sometimes provided. School assists in locating housing.
Academic Calendar: September–July.
Contact: Jim Graham, Headmaster, Sibford School, Sibford Ferris, nr. Banbury, Oxon OX15 5QL, United Kingdom. *Phone:* (44-29) 578-441.

SUNDERLAND

255 SUNDERLAND POLYTECHNIC

This is a public coed postsecondary vocational/technical school, professional college, adult/continuing education program, and university. Current enrollment is 6,000; 3 of the faculty are U.S. nationals.
Language of Instruction: English.
Opportunities: *General:* Full-time positions may be available. *ESL:* None. *Administrators:* None.
Requirements: Master's or doctor's degree in subject taught is preferred. Teaching experience is preferred.
Duration: Staff are mostly tenured with some part-time teachers; for part-time teachers, contract is renewable annually.
Salary: £11,000–£16,000 per calendar year.
Benefits: Appointee qualifies for National Health benefit after living in the U.K. for 6 months.
Academic Calendar: September–June.
Orientation: 2 days as needed.
Application Deadline: June 30.
Contact: The Admissions Office, Sunderland Polytechnic, Edinburgh Building, Chester Rd., Sunderland SR1 3SD, United Kingdom. *Phone:* (44-91) 567 6191.

THORPE

256 TASIS ENGLAND AMERICAN SCHOOL

This private coed primary/secondary school was founded in 1976. Current enrollment is 500; 70% of the faculty are U.S. nationals.
Language of Instruction: English.
Opportunities: *Teachers:* 15 positions for teachers on the primary level; positions for teachers of English, mathematics, science, history, French, Spanish, and German on the secondary level. *Administrators:* None.
Requirements for General Teachers: Bachelor's degree is required; master's degree is preferred. 2 years of teaching experience is required.
Requirements for ESL Teachers: Bachelor's or master's degree in applied linguistics is preferred. 2 years of teaching experience is required.
Duration: 2 years; renewable annually.
Salary: £7,500–£11,000 per academic year.
Benefits: 1-time travel allowance. Housing may be provided for appointee and dependents. Appointees are covered by National Health Service. Tuition for children enrolled at this school. Other benefits are provided.

Academic Calendar: September–June.
Orientation: 1 week in England.
Application Deadline: Open.
Contact: Mr. Lyle D. Rigg, Headmaster, TASIS England American School, Coldharbour Lane, Thorpe, Surrey TW20 8TE, United Kingdom. *Phone:* (44-932) 565252. *Telex:* 929172. *Or:* The TASIS Schools, 326 E. 69th St., New York, NY 10021. *Phone:* (212) 570-1066. *Telex:* 971912.

MIDDLE EAST AND NORTH AFRICA

ALGERIA

ALGIERS

257 AMERICAN SCHOOL OF ALGIERS
This private coed primary school was founded in 1964. Current enrollment is 115; 75% of the faculty are U.S. nationals.
Language of Instruction: English.
Opportunities: *General:* 12 full- and part-time positions for teachers of all subjects. *ESL:* 2–3 full- and part-time positions. *Administrators:* 2 full- and part-time positions.
Requirements for General Teachers: Bachelor's degree is required; master's degree is preferred. 2 years of teaching experience is required. Experience in a developing country is preferred. Language proficiency in French is preferred. Married teaching couples are preferred.
Requirements for ESL Teachers: Bachelor's degree in TESL/TEFL is required; master's degree is preferred. 2 years of teaching experience is required. Experience in a developing country is required. Language proficiency in French is preferred. Married teaching couples are preferred.
Requirements for Administrators: Master's degree in educational administration is required. 5 years of administrative experience is required. Experience in a developing country is required. Language proficiency in French is preferred.
Duration: 2 years; renewable indefinitely.
Salary: *Teachers:* $17,000–$28,000 per academic year. *Administrators:* $30,000–$34,000 per academic year.
Benefits: Round-trip transportation from U.S. for appointee and dependents. Housing for appointee and dependents. Paid home leave every 2 years. Health insurance. TIAA/CREF. Other benefits are provided.
Academic Calendar: September–June.
Application Deadline: None; interviews are held in the U.S. in February.
Contact: Wayne Halsema, Director, The American School of Algiers, Department of State/Algiers, Washington, DC 20520-6030. *Or:* The American School of Algiers, 5 Chemin Cheikh Bachir Brahimi, El Biar, Algiers, Algeria. *Phone:* (213-2) 60 37 72/60 14 25, Ext. 7150. *Telex:* (408) 66047 AMCO Alger DZ. *Cable:* AMEREMB ALGIERS.

CYPRUS

MORE THAN ONE CITY

258 MINISTRY OF EDUCATION
The Ministry reports that employment in public schools is available only to citizens of Cyprus. Private schools recruit local teachers; they employ foreigners only if no qualified local teachers are available.
Language of Instruction: *Primary:* Greek. *Other:* English, French.
Academic Calendar: September–June.
For General Information, Contact: Director General, Ministry of Education, Gregori Afxentiou St., Nicosia, Cyprus. *Phone:* 40-3331. *Telex:* 5760.

EGYPT

ALEXANDRIA

259 SCHUTZ AMERICAN SCHOOL
This private coed primary/secondary school was founded in 1924. Current enrollment is 180; 85% of the faculty are U.S. nationals.
Language of Instruction: English.
Opportunities: *General:* 6 full-time positions. *ESL:* 2 positions. *Administrators:* 1 full-time position.
Requirements for General Teachers: Bachelor's degree is required; master's degree is preferred. Teaching experience is preferred. International experience is preferred.
Requirements for ESL Teachers: Bachelor's degree is required; master's degree is preferred. International experience is preferred.
Requirements for Administrators: Bachelor's degree is required; master's degree is preferred. Administrative experience is preferred. International experience is preferred.
Duration: 1 year; renewable.
Salary: *Teachers:* $6,700 per academic year. *Administrators:* $6,700 per calendar year.
Benefits: Round-trip transportation from U.S. for appointee only. Housing for appointee only. Health and life insurance. Retirement plan. Other benefits are provided.
Academic Calendar: September–June.
Orientation: 1 week.
Contact: Headmaster, Schutz American School/Alexandria, Box 27, FPO NY 09527-6090. *Or:* Georhge W. Meloy, Headmaster, Schutz American School, P.O. Box 1000, Alexandria, Egypt. *Phone:* (20-3) 570-1435/571-2205. *Telex:* 54314 CARSE UN. *Cable:* INCLUCATE.

CAIRO

260 AMERICAN UNIVERSITY IN CAIRO
This private coed university was founded in 1919. Current enrollment is 2,750 academic, 12,000 adult education; 40% of the faculty are U.S. nationals.
Language of Instruction: *Primary:* English. *Other:* Arabic.
Opportunities: *General:* 15 full-time positions for teachers of liberal arts, business administration, and engineering. *ESL:* 5 full-time positions. *Administrators:* 3 full-time positions.
Requirements for General Teachers: Doctor's degree is required. 3 years of teaching experience is required. International experience is preferred.
Requirements for ESL Teachers: Master's degree in TEFL is required. Teaching experience is preferred. International experience is preferred.
Requirements for Administrators: Administrative experience is required. International experience is preferred.
Duration: 2 years; tenure possible.
Salary: Contact university for information.
Benefits: Round-trip transportation from U.S. for appointee and dependents. Housing for appointee and dependents. Paid home leave every 2 years. Health insurance. TIAA/CREF. School tuition for children. Other benefits are provided.
Academic Calendar: September–August.
Orientation: 10 days in Cairo.

All information is subject to change without notice
and must be confirmed directly with the employer.

49

Application Deadline: Dec. 1.
Contact: Dr. George H. Gibson, Dean of the Faculty, The American University in Cairo, 866 United Nations Plaza, New York, NY 10017. *Phone:* (212) 421-6320. *Telex:* 235515 AUC UR. *Cable:* VICTORIOUS.

ISRAEL

MORE THAN ONE CITY

261 CONSULATE GENERAL OF ISRAEL
The Consulate reports that there is no need for U.S. teachers or educational administrators at this time.
Language of Instruction: *Primary:* Hebrew. *Other:* Arabic.
Academic Calendar: September–June.
For General Information, Contact: Information Department, Consulate General of Israel, 800 Second Ave., New York, NY 10017. *Or:* Embassy of Israel, 3514 International Dr. NW, Washington, DC 20008.

JERUSALEM

262 FRIENDS WORLD COLLEGE—MIDDLE EAST/ISRAEL CENTER
This private coed university was founded in 1965. Current enrollment is 12; 50% of the faculty are U.S. nationals. Faculty exchanges for sabbatical leave recipients will be considered.
Language of Instruction: English.
Opportunities: *General:* 1 part-time position. *ESL:* None. *Administrators:* Less than 1 position per year.
Requirements for Teachers: Doctor's degree is required. Teaching experience is preferred or relevant work in the country or region is required. International experience is required. Language proficiency in Hebrew and/or Arabic on the advanced level is required.
Requirements for Administrators: Doctor's degree is required. Administrative experience is required. International experience is required. Language proficiency in Hebrew and/or Arabic on the advanced level is required.
Duration: 1 year; renewable indefinitely.
Salary: *Teachers:* $18,000–$20,000 per calendar year. *Administrators:* $22,000 per calendar year.
Benefits: Round-trip transportation from U.S. for appointee only. University assists in locating housing. Health insurance. Other benefits are provided.
Academic Calendar: September–June.
Orientation: At North American Center in Huntington, New York.
Application Deadline: Rolling.
Contact: Jane Ann Smith, Academic Vice President, Friends World College—Middle East/Israel Center, Rehov Tiveria 37, Jerusalem, Israel. *Phone:* (972-2) 248252; in U.S.: (516) 549-5000.

KFAR SHMARYAHU

263 AMERICAN INTERNATIONAL SCHOOL IN ISRAEL
This private coed primary/secondary school was founded in 1957. Current enrollment is 450; 60% of the faculty are U.S. nationals.
Language of Instruction: English.
Opportunities: *General:* 8–13 positions for teachers of all subjects. *ESL:* 1–2 positions.
Requirements for General Teachers: Bachelor's degree in elementary education is required; master's degree in education is preferred. 2 years of teaching experience is required. International experience is preferred.
Requirements for ESL Teachers: Master's degree in TEFL is preferred. 2 years of teaching experience is required. International experience is preferred.
Duration: 2 years; renewable.
Salary: $10,000–$13,100.
Benefits: Round-trip transportation from U.S. for appointee and dependents. Housing allowance.
Academic Calendar: September–June.
Orientation: 1 week.
Application Deadline: Feb. 15.
Contact: American International School in Israel, Kfar Shmaryahu, Israel.

TEL AVIV

264 TEL AVIV UNIVERSITY
This public coed university was founded in 1953. Current enrollment is 27,000; none of the faculty are U.S. nationals.
Language of Instruction: *Primary:* Hebrew. *Other:* Arabic, French, and English.
Opportunities: *General:* Full- and part-time positions. *ESL:* Full- and part-time positions. *Administrators:* Full- and part-time positions.
Academic Calendar: October–June.
Contact: Tel Aviv University, Ramat Aviv, Tel Aviv 69978, Israel. *Phone:* (972-3) 420111. *Telex:* 342171.
For General Information, Contact: Bluma B. Stoler, Director, Student Programs, Tel Aviv University, 360 Lexington Ave., New York, NY 10017. *Phone:* (212) 687-5651.

JORDAN

AMMAN

265 UNIVERSITY OF JORDAN
This private coed university was founded in 1962. Current enrollment is 13,000. The university participates in the Fulbright Exchange Program in addition to recruiting teachers itself.
Language of Instruction: *Primary:* Arabic. *Other:* English.
Opportunities: *General:* Positions available. *ESL:* Full- and part-time positions. *Administrators:* None.
Requirements for Teachers: Doctor's degree is required. Teaching experience is preferred.
Duration: 1 year; renewable for 1 year.
Salary: 420–800 dinar per semester.
Benefits: Housing for appointee and dependents. Health and life insurance. Pension plan.
Academic Calendar: September–May.
Application Deadline: 2 months prior to start.
Contact: Mohammed Sahel Abdel Ati, Secretary General, University of Jordan, Amman, Jordan. *Phone:* (962-6) 843555. *Telex:* 21629 UNVJ JO.

KUWAIT

HAWALLI

266 AMERICAN SCHOOL OF KUWAIT
This private coed primary/secondary school was founded in 1967. Current enrollment is 900; 80% of the faculty are U.S. nationals.
Language of Instruction: *Primary:* English. *Other:* Arabic and French.
Opportunities: *General:* 12 full-time positions for teachers of all subjects and special education. *ESL:* Less than 1 position per year. *Administrators:* Less than 1 position per year.
Requirements for General Teachers: Bachelor's degree in subject taught is required; master's degree is preferred. 2 years of teaching experience is required. International experience is preferred.
Requirements for ESL Teachers: Bachelor's degree in English or ESL is required; master's degree is preferred. 2 years of teaching experience is required. International experience is preferred.
Requirements for Administrators: Bachelor's degree is required; master's degree in administration is preferred; doctor's degree is preferred for superintendent. Administrative experience is preferred. International experience is preferred.
Duration: 2 years; renewable indefinitely.
Salary: *Teachers:* $13,000–$22,000 per calendar year. *Administrators:* $25,000 per calendar year.
Benefits: Round-trip transportation from U.S. for appointee and dependents. Housing for appointee and dependents. Paid home leave every 1 year. Health insurance. Other benefits are provided.
Academic Calendar: August–June.
Application Deadline: Feb. 1.

All information is subject to change without notice
and must be confirmed directly with the employer.

Contact: Brian McCauley, Superintendent, The American School of Kuwait, P.O. Box 6735, Hawalli 32042, Kuwait. *Phone:* (965) 531 4107. *Telex:* 46667 SchoolServ.

MOROCCO

MORE THAN ONE CITY

267 AMERICAN LANGUAGE CENTER
Founded in the late 1950s, ALC serves African teachers, educational administrators, curriculum developers, guidance counselors, library faculty, professionals, and students. There are ALC offices in Casablanca, Fes, Marrakech, Rabat, and Tanger-Tetouan.
Opportunities: *General:* None. *ESL:* 4–5 positions on all levels. *Administrators:* None.
Requirements: Bachelor's degree is required; master's degree in linguistics, applied linguistics, English literature, anthropology, sociology, or related fields is preferred. 1–2 years of teaching experience is preferred.
Duration: 2 years; renewable for 1 year.
Salary: 46–70 dirhams per hour.
Benefits: Health care. Retirement plan.
Orientation: 2 days in Morocco.
Academic Calendar: Starts in October.
Application Deadline: April.
Contact: Director, American Language Center, 1 Place de la Fraternite, Casablanca 01, Morocco. *Phone:* (212) 27 77 65/27 52 70.

CASABLANCA

268 CASABLANCA AMERICAN SCHOOL
This private coed pre-K and primary/secondary school was founded in 1973. Current enrollment is 165; 65% of the faculty are U.S. nationals.
Language of Instruction: *Primary:* English. *Other:* French and Arabic.
Opportunities: *General:* 5–10 full- and part-time positions for primary school teachers of all subjects and secondary school teachers of biology, chemistry, and physics. *ESL:* 1–5 full- and part-time positions. *Administrators:* Less than 1 position per year.
Requirements for General Teachers: Bachelor's degree in subject taught is required; master's or doctor's degree is preferred. 3 years of teaching experience is required. International experience is preferred. Language proficiency in French and/or Arabic on the beginning level is preferred.
Requirements for ESL Teachers: Master's degree in TEFL is required; doctor's degree is preferred. Teaching experience is required. International experience is preferred. Language proficiency in French and/or Arabic is preferred.
Requirements for Administrators: Master's degree in education/administration is required; doctor's degree is preferred. 5 years of administrative experience is required. International experience is required. Language proficiency in French is preferred.
Duration: 2 years; renewable indefinitely.
Salary: *Teachers:* $14,000–$18,000 per academic year. *Administrators:* $18,000–$20,000 per academic year.
Benefits: Round-trip transportation from U.S. for appointee only. Housing allowance. School assists in locating housing. Paid home leave at end of 2-year contract if renewed. Health insurance.
Academic Calendar: September–July.
Orientation: 2–3 weeks on-site.
Application Deadline: None.
Contact: John J. Randolph, Director, Casablanca American School, 9 Ouled Bouzid (ex. rue Bartholdi) Ain-Diab, Casablanca, Morocco. *Phone:* (212) 36-7473/36-4440. *Telex:* 23701M Gemaplan ATTN: Ecole Americain.

RABAT

269 RABAT AMERICAN SCHOOL
This private coed primary/secondary school was founded in 1962. Current enrollment is 245.
Language of Instruction: *Primary:* English. *Other:* French and Arabic.

Opportunities: *General:* 30 full- and part-time positions for teachers of all subjects and special education. *ESL:* 1–2 full- and part-time positions. *Administrators:* 2 full- and part-time positions.
Requirements for General Teachers: Bachelor's degree in elementary education, English, mathematics, science, history is required; master's degree is preferred. Teaching experience is required. International experience is preferred. Language proficiency in French is preferred.
Requirements for ESL Teachers: Bachelor's degree in English or ESL is required; master's degree is preferred. 2 years of teaching experience is required. International experience is preferred.
Requirements for Administrators: Master's degree in an academic discipline/education is required. 5 years of administrative experience is required. International experience is required. Language proficiency in French and/or Arabic is preferred.
Duration: 1–2 years; renewable.
Salary: *Teachers:* $15,500–24,000 per academic year. *Administrators:* $28,000–$35,000 per calendar year.
Benefits: Round-trip transportation from U.S. for appointee and dependents. Housing allowance. Health insurance. Retirement plan.
Academic Calendar: September–June.
Application Deadline: March.
Contact: Mr. Emmanuel J. Pavlos, Director, Rabat American School, c/o American Embassy Rabat, APO New York 09284. *Phone:* (212-7) 714-76/709-63.

SAUDI ARABIA

DHAHRAN

270 ARAMCO SCHOOLS
This private coed primary school was founded in 1947. Current enrollment is 1,853; 97% of the faculty are U.S. nationals.
Language of Instruction: English.
Opportunities: *General:* 10 full- and part-time positions for teachers of general subjects and special education (speech, learning disabilities, remedial reading). *ESL:* 2 full-time positions. *Administrators:* Full-time positions.
Requirements for General Teachers: Bachelor's degree in education is required; master's degree is preferred. 3 years of teaching experience is required.
Requirements for ESL Teachers: Bachelor's degree in education is required; master's degree in TESL is preferred. 3 years of teaching experience is required.
Requirements for Administrators: Bachelor's degree in education is required; master's degree in administration is required. 3 years of administrative experience is required.
Duration: No contract; educational personnel are employees of Arabian American Oil Company.
Salary: Contact company for information.
Benefits: Round-trip transportation from U.S. for appointee and dependents. Housing for appointee and dependents. Paid home leave every year. Health insurance. Educational opportunities. Other benefits are provided.
Academic Calendar: September–July.
Orientation: 1 week in Houston, Texas.
Application Deadline: None.
Contact: Dee Langley, Representative, Aramco Services Company, Career Development, MS-1098, P.O. Box 4534, Houston, TX 77210-4534. *Phone:* (713) 432-4167. *Telex:* 462-0667.

271 KING FAHD UNIVERSITY OF PETROLEUM AND MINERALS
This public male-only university was founded in 1963. Current enrollment is 4,200; 25% of the faculty are U.S. nationals.
Language of Instruction: *Primary:* English. *Other:* Arabic.
Opportunities: *General:* Full-time positions for teachers of sciences, engineering, industrial management, environmental design, computer science, and continuing education. *ESL:* Full-time positions. *Administrators:* None.
Requirements for General Teachers: Doctor's degree in subject taught is required. Teaching experience is required. International experience is preferred. Language proficiency in Arabic on the beginning level is preferred.

Requirements for ESL Teachers: Bachelor's degree in English is required; master's or doctor's degree is preferred. Teaching experience is required. International experience is preferred. Language proficiency in Arabic on the beginning level is preferred.
Duration: 2 years; renewable.
Salary: 45,120–228,000 riyals per calendar year.
Benefits: Round-trip transportation from U.S. for appointee and up to 3 dependents. Housing for appointee and dependents. Paid home leave every year. Children's educational grants. Other benefits are provided.
Academic Calendar: September–June/July.
Application Deadline: February.
Contact: Dr. Jasem M. Al-Ansari, Dean of Faculty and Personnel Affairs, King Fahd University of Petroleum and Minerals, Dhahran 31261, Saudi Arabia. *Phone:* (966-3) 860-2400. *Telex:* 801060 UPM SJ. *Cable:* AL-JAMAAH.

272 **SAUDI ARABIAN INTERNATIONAL SCHOOLS—DHAHRAN DISTRICT**
This private coed pre-K and primary school was founded in 1963. Current enrollment is 2,400; 75% of the faculty are U.S. nationals.
Language of Instruction: *Primary:* English. *Other:* French and Arabic.
Opportunities: *General:* Full- and part-time positions. *ESL:* Full- and part-time positions. *Administrators:* Full-time positions.
Requirements for General Teachers: Bachelor's degree is required. 2 years of teaching experience is required. International experience is preferred.
Requirements for ESL Teachers: Bachelor's degree is required; master's or doctor's degree is preferred. Teaching experience is required. International experience is preferred.
Requirements for Administrators: Bachelor's degree in education or school administration is required; master's or doctor's degree is preferred. 2 years of administrative experience is required. International experience is preferred.
Duration: 2 years; renewable for 1-year terms.
Salary: *Teachers:* $15,435–$28,216 per academic year. *Administrators:* $32,533–$82,512 per calendar year.
Benefits: Round-trip transportation from U.S. for appointee and dependents up to age 18. Housing for appointee and dependents. Paid home leave every year. Health insurance. Other benefits are provided.
Academic Calendar: September–June.
Orientation: 3–5 days on-site.
Application Deadline: None.
Contact: C.H. Rieske, Personnel Director, Saudi Arabian International Schools—Dhahran District, P.O. Box 81, Dhahran Airport, Dhahran 31932, Saudi Arabia. *Phone:* (966-3) 891-3842. *Telex:* 801937 YES SJ.

JEDDAH

273 **SAUDIA—S.A.I.S.**
This public coed primary/secondary school was founded in 1952. Current enrollment is 1,014; 85% of the faculty are U.S. nationals. This is an exchange program with the Shawnee Mission School District, Kansas.
Language of Instruction: English.
Opportunities: *General:* 50 full-time positions for teaching couples. *ESL:* 2 full-time positions. *Administrators:* 5 full-time positions.
Requirements for General Teachers: Bachelor's degree is required. 2 years of teaching experience is required. International experience is preferred.
Requirements for ESL Teachers: Bachelor's degree is required. 2 years of teaching experience is required.
Requirements for Administrators: Master's degree is required. 4 years of administrative experience is required. International experience is preferred.
Duration: 2 years; renewable for 2 years.
Salary: *Teachers:* $25,000–$38,000 per academic year. *Administrators:* $40,000 per academic year.
Benefits: Round-trip transportation from U.S. for appointee and dependents. Housing for appointee and dependents. Paid home leave every year. Other benefits are provided.
Academic Calendar: September–June.
Application Deadline: None.

Contact: John C. Thomas, Superintendent, Saudia-S.A.I.S., Saudi Arabian Airlines, c.c. 100, P.O. Box 167, Jeddah 21231, Saudi Arabia. *Phone:* (966-2) 667-4566, Ext. 203. *Telex:* 600184.

RIYADH

274 **SAUDI ARABIAN INTERNATIONAL SCHOOL—RIYADH**
This private coed pre-K and primary school was founded in 1965. Current enrollment is 1,950; 85% of the faculty are U.S. nationals.
Language of Instruction: *Primary:* English. *Other:* Arabic and French.
Opportunities: *General:* 10 full-time positions. *ESL:* 1 full-time position. *Administrators:* Less than 1 position per year.
Requirements for General Teachers: Bachelor's degree in education is required. 3–5 years of teaching experience is required. International experience is preferred.
Requirements for ESL Teachers: Bachelor's degree in TESL/TEFL is required. 3–5 years of teaching experience is required. International experience is preferred.
Requirements for Administrators: Master's degree in educational administration is required. 5–10 years of administrative experience is required. International experience is preferred.
Duration: 2 years; renewable.
Salary: *Teachers:* $23,000–$25,000 per academic year. *Administrators:* $35,000–$40,000 per calendar year.
Benefits: Round-trip transportation from U.S. for appointee, spouse, and dependents under age 18. Housing for appointee and dependents. Paid home leave every year. Health, life, and disability insurance. Other benefits are provided.
Academic Calendar: September–June.
Application Deadline: Feb. 1.
Contact: Robert Tinney, Coordinator of Personnel Services, Saudi Arabian International School—Riyadh, P.O. Box 990, Riyadh 11421, Saudi Arabia. *Phone:* (966-1) 491-4270. *Telex:* 403924 RICS SJ.

SYRIA

DAMASCUS

275 **DAMASCUS COMMUNITY SCHOOL**
This private coed primary/secondary school was founded in 1954. Current enrollment is 251; 48% of the faculty are U.S. nationals.
Language of Instruction: *Primary:* English. *Other:* French, German, and Arabic.
Opportunities: *General:* 3 full-time positions. *ESL:* 5 full-time positions. *Administrators:* 5 full-time positions.
Requirements for General Teachers: Bachelor's degree is required; master's degree is preferred. 2 years of teaching experience is required. International experience is preferred.
Requirements for Administrators: Master's degree in administration is required; doctor's degree is preferred. 3 years of administrative experience is required.
Duration: 2 years; renewable for 1–2 years.
Salary: *Teachers:* $15,000–$25,000 per calendar year. *Administrators:* $35,000–$45,000 per calendar year.
Benefits: Round-trip transportation from U.S. for appointee and dependents. Housing for appointee and dependents. Health and life insurance. Pension plan. Other benefits are provided.
Academic Calendar: August–June.
Application Deadline: Feb. 1.
Contact: R.A. Crawford, Director, Damascus Community School, c/o American Embassy Damascus Syria, Department of State, Washington, DC 20520. *Phone:* 337737. *Telex:* USDAMA 411919.

TUNISIA

TUNIS

276 **AMERICAN COOPERATIVE SCHOOL OF TUNIS**
This is a private coed primary school. Current enrollment is 103; 80% of the faculty are U.S. nationals.
Language of Instruction: *Primary:* English. *Other:* French.

All information is subject to change without notice and must be confirmed directly with the employer.

52

Opportunities: *General:* Positions for 1 teacher of general subjects and 1 math/computer teacher. *ESL:* None. *Administrators:* None.
Requirements: Bachelor's degree in subject taught is required; master's degree is preferred. 2 years of teaching experience is preferred. International experience is preferred. Language proficiency in French on the beginning or intermediate level is preferred.
Duration: 2 years; renewable.
Salary: Varies.
Benefits: Round-trip transportation from U.S. for appointee and dependents. Housing for appointee and dependents. Health insurance.
Academic Calendar: September–June.
Orientation: 5 days on-site.
Application Deadline: Feb. 1.
Contact: Director, American Cooperative School of Tunis, Department of State, Washington, DC 20520-2360. *Or:* American Cooperative School of Tunis, c/o U.S. Embassy, 144 Avenue de la Liberte, Tunis, Tunisia. *Phone:* (216-1) 760-905/760-517. *Telex:* 13379 AMBTUN TN.

277 BOURGUIBA INSTITUTE OF MODERN LANGUAGES
This public coed adult/continuing education program and university was founded in 1963 and is part of the University of Tunis. Current enrollment is 4,000; 7% of the faculty are U.S. nationals.
Language of Instruction: *Primary:* French and Arabic. *Other:* English.
Opportunities: *General:* 7 full- and part-time positions. *ESL:* 7–10 full- and part-time positions. *Administrators:* 1 full-time position.
Requirements for General Teachers: Bachelor's degree in English/linguistics is required; master's or doctor's degree is preferred. Teaching experience is preferred. International experience is preferred. Language proficiency in Arabic and French is preferred.
Requirements for ESL Teachers: Bachelor's degree in English/linguistics is required; master's or doctor's degree is preferred. Teaching experience is preferred. International experience is preferred. Language proficiency in Arabic and French is preferred.
Requirements for Administrators: Master's degree in English/linguistics is required; doctor's degree is preferred. Administrative experience is preferred. International experience is preferred. Language proficiency in Arabic and French is preferred.
Duration: 2 years; renewable.
Salary: *Teachers:* 300–600 dinars per month. *Administrators:* 300–600 dinars per month.
Benefits: Round-trip transportation from U.S. for appointee and dependents. School assists in locating housing. Other benefits are provided.
Academic Calendar: September–June.
Application Deadline: March 15.
Contact: Dr. Mohamed Maamouri, Director, Bourguiba Institute of Modern Languages, 47 Avenue de la Liberte, 1002 Belvedere, Tunis, Tunisia. *Phone:* (216-1) 282-418/282-923.

278 UNIVERSITE DE TUNIS, FACULTE DES LETTRES
This public coed university was founded in 1959. Current enrollment is 4,000; 1% of faculty are U.S. nationals. The university participates in the Fulbright Program in addition to recruiting teachers itself.
Language of Instruction: *Primary:* Arabic and French. *Other:* English, Spanish, German, Russian, and Italian.
Opportunities: *General:* 4 full- and part-time positions for teachers of U.S. studies, British studies, linguistics. *ESL:* 4 full- and part-time positions. *Administrators:* None.
Requirements for General Teachers: Master's or doctor's degree in English, linguistics, or civilization is required. 3 years of teaching experience is required. Language proficiency in Arabic or French on the beginning level is preferred.
Requirements for ESL Teachers: Master's or doctor's degree in English or linguistics is required. 3 years of teaching experience is required. Language proficiency in Arabic or French on the beginning level is preferred.
Duration: 2 years; renewable for 6–8 years.
Salary: 500–900 dinars per month.
Benefits: Round-trip transportation from U.S. for appointee and dependents. University assists in locating housing. Paid home leave every 2 years. Health insurance and health care.
Academic Calendar: September–June.
Application Deadline: May 31.

Contact: Chairman of the English Department, Universite de Tunis, Faculte des Lettres, 2010 Manouba, Tunis, Tunisia. *Phone:* (216-1) 514 163.

TURKEY

ADANA

279 UNIVERSITY OF CUKUROVA
This public coed university was founded in 1973. Current enrollment is 14,000; few of the faculty are U.S. nationals.
Language of Instruction: *Primary:* Turkish. *Other:* English.
Opportunities: *General:* None. *ESL:* 10 full-time positions. *Administrators:* None.
Requirements: Bachelor's degree in TEFL is required; master's or doctor's degree is preferred. 5 years of teaching experience is preferred. International experience is preferred.
Duration: 1 year; renewable indefinitely.
Salary: $500–$700.
Benefits: Housing for appointee only. Other benefits are provided.
Academic Calendar: October–August.
Contact: Prof. Dr. Mithat Ozsan, Rector, University of Cukurova, Balcali, Adana 01330, Turkey. *Phone:* (90-711) 37552.

ANKARA

280 BRITISH EMBASSY STUDY GROUP
This private coed pre-K and primary school was founded in 1959. Current enrollment is 105; 25% of the faculty are U.S. nationals. Positions are advertised locally.
Language of Instruction: English.
Opportunities: *General:* 1 position. *ESL:* None. *Administrators:* None.
Requirements: Bachelor's degree in English is required. 3 years of teaching experience is required. International experience is preferred.
Duration: 2 years; renewable.
Salary: 592,000–887,000 lira per month.
Academic Calendar: September–July.
Contact: D.R. Clark, Headmaster, British Embassy Study Group, Sehit Ersan Caddesii 46/A, Cankaya, Ankara, Turkey. *Phone:* (90-41) 127 43 10, Ext. 208. *Telex:* 42320 (prod TR).

BURSA

281 CIZAKCA LISESI
This private coed secondary school was founded in 1942. Current enrollment is 1,000; 10–15% of the faculty are U.S. nationals.
Language of Instruction: English/Turkish.
Opportunities: *General:* Full-time positions for teachers of mathematics and science. *ESL:* 7 full-time positions. *Administrators:* None.
Requirements for General Teachers: Bachelor's degree in mathematics or science is required; master's or doctor's degree is preferred. Teaching experience is preferred, but new graduates are encouraged to apply. Teaching certificate is required. International experience is preferred.
Requirements for ESL Teachers: Bachelor's degree in TESL/TEFL or English is required; master's or doctor's degree is preferred. Teaching experience is preferred, but new graduates are encouraged to apply. Teaching certificate is required. International experience is preferred.
Duration: 1 year; renewable.
Salary: 300,000–350,000 lira per month.
Benefits: Round-trip transportation from U.S. for appointee only. Housing for appointee and dependents. Paid home leave if contract is renewed. Health insurance. Pension plan. Other benefits are provided.
Academic Calendar: September–June.
Orientation: 1 week on-site.
Application Deadline: June.
Contact: Dr. Murat Cizakca, Cizakca Lisesi, Sirameseler, Bursa, Turkey. *Phone:* (90-241) 361990/362258.

All information is subject to change without notice
and must be confirmed directly with the employer.

ESKISEHIR

282 ANADOLU UNIVERSITY

This is a public coed university. Current enrollment is 300; 2% of the faculty are U.S. nationals.
Language of Instruction: *Primary:* Turkish. *Other:* English.
Opportunities: *General:* 10 full-time positions for teachers of computer science, journalism, mass communication, education, social sciences. *ESL:* 5 full-time positions. *Administrators:* None.
Requirements for General Teachers: Master's degree in subject taught is required. 2–3 years of teaching experience is required. International experience is preferred. Language proficiency in Turkish on the intermediate level is preferred.
Requirements for ESL Teachers: Bachelor's degree in English is required; master's degree is preferred. 2–3 years of teaching experience is required. Language proficiency in Turkish on the intermediate level is preferred.
Duration: 1 year; renewable for 1 year.
Salary: 700,000 lira per month.
Benefits: Round-trip transportation from U.S. for appointee only. Housing for appointee and dependents. Health service. Other benefits are provided.
Academic Calendar: September–July.
Orientation: 15 days on-site.
Application Deadline: Aug. 31.
Contact: Prof. Dr. Semih Buker, Dean, Anadolu University—Open Faculty, Anadolu Universitesi, Yunusemre Kampusu, Eskisehir 26470, Turkey. *Phone:* (90-221) 53455. *Telex:* 35174 TR.

ISTANBUL

283 ISTANBUL INTERNATIONAL COMMUNITY SCHOOL

This private coed pre-K and primary school was founded in 1911. Current enrollment is 315; 75% of the faculty are U.S. nationals.
Language of Instruction: English.
Opportunities: *General:* 2 full- and part-time positions for teachers of music and computer science. *ESL:* 1 full-time position. *Administrators:* None.
Requirements for General Teachers: Master's degree is required. 2 years of teaching experience is required. International experience is preferred.
Requirements for ESL Teachers: Master's degree is required. Teaching experience is required. International experience is preferred.
Duration: 2 years; renewable.
Salary: $15,000–$30,000 per calendar year.
Benefits: Round-trip transportation from U.S. for appointee and dependents. Housing for appointee and dependents. Paid home leave every 3 years. Health and life insurance. Other benefits are provided.
Academic Calendar: September–June.
Orientation: 1 week on-site.
Application Deadline: March.
Contact: Carol Fonger, Principal, Istanbul International Community School, Robert College, Arnavutkoy, P.K. 1, Istanbul 80820, Turkey. *Phone:* (90-1) 165 1591.

284 ROBERT COLLEGE OF ISTANBUL

This is a private coed secondary school. Current enrollment is 911; 36% of the faculty are U.S. nationals.
Language of Instruction: *Primary:* English. *Other:* Turkish.
Opportunities: *General:* 4–12 positions for teachers of mathematics, science, and physical education. *ESL:* Positions available. *Administrators:* None.
Requirements for General Teachers: Bachelor's degree in subject taught is required; master's degree is preferred. 2 years of teaching experience is preferred. Teaching certificate or significant teaching experience is required. International experience is preferred.
Requirements for ESL Teachers: Bachelor's degree in English is required; master's degree is preferred. 2 years of teaching experience is preferred. International experience is preferred.
Duration: 2 years; renewable.
Salary: $10,000–$23,000 per academic year.
Benefits: Round-trip transportation from U.S. for appointee and dependents. Housing for appointee and dependents. Paid home leave every 3 years. Health insurance. TIAA/CREF. Tuition for children enrolled at this school. Other benefits are provided.
Academic Calendar: September–June.
Orientation: 2 weeks on-site.
Application Deadline: March 1.
Contact: Dr. Harry A. Dawe or Dr. Jayne Warner, Robert College of Istanbul, 850 Third Avenue, New York, NY 10022. *Or:* Robert College of Istanbul, Arnavutkoy, P.K. 1, Istanbul 80820, Turkey. *Phone:* (90-1) 165 3430/39.

IZMIR

285 OZEL IZMIR AMERIKAN LISESI

This private coed secondary school was founded in 1876. Current enrollment is 1,037; 40% of the faculty are U.S. and British nationals.
Language of Instruction: *Primary:* English. *Other:* Turkish.
Opportunities: *General:* Full-time positions for teachers of literature, science, mathematics, art, and physical education. *ESL:* Full-time positions. *Administrators:* Full-time positions.
Requirements for General Teachers: Bachelor's degree in subject taught is required. Teaching experience is preferred. Teaching certificate is required. International experience is preferred.
Requirements for ESL Teachers: Bachelor's degree in English is required; master's degree is preferred. Teaching experience is preferred.
Requirements for Administrators: Bachelor's degree in English, mathematics, or science is required. Administrative experience is required. International experience is preferred. Language proficiency in Turkish is preferred.
Duration: 2 years; renewable for 1–2 years.
Salary: *Teachers:* $4,320 plus 1,560,000 lira per calendar year.
Benefits: Round-trip transportation from U.S. for appointee only. Housing for appointee only. Paid home leave every 2 years. Health insurance. Other benefits are provided.
Academic Calendar: September–June.
Orientation: 3 weeks in Istanbul.
Contact: Middle East Office, United Church Board for World Ministries, 475 Riverside Dr., New York, NY 10115. *Phone:* (212) 870-2835. *Telex:* 420 423 UBWM UI. *Cable:* FERNSTALK NEW YORK. *Or:* Marianne Miller, Principal, Ozel Izmir Amerikan Lisesi, Gozrepe, Izmir 35290, Turkey. *Phone:* (90-51) 15 34 01. *Telex:* 52590 IG TX TR235. *Cable:* Americol.

TARSUS

286 TARSUS AMERICAN SCHOOL

This private coed secondary school was founded in 1888. Current enrollment is 750; 40% of the faculty are U.S. nationals.
Language of Instruction: Turkish and English.
Opportunities: *General:* 6–8 full-time positions for teachers of mathematics, science, and art. *ESL:* 4–6 full-time positions. *Administrators:* Less than 1 position per year.
Requirements for General Teachers: Bachelor's degree in subject taught is required. 2 years of teaching experience is preferred. Teaching certificate is required. International experience is preferred.
Requirements for ESL Teachers: Bachelor's or master's degree in English, TESL, or TEFL is required. 2 years of teaching experience is preferred. International experience is preferred.
Requirements for Administrators: Bachelor's degree in English, mathematics, science, or art is required; master's degree in educational administration is preferred. 2 years of administrative experience is required. International experience is preferred. Language proficiency in Turkish is preferred.
Duration: 2 years; renewable.
Salary: *Teachers:* From $6,000 per calendar year. *Administrators:* From $6,000 per calendar year.
Benefits: Round-trip transportation from U.S. for appointee only. Housing for appointee only. Health insurance. Other benefits are provided.
Academic Calendar: September–May.
Orientation: 1 month in Istanbul.
Application Deadline: None.
Contact: Wallace M. Robeson, Principal, Tarsus American School, P.K. 6, Tarsus, Turkey. *Phone:* (90-761) 11198. *Telex:* 63822 CUMT TR.

All information is subject to change without notice and must be confirmed directly with the employer.

UNITED ARAB EMIRATES

ABU DHABI

287 AMERICAN COMMUNITY SCHOOL OF ABU DHABI
This private coed pre-K and primary school was founded in 1973.
Current enrollment is 300; 80% of the faculty are U.S. nationals.
Language of Instruction: English.
Opportunities: *General:* 2–3 full-time positions. *ESL:* Less than 1
position per year. *Administrators:* Less than 1 position per year.
Requirements for General Teachers: Bachelor's degree is required;
master's degree is preferred. 5 years of teaching experience is required.
Teaching certificate is required. International experience is preferred.
Requirements for ESL Teachers: Bachelor's degree is required;
master's degree is preferred. Teaching experience is required.
International experience is preferred. Language proficiency in Arabic is
preferred.
Requirements for Administrators: Bachelor's and master's degree is
required. 5 years of administrative experience is required. International
experience is preferred.
Duration: 2 years; renewable for 3–4 years.
Salary: *Teachers:* $20,000–$37,000 per calendar year. *Administrators:*
$39,000–$61,000 per calendar year.
Benefits: Round-trip transportation from U.S. for appointee and
dependents. Housing for appointee and dependents. Paid home leave
every year. Other benefits are provided.
Academic Calendar: September–June.
Orientation: On-site.
Application Deadline: January.
Contact: James M. Ambrose, Superintendent, American Community
School of Abu Dhabi, P.O. Box 4005, Abu Dhabi, United Arab
Emirates. *Phone:* (971-2) 361461. *Telex:* 22275 EM.

288 INTERNATIONAL SCHOOL OF CHOUEIFAT
This private coed primary/secondary school was founded in 1886.
Current enrollment is 1,810; 2% of the faculty are U.S. nationals.
Language of Instruction: English.
Opportunities: *General:* 2 full-time positions. *ESL:* 1 full-time position.
Administrators: None.
Requirements: Bachelor's degree in English, physics, mathematics, or
chemistry is required. Teaching experience is preferred. International
experience is preferred.
Duration: 1 year; renewable.
Salary: From $12,500 per calendar year.
Benefits: Round-trip transportation from London for appointee only.
Housing for appointee only. Paid home leave every year.
Academic Calendar: September–June.
Application Deadline: Jan. 31.
Contact: Mr. R.N. Germanos, Director, International School of
Choueifat, P.O. Box 7212, Abu Dhabi, United Arab Emirates. *Phone:*
(971-2) 461444. *Telex:* 23308 School.

AL-AIN

289 UNITED ARAB EMIRATES UNIVERSITY
This public university was founded in 1976. Current enrollment is
7,500; 12% of the faculty are U.S. nationals.
Language of Instruction: *Primary:* Arabic. *Other:* English.
Opportunities: *General:* 10–20 full-time positions. *ESL:* 2–5 full-time
positions. *Administrators:* 5–10 full-time positions.
Requirements for General Teachers: Doctor's degree is required.
Teaching experience is required. International experience is required.
Language proficiency in French on the advanced level is preferred.
Requirements for ESL Teachers: Master's or doctor's degree is
required. 5 years of teaching experience is required.
Requirements for Administrators: Master's or doctor's degree is
required. 5 years of administrative experience is required. Language
proficiency in French is preferred.
Duration: 3 years; renewable for 3 years.
Salary: *Teachers:* $3,000 per month. *Administrators:* Contact university
for information.
Benefits: Housing for appointee and dependents. Paid home leave every
year. Other benefits are provided.
Academic Calendar: September–June.
Application Deadline: December.
Contact: General Secretary, United Arab Emirates University, P.O. Box
15551, Al-Ain, United Arab Emirates. *Phone:* (971-3) 652500. *Telex:*
33521 JAMEAH EM.

YEMEN ARAB REPUBLIC

SANAA

290 SANAA INTERNATIONAL SCHOOL
This private coed primary/secondary school was founded in 1971.
Current enrollment is 200; 50% of the faculty are U.S. nationals.
Language of Instruction: English.
Opportunities: *General:* 5 full-time positions. *ESL:* 1 full-time position.
Administrators: Less than 1 position per year.
Requirements for General Teachers: Bachelor's degree is required;
master's degree is preferred. 2 years of teaching experience is required.
International experience is preferred. Applicants must be nonsmokers.
Requirements for ESL Teachers: Bachelor's degree is required;
master's degree is preferred. Teaching experience is required.
International experience is preferred. Applicants must be nonsmokers.
Requirements for Administrators: Master's degree is required. 10–15
years of administrative experience is required. International experience is
preferred.
Duration: 2 years; renewable.
Salary: *Teachers:* $14,800–$22,000 per calendar year. *Administrators:* 60%
more than teachers' salaries.
Benefits: Round-trip transportation from U.S. for appointee and
dependents. Housing for appointee and dependents. Health insurance.
Academic Calendar: September–July.
Application Deadline: None.
Contact: James E. Gilson, Director, Sanaa International School, Box
2002, Sanaa, Yemen Arab Republic. *Telex:* 2697 EMBSAN YE. *Cable:*
SANINTSCHOOL.

WESTERN HEMISPHERE

ARGENTINA

GENERAL ROCA

291 UNIVERSIDAD NACIONAL DEL COMAHUE, ESCUELA SUPERIOR DE IDIOMAS
This public coed university was founded in 1972. Current enrollment is 120; none of the faculty are U.S. nationals.
Language of Instruction: *Primary:* English. *Other:* Spanish.
Opportunities: *General:* None. *ESL:* 2 full-time positions. *Administrators:* None.
Requirements: Master's degree in English or doctor's degree in linguistics is preferred. Teaching or practical experience is preferred. International experience is preferred. Language proficiency in Spanish on the intermediate level is preferred.
Duration: 1 year; renewable indefinitely.
Salary: 1,000 australes per month.
Benefits: University assists in locating housing. Health and life insurance. Pension plan.
Academic Calendar: March–November.
Application Deadline: February.
Contact: Prof. Pascual Jose Masullo, Director, Escuela Superios de Idiomas, Universidad Nacional del Comahue, Mendoza y Peru, General Roca 8332, Argentina. *Phone:* (54-941) 22057/22503/22468.

BAHAMAS

NASSAU

292 LYFORD CAY SCHOOL
This private coed primary school was founded in 1960. Current enrollment is 150; 33% of the faculty are U.S. nationals.
Language of Instruction: English.
Opportunities: *General:* 2 full- and part-time positions for teachers of all subjects including music, science, and sports. *ESL:* None. *Administrators:* None.
Requirements: Bachelor's degree in education is required; master's degree is preferred. 3 years of teaching experience is required. International experience is preferred. Language proficiency in French or Spanish on the intermediate level is preferred.
Duration: 1–2 years; renewable for 5 years.
Salary: BA $12,500–$18,000 per calendar year.
Benefits: School assists in locating housing. Health insurance.
Academic Calendar: September–June.
Application Deadline: Feb. 28.
Contact: Mrs. V. Campbell, Headmistress, Lyford Cay School, P.O. Box N7776, Nassau, Bahamas. *Phone:* (809) 326-4774.

BARBADOS

MORE THAN ONE CITY

293 MINISTRY OF EDUCATION AND CULTURE
The Ministry reports that there is no need for U.S. teachers or educational administrators at this time.

For General Information, Contact: Ministry of Education and Culture, Jemmott's Lane, Bridgetown, Barbados.

BELIZE

MORE THAN ONE CITY

294 MINISTRY OF EDUCATION
The Ministry reports that there is no need for U.S. teachers or educational administrators at this time.
Language of Instruction: English.
Academic Calendar: September–June.
For General Information, Contact: Ministry of Education, Belmopan, Belize.

BERMUDA

MORE THAN ONE CITY

295 MINISTRY OF EDUCATION
The Ministry reports a need for U.S. nationals as teachers at the primary, secondary, and secondary vocational/technical levels, and for teachers of special education.
Language of Instruction: English.
Opportunities: *General:* 8–12 positions for teachers of remedial instruction on the primary level, and science and industrial arts on the secondary and vocational/technical level. Special education teachers are needed for the physically handicapped and hearing-disabled. *ESL:* None. *Administrators:* None.
Requirements: Bachelor's degree in education is required; master's degree in subject taught is preferred. 5 years of teaching experience is preferred, or experience in industry or commerce is required. Teaching certificate is required.
Duration: 3 years; renewable for at least 3 years.
Salary: BD $21,922–$41,301 per academic year.
Benefits: Housing allowance may be provided. School assists in locating housing. Paid home leave every 3 years. Health insurance. Pension plan. Other benefits are provided.
Academic Calendar: September–August.
Application Deadline: April 30.
Contact: Mrs. Veronica Todd, Acting/Senior Education Officer, Ministry of Education, 7 Point Finger Rd., Paget DV04, P.O. Box HM 1185, Hamilton HM EX, Bermuda. *Phone:* (809) 296-6904.

FERRY REACH

296 BERMUDA BIOLOGICAL STATION FOR RESEARCH
This private coed educational-research institute was founded in 1903. Current enrollment is 20–100; 80% of the faculty are U.S. nationals.
Language of Instruction: English.
Opportunities: Positions for teacher/administrators.
Requirements: Master's or doctor's degree in marine science is preferred. Teaching and administrative experience is preferred. International experience is preferred.

Duration: 1 year; renewable for 1 year.
Salary: From $19,000.
Benefits: Institute assists in locating housing. Other benefits are provided.
Academic Calendar: Year-round.
Application Deadline: None.
Contact: Dr. Susan Cook, Education Director, Bermuda Biological Station for Research Inc., 17 Biological Lane, Ferry Reach GE01, Bermuda. *Phone:* (809) 297-1880. *Telex:* BA 3246. *Cable:* BIOSTATION BERMUDA.

PEMBROKE

297 BERMUDA HIGH SCHOOL
This private female-only primary/secondary school (coed postgraduate year) was founded in 1894. Current enrollment is 500; 10% of the faculty are U.S. nationals.
Language of Instruction: English.
Opportunities: *General:* 2–3 full- and part-time positions. *ESL:* None. *Administrators:* Full- and part-time positions.
Requirements for Teachers: Bachelor's degree in subject taught is required. 5 years of teaching experience is preferred. International experience is preferred.
Requirements for Administrators: Master's degree in administration is preferred. 5 years of administrative experience is required. International experience is preferred.
Duration: 3 years; renewable for 3 years.
Salary: *Teachers:* $25,000 per calendar year. *Administrators:* $30,000 per calendar year.
Benefits: Round-trip transportation from U.S. for appointee only. Health and life insurance. Pension plan.
Academic Calendar: September–June.
Orientation: 2 days on-site.
Application Deadline: January.
Contact: Brian W. Porter, Principal, The Bermuda High School, 27 Richmond Road, Pembroke HM 08, Bermuda. *Phone:* (809) 295-6153.

BOLIVIA

LA PAZ

298 AMERICAN COOPERATIVE SCHOOL
This private coed primary/secondary school was founded in 1955. Current enrollment is 597; 80% of the faculty are U.S. nationals.
Language of Instruction: English.
Opportunities: *General:* 7 full- and part-time positions for teachers of all subjects. *ESL:* Full-time positions. *Administrators:* None.
Requirements for General Teachers: Bachelor's degree is required. 3 years of teaching experience is required. International experience is preferred. Language proficiency in Spanish is preferred.
Requirements for ESL Teachers: Bachelor's degree is required. Teaching experience is required. International experience is preferred.
Duration: 2 years; renewable indefinitely.
Salary: $11,000–$21,000 per academic year.
Benefits: Round-trip transportation from U.S. for appointee and dependents. Housing for appointee and dependents. Paid home leave every 2 years. Health insurance. Retirement plan.
Academic Calendar: August–June.
Orientation: 3 days on-site.
Contact: Herm Penland, Superintendent, American Cooperative School, U.S. Embassy, La Paz, Bolivia. *Phone:* (591-2) 792302/794750.

SANTA CRUZ

299 SANTA CRUZ COOPERATIVE SCHOOL
This private coed primary/secondary school was founded in 1959. Current enrollment is 470; 70% of the faculty are U.S. nationals.
Language of Instruction: *Primary:* English. *Other:* Spanish.
Opportunities: *General:* 22 full-time positions for teachers of all subjects (all primary teachers teach ESL). *ESL:* None. *Administrators:* 2 full-time positions.

Requirements for Teachers: Bachelor's degree in education is required. Teaching certificate is required. Teaching experience is preferred. International experience is preferred. Language proficiency in Spanish is preferred. Teachers with no dependents are preferred.
Requirements for Administrators: Master's degree in educational administration or education is required. 2 years of administrative experience is required. International experience is preferred. Language proficiency in Spanish is preferred.
Duration: 2 years; renewable.
Salary: *Teachers:* $16,000–$24,000 per calendar year. *Administrators:* $34,000–$45,000 per calendar year.
Benefits: Round-trip transportation from U.S. for appointee and dependents. Housing allowance for administrators only. Paid home leave every year after 2 years. Health insurance.
Academic Calendar: August–June.
Orientation: 1 week on-site.
Application Deadline: January.
Contact: Eric Spindler, Director, Santa Cruz Cooperative School, Casilla 753, Santa Cruz, Bolivia. *Phone:* (591-33) 32993.

BRAZIL

MORE THAN ONE CITY

300 COMMISSION FOR EDUCATIONAL EXCHANGE BETWEEN THE U.S.A. AND BRAZIL (FULBRIGHT COMMISSION)
The Commission reports that there is more of an interest in than a need for U.S. lecturers, ESL teachers, and researchers in university, vocational/technical, and professional education. Legal restrictions limit teaching possibilities for U.S. nationals to those sponsored by the Fulbright Program, Ford Foundation, U.S. Information Agency, home or host institution, or Brazilian Ministry of Education.

A permanent visa is required, but is issued only to a teacher with a contract. Obtaining a contract generally requires that the teacher be licensed in Brazil, which entails having one's U.S. diploma(s) recognized in Brazil.

For ESL teachers, there is the common problem of needing to present a contract to obtain a permanent visa but needing a permanent visa in order to obtain a contract.
For General Information, Contact: Commission for Educational Exchange Between the U.S.A. and Brazil, Casa Thomas Jefferson, SEP Sul—W-4 EQ 706/906, 70350 Brasilia (D.F.), Brazil.

BELEM

301 AMAZON VALLEY ACADEMY
This private coed primary/secondary school was founded in 1959. Current enrollment is 119; 65% of the faculty are U.S. nationals. The school recruits only volunteer teachers and administrators who are full-time missionaries with UFM International, an evangelical fundamentalist Protestant mission organization.
Language of Instruction: *Primary:* English. *Other:* German.
Opportunities: *General:* 4 full-time positions. *ESL:* None. *Administrators:* Less than 1 position per year.
Requirements for Teachers: Bachelor's degree in subject taught is required; master's degree is preferred. 2 years of teaching experience is required. International experience is preferred.
Requirements for Administrators: Bachelor's degree is required; master's degree is preferred. 4 years of administrative experience is required. International experience is preferred. Language proficiency in Portuguese on the intermediate level is preferred.
Duration: 4 years; renewable for 4 years.
Salary: None; teachers and administrators are volunteers.
Academic Calendar: August–June.
Orientation: On-site.
Contact: Albert F. Roth, Principal, Amazon Valley Academy, Caixa Postal 3030, Agencia Independencia, 66000 Belem (Para), Brazil. *Phone:* (55-91) 235-2166. *Or:* UFM International, Box 306, Bala-Cynwyd, PA 19004.

BELO HORIZONTE

302 AMERICAN SCHOOL OF BELO HORIZONTE

This private coed primary/secondary school was founded in 1956. Current enrollment is 65; 90% of the faculty are U.S. nationals. The school exchanges teachers with the Greensville County School in Virginia.
Language of Instruction: English.
Opportunities: *General:* 2–4 full-time positions for teachers of all subjects. *ESL:* None. *Administrators:* 1 full-time position.
Requirements for Teachers: Bachelor's degree in subject taught is required; master's degree is preferred. 2 years of teaching experience is required. International experience is preferred.
Requirements for Administrators: Master's degree in education is required. 2 years of administrative experience is required. International experience is preferred.
Duration: 2 years; renewable for 2 years.
Salary: *Teachers:* $10,000–$18,000 per calendar year. *Administrators:* $30,000–$60,000 per calendar year.
Benefits: Round-trip transportation from U.S. for appointee and dependents. Housing for appointee and dependents. Paid home leave every 2 years. Health insurance. Pension plan. Other benefits are provided.
Academic Calendar: August–June.
Orientation: 2 days on-site.
Application Deadline: None.
Contact: Sidney Stewart, Director, American School of Belo Horizonte, Caixa Postal 2501, 30000 Belo Horizonte, Brazil. *Phone:* (55-31) 312-2711.

BRASILIA

303 AMERICAN SCHOOL OF BRASILIA

This private coed primary/secondary school was founded in 1964. Current enrollment is 630; 80% of the faculty are U.S. nationals.
Language of Instruction: *Primary:* English. *Other:* Portuguese and French.
Opportunities: *General:* 5–7 full-time positions for teachers of all subjects and special education. *ESL:* Less than 1 position per year. *Administrators:* Less than 1 position per year.
Requirements for General Teachers: Bachelor's degree in elementary/secondary education is required; master's degree is preferred. 3 years of teaching experience is required. International experience is preferred.
Requirements for ESL Teachers: Bachelor's degree in elementary/secondary education is required; master's degree is preferred. 3 years of teaching experience is required. International experience is preferred.
Requirements for Administrators: Master's degree in administration is required. 3 years of administrative experience is required. International experience is preferred.
Duration: 2 years; renewable for 2 years.
Salary: *Teachers:* $13,500–$27,000 per calendar year. *Administrators:* $32,000 per calendar year.
Benefits: Round-trip transportation from U.S. for appointee and dependents. Housing for appointee and dependents. Paid home leave every 2 years. Health insurance. Pension plan. Other benefits are provided.
Academic Calendar: August–June.
Application Deadline: None.
Contact: William D. Rose, Headmaster, American School of Brasilia, L-2 Sul Q605-E, 70200 Brasilia (D.F.), Brazil. *Phone:* (55-61) 243-3237. *Telex:* 611091. *Cable:* AM EMBASSY—BRASILIA.

304 CASA THOMAS JEFFERSON

This private coed binational center was founded in 1970. Current enrollment is 4,600; 5% of the faculty are U.S. nationals. The center reports that due to visa restrictions, it is difficult to hire anyone from outside the country. However, the center will interview candidates who obtain a temporary visa and wish to visit the Casa Thomas Jefferson.
Language of Instruction: *Primary:* English. *Other:* Portuguese.
Opportunities: *Teachers:* Full- and part-time positions. *Administrators:* None.
Contact: Angela Nogueira, Language Coordinator, Casa Thomas Jefferson, SEP/Sul Entrequadras 706/906, Caixa Postal 07-1201, 70390 Brasilia (D.F.), Brazil. *Phone:* (55-61) 243-6588, Ext. 32. *Telex:* 1592.

CAMPINAS

305 ESCOLA AMERICANA DE CAMPINAS

This private coed primary/secondary school was founded in 1957. Current enrollment is 235; 33% of the faculty are U.S. nationals.
Language of Instruction: *Primary:* English. *Other:* Portuguese.
Opportunities: *General:* 1 full-time position. *ESL:* None. *Administrators:* Less than 1 position per year.
Requirements for Teachers: Bachelor's or master's degree is required; doctor's degree may be preferred. 2–5 years of teaching experience is required. Teaching certificate is required. International experience is preferred. Language proficiency in Portuguese on the beginning level is preferred.
Requirements for Administrators: Master's degree is required; doctor's degree is preferred. 5 years of administrative experience is required. Administrative certificate is required. International experience is required. Language proficiency in Portuguese on the beginning level is required.
Duration: 2 years; renewable indefinitely.
Salary: *Teachers:* $15,519–$24,780 per calendar year. *Administrators:* $25,000–$40,000 per calendar year.
Benefits: Round-trip transportation from U.S. for appointee and dependents. School assists in locating housing. Paid home leave every 2 years. Health insurance.
Academic Calendar: August–June.
Application Deadline: February.
Contact: Stephen Field, Superintendent, Escola Americana de Campinas, Caixa Postal 1183, 13001 Campinas, Brazil. *Phone:* (55-192) 51-7377.

CURITIBA

306 INTERNATIONAL SCHOOL OF CURITIBA

This private coed primary/secondary school was founded in 1959. Current enrollment is 142; 25% of the faculty are U.S. nationals.
Language of Instruction: *Primary:* English. *Other:* Portuguese.
Opportunities: *General:* 2 full-time positions. *ESL:* None. *Administrators:* 1 position every 2 years.
Requirements for Teachers: Bachelor's degree is required. 3 years of teaching experience is required. International experience is preferred.
Requirements for Administrators: 3 years of administrative experience is required. Language proficiency in Portuguese is preferred.
Duration: 2 years; renewable for 2 years.
Salary: Contact school for information.
Benefits: Round-trip transportation from U.S. for appointee. Housing for appointee and dependents. Health insurance.
Academic Calendar: August–June.
Application Deadline: February.
Contact: Karl M. Lorenz, Director, International School of Curitiba, Caixa Postal 7004, 80520 Curitiba (Parana), Brazil. *Phone:* (55-41) 234-5545.

PIRACICABA

307 UNIVERSIDADE METODISTA DE PIRACICABA

This is a private university, founded in 1975. Current enrollment is about 6,600. Although faculty is primarily recruited locally, the administration indicates interest in hiring U.S. nationals.
Language of Instruction: Spanish.
Opportunities: *Teachers:* Positions available. *Administrators:* None.
Contact: Almir de Souza Maia, President, Universidade Metodista de Piracicaba, Rue Rangel Pestana 762, Caixa Postal 68, 13400 Piracicaba (SP), Brazil. *Phone:* (55-194) 33-5011. *Telex:* 019-1914 UMEP BR.

PORTO ALEGRE

308 PAN AMERICAN SCHOOL OF PORTO ALEGRE
This private coed primary and correspondence secondary school was founded in 1966. Current enrollment is 52; 50% of the faculty are U.S. nationals.
Language of Instruction: *Primary:* English. *Other:* Portuguese.
Opportunities: *General:* 1–2 full- and part-time positions for teachers. *ESL:* Less than 1 position per year. *Administrators:* Less than 1 position per year.
Requirements for General Teachers: Bachelor's degree in subject taught is required. Teaching experience is preferred or practical experience is required. International experience is preferred. Language proficiency in Portuguese on the beginning level is preferred.
Requirements for ESL Teachers: Bachelor's degree in ESL is required. Teaching experience is preferred or practical experience is required. International experience is preferred. Language proficiency in Portuguese is preferred.
Requirements for Administrators: Master's degree in educational administration is required. Administrative experience is preferred. International experience is preferred. Language proficiency in Portuguese on the beginning level is preferred.
Duration: 2 years; renewable indefinitely.
Salary: *Teachers:* $9,000–$15,000 per calendar year. *Administrators:* $25,000–$35,000 per calendar year.
Benefits: Round-trip transportation from U.S. for appointee and dependents. Housing allowance. Paid home leave every 2 years. Health care. Tuition for children enrolled at this school. Other benefits are provided.
Academic Calendar: August–June.
Orientation: 1 week in Porto Alegre.
Application Deadline: February.
Contact: Ronald McCluskey, Director, Pan American School of Porto Alegre, Rua Joao Paetzel 440, 91330 Porto Alegre, Brazil. *Phone:* (55-512) 34-5866.

RECIFE

309 AMERICAN SCHOOL OF RECIFE
This private coed pre-K and primary/secondary school was founded in 1957. Current enrollment is 237; 50% of the faculty are U.S. nationals. Faculty are recruited locally.
Language of Instruction: *Primary:* English. *Other:* Portuguese.
Opportunities: *General:* Less than 1 position per year. *ESL:* Less than 1 position per year. *Administrators:* Less than 1 position per year.
Contact: American School of Recife, Rua Sa' e Souza 408, 51030 Recife, Brazil. *Phone:* (55-81) 341-4716/0142. *Or:* American School of Recife, c/o U.S. Consulate/Recife, APO Miami, FL 34030.

RIO DE JANEIRO

310 ESCOLA AMERICANA DO RIO DE JANEIRO
This private coed primary/secondary school was founded in 1937. Current enrollment is 900; 25% of the faculty are U.S. nationals.
Language of Instruction: *Primary:* English. *Other:* Portuguese.
Opportunities: *General:* 4 full-time positions for primary school teachers of all subjects and secondary school teachers of mathematics and English. *ESL:* 1 full-time position. *Administrators:* Less than 1 position per year.
Requirements for General Teachers: Bachelor's degree in subject taught is required; master's degree is preferred. 3 years of teaching experience is required. International experience is preferred.
Requirements for ESL Teachers: Bachelor's degree in TESL or TEFL is required; master's degree is preferred. 3 years of teaching experience is required. International experience is preferred. Language proficiency in Portuguese is preferred.
Requirements for Administrators: Master's degree in educational administration is required. 5 years of administrative experience is required. International experience is preferred.
Duration: 2 years; renewable indefinitely.
Salary: *Teachers:* $11,000 per academic year. *Administrators:* $40,000 per academic year.

Benefits: Round-trip transportation from U.S. for appointee, spouse, and dependents under age 18. Housing for appointee and dependents. Paid home leave every 2 years.
Academic Calendar: August–June.
Orientation: 8 days on-site.
Application Deadline: March 1.
Contact: Les Landers, Headmaster, Escola Americana, 132 Estrada da Gavea, 22451 Rio de Janeiro, Brazil. *Phone:* (55-21) 322-0825.

SALVADOR

311 PAN AMERICAN SCHOOL OF BAHIA
This private coed primary/secondary school was founded in 1960. Current enrollment is 389; 60% of the faculty are U.S. nationals. The school exchanges faculty with Ridgewood (New Jersey) Schools.
Language of Instruction: *Primary:* English. *Other:* Portuguese.
Opportunities: *General:* 15 full-time positions for teachers of all subjects. *ESL:* None. *Administrators:* 2 full-time positions.
Requirements for Teachers: Bachelor's degree in elementary education or subject taught is required; master's degree is preferred. 3 years of teaching experience is required. Language proficiency in Portuguese or Spanish is preferred. Teachers without dependents are preferred.
Requirements for Administrators: Doctor's degree in school administration is preferred. 3 years of administrative experience is required. Administrators without dependents are preferred.
Duration: 2 years; renewable for 2 years.
Salary: *Teachers:* From $12,000 per calendar year. *Administrators:* From $15,000 per calendar year.
Benefits: Round-trip transportation from U.S. for appointee and dependents. Housing for appointee only. Paid home leave every 2 years. Health insurance. Other benefits are provided.
Academic Calendar: August–June.
Orientation: 2 days on-site.
Application Deadline: Jan. 30.
Contact: Cecilia Lingerfelt, Administrative Assistant, Pan American School of Bahia, Caixa Postal 231, 40000 Salvador, Bahia, Brazil. *Phone:* (55-71) 249-9099.

SAO LUIS

312 MARANHAO AMERICAN SCHOOL
This is a private coed primary school. Current enrollment is 15; 66% of the faculty are U.S. nationals.
Language of Instruction: *Primary:* English. *Other:* Portuguese.
Opportunities: *General:* 1 full-time position. *ESL:* None. *Administrators:* 1 full-time position.
Requirements for Teachers: Bachelor's degree in elementary education is required. 2 years of teaching experience is required. International experience is preferred.
Requirements for Administrators: Master's degree in education is required. 2 years of administrative experience is required. International experience is preferred.
Duration: 1 year; renewable indefinitely.
Salary: *Teachers:* $18,000 per calendar year. *Administrators:* $25,000 per calendar year.
Benefits: Round-trip transportation from U.S. for appointee and dependents. Housing for appointee and dependents. Paid home leave every year. Health and life insurance. Pension plan.
Academic Calendar: August–June.
Application Deadline: February.
Contact: Jackie Turner, Vice President, International Schools Services, P.O. Box 5910, Princeton, NJ 08543. *Phone:* (609) 452-0990. *Telex:* 843 308. *Cable:* SCHOLSERV PRINCETON. *Or:* Bruce Goforth, Principal, Maranhao American School, Sao Luis, Brazil, 1501 Alcoa Bldg., Pittsburgh, PA 15219. *Phone:* In Brazil: (55-95) 226-0203/2457.

SAO PAULO

313 ESCOLA GRADUADA DE SAO PAULO
This private coed primary/secondary school was founded in 1920. Current enrollment is 975; 40% of the faculty are U.S. nationals.
Language of Instruction: *Primary:* English. *Other:* Portuguese.

Opportunities: *General:* 10 full- and part-time positions. *ESL:* Less than 1 position per year. *Administrators:* 1 full-time position.
Requirements for General Teachers: Bachelor's degree in subject taught is required. 3 years of teaching experience is required. Teaching certificate is required.
Requirements for ESL Teachers: Bachelor's degree in TESL/applied linguistics is required. 3 years of teaching experience is required. Teaching certificate is required. International experience is preferred.
Requirements for Administrators: Master's degree in school administration or related field is required. 5 years of administrative experience is required. International experience is preferred.
Duration: 2 years; renewable indefinitely.
Salary: *Teachers:* $16,000–$25,000 per calendar year. *Administrators:* $35,000–$45,000 per calendar year.
Benefits: Round-trip transportation from U.S. for appointee and dependents. Housing for appointee and dependents. Paid home leave every year after 2 years. Health insurance. Pension plan.
Academic Calendar: August–June.
Orientation: 2 weeks on-site.
Application Deadline: January.
Contact: Victor J. Huser, Dean of Personnel, Escola Graduada de Sao Paulo, Caixa Postal 7432, 01051 Sao Paulo (SP), Brazil. *Phone:* (55-11) 842-2499.

314 ESCOLA MARIA IMACULADA (CHAPEL AMERICAN SCHOOL)

This private coed primary/secondary school was founded in 1947. Current enrollment is 740; 18% of the faculty are U.S. nationals.
Language of Instruction: *Primary:* English. *Other:* Portuguese.
Opportunities: *General:* 7 full-time positions. *ESL:* None. *Administrators:* 1 full-time position.
Requirements for Teachers: Bachelor's degree in education is required; master's degree is preferred. 3 years of teaching experience is required. International experience is preferred. Language proficiency in Portuguese is preferred.
Requirements for Administrators: Master's degree in administrative education is required. Administrative experience is required. International experience is preferred. Language proficiency in Portuguese on the beginning level is preferred.
Duration: 2 years; renewable annually.
Salary: *Teachers:* $13,694–$23,827 per calendar year.
Benefits: Round-trip transportation from U.S. for appointee and dependents. Housing for appointee and dependents. Paid home leave. Health, life, and accident insurance. Tuition for children enrolled at this school. Other benefits are provided.
Academic Calendar: August–June.
Orientation: 1 week on-site.
Application Deadline: March 1.
Contact: William A. Sheehan, Director, Escola Maria Imaculada (Chapel American School), Caixa Postal 21293—Brooklin, 04698 Sao Paulo (SP), Brazil. *Phone:* (55-11) 247-7455.

CANADA

MORE THAN ONE CITY

315 CANADIAN CONSULATE GENERAL

The Consulate reports that there is no need for U.S. teachers or educational administrators at this time.
Language of Instruction: English and French.
Academic Calendar: September–May.
For General Information, Contact: Canadian Consulate General, 1251 Avenue of the Americas, New York, NY 10020-1175.

316 CANADIAN EDUCATION ASSOCIATION

Each of the 10 provinces and 2 territories in Canada is responsible for its own educational system. There is no federal office or national ministry of education. Candidates wishing to teach in an elementary or secondary school in Canada should write for information and guidance to the department or ministry of education in the capital city of the province or territory in which they are interested.

Requirements for permanent teacher certification and teaching positions usually include copies of diplomas and certificates, college transcripts, proficiency in English or French, and, in some provinces, Canadian citizenship. Temporary teaching opportunities are virtually nonexistent.

For a list of the provincial departments of education, write to the address below and request the booklet *Information for Teachers Thinking of Coming to Canada.*
For General Information, Contact: Canadian Education Association, 252 Bloor St. West, Suite 8-200, Toronto, Ontario M5S 1V5, Canada.

BEAMSVILLE

317 GREAT LAKES CHRISTIAN COLLEGE

This private coed secondary school and Bible college was founded in 1952. Current enrollment is 125; 20% of the faculty are U.S. nationals.
Language of Instruction: English.
Opportunities: *General:* 2 full-time positions. *ESL:* None. *Administrators:* 1 full-time position.
Requirements for Teachers: Bachelor's degree is required; master's degree is preferred. 3–5 years of teaching experience is preferred. International experience is preferred.
Requirements for Administrators: Bachelor's degree is required; master's degree is preferred. 5–10 years of administrative experience is preferred.
Duration: 1 year; renewable.
Salary: *Teachers:* CN $14,255–$31,071 per academic year. *Administrators:* CN $32,571–$33,148 per calendar year.
Benefits: Health, life, and disability insurance. Pension plan.
Academic Calendar: September–June.
Application Deadline: March 31.
Contact: Edwin Broadus, President, Great Lakes Christian College, Box 399, Beamsville, Ontario L0R 1B0, Canada. *Phone:* (416) 563-5374.

BURNABY

318 DORSET COLLEGE

This private coed secondary school and adult/continuing education program was founded in 1981. Current enrollment is 160; 6% of the faculty are U.S. nationals.
Language of Instruction: *Primary:* English. *Other:* Mandarin, French, Italian, Japanese, and Russian.
Opportunities: *General:* Less than 1 position per year for teachers of secondary school and adult education hospitality/tourism management programs. *ESL:* None. *Administrators:* None.
Requirements: Master's degree is required; doctor's degree is preferred. 2 years of teaching or practical experience is required. International experience is preferred. Language proficiency in any Pacific rim language on the intermediate and advanced level is preferred. British Columbia teacher certification is required.
Duration: 2 semesters; renewable indefinitely.
Salary: CN $2,200–$2,400 per month.
Academic Calendar: September–August.
Orientation: Several days in Vancouver.
Application Deadline: 1 month before semester begins.
Contact: C.W. Dick, Principal, Dorset College and Dorset College Continuing Education Division, 250 Willingdon Ave., Burnaby, BC V5C 5E9, Canada. *Phone:* (604) 291-8686. *Telex:* 04-54247. *Fax:* (604) 662-7934 Mr. E. Cheng.

THREE HILLS

319 PRAIRIE HIGH SCHOOL

This private coed secondary school was founded in 1938. Current enrollment is 275; 5–10% of the faculty are U.S. nationals. The school recruits only faculty with Canadian Landed Immigrant status.
Language of Instruction: English.
Opportunities: *General:* 1–2 full-time positions for teachers of all subjects. *ESL:* None. *Administrators:* 1 full-time position.
Requirements for Teachers: Bachelor's degree in education with a specific major is required; master's degree in education is preferred. 2 years of teaching experience is preferred. Alberta teaching certification is required.

All information is subject to change without notice and must be confirmed directly with the employer.

Requirements for Administrators: Bachelor's degree in education is required; master's degree in educational administration is preferred. 3 years of administrative experience is required. Experience in Christian school teaching and administration is required.
Duration: 1 year; renewable.
Salary: *Teachers:* CN $12,000–$16,000 per calendar year. *Administrators:* CN $12,000–$16,000 per calendar year.
Benefits: Housing for appointee and dependents. Health care. Life insurance. Pension plan.
Academic Calendar: September–June.
Orientation: On-site.
Application Deadline: February.
Contact: Rick Down, Vice-President of General Education, Prairie Bible Institute, Box 4032, Three Hills, Alberta T0M 2A0, Canada. *Phone:* (403) 443-5511, Ext. 86.

TORONTO

320 ST. CLEMENT'S SCHOOL
This private female-only primary/secondary school was founded in 1901. Current enrollment is 400; none of the faculty are U.S. nationals.
Language of Instruction: *Primary:* English. *Other:* French.
Opportunities: *General:* Less than 1 position per year. *ESL:* None. *Administrators:* Less than 1 position per year.
Requirements for Teachers: Bachelor's degree in education is required. Teaching experience is required.
Requirements for Administrators: Master's degree is required. 10 years of administrative experience is required.
Duration: 1 year; renewable.
Salary: *Teachers:* CN $23,121–$48,026 per calendar year. *Administrators:* CN $48,000 per calendar year.
Benefits: Life insurance. Other benefits are provided.
Academic Calendar: September–June.
Application Deadline: Jan. 1.
Contact: Miss H.W. Perkin, Principal, St. Clement's School, 21 St. Clement's Ave., Toronto, Ontario M4R 1G8, Canada. *Phone:* (416) 483-4835.

CHILE

SANTIAGO

321 INSTITUTO CHILENO-NORTEAMERICANO DE CULTURA
This private coed binational center was founded in 1938. Current enrollment is 2,500; 10% of the faculty are U.S. nationals.
Language of Instruction: English.
Opportunities: *General:* None. *ESL:* 4 full- and part-time positions. *Administrators:* None.
Requirements: Master's degree in TESOL is required. 5 years of teaching experience is required. International experience is preferred. Language proficiency in Spanish on the intermediate level is preferred.
Duration: 1 year; renewable for 1 year.
Benefits: Institute assists in locating housing. Health insurance. Pension plan. Other benefits are provided.
Academic Calendar: March–January.
Orientation: On-site.
Application Deadline: May 30.
Contact: Liliana Baltra, Academic Director, Instituto Chileno-Norteamericano de Cultura, Moneda 1467, Santiago, Chile. *Phone:* (56-2) 6963215.

322 INTERNATIONAL SCHOOL NIDO DE AGUILAS
This private coed primary/secondary school was founded in 1934. Current enrollment is 667; 47% of the faculty are U.S. nationals.
Language of Instruction: *Primary:* English. *Other:* Spanish and French.
Opportunities: *General:* 3 full-time positions for teachers of secondary school mathematics and English, and teachers of primary and secondary school special education. *ESL:* 1 full-time position. *Administrators:* 1 full-time position.

Requirements for General Teachers: Bachelor's degree in subject taught is required. 2 years of teaching experience is required. International experience is preferred.
Requirements for ESL Teachers: Master's degree in ESL is required. 2 years of teaching experience is required. International experience is preferred. Language proficiency in Spanish is preferred.
Requirements for Administrators: Master's degree in educational administration is required. 3 years of administrative experience is required.
Duration: 2 years; renewable indefinitely.
Salary: *Teachers:* $14,000–$17,000 per calendar year. *Administrators:* $15,500–$18,000 per calendar year.
Benefits: Round-trip transportation from U.S. for appointee and dependents. School assists in locating housing. Paid home leave every 2 years. Health insurance.
Academic Calendar: August–July.
Application Deadline: March.
Contact: Dale I. Swall, Headmaster, The International School Nido de Aguilas, Casilla 16211, Santiago 9, Chile. *Phone:* (56-2) 472555.

323 LINCOLN INTERNATIONAL ACADEMY
This private coed pre-K and primary/secondary school was founded in 1976. Current enrollment is 488; 5% of the faculty are U.S. nationals. Faculty are recruited from those presently residing in Chile.
Language of Instruction: *Primary:* English. *Other:* Spanish.
Opportunities: *Teachers:* Full-time positions. *Administrators:* Full-time positions.
Academic Calendar: March–December.
Contact: Veronica Caroca, Directora, Lincoln International Academy, Casilla 20000, Correo 20, Santiago, Chile. *Phone:* (56-2) 471907/242-4128.

324 REDLAND SCHOOL
This private coed primary/secondary school was founded in 1966. Current enrollment is 600; at present, none of the faculty are U.S. nationals.
Language of Instruction: *Primary:* Spanish. *Other:* English.
Opportunities: *General:* Positions available. *ESL:* Positions available. *Administrators:* None.
Requirements for General Teachers: Bachelor's degree in education is preferred. 6 years of teaching experience is required. International experience is preferred.
Requirements for ESL Teachers: Bachelor's degree in applied linguistics is preferred. 3 years of teaching experience is required. International experience is preferred.
Duration: 3 years; renewable for 2 years.
Benefits: Round-trip transportation from U.S. for appointee only. School assists in locating housing.
Academic Calendar: March–December.
Contact: Richard Collingwood-Selby, Headmaster, Redland School, Camino El Alba 11357, Las Condes, Santiago, Chile.

325 SANTIAGO LANGUAGE CENTER LIMITADA
This private coed adult/continuing education program was founded in 1974. Current enrollment is 1,500; 20% of the faculty are U.S. nationals.
Language of Instruction: *Primary:* English. *Other:* Spanish.
Opportunities: *General:* None. *ESL:* 8 full- and part-time positions. *Administrators:* None.
Requirements: 2 years of teaching experience is required. International experience is preferred.
Duration: 1 year; renewable for 1 year.
Salary: $4 per hour.
Benefits: Center assists in locating housing.
Academic Calendar: March–December.
Contact: Mrs. Toscha Tobias, Technical Director, Santiago Language Center Limitada, Irene Morales No. 11, Santiago, Chile. *Phone:* (56-2) 332599/398703.

COLOMBIA

BARRANQUILLA

326 COLEGIO KARL C. PARRISH
This private coed primary/secondary school was founded in 1938.
Current enrollment is 723; 25% of the faculty are U.S. nationals.
Language of Instruction: *Primary:* English. *Other:* Spanish.
Opportunities: *General:* Full-time positions for teachers of all subjects
and special education. *ESL:* 2 positions. *Administrators:* Full-time
positions.
Requirements for General Teachers: 2 years of teaching experience is
preferred. International experience is preferred. Language proficiency in
Spanish is preferred.
Requirements for Administrators: Master's degree in administration
and elementary or secondary education is required; doctor's degree is
preferred. 2 years of administrative experience is preferred. International
experience is preferred. Language proficiency in Spanish is preferred.
Duration: 10 months for teachers, 2 years for administrators; renewable.
Salary: *Teachers:* $16,000–$20,250 per academic year.
Benefits: Round-trip transportation from U.S. for appointee and
dependents. School assists in locating housing. Health insurance.
Academic Calendar: August–June.
Orientation: 2 days in Miami.
Contact: Dr. Robert Michael Farr, Director, Colegio Karl C. Parrish,
Apartado Aereo 52962, Barranquilla, Colombia. *Phone:* (57-5) 455449.

327 MARYMOUNT SCHOOL
This private coed primary/secondary school was founded in 1953.
Current enrollment is 1,300; 33% of the faculty are U.S. nationals.
Language of Instruction: *Primary:* English. *Other:* Spanish.
Opportunities: *General:* 4 full-time positions for teachers of
mathematics, social studies, and computer. *ESL:* 6 full-time positions.
Administrators: 1 full-time position.
Requirements for General Teachers: Bachelor's degree in subject
taught is required. 2 years of teaching experience is required. Teaching
certificate is required. International experience is preferred.
Requirements for ESL Teachers: Bachelor's degree is required.
Teaching experience is required. International experience is preferred.
Language proficiency in Spanish on the intermediate level is preferred.
Requirements for Administrators: Master's degree is required. 5 years
of administrative experience is required. International experience is
preferred. Language proficiency in Spanish on the intermediate level is
preferred.
Duration: 2 years; renewable for 1–2 years.
Salary: *Teachers:* $16,000–$20,000 per academic year. *Administrators:*
$21,000–$26,000 per calendar year.
Benefits: Round-trip transportation from U.S. for appointee only.
Housing allowance. School assists in locating housing. Health care.
Pension plan.
Academic Calendar: August–June.
Application Deadline: March 1.
Contact: Marylou Kumnick, Teacher Recruitment Officer, 148
Metacomet Dr., Meriden, CT 06450. *Phone:* (203) 237-5133. *Or:*
Kathleen Cunniffe, Principal, Marymount School, Apartado Aereo 1912,
Barranquilla, Colombia. *Phone:* (57-5) 342249.

BOGOTA

328 CENTRO COLOMBO AMERICANO
This private English language institute for adults was founded in 1942.
Current enrollment is 4,000; 15% of the faculty are U.S. nationals.
Language of Instruction: *Primary:* English. *Other:* Spanish.
Opportunities: *General:* None. *ESL:* 15 full-time positions.
Administrators: Less than 1 position per year.
Requirements for Teachers: Master's degree in TESL or TEFL is
required. International experience is preferred. Language proficiency in
Spanish on the intermediate level is preferred.
Requirements for Administrators: Bachelor's or master's degree in
TESL or TEFL is preferred. Language proficiency in Spanish on the
intermediate level is preferred.
Duration: 11 months; renewable.
Salary: *Teachers:* 1,940,000 pesos per calendar year.

Benefits: Round-trip transportation from U.S. for appointee only.
Health care. Other benefits are provided.
Academic Calendar: January–December.
Orientation: About 1 week on-site.
Application Deadline: Monthly.
Contact: Edward C. Stanford, Director of Studies, Centro Colombo
Americano, Avenida 19 No. 3-05, Bogota, Colombia. *Phone:* (57-1)
234-7640.

329 COLEGIO NUEVA GRANADA
This private coed primary/secondary school was founded in 1938.
Current enrollment is 1,332; 40% of the faculty are U.S. nationals.
Language of Instruction: *Primary:* English. *Other:* Spanish.
Opportunities: *General:* 25 full-time positions for teachers of all
subjects. *ESL:* 1 full-time position. *Administrators:* 1 full-time position.
Requirements for General Teachers: Bachelor's degree is required;
master's degree is preferred. Teaching experience is preferred, or
student teaching is required. Teaching certificate is required.
International experience is preferred. Language proficiency in Spanish
on the beginning level is preferred.
Requirements for ESL Teachers: Bachelor's degree is required;
master's degree is preferred. Teaching experience is required.
International experience is preferred. Language proficiency in Spanish is
required.
Requirements for Administrators: Master's degree is required.
Administrative experience is required. Administrative certificate is
required. International experience is preferred. Language proficiency in
Spanish on the intermediate level is preferred.
Duration: 2 years; renewable indefinitely.
Salary: *Teachers:* $8,500–$13,000 per calendar year. *Administrators:*
$30,000–$35,000 per calendar year.
Benefits: Round-trip transportation from U.S. for appointee and
dependents. Housing allowance. Paid home leave after 2 years, then
every year. Health insurance.
Academic Calendar: August–June.
Orientation: 2 days in Miami.
Application Deadline: February–April.
Contact: Peter R. Cooper, Director, Colegio Nueva Granada, Apartado
Aereo 51339, Bogota, Colombia. *Phone:* (57-1) 235-5350.

BUCARAMANGA

330 COLEGIO PANAMERICANO
This private coed primary/secondary school was founded in 1963.
Current enrollment is 300; 20% of the faculty are U.S. nationals.
Language of Instruction: *Primary:* English. *Other:* Spanish.
Opportunities: *General:* 5 full-time positions for primary school teachers
of all subjects and secondary school teachers of mathematics, computers,
biology, English, accounting, and business education. *ESL:* 3 full-time
positions. *Administrators:* 2 full-time positions.
Requirements for General Teachers: Bachelor's degree in mathematics,
biology, or elementary education is required. Teaching or practical
experience is preferred. International experience is preferred. Language
proficiency in Spanish on the beginning level is preferred.
Requirements for ESL Teachers: Bachelor's degree in English/TESL is
preferred. Teaching or practical experience is preferred. International
experience is preferred. Language proficiency in Spanish is preferred.
Requirements for Administrators: Bachelor's degree is required;
master's degree is preferred. Administrative experience is preferred.
International experience is preferred. Language proficiency in Spanish
on the intermediate level is required.
Duration: 2 years; renewable.
Salary: Negotiable.
Benefits: Round-trip transportation from U.S. for appointee only.
Housing for appointee only. Health insurance and health care.
Retirement plan. Other benefits are provided.
Academic Calendar: February–November.
Orientation: 1–2 weeks on-site.
Application Deadline: August.
Contact: Laura Garcia, Director, Colegio Panamericano, Apartado
Aereo 522, Bucaramanga, Colombia. *Phone:* (57-73) 386213/387336.

All information is subject to change without notice
and must be confirmed directly with the employer.

CALI

331 COLEGIO BOLIVAR
This private coed primary/secondary school was founded in 1947. Current enrollment is 930; 60% of the faculty are U.S. nationals. The school exchanges faculty with Greenhill School, Dallas, Texas.
Language of Instruction: *Primary:* English. *Other:* Spanish.
Opportunities: *General:* 12 full-time positions. *ESL:* None. *Administrators:* Less than 1 position per year.
Requirements for Teachers: Bachelor's degree in subject taught or education is required; master's degree is preferred. Teaching experience is required. Teaching certificate is required. International experience is preferred. Language proficiency in Spanish is preferred.
Requirements for Administrators: Master's degree in administration or curriculum is required. Administrative experience is required. International experience is preferred. Language proficiency in Spanish on the intermediate level is preferred.
Duration: 2 years; renewable indefinitely.
Salary: *Teachers:* $12,000–$14,000 per academic year. *Administrators:* $30,000–$55,000 per calendar year.
Benefits: Round-trip transportation from U.S. for appointee only. Housing allowance. Paid home leave every 2 years. Health insurance.
Academic Calendar: August–June.
Orientation: 2 days in Miami.
Application Deadline: December.
Contact: Martin Felton, Director, Colegio Bolivar, Apartado Aereo 4875, Cali, Colombia. *Phone:* (57-3) 39 32 01.

CARTAGENA

332 GEORGE WASHINGTON SCHOOL
This private coed primary/secondary school was founded in 1952. Current enrollment is 457; 50% of the faculty are U.S. nationals. The school exchanges faculty with Narragansett High School, Narragansett, Rhode Island.
Language of Instruction: *Primary:* English. *Other:* Spanish.
Opportunities: *General:* 5–8 full-time positions for primary school teachers of all subjects and secondary school teachers of English, science, and mathematics. *ESL:* None. *Administrators:* Less than 1 position per year.
Requirements for Teachers: Bachelor's degree in education is required. 2 years of teaching experience is preferred. Teacher certificate is required. International experience is preferred. Language proficiency in Spanish on the beginning level is preferred.
Requirements for Administrators: Bachelor's degree in education is required; master's degree in administration is required. Administrative experience is required. International experience is preferred. Language proficiency in Spanish is preferred.
Duration: 1 year; renewable.
Salary: *Teachers:* $9,500–$11,000 per academic year. *Administrators:* $15,000–$20,000 per calendar year.
Benefits: Round-trip transportation from U.S. for appointee only. Health insurance. Other benefits provided.
Academic Calendar: August–June.
Orientation: 3 days in Miami.
Application Deadline: February.
Contact: Joseph Nagy, Director, George Washington School, Apartado Aereo 2899, Cartagena, Colombia. *Phone:* (57-59) 54035.

MEDELLIN

333 COLUMBUS SCHOOL
This private coed primary/secondary school was founded in 1947. Current enrollment is 1,050.
Language of Instruction: *Primary:* English. *Other:* Spanish.
Opportunities: *General:* 15 full-time positions. *ESL:* None. *Administrators:* Less than 1 position per year.
Requirements for Teachers: Bachelor's degree in elementary education/secondary education is required; master's degree is preferred. 2 years of teaching experience is preferred. Teaching certificate is required. International experience is preferred. Language proficiency in Spanish on any level is preferred.
Requirements for Administrators: Master's degree in school administration is required. Administrative experience is required.

Administrative certificate is required. International experience is preferred. Language proficiency in Spanish on the advanced level is preferred.
Duration: 2 years; renewable.
Salary: *Teachers:* $8,000–$14,000 per calendar year.
Benefits: Round-trip transportation from U.S. for appointee and dependents. Housing for appointee and dependents. Health insurance.
Academic Calendar: August–June.
Orientation: 2 days in Miami.
Application Deadline: Dec. 31.
Contact: John K. Schober, Superintendent, The Columbus School, Apartado Aereo 5225, Medellin, Colombia. *Phone:* (57-42) 257-7531.

COSTA RICA

MORE THAN ONE CITY

334 EMBASSY OF COSTA RICA
The Embassy reports that there is no need for U.S. teachers or educational administrators at this time.
Language of Instruction: *Primary:* Spanish. *Other:* English and French.
Academic Calendar: March–December.
For General Information, Contact: Embassy of Costa Rica, 1825 Connecticut Ave. NW, Suite 211, Washington, DC 20009.

SAN JOSE

335 COLEGIO METODISTA
This private coed primary/secondary school was founded in 1921. Current enrollment is 1,272.
Language of Instruction: *Primary:* Spanish. *Other:* English and French.
Opportunities: *General:* 5 full- or part-time positions for teachers of English and science. *ESL:* 4 full-time positions. *Administrators:* 1 full-time position.
Requirements for General Teachers: Bachelor's degree in biology, chemistry, or English is required. 2 years of teaching experience is preferred. Language proficiency in Spanish on the intermediate level is required. Teachers should be Protestant and active in church work.
Requirements for ESL Teachers: Bachelor's degree in English is preferred. 2 years of teaching experience is preferred. Language proficiency in Spanish on the intermediate level is preferred.
Requirements for Administrators: Master's degree is required for the principal and director. 2 years of administrative experience is required. Language proficiency in Spanish on the advanced level is required. Administrators must be Protestants, preferably Methodists, and active in church work.
Duration: 1 year; renewable.
Salary: *Teachers:* 20,000–30,000 colones per year.
Benefits: School assists in locating housing. Paid home leave.
Academic Calendar: February–December.
Orientation: 1 week on-site.
Application Deadline: Nov. 30.
Contact: James D. Tuttle, Director, Colegio Metodista, Apartado 931, San Jose 1000, Costa Rica. *Phone:* (506) 25-06-55. *Cable:* METODISCO.

336 FRIENDS WORLD COLLEGE—LATIN AMERICAN CENTER
This private coed university was founded in 1965. Current enrollment is 20; 33% of the faculty are U.S. nationals.
Language of Instruction: *Primary:* English. *Other:* Spanish.
Opportunities: *General:* 1 full- or part-time position for a teacher of area studies, social and natural sciences, or the arts. *ESL:* None. *Administrators:* Less than 1 position per year.
Requirements for Teachers: Doctor's degree in subject taught is required. Teaching experience is required. Experience in the country or region is required. Language proficiency in Spanish on the advanced level is required. A faculty exchange for recipients of sabbatical leave can be considered.
Requirements for Administrators: Doctor's degree is required. Administrative experience is required. International experience is

required. Language proficiency in Spanish on the advanced level is required.
Duration: 1 year; renewable indefinitely.
Salary: *Teachers:* $16,000 per calendar year. *Administrators:* $18,000 per calendar year.
Benefits: Round-trip transportation from U.S. for appointee only. University assists in locating housing. Health insurance. Other benefits are provided.
Academic Calendar: September–June.
Orientation: In Huntington, New York.
Application Deadline: Open.
Contact: Rafael Bolanos, Director, Friends World College—Latin American Center, Apartado 8496, San Jose, Costa Rica. *Phone:* (506) 25-50-08.

337 LINCOLN SCHOOL
This private coed primary/secondary school was founded in 1939. Current enrollment is 1,550; 25% of the faculty are U.S. nationals.
Language of Instruction: *Primary:* English. *Other:* Spanish and French.
Opportunities: *General:* 20 full-time positions for teachers of all subjects. *ESL:* None. *Administrators:* 2 full-time positions.
Requirements for Teachers: Bachelor's degree is required; master's degree is preferred. 3 years of teaching experience is preferred. Language proficiency in Spanish is preferred.
Requirements for Administrators: Master's degree is required; doctor's degree is preferred. 2 years of administrative experience is preferred. International experience is preferred. Language proficiency in Spanish on the intermediate level is preferred.
Duration: 1 year; renewable indefinitely.
Salary: *Teachers:* $500 per month. *Administrators:* $1,400 per month.
Benefits: Round-trip transportation from U.S. for appointee only. Housing allowance. School assists in locating housing. Health insurance. Other benefits are provided.
Academic Calendar: February–November.
Orientation: 2 days on-site.
Application Deadline: Sept. 30.
Contact: Edward J. Feeney, Director, Lincoln School, Apartado 1919, San Jose, Costa Rica. *Phone:* (506) 35-77-33.

338 UNIVERSIDAD DE COSTA RICA
This public coed university was founded in 1941. Current enrollment is 30,000; none of the faculty are U.S. nationals.
Language of Instruction: Spanish.
Opportunities: *General:* Part-time positions. *ESL:* Part-time positions. *Administrators:* Part-time positions.
Requirements for General Teachers: Doctor's degree is required. 5 years of teaching experience is required. Language proficiency in Spanish on the advanced level is required.
Requirements for ESL Teachers: Doctor's degree is required. 5 years of teaching experience is required. Language proficiency in Spanish is required.
Requirements for Administrators: Doctor's degree is required. 5 years of administrative experience is required. Language proficiency in Spanish on the advanced level is required.
Duration: 1 month–1 year; renewable.
Salary: *Teachers:* $500–$700 per month. *Administrators:* $500–$700 per month.
Benefits: Health insurance. Other benefits are provided.
Academic Calendar: February–November.
Orientation: On-site.
Application Deadline: Not given.
Contact: Lic. Janina del Vecchio de Hidalgo, Vicerrectora de Docencia, Universidad de Costa Rica, Ciudad Universitaria Rodrigo Facio, San Jose, Costa Rica. *Phone:* (506) 24-37-06. *Telex:* 2544 UNICORI.

DOMINICAN REPUBLIC

SANTO DOMINGO

339 CAROL MORGAN SCHOOL OF SANTO DOMINGO
This private coed pre-K and primary/secondary school was founded in 1933. Current enrollment is 1,200; 50% of the faculty are U.S. nationals.
Language of Instruction: English.

Opportunities: *General:* Positions available. *ESL:* Positions may be available. *Administrators:* None.
Requirements for General Teachers: Bachelor's degree in subject taught is required; master's degree is preferred. 2 years of teaching experience is preferred. Language proficiency in Spanish on the beginning level is preferred.
Requirements for ESL Teachers: Bachelor's or master's degree in applied linguistics is required. Teaching experience is required. International experience is preferred. Language proficiency in Spanish on the beginning level is preferred.
Duration: 2 years; renewable.
Salary: $12,000–$25,000 per year.
Benefits: Round-trip transportation from U.S. for appointee and dependents. Housing allowance. Health and life insurance. Tuition for 1 child enrolled at this school. Other benefits are provided.
Academic Calendar: August–June.
Orientation: 1 week on-site.
Application Deadline: Feb. 1.
Contact: Robert B. Leggat, Superintendent, Carol Morgan School of Santo Domingo, Apartado 1169, Santo Domingo, Dominican Republic.

ECUADOR

MORE THAN ONE CITY

340 U.S. INFORMATION AGENCY
Teaching Assistantships in English.
Opportunities: Positions for ESL teachers on the secondary level.
Requirements: Bachelor's degree is required; master's degree is preferred. Teaching experience is preferred. Language proficiency in Spanish is required.
Duration: 9 months; not renewable.
Benefits: Round-trip transportation from U.S. for appointee. Housing may be provided. Health insurance. Other benefits are provided.
Academic Calendar: September–July or April–February.
Application Deadline: Oct. 31.
Contact: U.S. Student Programs, Institute of International Education, 809 United Nations Plaza, New York, NY 10017. *Phone:* (212) 984-5330.

QUITO

341 ACADEMIA COTOPAXI, AMERICAN INTERNATIONAL SCHOOL
This private coed primary/secondary school was founded in 1958. Current enrollment is 700; 77% of the faculty are U.S. nationals.
Language of Instruction: *Primary:* English. *Other:* Spanish and French.
Opportunities: *General:* Full-time positions. *ESL:* Full-time positions. *Administrators:* Full-time positions.
Requirements for General Teachers: Bachelor's degree is required for elementary school teachers; master's degree is preferred for secondary school teachers. 2 years of teaching experience is required. International experience is preferred. Language proficiency in Spanish is preferred.
Requirements for ESL Teachers: Master's degree is required. 2 years of teaching experience is preferred. International experience is preferred. Language proficiency in Spanish is preferred.
Requirements for Administrators: Master's degree is required. Administrative experience is required. International experience is preferred.
Duration: 2 years; renewable.
Salary: *Teachers:* $13,000 per calendar year. *Administrators:* $30,000 per calendar year.
Benefits: Round-trip transportation from U.S. for appointee and dependents. Housing for appointee and dependents. Health insurance. Other benefits are provided.
Academic Calendar: June–August.
Application Deadline: February.
Contact: Dr. Donald A. Fournier, Superintendent, Academia Cotopaxi, American International School, P.O. Box 199, Quito, Ecuador. *Phone:* (593-2) 433-602. *Telex:* 22298 ECUAME. *Or:* Director, Cotopaxi Academy, c/o American Embassy/Quito, APO Miami, FL 34039.

All information is subject to change without notice
and must be confirmed directly with the employer.

65

342 AMERICAN SCHOOL OF QUITO (COLEGIO AMERICANO DE QUITO)

This private coed primary/secondary school and junior college was founded in 1939. Current enrollment is 2,754; 19% of the faculty are U.S. nationals. The school exchanges teachers with Locke Haven University.

Language of Instruction: English and Spanish.
Opportunities: *General:* 8–10 full-time positions. *ESL:* 4–5 full-time positions. *Administrators:* About 1 full-time position.
Requirements for General Teachers: Bachelor's degree in subject taught is required; master's degree is preferred. 2 years of teaching experience is preferred. Teaching certificate is required. International experience is preferred. Language proficiency in Spanish is preferred.
Requirements for ESL Teachers: Bachelor's degree in English or ESL is required; master's degree is preferred. 2 years of teaching experience is preferred. International experience is preferred. Language proficiency in Spanish is preferred.
Requirements for Administrators: Master's degree in educational leadership or administration/supervision is required. 2 years of administrative experience is required. International experience is preferred. Language proficiency in Spanish is required.
Duration: 2 years; renewable for 2 years.
Salary: *Teachers:* $200 plus 60,000–75,000 sucres per month. *Administrators:* $200 plus 140,000 sucres per month.
Benefits: Round-trip transportation from U.S. for appointee only. Health insurance. Other benefits are provided.
Academic Calendar: October–July.
Orientation: 2 weeks in Quito.
Application Deadline: March–April.
Contact: Mary V. Sanchez, Director, Colegio Americano/American School of Quito, P.O. Box 157, Quito, Ecuador. *Phone:* (593-2) 472-972/975, Ext. 214. *Telex:* FTONIA 24029. *Cable:* AMERSCH.

EL SALVADOR

SAN SALVADOR

343 ESCUELA AMERICANA

This private coed primary/secondary school was founded in 1946. Current enrollment is 1,640; 50% of the faculty are U.S. nationals.
Language of Instruction: *Primary:* English. *Other:* Spanish.
Opportunities: *General:* 10–15 full-time positions. *ESL:* 2–3 full-time positions. *Administrators:* 1–2 full-time positions.
Requirements for General Teachers: Bachelor's degree is required. 2 years of teaching experience is preferred. Teaching certificate is required. International experience is preferred. Language proficiency in Spanish on the beginning level is preferred.
Requirements for ESL Teachers: Bachelor's degree is required; master's degree is preferred. 2 years of teaching experience is preferred. International experience is preferred. Language proficiency in Spanish on the intermediate level is preferred.
Requirements for Administrators: Master's degree is required. 2 years of administrative experience is preferred. Administrative certificate is required. International experience is preferred. Language proficiency in Spanish on the intermediate level is preferred.
Duration: 2 years; renewable annually.
Salary: *Teachers:* $12,000 per year. *Administrators:* $18,000 per year.
Benefits: Round-trip transportation from U.S. for appointee and 2 dependents. Housing allowance. Paid home leave every 2 years. Health and life insurance. Other benefits are provided.
Academic Calendar: August–May.
Application Deadline: January.
Contact: Larry D. Smith, Superintendent, Escuela Americana, P.O. Box 01-35, San Salvador, El Salvador. *Phone:* (503) 23-4353.

GUATEMALA

GUATEMALA CITY

344 AMERICAN SCHOOL OF GUATEMALA

This private coed primary/secondary school with a special education program was founded in 1945. Current enrollment is 1,400. The school is registered with International Schools Services (see listing 4).
Language of Instruction: *Primary:* Spanish. *Other:* English.
Opportunities: *General:* Full-time positions. *ESL:* 8 full-time positions. *Administrators:* None.
Requirements for General Teachers: Bachelor's degree is required. Teaching experience is preferred. Language proficiency in Spanish on the intermediate level is preferred.
Requirements for ESL Teachers: Bachelor's degree is required. Language proficiency in Spanish is preferred.
Duration: 1 year; not renewable.
Salary: $7,600 per academic year.
Benefits: Round-trip transportation from U.S. for appointee only. School assists in locating housing. Paid home leave. Health and life insurance. Retirement plan. Other benefits are provided.
Academic Calendar: January–October.
Contact: George G. Miller, Director, The American School of Guatemala, c/o U.S. Embassy/Guatemala, APO Miami, FL 34024. *Phone:* In Guatemala: (502-2) 690791-5. *Cable:* AMSCHOOL.

GUYANA

GEORGETOWN

345 GEORGETOWN AMERICAN SCHOOL

This private coed primary school was founded in 1971. Current enrollment is 58; 36% of the faculty are U.S. nationals.
Language of Instruction: English.
Opportunities: *General:* Positions. *ESL:* None. *Administrators:* 1 position.
Requirements for Administrators: Administrative experience is preferred. International experience is preferred.
Duration: 1 year; renewable for 1 year.
Salary: *Teachers:* $8,916–$12,612 per academic year. *Administrators:* $17,495 per calendar year.
Benefits: Reduced tuition for dependents.
Academic Calendar: September–June.
Contact: Mrs. Kala Seegopaul, Administrative Assistant, Georgetown American School, Georgetown, Department of State, Washington, DC 20520-3170. *Phone:* (592-2) 61595.

HAITI

PORT-AU-PRINCE

346 HAITIAN-AMERICAN INSTITUTE

This private coed adult/continuing education school was founded in 1942. Current enrollment is 1,000; 30% of the faculty are U.S. nationals. Faculty are recruited from permanent residents in Haiti.
Language of Instruction: *Primary:* English. *Other:* Creole.
Opportunities: *General:* None. *ESL:* 3 full- and part-time positions. *Administrators:* 1 full- or part-time position.
Requirements for Teachers: Bachelor's degree in English, social science, or education is required; master's degree in TESL/TEFL is preferred; doctor's degree in English or education is preferred. Teaching experience is required. International experience is required. Language proficiency in French or Creole on the beginning level is preferred.
Requirements for Administrators: Master's degree in educational administration or EFL is required; doctor's degree in educational administration or English is preferred. 5 years of administrative experience is required. International experience is required. Language proficiency in French or Creole on the intermediate level is required.
Salary: *Teachers:* $100–$126 per 1-hour class per month.

All information is subject to change without notice and must be confirmed directly with the employer.

66

Benefits: School assists in locating housing. Health insurance. Other benefits are provided.
Academic Calendar: January–December.
Orientation: 1 month on-site.
Contact: Eleanor Snare, Director, Haitian-American Institute, Angle Rue Capois et Rue St. Cyr, Port-au-Prince, Haiti. *Phone:* (509-1) 2-3715/4608.

HONDURAS

PUERTO CORTES

347 SAINT JOHN'S EPISCOPAL BILINGUAL SCHOOL
This private coed primary/secondary school was founded in 1974. Current enrollment is 250; 33% of the faculty are U.S. nationals.
Language of Instruction: *Primary:* English. *Other:* Spanish.
Opportunities: *General:* 5–6 full-time positions for teachers of all subjects. *ESL:* 5–6 full-time positions. *Administrators:* 1 full-time position.
Requirements for General Teachers: Bachelor's degree in subject taught is preferred. 2–3 years of teaching experience is preferred, although some recent graduates are accepted. Language proficiency in Spanish on the beginning level is preferred.
Requirements for ESL Teachers: Bachelor's or master's degree in English or education is preferred. 2–4 years of teaching experience is required. Language proficiency in Spanish on the beginning level is preferred.
Requirements for Administrators: Bachelor's degree is required; master's degree in administration is preferred. 3–4 years of administrative experience is preferred. International experience is preferred. Language proficiency in Spanish on the intermediate level is preferred.
Duration: 1–3 years; renewable for 1–3 years.
Salary: *Teachers:* $300–$400 per month. *Administrators:* $500–$600 per month.
Benefits: School assists in locating housing.
Academic Calendar: September–June.
Orientation: 1 month with the voluntary Episcopal Commission in New Jersey.
Application Deadline: May 30.
Contact: William S. Craigie, Headmaster, Saint John's Episcopal Bilingual School, Apartado Postal #16, Puerto Cortes, Honduras. *Phone:* (504) 55-02-00.

SAN PEDRO SULA

348 ESCUELA INTERNATIONAL SAMPEDRANO
This private coed pre-K and primary/secondary school was founded in 1946. Current enrollment is 1,100; 25% of the faculty are U.S. nationals.
Language of Instruction: *Primary:* English. *Other:* Spanish.
Opportunities: *General:* 20 full-time positions. *ESL:* 2 full-time positions. *Administrators:* 3 full-time positions.
Requirements for General Teachers: Bachelor's degree in elementary or secondary education is required; master's degree is preferred. Teaching experience is required. Teaching certificate is required. International experience is preferred. Language proficiency in Spanish is preferred.
Requirements for Administrators: Master's degree in administration and supervision is required. Administrative experience is preferred. International experience is preferred. Language proficiency in Spanish is preferred.
Duration: 2 years; renewable for 2 years.
Salary: *Teachers:* $11,000–$14,000 per academic year. *Administrators:* $1,500 per month.
Benefits: Round-trip transportation from U.S. for appointee and dependents. Paid home leave every 2 years. Health and life insurance. Other benefits are provided.
Academic Calendar: August–June.
Application Deadline: March.

Contact: Gregory Werner, Superintendant, Escuela International Sampedrano, Apartado #565, San Pedro Sula, Honduras. *Phone:* (504) 53-3677.

TEGUCIGALPA

349 AMERICAN SCHOOL IN TEGUCIGALPA
This private coed pre-K and primary/secondary school was founded in 1946. Current enrollment is 985; 37% of the faculty are U.S. nationals.
Language of Instruction: *Primary:* English. *Other:* Spanish.
Opportunities: *General:* 10 full- and part-time positions. *ESL:* 2 full-time positions. *Administrators:* 1 full-time position.
Requirements for General Teachers: Bachelor's degree in pre-school or elementary education, or subject taught is required. 2 years of teaching experience is preferred. Teaching certificate is required. International experience is preferred.
Requirements for ESL Teachers: Bachelor's degree in English is required. 2 years of teaching experience is preferred. Teaching certificate is required. International experience is preferred. Language proficiency in Spanish is preferred.
Requirements for Administrators: Master's degree in education is required; 15 graduate hours beyond master's degree in school administration is required. Administrative experience is required. International experience is preferred. Language proficiency in Spanish is preferred.
Duration: 2 years; renewable indefinitely.
Salary: *Teachers:* $10,525–$17,237 per academic year. *Administrators:* $18,000 per calendar year.
Benefits: Round-trip transportation from U.S. for administrative appointee only. Housing allowance. School assists in locating housing. Paid home leave every 2 years. Health insurance. Tuition discount for children enrolled at this school. Other benefits are provided.
Academic Calendar: August–June.
Application Deadline: Dec. 15.
Contact: Matilde A. Izaguirre, Director, American School, c/o U.S. Embassy, Tegucigalpa, Honduras. *Phone:* (504) 32-4696.

JAMAICA

KINGSTON

350 PRIORY SCHOOL
This private coed pre-K and primary/secondary school was founded in 1944. Current enrollment is 541; 2% of the faculty are U.S. nationals.
Language of Instruction: English.
Opportunities: *General:* 4 full-time positions for teachers of all subjects, special education, and a college guidance counselor. *ESL:* 1 full-time position. *Administrators:* None.
Requirements for General Teachers: Bachelor's degree is required. Teaching experience is required. International experience is preferred.
Requirements for ESL Teachers: Bachelor's degree is required. Teaching experience is required. International experience is preferred. Language proficiency in Spanish on the intermediate level is preferred.
Duration: 2 years; renewable annually.
Salary: $7,000–$10,000 per calendar year.
Benefits: School assists in locating housing. Health, accident, and life insurance. Pension plan. Other benefits are provided.
Academic Calendar: September–August.
Application Deadline: April.
Contact: Patrick C. Bourke, Director, The Priory School, 32 Hope Road, Kingston 10, Jamaica. *Phone:* (809) 926-4764.

MEXICO

CUERNAVACA

351 COLEGIO INTERNACIONAL DE CUERNAVACA
This private coed primary school was founded in 1975. Current enrollment is 200; 50% of the faculty are U.S. nationals.
Language of Instruction: *Primary:* English. *Other:* Spanish.

Opportunities: *General:* 6–7 full-time positions. *ESL:* 4–5 positions. *Administrators:* Less than 1 position per year.
Requirements for General Teachers: Bachelor's, master's, or doctor's degree is preferred.
Requirements for ESL Teachers: Bachelor's degree is preferred.
Requirements for Administrators: Bachelor's degree is preferred.
Duration: 1–2 years; renewable.
Salary: Varies.
Benefits: School assists in locating housing. Other benefits are provided.
Academic Calendar: September–June.
Orientation: On-site.
Application Deadline: July.
Contact: Yvonne Leonard Flores, Director, Colegio Internacional de Cuernavaca, Apartado Postal 1334, Cuernavaca, Mexico. *Phone:* (73) 13-29-05/13-08-30.

GUADALAJARA

352 AMERICAN SCHOOL FOUNDATION OF GUADALAJARA
This private coed primary/secondary school and adult/continuing education program was founded in 1956. Current enrollment is 1,150; 40% of the faculty are U.S. nationals.
Language of Instruction: *Primary:* English. *Other:* Spanish and French.
Opportunities: *Teachers:* 20 positions. *Administrators:* None.
Requirements for General Teachers: Bachelor's degree is required. 2 years of teaching experience is preferred. Teaching certificate is required. International experience is preferred.
Requirements for ESL Teachers: Bachelor's degree in English is preferred. 2 years of teaching experience is preferred. Foreign language proficiency on the intermediate level is preferred.
Academic Calendar: September–June.
Contact: Director, American School Foundation of Guadalajara, Apartado Postal 6-1074, Guadalajara, Mexico.

MEXICO CITY

353 AMERICAN SCHOOL FOUNDATION
This private coed pre-K and primary/secondary school was founded in 1888; a small facility for students with learning disabilities was added in 1983. Current enrollment is 2,000; 60% of the faculty are U.S. nationals.
Language of Instruction: *Primary:* English and Spanish. *Other:* French · and Italian.
Opportunities: *General:* About 20 full-time positions annually for elementary school teachers; accounting, English, computer science, mathematics, science, social studies, gymnastics, and physical education teachers on the secondary level; and special education. *ESL:* About 10 full-time positions. *Administrators:* Full-time positions, especially for counselors and high school principal.
Requirements for General Teachers: Bachelor's degree in subject taught is required. 1–2 years of teaching experience is preferred. International experience is preferred.
Requirements for ESL Teachers: Bachelor's degree in linguistics or TESL is required. 1–2 years of teaching experience is preferred. International experience is preferred.
Requirements for Administrators: Master's degree is required; doctor's degree is required for superintendent. Previous administrative or counseling experience is required. International experience is preferred.
Duration: 1 year; renewable indefinitely.
Salary: *Teachers:* 733,000–1,430,000 pesos per month, depending on training and experience. *Administrators:* Varies.
Benefits: Round-trip transportation from U.S. for appointee only. Housing for appointee and dependents. Tuition discounts for dependent children. Paid home leave every 2 years. Health and life insurance. Other benefits.
Academic Calendar: September–June.
Orientation: 2 weeks on-site.
Application Deadline: Open; most hiring done in May.
Contact: Personnel Officer, American School Foundation, Bondojito 215, Tacubaya, 01120 Mexico D.F., Mexico. *Phone:* (90-5) 516-07-20.

354 GREENGATES SCHOOL
This private coed primary/secondary school was founded in 1951. Current enrollment is 880; 15% of the faculty are U.S. nationals. Faculty are recruited from those presently residing in Mexico.
Language of Instruction: English.
Opportunities: *Teachers:* Full-time positions. *Administrators:* Positions available.
Contact: Susan Martinez-Mayer, Principal, Greengates School, Apartado Postal 41-659, 11000 Mexico D.F., Mexico. *Phone:* (90-5) 373-0088.

355 INSTITUTO MEXICANO NORTEAMERICANO DE RELACIONES CULTURALES
This private coed binational center was founded in 1943. Current enrollment is 7,000; 40% of the faculty are U.S. nationals.
Language of Instruction: English and Spanish.
Opportunities: *General:* None. *ESL:* 3–4 full-time positions. *Administrators:* Less than 1 position per year.
Requirements for Teachers: Bachelor's or master's degree in TESOL/education/English is preferred. 3 years of teaching experience is required. International experience is preferred. Language proficiency in Spanish is preferred. Knowledge of Mexican culture, history, and lifestyles is required.
Requirements for Administrators: Bachelor's or master's degree in education/business administration is preferred. 3–5 years of administrative experience is required. International experience is preferred. Language proficiency in Spanish on the intermediate level is preferred. Knowledge of Mexican culture, history, and lifestyles is required.
Duration: 2 years; renewable indefinitely.
Salary: *Teachers:* $5,700 per calendar year. *Administrators:* $9,000 per calendar year.
Benefits: Health care. Life insurance. Other benefits are provided.
Academic Calendar: January–December.
Application Deadline: Open.
Contact: Barbara de los Reyes, Director of Courses, Instituto Mexicano Norteamericano de Relaciones Culturales, Hamburgo No. 115, 06600 Mexico, D.F., Mexico. *Phone:* (90-5) 525-3357.

356 UNITED STATES INTERNATIONAL UNIVERSITY— MEXICO
This private coed university, founded in 1952, is also known as the Universidad Internacional de Mexico. Current enrollment is 100; 33% of the faculty are U.S. nationals.
Language of Instruction: English.
Opportunities: *General:* Part-time positions for teachers of business administration, international relations, and social psychology. *ESL:* 1 part-time position. *Administrators:* 1 full-time position.
Requirements for General Teachers: Master's or doctor's degree in subject taught is required. Teaching experience is preferred.
Requirements for ESL Teachers: Bachelor's degree in TESL is required; master's degree is preferred. Teaching or practical experience is preferred. International experience is preferred. Language proficiency in Spanish is preferred.
Requirements for Administrators: Doctor's degree is required. Previous administrative experience is required. International experience is preferred. Language proficiency in Spanish on the advanced level is preferred.
Duration: 10 weeks; renewable indefinitely.
Salary: *Teachers:* $700 per course. *Administrators:* Varies.
Benefits: University assists in locating housing.
Academic Calendar: September–August.
Application Deadline: Rolling.
Contact: Noel Osborn, Director, United States International University—Mexico, La Otra Banda 40, 01090 Mexico, D.F., Mexico. *Phone:* (90-5) 548-7646/550-4073. *Telex:* 1771300 (for UIM).

PUEBLA

357 UNIVERSIDAD POPULAR AUTONOMA DEL ESTADO DE PUEBLA
This private coed university was founded in 1973. Current enrollment is 5,000; 0.002% of the faculty are U.S. nationals. The university exchanges faculty with the University of Southern California.
Language of Instruction: Spanish.

All information is subject to change without notice
and must be confirmed directly with the employer

Opportunities: *General:* Positions available. *ESL:* None. *Administrators:* None.
Requirements: Language proficiency in Spanish is preferred.
Duration: 6 months; renewable.
Salary: $300 per month.
Benefits: University assists in locating housing. Other benefits are provided.
Academic Calendar: January–July and August–December.
Orientation: 1 week on-site.
Contact: Ing. Urbano Ponee, Director, 21 Sur 1103, 72000 Puebla (CP), Mexico. *Phone:* (22) 42-59-21, Ext. 20.

XALAPA

358 UNIVERSIDAD VERACRUZANA
This public coed university and adult/continuing education program was founded in 1946. Current enrollment is 77,000; 0.1% of the faculty are U.S. nationals.
Language of Instruction: *Primary:* Spanish. *Other:* English.
Opportunities: *General:* None. *ESL:* Part-time positions. *Administrators:* None.
Requirements: Doctor's degree is required.
Duration: 6 months; renewable for 6 months.
Benefits: Housing allowance. Health and accident insurance. Other benefits are provided.
Academic Calendar: September–July.
Orientation: On-site.
Contact: Universidad Veracruzana, Lomas del Estadio s/n, Xalapa, Veracruz, Mexico. *Phone:* (29) 7-94-83.

NICARAGUA

MANAGUA

359 AMERICAN-NICARAGUAN SCHOOL
This private coed primary/secondary school was founded in 1939. Current enrollment is 580; 40% of the faculty are U.S. nationals.
Language of Instruction: *Primary:* English. *Other:* Spanish.
Opportunities: *General:* 4–7 full-time positions. *ESL:* Less than 1 position per year. *Administrators:* Less than 1 position per year.
Requirements for General Teachers: Bachelor's degree in primary or secondary education is required; master's degree is preferred. 2 years of teaching experience or student/intern teaching experience is preferred. Teaching certificate is required. International experience is preferred. Language proficiency in Spanish on the beginning level is preferred.
Requirements for ESL Teachers: Bachelor's degree is required. 2 years of teaching experience is required. Teaching certificate is required. International experience is preferred. Language proficiency in Spanish is required.
Requirements for Administrators: Master's degree in administration/supervision is required; doctor's degree is preferred. 5 years of administrative experience is required. Administrative certificate is required. Language proficiency in Spanish is preferred.
Duration: 2 years; renewable for 2-year periods.
Salary: *Teachers:* $8,000–$10,000 per calendar year. *Administrators:* $25,000–$35,000 per calendar year.
Benefits: Round-trip transportation from U.S. for appointee and dependents. Housing allowance. Paid leave to Miami every 2 years. Health insurance. Other benefits are provided.
Academic Calendar: August–July.
Orientation: 3 days on-site.
Application Deadline: Nov. 1.
Contact: Richard C. Chesley, Director, American-Nicaraguan School, P.O. Box 2670, Managua, Nicaragua. *Phone:* (505-2) 70111/2/3.

PANAMA

MORE THAN ONE CITY

360 EMBASSY OF PANAMA
The Embassy reports that there is no need for U.S. teachers or educational administrators at this time.
Language of Instruction: *Primary:* Spanish. *Other:* English and French.
Academic Calendar: April–December.
For General Information, Contact: Embassy of Panama, 2862 McGill Terrace NW, Washington, DC 20008.

PERU

MORE THAN ONE CITY

361 COMMISSION FOR EDUCATIONAL EXCHANGE BETWEEN THE U.S.A. AND PERU (FULBRIGHT COMMISSION)
USIA Fulbright Scholar Program.
Opportunities: 2–3 positions for educational administrators, educational psychology, and curriculum development on the university level.
Requirements: Bachelor's degree is required; master's or doctor's degree is preferred. Teaching experience is preferred. Language proficiency in Spanish on the intermediate or advanced level is preferred.
Duration: 5 months; renewable for 3 months.
Salary: $1,500–$2,000.
Benefits: Round-trip transportation from U.S. for appointee only. Health and accident insurance. Other benefits are provided.
Orientation: 1 day in Lima.
Application Deadline: June 30.
Contact: Council for International Exchange of Scholars, 11 Dupont Circle NW, Suite 300, Washington, DC 20036. *Phone:* (202) 939-5401.

LIMA

362 AMERICAN SCHOOL OF LIMA (COLEGIO ROOSEVELT)
This private coed primary/secondary school was founded in 1947. Current enrollment is 1,215; 45% of the faculty are U.S. nationals.
Language of Instruction: *Primary:* English. *Other:* Spanish.
Opportunities: *General:* 8 full-time positions. *ESL:* None. *Administrators:* 1 full-time position.
Requirements for Teachers: Bachelor's degree is required; master's degree is preferred. 2 years of teaching experience is required. International experience is preferred.
Requirements for Administrators: Master's degree is required. Administrative experience is required. International experience is preferred.
Duration: 2 years; renewable yearly.
Salary: *Teachers:* $10,000–$19,000 per year. *Administrators:* From $25,000 per calendar year.
Benefits: Round-trip transportation from U.S. for appointee only. Housing allowance. Paid home leave every 2 years if contract is renewed. Health insurance.
Academic Calendar: August–June.
Application Deadline: Rolling.
Contact: Dr. Fred J. Pasquale, Superintendent, American School of Lima, Apartado 18-0977 Miraflores, Lima 18, Peru. *Phone:* (51-14) 35-08-90.

PUERTO RICO

MORE THAN ONE CITY

363 DEPARTMENTO DE INSTRUCCION PUBLICA
The Department of Public Instruction reports that there is no need for U.S. teachers or educational administrators at this time.
For General Information, Contact: Departamento de Instruccion Publica, Hato Rey, Puerto Rico 00919.

All information is subject to change without notice and must be confirmed directly with the employer.

69

BAYAMON

364 CARIBBEAN UNIVERSITY COLLEGE
This private coed university was founded in 1969.
Language of Instruction: *Primary:* Spanish. *Other:* English.
Opportunities: *General:* Full- and part-time positions. *ESL:* Full- and part-time positions. *Administrators:* Full- and part-time positions.
Requirements for General Teachers: Master's degree is required; doctor's degree is preferred. 1 year of teaching experience is preferred. Language proficiency in Spanish is required.
Requirements for ESL Teachers: Master's degree in education or English is required; doctor's degree is preferred. 1 year of teaching experience is required. Language proficiency in Spanish on the beginning or intermediate level is required.
Requirements for Administrators: Bachelor's degree is required; master's degree is preferred. 1 year of administrative experience is preferred. Language proficiency in Spanish is required.
Duration: 4 months; renewable.
Salary: *Teachers:* $886–$995 per month. *Administrators:* $1,000–$1,700 per month.
Benefits: Health and life insurance. Other benefits are provided.
Academic Calendar: January–December.
Contact: Francisco Batista, Personnel Director, Caribbean University College, Box 493, Bayamon, Puerto Rico 00621. *Phone:* (809) 780-0070, Ext. 204/205.

MAYAGUEZ

365 SOUTHWESTERN EDUCATIONAL SOCIETY
This private coed primary/secondary school was founded in 1973. Current enrollment is 560; 4% of the faculty are U.S. nationals.
Language of Instruction: *Primary:* English. *Other:* Spanish.
Opportunities: *General:* 1 full-time position. *ESL:* 1 full-time position. *Administrators:* 1 full-time position.
Requirements for General Teachers: Bachelor's degree is required. Teaching experience is required. Teacher's certificate is required. International experience is preferred. Language proficiency in Spanish is preferred.
Requirements for ESL Teachers: Bachelor's degree is required. Teaching experience is required. Teacher's certificate is required. Language proficiency in Spanish is preferred.
Requirements for Administrators: Bachelor's degree is required; master's degree in counseling is preferred. Administrative experience is required. Administrative certificate is required. Language proficiency in Spanish is preferred.
Duration: 1 years; renewable.
Salary: *Teachers:* $8,000–$9,769 per academic year. *Administrators:* Varies.
Benefits: School assists in locating housing. Health insurance. Other benefits are provided.
Academic Calendar: August–May.
Orientation: On-site.
Application Deadline: March.
Contact: Elena Martinez, Principal, Southwestern Educational Society, P.O. Box 40, Mayaguez, Puerto Rico 00709. *Phone:* (809) 834-2150/833-6823.

TRINIDAD

MORE THAN ONE CITY

366 MINISTRY OF EDUCATION
The Ministry reports that there is no need for U.S. teachers or educational administrators at this time.
For General Information, Contact: Ministry of Education, Alexandra Street, St. Clair, Port-of-Spain, Trinidad. *Phone:* (809) 622-2815.

U.S. VIRGIN ISLANDS

ST. THOMAS

367 ANTILLES SCHOOL
This private coed primary/secondary school was founded in 1950. Current enrollment is 355; 85% of the faculty are U.S. nationals.
Language of Instruction: English.
Opportunities: *General:* 3–6 positions for teachers of specific secondary subjects, self-contained primary classes, U.S. college-preparatory curriculum, and reading specialists for students with minor learning disabilities. *ESL:* None. *Administrators:* None.
Requirements: Bachelor's degree in subject taught is required; master's or doctor's degree is preferred. 3 years of teaching experience is preferred.
Duration: 1 year; renewable.
Salary: $15,500–$17,000 per year.
Benefits: Health and life insurance. Retirement plan.
Academic Calendar: September–June.
Application Deadline: February–April.
Contact: Headmaster, Antilles School, P.O. Box 7280, St. Thomas, VI 00801.

368 UNIVERSITY OF THE VIRGIN ISLANDS
This public coed university was founded in 1962. Current enrollment is 2,500; 80% of the faculty are U.S. nationals.
Language of Instruction: English.
Opportunities: *General:* 10 full- and part-time positions. *ESL:* None. *Administrators:* 2 full- and part-time positions.
Duration: 1–3 years; renewable.
Salary: *Teachers:* $24,114–$45,824 per academic year. *Administrators:* $28,679–$64,782 per calendar year.
Benefits: Round-trip transportation from U.S. for appointee and dependents. Other benefits are provided.
Academic Calendar: August–June.
Application Deadline: Varies.
Contact: William P. MacLean, Vice President for Academic Affairs, University of the Virgin Islands, St. Thomas, VI 00802. *Phone:* (809) 776-9200. *Telex:* 3470102 UVI.

URUGUAY

MONTEVIDEO

369 URUGUAYAN AMERICAN SCHOOL
This private coed primary/secondary school was founded in 1959. Current enrollment is 200; 25% of the faculty are U.S. nationals.
Language of Instruction: *Primary:* English. *Other:* Spanish and French.
Opportunities: *General:* 2 full- and part-time positions for teachers of self-contained classes, remedial reading, and mathematics on the primary level, and U.S. history, social studies, mathematics, and sciences on the secondary level. *ESL:* None. *Administrators:* Less than 1 position per year.
Requirements for Teachers: Bachelor's degree in subject taught is required; master's degree in subject taught or education is preferred. 3 years of teaching experience is required. International experience is preferred. Language proficiency in Spanish on the beginning level is preferred.
Requirements for Administrators: Master's degree in administration is required; doctor's degree is preferred. 5 years of administrative experience is required. International experience is preferred. Language proficiency in Spanish on the intermediate level is preferred.
Duration: 2 years; renewable for 2 years.
Salary: *Teachers:* $10,000–$15,000 per calendar year. *Administrators:* $25,000–$35,000 per calendar year.
Benefits: Round-trip transportation from U.S. for appointee and dependents. Paid home leave every 2 years. Health insurance.
Academic Calendar: August–June.
Application Deadline: January.
Contact: William F. Johnston, Director, Uruguayan American School, Administrative Officer (UAS), U.S. Embassy/Montevideo, Washington, DC 20520-3360. *Phone:* In Uruguay: (598-2) 50 63 16/50 76 81.

VENEZUELA

CARACAS

370 ESCUELA CAMPO ALEGRE
This private coed primary/secondary school was founded in 1937. Current enrollment is 850; 75% of the faculty are U.S. nationals.
Language of Instruction: *Primary:* English. *Other:* Spanish and French.
Opportunities: *General:* 1–4 positions. *ESL:* None. *Administrators:* None.
Requirements for General Teachers: Bachelor's degree in education is required; master's or doctor's degree is preferred. 2 years of teaching experience is required. International experience is preferred.
Duration: 2 years; renewable.
Benefits: Round-trip transportation from U.S. for appointee only. Health insurance. Tuition benefits for dependent children. Other benefits are provided.
Academic Calendar: August–June.
Orientation: 3–4 days on-site.
Application Deadline: March–April.
Contact: Dr. George G. Takacs, Superintendent, Escuela Campo Alegre, Apdo. del Este 60382, Caracas 1060-A, Venezuela. *Phone:* (58-2) 92 47 31. *Cable:* ESCAAL.

VALENCIA

371 COLEGIO INTERNACIONAL DE CARABOBO
This is a private coed primary/secondary school. Current enrollment is 300; 83% of the faculty are U.S. nationals. Positions available for single teachers or teaching couples without dependents.
Language of Instruction: *Primary:* English. *Other:* Spanish.
Opportunities: *General:* 6–10 positions. *ESL:* None. *Administrators:* None.
Requirements: Bachelor's degree in subject taught is required; master's degree is preferred. 3 years of teaching experience is required.
Duration: 1 year; renewable.
Salary: $15,000–$22,000 per year.
Benefits: Round-trip transportation from U.S. for appointee only. Housing for appointee only. Health insurance.
Academic Calendar: August–June.
Orientation: 1 week on-site.
Application Deadline: January.
Contact: Frank Anderson, Colegio Internacional de Carabobo, Apdo. 103, Valencia, Venezuela.

TEACHING ABROAD

PART 2

Study Opportunities Abroad for Teachers

WORLDWIDE

372 AFS INTERNATIONAL INTERCULTURAL PROGRAMS
AFS Teachers Programs.
Location: Argentina, Chile, China, Costa Rica, Peru, Thailand, USSR.
Dates: 7-week, 10-week, and 1-year programs.
Subjects: Culture, education system, language of host country.
Credit: Graduate credit available.
Eligibility: Teachers, adults. Minimum/maximum age requirements for some programs. Requires strong interest in area studies, social studies, or education.
Instruction: In English or language of host country. Students attend classes arranged for the group, special courses for foreigners, and teaching assignments in foreign schools.
Highlights: 3-day orientation. Excursions and field trips.
Costs: Depend upon program selected and length of stay.
Housing: In residence halls, private homes.
Deadline: April 1; June 1/Jan. 31 for China.
Contact: Craig H. Brown, Program Information Manager, or Carol Byrne, Program Administrator, AFS, 313 E. 43rd St., New York, NY 10017. *Phone:* (800) AFS-INFO/(212) 949-4242. *Telex:* (ITT) 424031 AFSI UI; (WUI) AFSIUI 666379 UW.

373 SIVANANDA YOGA VEDANTA CENTER
Yoga Teachers Training Course.
Location: Bahamas, Canada, India.
Dates: 4 weeks: July in Quebec; January in Trivandrum, India; February in Nassau, Bahamas.
Subjects: Yoga philosophy, physiology, Bhagavad Gita, chanting, meditation.
Credit: None.
Eligibility: Adults. Average age 35.
Instruction: In English, French, Spanish, German. Students attend regular classes at local branch of Center.
Highlights: Program began in 1969.
Costs: $500 for 4 weeks in India, $800 for 4 weeks in Canada and Bahamas, includes tuition, meals, books.
Housing: In tents (participants furnish their own).
Deadline: Until program is filled.
Contact: Sivananda Yoga Vedanta Center, 243 W. 24th St., New York, NY 10011.

373A U.S. DEPARTMENT OF EDUCATION
Fulbright Seminars Abroad Program.
Location: Brazil, China, Egypt, India, Israel, Japan, Korea, Malaysia, Pakistan, Thailand, Yugoslavia; countries vary from year to year.
Dates: 4–8 weeks, summer.
Subjects: Education, focusing on the social sciences, humanities, and social studies.
Credit: None.
Eligibility: Secondary school teachers, college faculty, social studies curriculum specialists. Requires U.S. citizenship, bachelor's degree, 3 years of teaching or administrative experience and current position in social studies, humanities, or social sciences. Language proficiency required for Japan seminars.
Instruction: In English. Students attend courses arranged for the group.
Highlights: Program began in 1961. Briefings by experts in the field. Excursions and field trips.
Costs: Fulbright grant covers tuition, housing, meals, round-trip transportation, all travel in host country.
Housing: In hotels.
Deadline: October–Dec. 5.
Contact: Ms. Lungching Chiao, Senior Program Officer, Center for International Education, International Studies Branch, U.S. Department of Education (Mail Stop: 3308), 400 Maryland Ave. SW, Washington, DC 20202. *Phone:* (202) 732-3292/3.

374 UNIVERSITY OF CALIFORNIA, SANTA BARBARA EXTENSION
Expanding Your Classroom with Travel Study.
Location: Any country.
Dates: 10 days minimum.
Subjects: Any field.
Credit: 2–5 graduate quarter units.
Eligibility: Teachers, educators, librarians, administrators, graduates, adults.
Instruction: In English. Students attend independent study arrangements.
Highlights: Program began in 1977. Independent travel only.
Costs: $40 per quarter unit, includes tuition.
Housing: Students make own arrangements.
Deadline: Rolling admissions.
Contact: Lily Byall, Coordinator, Travel Study, University of California Extension, Santa Barbara, CA 93106. *Phone:* (805) 961-4200. *Or:* Steven Tash, Travel Study Instructor, University of California, P.O. Box 16501, Irvine, CA 92713. *Phone:* (714) 786-7857.

All program information is subject to change without notice
and must be confirmed directly with the sponsor.

73

AFRICA, SOUTH OF THE SAHARA

IVORY COAST

MORE THAN ONE CITY

375 **PARSONS SCHOOL OF DESIGN**
   Parsons in West Africa: Ivory Coast.
Location: Abidjan, Senufo and Baule regions.
Dates: About 4 weeks, July.
Subjects: African culture, archaeology, art history; African arts, including ceramics, fibers, metals, photography.
Credit: 6 undergraduate credits. Graduate credit available.
Eligibility: Undergraduates, graduates, teachers, professionals. Requires submission of portfolio for studio classes. Knowledge of French recommended.
Instruction: In English. Students attend courses arranged for the group taught by U.S. and foreign faculty.
Highlights: Program began in 1984. Offered in cooperation with the Society for International Exchange. 2-day orientation abroad. Excursions and field trips.
Costs: About $3,820 includes tuition, housing, some meals, round-trip transportation, excursions, fees.
Housing: In residence halls, hotels.
Deadline: April 15.
Contact: Office of Special Programs, Parsons School of Design, 66 Fifth Ave., New York, NY 10011. *Phone:* (212) 741-8975.

MALI

MORE THAN ONE CITY

376 **PARSONS SCHOOL OF DESIGN**
   Parsons in West Africa: Mali.
Location: Bamako, Djenne, Dogon country, Mopti, Timbuctou.
Dates: About 3 weeks, August.
Subjects: History of African art and architecture.
Credit: 4 undergraduate credits. Graduate credit available.
Eligibility: Undergraduates, graduates, teachers, professionals. Requires submission of portfolio for studio classes. Knowledge of French recommended.
Instruction: In English. Students attend courses arranged for the group taught by U.S. and foreign faculty.
Highlights: Program began in 1984. Offered in cooperation with the Society for International Exchange. 2-day orientation in Abidjan, Ivory Coast. Excursions and field trips.
Costs: About $3,750 includes tuition, housing, some meals, round-trip transportation, excursions, fees.
Housing: In residence halls, hotels, camps.
Deadline: April 15.
Contact: Office of Special Programs, Parsons School of Design, 66 Fifth Ave., New York, NY 10011. *Phone:* (212) 741-8975.

All program information is subject to change without notice
and must be confirmed directly with the sponsor.

75

ASIA AND OCEANIA

AUSTRALIA

MELBOURNE

377 UNIVERSITY OF LOUISVILLE, INTERNATIONAL CENTER
Education in Australia.
Location: Melbourne.
Dates: 2 weeks, July 7–22.
Subjects: Special education and reading.
Credit: 6 undergraduate credits. 6 graduate credits.
Eligibility: Juniors, seniors, graduates, adults, teachers, educators. Requires approval of instructors.
Instruction: In English. Students attend courses arranged for the group taught by U.S. and foreign faculty.
Highlights: Program begins in 1988. 3-day orientation in U.S. and abroad. Excursions.
Costs: Contact sponsor for information.
Housing: In residence halls.
Deadline: April 15.
Contact: Arthur Neisberg, Coordinator of International Programs, University of Louisville, International Center, Louisville, KY 40292. *Phone:* (502) 588-6602.

NEWCASTLE

378 UNIVERSITY OF NEWCASTLE
Master/Bachelor of Educational Studies.
Location: Newcastle.
Dates: February–October; students must enroll for entire period.
Subjects: Education, including history, philosophy, psychology, and sociology of education, educational administration, computers in education, curriculum studies.
Credit: Degree.
Eligibility: Graduates, adults, teachers. Requires bachelor's degree with major in education or teacher training course.
Instruction: In English. Students attend regular classes at the University of Newcastle.
Highlights: Program began in 1976. Contact with previous participants available.
Costs: About $500 per year, includes tuition, fees.
Housing: Sponsor assists in locating housing.
Deadline: Dec. 31.
Contact: The Faculty Secretary, Faculty of Education, University of Newcastle, Newcastle, N.S.W. 2308, Australia. *Phone:* (61-49) 685417.

CHINA/HONG KONG

MORE THAN ONE CITY

379 COUNCIL ON INTERNATIONAL EDUCATIONAL EXCHANGE (CIEE)
U.S.-China Educator Exchange.
Location: Beijing, Hong Kong, Nanjing, Shanghai, Xi'an, and other cities.

Dates: 3 weeks, June–July.
Subjects: Study tour focusing on education in China.
Credit: None.
Eligibility: Teachers, and other professionals in the field of education. Requires good physical health.
Instruction: In English. Students attend study tour arranged for the group led by U.S. faculty.
Highlights: Program began in 1986. This is a reciprocal exchange program, offered in cooperation with the Chinese Education Association for International Exchanges (CEAIE). Visits to secondary schools, universities, teacher training institutes; meetings with Chinese teachers and students. Postsession review.
Costs: About $3,000 includes housing, most meals, round-trip transportation from the West Coast, excursions, fees.
Housing: In hotels.
Deadline: April 27.
Contact: U.S.-China Educator Exchange, Council on International Educational Exchange (CIEE), 205 E. 42nd St., New York, NY 10017. *Phone:* (212) 661-1414, Ext. 1207.

380 EASTERN MICHIGAN UNIVERSITY
Education in the Orient.
Location: Beijing, Chengdu, Guangzhou, Hong Kong, Kunming, Lhasa, Xi'an, Xigaze.
Dates: June 24–July 16.
Subjects: Teacher education.
Credit: 2 graduate credits.
Eligibility: Seniors, graduates, teachers, adults. Requires 2.0 GPA.
Instruction: In English. Students attend courses arranged for the group taught by U.S. and foreign faculty.
Highlights: Program begins in 1988. Orientation by mail in U.S. Excursions and field trips to schools, colleges, clinics, family service agencies, child care centers. Postsession review.
Costs: About $4,000 includes tuition, housing, meals, round-trip transportation, excursions, field trips, fees.
Housing: In hotels.
Deadline: April 1.
Contact: Dr. George Klein, Office of International Studies, Eastern Michigan University, 333 Goodison Hall, Ypsilanti, MI 48197. *Phone:* (313) 487-2424.

381 WESTERN WASHINGTON UNIVERSITY
Summer Studies in China: Educational Curriculum and Social Change.
Location: Beibei, Chongqing (Sichuan province).
Dates: 6 weeks, June 14–July 28.
Subjects: Beginning conversational Chinese language; Chinese history, culture, and educational system; teacher resource package, East Asian studies.
Credit: 12 undergraduate credits. 12 graduate credits available.
Eligibility: Juniors, seniors, graduates, adults, teachers, educators/administrators. Requires 2.5 GPA.
Instruction: In English. Students attend courses arranged for the group taught by U.S. and foreign faculty and special courses for foreigners at Southwest China Teachers University in Beibei or Chongqing University in Chongqing.
Highlights: Program began in 1987. Offered in cooperation with Southwest China Teachers University in Beibei and Chongqing University in Chongqing. 2-day orientation in U.S. Program-related

All program information is subject to change without notice and must be confirmed directly with the sponsor.

77

travel in China. Excursions and cultural events. Contact with previous participants available.
Costs: About $2,400 includes tuition, housing, some meals, round-trip transportation, most books, excursions, fees.
Housing: In furnished apartments.
Deadline: March 15.
Contact: Art Kimmel, Director, Foreign Study Office, Western Washington University, Old Main 400, Bellingham, WA 98225. *Phone:* (206) 676-3298/3299. *Or:* Dr. Roberta Wong Bouverat, Professor of Education, Western Washington University, Miller 324-B, Bellingham, WA 98225. *Phone:* (206) 676-3347.

BEIJING

382 STATE OF OREGON COLLEGES OF EDUCATION
Oregon Teacher Education Program in China.
Location: Beijing.
Dates: Sept. 1–Dec. 18.
Subjects: Beginning Chinese language; Chinese culture, history; education.
Credit: Undergraduate credit available. Graduate credit.
Eligibility: Sophomores, juniors, seniors, graduates. Requires 2.5 GPA.
Instruction: In English. Students attend courses arranged for the group taught by U.S. and foreign faculty and special courses for foreigners at Beijing Teachers College.
Highlights: Program began in 1986. 1-day orientation in U.S. Excursions. Program-related travel to Hangzhou, Shanghai, Xiamen. Contact with previous participants available.
Costs: About $3,472 includes housing, meals, round-trip transportation, books, excursions, fees.
Housing: In residence halls.
Deadline: April 1.
Contact: Dr. Christine Sproul or Shelly Black, Office of International Education, Oregon State System of Higher Education, Oregon State University, Corvallis, OR 97331. *Phone:* (503) 754-2394. *Telex:* 510-596-0682 OSU COVS.

HOHHOT

383 WESTERN WASHINGTON UNIVERSITY
Mongolian Language.
Location: Hohhot.
Dates: June 13–Aug. 6.
Subjects: Beginning and intermediate Mongolian language; beginning Chinese language.
Credit: Undergraduate credit available. No graduate credit.
Eligibility: Undergraduates, graduates, teachers, adults.
Instruction: In Mongolian, English. Students attend courses arranged for the group taught by foreign faculty at Inner Mongolia University.
Highlights: Program began in 1981. 3-day orientation in U.S. Program evaluations available to prospective participants. 1 week of program-related travel in grassland areas.
Costs: About $2,750 includes tuition, housing, meals, round-trip transportation, books, excursions, fees.
Housing: In residence halls, furnished rooms.
Deadline: March 1.
Contact: Prof. Henry G. Schwarz, Center for East Asian Studies, Western Washington University, Bellingham, WA 98225. *Phone:* (206) 676-3041.

XIAMEN

384 COUNCIL ON INTERNATIONAL EDUCATIONAL EXCHANGE (CIEE)
Views of China.
Location: Xiamen.
Dates: 3 weeks, April/May, with optional 2-week extensions.
Subjects: Chinese culture, history, traditional arts.
Credit: Certificate.
Eligibility: Adults, teachers. Requires good physical health.
Instruction: In English. Students attend courses arranged for the group taught by foreign faculty at Xiamen University.

Highlights: Program begins in 1988. Orientation in Hong Kong. Excursions and field trips. Optional program-related travel to (A) Beijing, Guangzhou, Guilin, Xi'an or (B) Yangzi River cruise, Beijing, Chongqing, Guangzhou, Wuhan. Postsession review.
Costs: About $2,260 includes tuition, housing, meals, round-trip transportation from the West Coast, excursions, fees; about $1,200 includes optional travel.
Housing: In hotels.
Deadline: Feb. 15, or until program is filled.
Contact: Professional and Secondary Education Programs, Council on International Educational Exchange (CIEE), 205 E. 42nd St., New York, NY 10017. *Phone:* (212) 661-1414, Ext. 1207.

XI'AN

385 UNIVERSITY OF MASSACHUSETTS AT AMHERST
Xi'an Summer Program.
Location: Xi'an.
Dates: Late June–early August.
Subjects: Chinese history and culture.
Credit: 4 undergraduate credits in history.
Eligibility: Undergraduates, graduates, teachers, university faculty.
Instruction: In English. Students attend special courses for foreigners.
Highlights: Program began in 1985. Extensive program-related travel in China. Contact with previous participants available.
Costs: $3,500 includes tuition, housing, meals, round-trip transportation, excursions.
Housing: Provided.
Deadline: March 31.
Contact: International Programs, University of Massachusetts at Amherst, Amherst, MA 01003. *Phone:* (413) 545-2710.

386 UNIVERSITY OF PENNSYLVANIA
Penn-in-Xi'an.
Location: Xi'an.
Dates: June 6–July 24.
Subjects: Beginning Chinese language; Chinese archaeology, history.
Credit: 3 undergraduate credits.
Eligibility: Undergraduates, graduates, adults, teachers, precollege. Requires good academic standing. Background in Chinese language, history, or archaeology helpful.
Instruction: In English. Students attend courses arranged for the group taught by U.S. and foreign faculty at Northwest University in Xi'an.
Highlights: Program began in 1983. Orientation in U.S. and abroad. 2 weeks of program-related travel in China. Contact with previous participants available.
Costs: $2,200 includes tuition, housing, meals, excursions.
Housing: In residence halls.
Deadline: April 1.
Contact: Elizabeth Sachs, Penn Summer Abroad, University of Pennsylvania, 210 Logan Hall/CN, Philadelphia, PA 19104. *Phone:* (215) 898-5738.

JAPAN

MORE THAN ONE CITY

387 COUNCIL ON INTERNATIONAL EDUCATIONAL EXCHANGE (CIEE)
Views of Japan.
Location: Kyoto, Nagoya, Takayama, Tokyo.
Dates: 3 weeks, June–July.
Subjects: Contemporary Japanese civilization, including architecture, business, education, religion, technology.
Credit: Up to 3 graduate credits available by arrangement.
Eligibility: Graduates, adults, teachers. Requires good physical health.
Instruction: In English. Students attend courses arranged for the group taught by foreign faculty.
Highlights: Program began in 1970. Orientation in Tokyo. 1-week homestay. Excursions and field trips to businesses, schools, Buddhist monastery, Gion Festival. Optional independent travel.

All program information is subject to change without notice
and must be confirmed directly with the sponsor.

78

Costs: About $2,950 includes housing, some meals, round-trip transportation from the West Coast, excursions, fees.
Housing: In hotels, monastery, inns, private homes.
Deadline: May 15.
Contact: Professional and Secondary Education Programs, Council on International Educational Exchange (CIEE), 205 E. 42nd St., New York, NY 10017. *Phone:* (212) 661-1414, Ext. 1207.

388 **SOUTHERN ILLINOIS UNIVERSITY AT CARBONDALE**
   Special Education in Japan.
Location: Kyoto, Tokyo.
Dates: 10 days, July 17–27.
Subjects: Special education.
Credit: 1–3 graduate credits.
Eligibility: Graduates and teachers preferred; qualified undergraduates. Requires background in education and rehabilitation.
Instruction: In English. Students attend courses arranged for the group taught by U.S. and foreign faculty.
Highlights: Program began in 1980. 1-day orientation abroad. Excursions and field trips. Postsession review. Contact with previous participants available.
Costs: About $1,730 includes housing, some meals, books, excursions, fees, insurance.
Housing: In hotels, inn.
Deadline: April 1.
Contact: Thomas A. Saville, Coordinator, Study Abroad Programs, International Programs and Services, Southern Illinois University at Carbondale, Carbondale, IL 62901-6514. *Phone:* (618) 453-5774. *Telex:* 910-996-2540. *Or:* Prof. Toshiaki Hisama, Special Education, Southern Illinois University at Carbondale, Carbondale, IL 62901. *Phone:* (618) 453-2311. *Telex:* 910-996-2540.

TOKYO

389 **TOKYO JAPANESE ACADEMY**
   Japanese Language Course.
Location: Tokyo.
Dates: 12-week terms, year-round; students may enroll for 1 or more terms.
Subjects: Japanese language on all levels.
Credit: None.
Eligibility: Undergraduates, graduates, adults, teachers.
Instruction: In Japanese. Students attend special courses for foreigners at Tokyo Japanese Academy.
Highlights: Program began in 1979. Excursions. Contact with previous participants available.
Costs: 149,000 yen per term, includes tuition, fees.
Housing: Sponsor assists in locating housing.
Deadline: None.
Contact: Ms. Y. Nakashima, Tokyo Japanese Academy, 201 Yoyogi Residence, 2-27 Yoyogi, Shibuya-ku, Tokyo, Japan. *Phone:* (81-3) 379-5245.

KOREA

SEOUL

390 **YONSEI UNIVERSITY**
   Graduate Program in International Studies.
Location: Seoul.
Dates: August–December and/or February–June; students may enroll for 1 or both semesters.

Subjects: Korean language on all levels; Korean and East Asian studies, including culture, history, philosophy, sociology; business administration, economics, political science, public administration, with emphasis on East Asia. 2-year master's program available.
Credit: 9 graduate credits per semester.
Eligibility: Graduates, teachers. Requires bachelor's degree from non-Korean college or university.
Instruction: In English. Students attend special courses for foreigners at Yonsei University Graduate School of International Studies.
Highlights: Program began in 1966. Offered in cooperation with the United Board for Christian Higher Education in Asia. 3-day orientation. Excursions. Contact with previous participants available.
Costs: About $6,000 per year, includes tuition, housing, meals, books, excursions, fees, insurance. Work-study available.
Housing: In residence halls.
Deadline: June 30 for fall; Jan. 10 for spring.
Contact: Dr. Horace H. Underwood, Associate Dean, Graduate School of International Studies, Yonsei University, Seoul, Korea. *Phone:* (82-2) 392-0131, Ext. 2911/2701. *Telex:* YONSEI K29127. *Or:* The United Board for Christian Higher Education in Asia, Room 1221, 475 Riverside Dr., New York, NY 10115. *Phone:* (212) 870-2608.

391 **YONSEI UNIVERSITY**
   Korean Language Institute.
Location: Seoul.
Dates: 10-week terms, April–June, July–September, October–December, January–March.
Subjects: Korean language on all levels; Korean culture.
Credit: 10 undergraduate credit hours.
Eligibility: Sophomores, juniors, seniors, graduates, adults, teachers.
Instruction: In English, Korean. Students attend special courses for foreigners at Yonsei University.
Highlights: Program began in 1959. Orientation. Excursions and cultural activities. Contact with previous participants available.
Costs: About $460 (1987) per term, includes tuition. Scholarships available.
Housing: In residence halls.
Deadline: Apply early.
Contact: Director, Korean Language Institute, Yonsei University, Seoul 120, Korea. *Phone:* (82-2) 392-6405/392-0131, Ext. 2576/7.

SRI LANKA

COLOMBO

392 **UNIVERSITY OF COLOMBO**
   Diploma in English Language Teaching (Tertiary).
Location: Colombo.
Dates: January–January; students must enroll for entire period.
Subjects: Teaching English.
Credit: Diploma. Graduate credit by special arrangement.
Eligibility: Teachers.
Instruction: In English. Students attend regular classes at the University of Colombo.
Highlights: Program begins in 1988.
Costs: Contact sponsor for information.
Housing: Students make own arrangements.
Deadline: Oct. 31.
Contact: Registrar, University of Colombo, College House, P.O. Box 1490, Colombo 3, Sri Lanka. *Phone:* (94-1) 583818. *Telex:* 22039.

All program information is subject to change without notice and must be confirmed directly with the sponsor.

79

EUROPE

MORE THAN ONE COUNTRY

393 COUNCIL ON INTERNATIONAL EDUCATIONAL EXCHANGE (CIEE)
Views of Germany.
Location: East Germany: Berlin, Dresden, Erfurt, Jena, Weimar, Wittenberg; West Germany: Bonn, Berlin, Frankfurt.
Dates: 3 weeks, July–August.
Subjects: Contemporary East/West German education, history, media, politics.
Credit: Up to 3 graduate credits available by arrangement.
Eligibility: Graduates, adults, teachers. Requires good physical health.
Instruction: In English. Students attend courses arranged for the group taught by foreign faculty at Bonn University.
Highlights: Program begins in 1988. Orientation in Bonn. 3-day homestay. Excursions and field trips. Optional independent travel. Postsession review.
Costs: About $2,320 includes housing, some meals, round-trip transportation, excursions, fees.
Housing: In residence halls, hotels, private homes.
Deadline: April 15.
Contact: Professional and Secondary Education Programs, Council on International Educational Exchange (CIEE), 205 E. 42nd St., New York, NY 10017. *Phone:* (212) 661-1414, Ext. 1207.

394 EASTERN MICHIGAN UNIVERSITY
European Travel Study Program.
Location: Corsica, France, Germany, Portugal, Spain, Switzerland.
Dates: June 25–Aug. 5.
Subjects: History.
Credit: 2–6 undergraduate credits. Graduate credit.
Eligibility: Undergraduates, graduates, teachers, professionals.
Instruction: In English. Students attend courses arranged for the group taught by U.S. faculty.
Highlights: Program began in 1959. Orientation in U.S. Excursions and cultural events. Contact with previous participants available.
Costs: About $2,000 includes tuition, housing, some meals, excursions, fees.
Housing: In hotels.
Deadline: May 1.
Contact: Dr. George Klein, Office of International Studies, Eastern Michigan University, 333 Goodison Hall, Ypsilanti, MI 48197. *Phone:* (313) 487-2424.

395 KEARNEY STATE COLLEGE
Summer Studies Abroad.
Location: France, Germany, Spain.
Dates: June and July; students may enroll for 2 weeks or more.
Subjects: French, German, and Spanish languages on all levels; business, linguistics, teacher training.
Credit: Available.
Eligibility: Undergraduates, graduates, teachers, adults.
Instruction: In French, German, Spanish, English. Students attend courses arranged for the group taught by U.S. and foreign faculty.
Highlights: Orientation abroad. Excursions. Contact with previous participants available.
Costs: $1,300–$2,500 includes tuition, housing, some meals, round-trip transportation, excursions. Scholarships available.

Housing: In residence halls, hotels.
Deadline: Dec. 15.
Contact: J. Thomas York, Chairman, Dept. of Foreign Languages, Kearney State College, Kearney, NE 68849. *Phone:* (308) 234-8536. *Or:* Betty Becker-Theye, Dean, School of Fine Arts and Humanities, Kearney State College, Kearney, NE 68849. *Phone:* (308) 234-8521.

396 MICHIGAN STATE UNIVERSITY
Science Museums in Europe.
Location: London, England; Munich, Germany; Paris, France.
Dates: 3 weeks, July 25–Aug. 12.
Subjects: Physical science, biological science.
Credit: 3 undergraduate credits. 3 graduate credits.
Eligibility: Juniors, seniors, graduates, adults, teachers.
Instruction: In English. Students attend courses arranged for the group taught by U.S. faculty.
Highlights: Program began in 1986. 1-day orientation in U.S. and 1 day abroad. Excursions and field trips. Postsession review. Contact with previous participants available.
Costs: About $2,100 includes tuition, housing, some meals, excursions, fees. Scholarships available.
Housing: In hotels.
Deadline: April 22.
Contact: Dr. Charles Gliozzo, Director, or Nona Anderson, Assistant Director, Office of Overseas Study, Michigan State University, 108 International Center, East Lansing, MI 48824-1035. *Phone:* (517) 353-8920. *Telex:* 650-277-3148 MCI.

397 SOUTHERN ILLINOIS UNIVERSITY AT CARBONDALE
The History of Chemistry.
Location: Belgium, Czechoslovakia, France, East and West Germany, Great Britain, Italy, Netherlands, Switzerland.
Dates: 8 weeks, June–July; students may enroll for 2 weeks; offered next in 1989.
Subjects: Chemistry, independent study.
Credit: 6 undergraduate credits. 6 graduate credits.
Eligibility: Juniors, seniors, graduates, teachers, chemists. Requires background in chemistry, interest in history of chemistry.
Instruction: In English. Students attend courses arranged for the group taught by U.S. and foreign faculty.
Highlights: Program began in 1972. Orientation in U.S. Field trips to science museums, university and industrial laboratories. Program evaluations available to prospective participants.
Costs: About $3,800 (1987) includes housing, meals, books, fees, all travel in Europe.
Housing: In hotels, guest houses.
Deadline: April 1, or until program is filled.
Contact: Thomas A. Saville, Coordinator, Study Abroad Programs, International Programs & Services, Southern Illinois University at Carbondale, Carbondale, IL 62901-6514. *Phone:* (618) 453-5774. *Telex:* 910-996-2540.

398 VERGILIAN SOCIETY OF AMERICA
Travel Study Sessions.
Location: Germany, Italy.
Dates: 6 sessions, July–August.
Subjects: Archaeology, civilization, classical studies, Greek/Roman art.
Credit: Available by arrangement.
Eligibility: Undergraduates, graduates, teachers, precollege.

All program information is subject to change without notice
and must be confirmed directly with the sponsor.

81

Instruction: In English. Students attend courses arranged for the group taught by U.S. faculty.
Highlights: Program began in 1952. Orientation abroad.
Costs: Vary. Scholarships available.
Housing: Provided.
Deadline: April 1; Feb. 1 for scholarships.
Contact: Prof. R.J. Rowland, Jr., Vergilian Society of America, c/o Classics Dept., University of Maryland—College Park, College Park, MD 20742. *Phone:* (301) 454-2510.

399 WESTERN ILLINOIS UNIVERSITY
Independent Travel-Study.
Location: London and other Western European cities.
Dates: June 1–Aug. 20; students may enroll for minimum of 1 week.
Subjects: Archaeology, art, education, history, geography, international relations, sociology, urban affairs, independent study.
Credit: Up to 6 undergraduate semester hours. Graduate credit available.
Eligibility: Undergraduates, graduates, teachers.
Instruction: In English, language of host country. Students attend independent study projects.
Highlights: Program began in 1970. Orientation abroad.
Costs: About $50 per semester hour, includes tuition.
Housing: Students make own arrangements.
Deadline: July 15.
Contact: Dr. William L. Burton, International Programs, Western Illinois University, 100 Memorial Hall, Macomb, IL 61455. *Phone:* (309) 298-2427.

AUSTRIA

MORE THAN ONE CITY

400 BOWLING GREEN STATE UNIVERSITY
Summer Programs in Salzburg.
Location: Salzburg, Zell am See.
Dates: 3 or 4 weeks, July–August.
Subjects: German language on all levels; art, music, sports, theater.
Credit: Undergraduate credit. Graduate credit.
Eligibility: Undergraduates, graduates, adults, teachers.
Instruction: In German. Students attend special courses for foreigners at Internationale Ferienkurse fuer Deutsche Sprache und Germanistik.
Highlights: Program began in 1977. Offered in cooperation with the University of Salzburg. Excursions. Contact with previous participants available.
Costs: $600–$1,025 depending on program selected, includes tuition, housing, some meals, books, excursions, fees.
Housing: In residence halls, private homes.
Deadline: May 20.
Contact: Dr. Joseph L. Gray, Chair, Dept. of German, Russian, and East Asian Languages, Bowling Green State University, Bowling Green, OH 43403. *Phone:* (419) 372-2268.

GRAZ

401 LOUISIANA STATE UNIVERSITY
LSU in Austria.
Location: Graz.
Dates: 6 weeks, July–August.
Subjects: German language on all levels; Austrian civilization, literature.
Credit: 5–9 undergraduate credits. 3–6 graduate credits.
Eligibility: Sophomores, juniors, seniors, graduates, teachers. Requires 2.5 GPA for undergraduates, 3.0 GPA for graduates, 1 year of German.
Instruction: In German. Students attend courses arranged for the group taught by U.S. faculty.
Highlights: Orientation in U.S. Excursions.
Costs: About $2,100 (1987) includes tuition, housing, meals, round-trip transportation, excursions, fees.
Housing: In student hotels.
Deadline: April 15.
Contact: Prof. James Hintze, Foreign Languages, Louisiana State University, Baton Rouge, LA 70803. *Phone:* (504) 388-6616.

INNSBRUCK

402 SPRACHSCHULE LERCH
German Language Courses for Foreigners.
Location: Innsbruck.
Dates: 4-week courses, June–Sept; students may enroll for 2 weeks.
Subjects: German language on all levels; Austria culture, literature; special courses for teachers of German.
Credit: None.
Eligibility: Adults, teachers, precollege. Minimum age 14; average age 17–25.
Instruction: In German. Students attend special courses for foreigners at Sprachschule Lerch.
Highlights: Program began in 1959. Excursions.
Costs: AS 4,600 per week, AS 18,400 for 4 weeks, includes tuition, housing, meals, excursions. Scholarships available.
Housing: In private homes.
Deadline: 1 month before course begins; 3 months prior for scholarships.
Contact: Helmut Lerch, Director, Sprachschule Lerch, Kapuzinergasse 10, A-6020 Innsbruck, Austria. *Phone:* (43-5222) 28957.

SALZBURG

403 IFK (INTERNATIONALE FERIENKURSE FUER DEUTSCHE SPRACHE UND GERMANISTIK)
German Courses.
Location: Salzburg.
Dates: 3–4 weeks, July–August; 10 weeks in fall, winter, spring.
Subjects: German language on all levels, including intensive courses, special group programs, courses for teachers of German; German literature, Austrian civilization.
Credit: None.
Eligibility: Adults, precollege, teachers. Minimum age 16.
Instruction: In German. Students attend special classes for foreigners at IFK.
Highlights: Program began in 1948. Offered in cooperation with the Universitaet Salzburg. Orientation abroad. Excursions and cultural events.
Costs: About AS 9,000–12,000 includes tuition, housing, some meals, books, excursions, fees.
Housing: In hostels, private homes.
Deadline: 2 weeks before course begins.
Contact: Internationale Ferienkurse fuer Deutsche Sprache und Germanistik (IFK), Franz-Josef-Strasse 19, A-5020 Salzburg, Austria. *Phone:* (43-662) 76595.

STROBL

404 UNIVERSITY OF VIENNA
Summer School.
Location: Strobl.
Dates: July 17–Aug. 26; students may enroll for 3 weeks.
Subjects: Regular and intensive German language on all levels; workshop for teachers of German; Austrian culture, international relations, social sciences.
Credit: Certificate/diploma.
Eligibility: Juniors, seniors, graduates, adults, teachers. Requires 2 years of college or education equivalent to 1 year at a European university.
Instruction: In English, German. Students attend regular classes at the University of Vienna Summer School.
Highlights: Program began in 1949. Excursions and Salzburg Festival events. Program evaluations available to prospective participants.
Costs: About AS 20,800 for 6 weeks, includes tuition, housing, meals, excursions, fees. Scholarships available.
Housing: In residence halls, guest houses, private homes.
Deadline: June 1; March 1 for scholarships.
Contact: Dr. Peter Gerlich, Director of Summer School, University of Vienna, Wahringerstrasse 17, A-1090 Vienna, Austria. *Phone:* (43-222) 436141/60.

All program information is subject to change without notice and must be confirmed directly with the sponsor.

VIENNA

405 WIENER INTERNATIONALE HOCHSCHULKURSE
Deutsche Sprachkurse fuer Auslaender.
Location: Vienna.
Dates: July 11–Aug. 6, Aug. 8–Sept. 3, Sept. 5–24.
Subjects: German language on all levels; courses for teachers of German.
Credit: None.
Eligibility: Adults, teachers, precollege. Minimum age 16.
Instruction: In German. Students attend special courses for foreigners at the Wiener Internationale Hochschulkurse.
Highlights: Program began in 1922. Excursions.
Costs: About AS 7,800 includes tuition, housing.
Housing: In student residences.
Deadline: 1 month before course begins.
Contact: Dr. Theodor Kriesch, Wiener Internationale Hochschulkurse, Universitaet, A-1010 Vienna, Austria. *Phone:* (43-222) 424737.

406 WIENER INTERNATIONALE HOCHSCHULKURSE
German Language Courses at the University of Vienna.
Location: Vienna.
Dates: 9-week terms, Oct. 17–Dec. 17, Jan. 16–March 18, April 3–June 3; students may enroll for 1 or more terms.
Subjects: German language on all levels.
Credit: Available by special arrangement.
Eligibility: Undergraduates, graduates, adults, teachers. Minimum age 16.
Instruction: In German. Students attend special courses for foreigners at Wiener Internationale Hochschulkurse.
Highlights: Program began in 1922.
Costs: About AS 1,560 per term, includes tuition.
Housing: Students make own arrangements.
Deadline: None.
Contact: Wiener Internationale Hochschulkurse, University of Vienna, A-1010 Wien, Austria. *Phone:* (43-222) 42 12 54/42 47 37.

DENMARK

SNEDSTED

407 NORDENFJORD WORLD UNIVERSITY
Global Folkelighed—World Democracy.
Location: Snedsted.
Dates: 9 weeks, Oct. 1–Dec. 10.
Subjects: Beginning Danish language; Danish culture, folk high schools, history; community development, democracy, mythology. Internships.
Credit: 12 undergraduate credits. 10 graduate credits.
Eligibility: Sophomores, juniors, seniors, graduates, adults, teachers. Minimum age 18; maximum age 62.
Instruction: In English. Students attend regular classes at Nordenfjord World University.
Highlights: Program began in 1949. Offered in cooperation with the Association for World Education. 4-day orientation. Excursions and field trips. Contact with previous participants available.
Costs: About Dkr. 13,800 per term, includes tuition, housing, meals, books, insurance.
Housing: In residence halls.
Deadline: 4 months before course begins.
Contact: Johan Toft, Director, Nordenfjord World University, 7752 Snedsted, Denmark. *Phone:* (45-7) 93 62 34. *Or:* Aage Rosendal Nielsen, President, Association of World Education, 7752 Snedsted, Denmark. *Phone:* (45-7) 93 62 77.

FINLAND

HELSINKI

408 COUNCIL FOR INSTRUCTION OF FINNISH FOR FOREIGNERS
Courses in Finnish Language and Culture.
Location: Helsinki.
Dates: 4 weeks, July.
Subjects: Finnish language on all levels; Finnish culture.
Credit: None.
Eligibility: Undergraduates, graduates, adults, teachers, professionals. Intermediate and advanced courses require previous study of Finnish.
Instruction: In Finnish. Students attend special courses for foreigners.
Highlights: Contact sponsor for information.
Costs: Free tuition, housing, books. Scholarships available.
Housing: Students make own arrangements.
Deadline: Feb. 28.
Contact: Council for Instruction of Finnish for Foreigners, Vuorikatu 5 B 18, SF-00100 Helsinki, Finland.

KUOPIO

409 COUNCIL FOR INSTRUCTION OF FINNISH FOR FOREIGNERS
Courses in Finnish Language and Culture.
Location: Kuopio.
Dates: 4 weeks, July.
Subjects: Finnish language on all levels; Finnish culture.
Credit: None.
Eligibility: Undergraduates, graduates, adults, teachers, professionals. Intermediate and advanced courses require previous study of Finnish.
Instruction: In Finnish. Students attend special courses for foreigners.
Highlights: Contact sponsor for information.
Costs: Free tuition, housing, books. Scholarships available.
Housing: Students make own arrangements.
Deadline: Feb. 28.
Contact: Council for Instruction of Finnish for Foreigners, Vuorikatu 5 B 18, SF-00100 Helsinki, Finland.

LAPPEENRANTA

410 COUNCIL FOR INSTRUCTION OF FINNISH FOR FOREIGNERS
Courses in Finnish Language and Culture.
Location: Lappeenranta.
Dates: 4 weeks, July.
Subjects: Finnish language on all levels; Finnish culture.
Credit: None.
Eligibility: Undergraduates, graduates, adults, teachers, professionals. Intermediate and advanced courses require previous study of Finnish.
Instruction: In Finnish. Students attend special courses for foreigners.
Highlights: Contact sponsor for information.
Costs: Free tuition, housing, books. Scholarships available.
Housing: Students make own arrangements.
Deadline: Feb. 28.
Contact: Council for Instruction of Finnish for Foreigners, Vuorikatu 5 B 18, SF-00100 Helsinki, Finland.

RAUMA

411 COUNCIL FOR INSTRUCTION OF FINNISH FOR FOREIGNERS
Courses in Finnish Language and Culture.
Location: Rauma.
Dates: 4 weeks, July.
Subjects: Finnish language on all levels; Finnish culture.
Credit: None.
Eligibility: Undergraduates, graduates, adults, teachers, professionals. Intermediate and advanced courses require previous study of Finnish.
Instruction: In Finnish. Students attend special courses for foreigners.
Highlights: Contact sponsor for information.
Costs: Free tuition, housing, books. Scholarships available.
Housing: Students make own arrangements.

All program information is subject to change without notice and must be confirmed directly with the sponsor.

83

Deadline: Feb. 28
Contact: Council for Instruction of Finnish for Foreigners, Vuorikatu 5 B 18, SF-00100 Helsinki, Finland.

FRANCE

MORE THAN ONE CITY

412 PARSONS SCHOOL OF DESIGN
Parsons in Paris: 6-Week Program.
Location: Paris and either Dordogne region of France or Tuscany, Italy.
Dates: About July 1–Aug. 15.
Subjects: Beginning French language; French history, literature; prehistoric archaeology, art history, drawing, landscape painting, painting.
Credit: 6–9 undergraduate credits. Graduate credit available.
Eligibility: Undergraduates, graduates, adults, teachers, professionals. Requires submission of portfolio for studio classes.
Instruction: In English. Students attend courses arranged for the group taught by U.S. and foreign faculty.
Highlights: Program began in 1976. 1-day orientation abroad.
Costs: About $3,000–$3,500 includes tuition, housing, some meals, round-trip transportation, excursions, fees.
Housing: In residence halls, hotels.
Deadline: May 1.
Contact: Office of Special Programs, Parsons School of Design, 66 Fifth Ave., New York, NY 10011. *Phone:* (212) 741-8975.

413 UNIVERSITY OF KENTUCKY
Tour de France: French 375.
Location: Various sites throughout France.
Dates: 4 weeks, June 10–July 10.
Subjects: Advanced French language; cultural history of France.
Credit: 4 undergraduate credits. 3 graduate credits.
Eligibility: Juniors, seniors, graduates, teachers. Minimum age 18. Requires 2 semesters of intermediate French.
Instruction: In French. Students attend courses arranged for the group taught by U.S. faculty.
Highlights: Program began in 1978. 3-day orientation in U.S. and abroad. Excursions and field trips. Contact with previous participants available.
Costs: About $2,200 includes housing, meals, round-trip transportation, excursions. Scholarships and work-study available.
Housing: In residence halls, pensions.
Deadline: March 15.
Contact: Dr. Jean Charron or Dr. Rupert T. Pickens, University of Kentucky, 1015 Patterson Office Tower, Lexington, KY 40506. *Phone:* (606) 257-5721. *Telex:* 204009.

ANGERS

414 UNIVERSITY OF NORTHERN IOWA
Summer Institute in France for Teachers of French.
Location: Angers.
Dates: June 27–Aug. 12.
Subjects: Intensive French language for teachers of French.
Credit: 8 graduate semester hours.
Eligibility: Teachers, graduates.
Instruction: In French. Students attend special courses for foreigners at a university in Angers.
Highlights: Program began in 1967. 2 weeks of program-related travel in Bretagne.
Costs: $1,650 includes tuition, housing, meals, books, excursions, fees.
Housing: In private homes.
Deadline: April 1.
Contact: Andre Walther, Dept. of Modern Languages, University of Northern Iowa, Cedar Falls, IA 50614. *Phone:* (319) 273-2200/2404.

AUCH

415 BORDEAUX INTERNATIONAL SCHOOL
Intensive Course in Languages.
Location: Auch, Gers (southwest France).
Dates: September–December or January–April. Summer program also available.
Subjects: French, German, and Spanish languages on all levels. Internships in business, tourism.
Credit: None.
Eligibility: Undergraduates, graduates, adults, teachers, professionals. Minimum age 15.
Instruction: In French, German, or Spanish. Students attend special courses for foreigners and regular classes at the Bordeaux International School.
Highlights: Program began in 1985. Excursions. Postsession review. Contact with previous participants available.
Costs: Fr. 18,900 includes tuition, housing, meals, some books, excursions, fees.
Housing: In private homes.
Deadline: First day of class.
Contact: Mrs. M. Strudwick, Director, or Mlle C. Cussac, Deputy Director, Bordeaux International School, 10 bis rue de l'Egalite, 32000 Auch, France. *Phone:* (33) 62 35 67 41/62 28 92 44.

BEZIERS

416 ECOLE DE LANGUES HOBSON
French Courses for Foreigners.
Location: Beziers.
Dates: January–July; students must enroll for entire period.
Subjects: French, German, Italian, and Spanish languages on all levels; commercial French, art history, French literature.
Credit: None.
Eligibility: Undergraduates, graduates, adults, teachers, professionals.
Instruction: In French. Students attend special courses for foreigners at Ecole de Langues Hobson.
Highlights: Program begins in 1988. Excursions.
Costs: About Fr. 6,000 per semester, includes tuition, books, excursions, rail passes.
Housing: In private homes.
Deadline: Dec. 15.
Contact: Jacqueline Hobson, Director, Ecole de Langues Hobson, 57 Avenue St. Saens, 34500 Beziers, France. *Phone:* (33) 67 76 70 33.

CAEN

417 UNIVERSITE DE CAEN
Centre d'Etudes Francaises pour l'Etranger (CEFPE).
Location: Caen, Normandy.
Dates: Oct. 1–June 30; students may enroll for 1 or both semesters.
Subjects: French language on all levels; French civilization, literature; teaching French as a foreign language; student teaching.
Credit: Certificate/diploma. Credit by special arrangement.
Eligibility: Undergraduates, graduates, adults, teachers, professionals. Minimum age 18. Requires high school diploma.
Instruction: In French. Students attend special courses for foreigners at the Universite de Caen.
Highlights: Program began in 1947. 1-week orientation. Excursions and field trips. Contact with previous participants available.
Costs: Fr. 1,530 (1987) per semester, includes tuition. Scholarships available.
Housing: Sponsor assists in locating housing.
Deadline: Feb. 1 for fall/academic year; Oct. 1 for spring.
Contact: CEFPE, Universite de Caen, 14032 Caen, France. *Phone:* (33-31) 93 26 76.

418 UNIVERSITE DE CAEN
Cours Internationaux d'Ete.
Location: Caen.
Dates: July 3–21, July 24–Aug. 11, Aug. 14–Sept. 1, Sept. 4–22.
Subjects: French language on all levels; French civilization, literature; special classes for teachers of French.
Credit: None.

All program information is subject to change without notice and must be confirmed directly with the sponsor.

84

Eligibility: Undergraduates, adults, teachers. Minimum age 18; average age 27.
Instruction: In French. Students attend special classes for foreigners at the Universite de Caen.
Highlights: Program began in 1947. Excursions.
Costs: About $580 for 3 weeks, includes tuition, housing, meals. Scholarships available.
Housing: In residence halls, apartments.
Deadline: 3 weeks before course begins.
Contact: J. Chauvin, C.I.E., Universite de Caen, F-14032 Caen, France. *Phone:* (33-31) 93 26 76. *For scholarships, contact:* Services Culturels, Ambassade de France, 972 Fifth Ave., New York, NY 10021.

CANNES

419 AMERICAN INSTITUTE FOR FOREIGN STUDY (AIFS)
College International de Cannes.
Location: Cannes.
Dates: July–August; students may enroll for 4 weeks.
Subjects: French language on all levels.
Credit: 8 undergraduate credits.
Eligibility: Undergraduates, graduates, teachers of French. Minimum age 17. Requires 2.5 GPA.
Instruction: In French. Students attend regular classes at College International de Cannes.
Highlights: Program began in 1987. Offered in cooperation with College International de Cannes. 1-day orientation abroad. Excursions.
Costs: About $2,799 includes tuition, housing, meals, round-trip transportation, excursions, fees.
Housing: In residence halls.
Deadline: April 1.
Contact: Gerry Thompson, SVP, College Division, American Institute for Foreign Study, 102 Greenwich Ave., Greenwich, CT 06830. *Phone:* (203) 869-9090.

420 COLLEGE INTERNATIONAL DE CANNES, UNIVERSITE LIBRE DE LA COTE D'AZUR
Cours de Francais pour Etrangers.
Location: Cannes.
Dates: 4-week courses, year-round. 3-month terms, late September–mid-December, early January–late March, early May–late June.
Subjects: French language on all levels; business French, phonetics, theatrical expression; French art history, cinema, history, literature, politics, society; student teaching.
Credit: Available.
Eligibility: Undergraduates, graduates, adults, professionals, teachers of French. Minimum age 16.
Instruction: In English, French. Students attend special courses for foreigners and regular classes at College International de Cannes.
Highlights: Program began in 1969. Excursions. Contact with previous participants available.
Costs: Contact sponsor for information.
Housing: In residence halls, furnished rooms, apartments, private homes.
Deadline: Apply early.
Contact: Patrick de Bouter, Secretaire General, College International, 1 Avenue du Dr. Pascal, 06400 Cannes, France. *Phone:* (33-93) 67 39 29. *Telex:* 214235 MISSITEX CICANNES.

DIJON

421 GEORGETOWN UNIVERSITY, SCHOOL FOR SUMMER AND CONTINUING EDUCATION
Summer Session in Dijon.
Location: Dijon.
Dates: 6 weeks, early July–August.
Subjects: French on all levels, conversation, composition, translation; French art, civilization, culture, drama, history, literature.
Credit: 6–8 undergraduate credits. Graduate credit.
Eligibility: Undergraduates, graduates, adults, teachers. Minimum age 18. Knowledge of French recommended for beginning course.
Instruction: In French. Students attend courses arranged for the group taught by foreign faculty.

Highlights: Program began in 1964. Orientation abroad. Excursions and field trips. Contact with previous participants available.
Costs: About $2,300 includes tuition, round-trip transportation, books, excursions, fees, insurance.
Housing: In private homes.
Deadline: April 30.
Contact: Dr. Anthony T. Moore, School for Summer and Continuing Education, ICC #306, Georgetown University, Washington, DC 20057. *Phone:* (202) 625-3017. *Or:* Dr. Pierre Maubrey, Dijon Program, School for Summer and Continuing Education, Georgetown University, Washington, DC 20057. *Phone:* (202) 625-3001.

422 UNIVERSITE DE BOURGOGNE, CENTRE INTERNATIONAL D'ETUDES FRANCAISES
Cours Annuels pour Etudiants Etrangers.
Location: Dijon.
Dates: October–June; students may enroll for 1 or both semesters.
Subjects: French language on all levels; French studies, including art history, civilization, history, literature, philosophy.
Credit: None.
Eligibility: Undergraduates, graduates, adults, teachers, professionals. Minimum age 17. Requires high school diploma.
Instruction: In French. Students attend special courses for foreigners and regular classes at the Centre International d'Etudes Francaises of the Universite de Bourgogne.
Highlights: Program began in 1902. 1-day orientation. Excursions.
Costs: About Fr. 4,230 per semester, includes tuition, fees.
Housing: In residence halls.
Deadline: Apply early.
Contact: Centre International d'Etudes Francaises, 36 rue Chabot-Charny, 21000 Dijon, France. *Phone:* (33-80) 66 20 49.

423 UNIVERSITY OF MASSACHUSETTS AT AMHERST
Summer Studies in France.
Location: Dijon.
Dates: July 5–Aug. 13.
Subjects: French language, phonetics; special courses for teachers of French; French art history, civilization, history, literature, political science.
Credit: 6 undergraduate credits.
Eligibility: Undergraduates, graduates, teachers. Requires 1 year of French for undergraduates; requires fluency in French for graduates and for enrollment in history, political science, and art courses.
Instruction: In French. Students attend special courses for foreigners and regular classes at the Universtiy of Dijon.
Highlights: Program began in 1970. Excursions. Program evaluations available to prospective participants.
Costs: About $1050 includes tuition, housing, excursions.
Housing: In residence halls.
Deadline: Feb. 1.
Contact: French and Italian Dept., University of Massachusetts, Amherst, MA 01003. *Phone:* (413) 545-2314.

LISIEUX

424 FRENCH AMERICAN STUDY CENTER
French for English-Speaking People.
Location: Lisieux.
Dates: 10-week programs beginning in early September, late March. Shorter courses and summer program also available.
Subjects: French and German languages on all levels; architecture and culture of Normandy, French history. Internships.
Credit: 16 undergraduate credits.
Eligibility: Undergraduates, graduates, adults, teachers, professionals. Minimum age 15.
Instruction: In French, English. Students attend special courses for foreigners and regular classes.
Highlights: Program began in 1975. Offered in cooperation with the University of Caen and the University of Central Florida. Orientation. Excursions. Contact with previous participants available.
Costs: $3,453 for fall term, $3,864 for spring term, includes tuition, housing, some meals, excursions. Work-study available.
Housing: In residence halls, private homes.
Deadline: 1 month before course begins.

All program information is subject to change without notice
and must be confirmed directly with the sponsor.

Contact: Dr. Almeras, French American Study Center, B.P. 176, Lisieux 14104, France. *Phone:* (33) 31 31 22 01. *Telex:* 171 439 Attention FASC. *Or:* Dr. Barsch, University of Central Florida at Orlando, Dept. of Foreign Languages, Orlando, FL 32816. *Phone:* (305) 275-2466.

NICE

425 CENTRE INTERNATIONAL DE FORMATION MUSICALE
Summer Sessions in Music, Dance, and Fine Arts.
Location: Nice.
Dates: July 9–23, July 25–Aug. 8; students may enroll for 1 or both sessions. Special flute symposium, July 4–7.
Subjects: French language on all levels; contemporary and classical dance; fine arts; master classes in music, including chamber, choral, instrumental, orchestra, voice.
Credit: None.
Eligibility: Advanced music/dance students, adults, teachers, professionals. Minimum age 16. Music/dance classes require considerable previous study; no previous study required for language/fine arts courses.
Instruction: In French, English. Students attend special courses for foreigners and regular classes at CIFM.
Highlights: Program began in 1958. Offered in cooperation with the Municipality of Nice.
Costs: About Fr. 4,550 per session, includes tuition, housing, some meals, fees.
Housing: In residence halls, or students make own arrangements.
Deadline: Apply early.
Contact: Mme. Nadine Haas, Secretaire Generale, Centre International de Formation Musicale (CIFM), 24 Blvd. de Cimiez, F-06000 Nice, France. *Phone:* (33) 93 81 01 23/93 81 57 18.

426 GEORGE MASON UNIVERSITY
GMU Summer Study in Nice.
Location: Nice.
Dates: July 3–29.
Subjects: French language on all levels; French literature; teaching French; scientific, commercial, and juridical French.
Credit: 6 undergraduate credits. 3 graduate credits.
Eligibility: Undergraduates, graduates, teachers. Minimum age 18.
Instruction: In French. Students attend special courses for foreigners at the Centre International d'Etudes Francaises, Universite de Nice.
Highlights: Program began in 1985. 2-day orientation in U.S. Postsession review. Contact with previous participants available.
Costs: About $1,500 for Virginia residents, includes tuition, housing, meals, insurance.
Housing: In residence halls.
Deadline: April 1.
Contact: Neal Dwyer, Study Abroad Advisor, or Dr. Louis E. Guzman, International Studies Coordinator, George Mason University, 4400 University Dr., Fairfax, VA 22030. *Phone:* (703) 323-2652.

427 INTERNATIONAL COUNCIL FOR CULTURAL EXCHANGE
French Language, Art, and Music in Nice.
Location: Nice and the Riviera.
Dates: 3–4 weeks in summer. Year-round courses also available.
Subjects: French on all levels; art, music (vocal, instrumental, dance).
Credit: Available.
Eligibility: Undergraduates, graduates, precollege, adults, teachers, professionals.
Instruction: In French, English. Students attend courses arranged for the group taught by U.S. and foreign faculty and regular classes at International Center of French Studies, University of Nice, and other institutions.
Highlights: Program began in 1985. Orientation in U.S. Program-related travel throughout the French Riviera. Program evaluations available to prospective participants.
Costs: About $2,279 for 4 weeks, includes tuition, housing, meals, round-trip transportation, excursions, fees.
Housing: In residence halls, hotels, private homes.
Deadline: 1 month before course begins.

Contact: Dr. Stanley Gochman, International Council for Cultural Exchange, Inc., 1559 Rockville Pike, Rockville, MD 20852. *Phone:* (301) 983-9479. *Telex:* 440730 ITS UI.

PARIS

428 ALLIANCE FRANCAISE DE PARIS
French in France.
Location: Paris.
Dates: 2–4 months, year-round. Shorter courses also available.
Subjects: Intensive and regular French language on all levels; business French, linguistics, literature, translation; special training programs for teachers of French and translators.
Credit: Certificate/diploma. Credit by special arrangement.
Eligibility: Undergraduates, graduates, adults, teachers, professionals. Minimum age 16.
Instruction: In French. Students attend special courses for foreigners at the Alliance Francaise.
Highlights: Program began in 1883. Excursions.
Costs: Contact sponsor for information.
Housing: Sponsor assists in locating housing.
Deadline: Rolling.
Contact: M. Perez, Alliance Francaise, 101 Blvd. Raspail, F-75270 Paris Cedex 06, France. *Phone:* (33-1) 45 44 38 28. *Telex:* 204 941.

429 AMERICAN COLLEGE IN PARIS
Summer Institute for French Teachers.
Location: Paris.
Dates: 4 weeks, July.
Subjects: French language; contemporary French culture, history, literature, teaching methods, AP and IB workshops.
Credit: Graduate credit.
Eligibility: Teachers of French.
Instruction: In French. Students attend courses arranged for the group taught by U.S. and foreign faculty.
Highlights: Program began in 1985. Excursions.
Costs: About $1,000 includes tuition, housing, some meals, fees. Some scholarships available.
Housing: In residence halls, hotels.
Deadline: April 15.
Contact: Mr. G. Stephen Ryer, The American College in Paris, 31 Ave. Bosquet, 75007 Paris, France. *Phone:* (33-1) 4555-9173.

430 CHAMBRE DE COMMERCE ET D'INDUSTRIE DE PARIS
Business French A1.
Location: Paris.
Dates: 1 week, June 22–28.
Subjects: Intensive program in business French; French economics and business environment for teachers.
Credit: None.
Eligibility: Adults, businesspeople, teachers of French. Requires previous study of French.
Instruction: In French. Students attend special courses for foreigners at the Chambre de Commerce et d'Industrie.
Highlights: Program began in 1987.
Costs: About Fr. 3,000 includes tuition, housing, meals.
Housing: In residence halls, hotels.
Deadline: 4 weeks before course begins; 8 weeks if housing is requested.
Contact: Direction de l'Enseignement, Chambre de Commerce et d'Industrie de Paris, 42 rue du Louvre, 75001 Paris, France. *Phone:* (33-1) 45 08 37 34. *Telex:* 213509 DE CCIP.

431 CHAMBRE DE COMMERCE ET D'INDUSTRIE DE PARIS
Business French A2.
Location: Paris.
Dates: 2 weeks, June 30–July 13.
Subjects: The teaching of business French: methods, materials.
Credit: None.
Eligibility: Adults, teachers of French. Requires previous experience teaching French.
Instruction: In French. Students attend special courses for foreigners at the Chambre de Commerce et d'Industrie.

All program information is subject to change without notice and must be confirmed directly with the sponsor.

Highlights: Program began in 1987. Visits to French businesses and financial organizations.
Costs: About Fr. 4,600 includes tuition, housing, meals, field trips.
Housing: In residence halls, hotels.
Deadline: 5 weeks before course begins; 8 weeks if housing is requested.
Contact: Direction de l'Enseignement, Chambre de Commerce et d'Industrie de Paris, 42 rue du Louvre, 75001 Paris, France. *Phone:* (33-1) 45 08 37 34. *Telex:* 213509 DE CCIP.

432 CHAMBRE DE COMMERCE ET D'INDUSTRIE DE PARIS
Business French B.
Location: Paris.
Dates: 3 weeks, June 30–July 22.
Subjects: French business environment. Internship in French business.
Credit: None.
Eligibility: Adults, businesspeople, teachers and advanced students of French, advanced students. Requires previous study of French.
Instruction: In French. Students attend special courses at the Chambre de Commerce et d'Industrie.
Highlights: Program began in 1987. Program includes 1 week of classes, 1-week field trip to a French province, and 1-week internship in a French company.
Costs: About Fr. 7,000 includes tuition, housing, meals, field trip.
Housing: In residence halls, hotels.
Deadline: 4 weeks before course begins; 8 weeks if housing is requested.
Contact: Direction de l'Enseignement, Chambre de Commerce et d'Industrie de Paris, 42 rue du Louvre, 75001 Paris, France. *Phone:* (33-1) 45 08 37 34. *Telex:* 213509 DE CCIP.

433 CHAMBRE DE COMMERCE ET D'INDUSTRIE DE PARIS
Business French C.
Location: Paris.
Dates: 1 week, June 22–28.
Subjects: Current social, political, and economic aspects of France.
Credit: None.
Eligibility: Adults, businesspeople, teachers of French, advanced students. Requires previous study of French.
Instruction: In French. Students attend special courses for foreigners at the Chambre de Commerce et d'Industrie.
Highlights: Program began in 1987. Visits to French businesses and financial organizations.
Costs: About Fr. 2,800 includes tuition, housing, meals, field trips.
Housing: In residence halls, hotels.
Deadline: 4 weeks before course begins; 8 weeks if housing is requested.
Contact: Direction de l'Enseignement, Chambre de Commerce et d'Industrie de Paris, 42 rue du Louvre, 75001 Paris, France. *Phone:* (33-1) 45 08 37 34. *Telex:* 213509 DE CCIP.

434 EUROCENTRES
Learn a Language—Live a Language.
Location: Paris.
Dates: 3, 4, or 12 weeks, year-round.
Subjects: French language on all levels; business/technical French; French culture, literature; courses for teachers of French.
Credit: None.
Eligibility: Undergraduates, adults, teachers. Minimum age 16; average age 28.
Instruction: In French. Students attend special courses for foreigners at Paris Eurocentre.
Highlights: Program began in 1973. Optional excursions.
Costs: About $1,100 for 4 weeks, $3,050–$3,600 for 12 weeks, includes tuition, housing, some meals.
Housing: In hotels, private homes.
Deadline: Apply early.
Contact: Head Office, Eurocentres, Seestrasse 247, CH-8038 Zurich, Switzerland. *Phone:* (41-1) 482-5040. *Telex:* 815250. *Or:* Eurocentre, 13 Passage Dauphine, 75006 Paris, France. *Phone:* (33-1) 43 25 81 40. *Telex:* 200403.

435 FONDATION POSTUNIVERSITAIRE INTERNATIONALE
Cours de Langue et de Civilisation Francaises.
Location: Paris.
Dates: 3 months, year-round. Shorter courses also available.

Subjects: French language on all levels, business French; French civilization. 1-month courses in teaching French as a foreign language.
Credit: None.
Eligibility: Juniors, seniors, graduates, adults, teachers. Minimum age 16.
Instruction: In English, French. Students attend special courses for foreigners at the Fondation Postuniversitaire.
Highlights: Program began in 1974. Language laboratory and video equipment.
Costs: About Fr. 1,255 per month, includes tuition.
Housing: In residence halls.
Deadline: None.
Contact: Fondation Postuniversitaire Internationale, 30 rue Cabanis, F-75014 Paris, France. *Phone:* (33-1) 45 89 84 20. *Telex:* FIAP 205 666. *Or:* Council for International Education (CIE), 326 South 500 East, Salt Lake City, UT 84102. *Phone:* (801) 355-3630. *Telex:* 495 2860.

436 PARSONS SCHOOL OF DESIGN
Fashion in Paris.
Location: Paris.
Dates: About July 1–30.
Subjects: History of European costume, contemporary trends in French fashion, fashion illustration.
Credit: Available.
Eligibility: Undergraduates, graduates, teachers, professionals. Requires current enrollment in fashion-related program or proven professional interest.
Instruction: In English. Students attend courses arranged for the group taught by U.S. and foreign faculty.
Highlights: Program began in 1980. 1-day orientation abroad. Excursions and field trips.
Costs: About $2,400–$3,000 includes tuition, housing, round-trip transportation, excursions, fees.
Housing: In residence halls, hotels.
Deadline: May 1.
Contact: Office of Special Programs, Parsons School of Design, 66 Fifth Ave., New York, NY 10011. *Phone:* (212) 741-8975.

437 PARSONS SCHOOL OF DESIGN
History of French Architecture/Studies in European Decorative Arts.
Location: Paris.
Dates: About July 1–30.
Subjects: Architecture, art, interior design.
Credit: Available.
Eligibility: Undergraduates, graduates, teachers, professionals. Requires current enrollment in design course or professional experience.
Instruction: In English. Students attend courses arranged for the group taught by U.S. and foreign faculty at Musee des Arts Decoratifs.
Highlights: Program began in 1978. 1-day orientation. Excursions and field trips.
Costs: About $3,100 includes tuition, housing, round-trip transportation, excursions, fees.
Housing: In hotels.
Deadline: May 1.
Contact: Office of Special Programs, Parsons School of Design, 66 Fifth Ave., New York, NY 10011. *Phone:* (212) 741-8975.

438 PARSONS SCHOOL OF DESIGN and NEW SCHOOL FOR SOCIAL RESEARCH
Photography in Paris.
Location: Paris.
Dates: About July 1–30.
Subjects: Photography.
Credit: Available.
Eligibility: Undergraduates, graduates, teachers, professionals. Requires submission of portfolio.
Instruction: In English. Students attend courses arranged for the group taught by U.S. faculty.
Highlights: Program began in 1979. 1-day orientation abroad. Excursions and field trips.
Costs: About $2,400–$3,000 includes tuition, housing, round-trip transportation, excursions, fees.
Housing: In residence halls, hotels.
Deadline: May 1.

All program information is subject to change without notice and must be confirmed directly with the sponsor.

Contact: Parsons School of Design, Office of Special Programs, 66 Fifth Ave., New York, NY 10011. *Phone:* (212) 741-8975.

439 UNIVERSITE DE PARIS—SORBONNE
Cours de Civilisation Francaise de la Sorbonne.
Location: Paris.
Dates: September–June; students may enroll for 1 or both semesters.
Subjects: French language on all levels; business French, French civilization.
Credit: By special arrangement.
Eligibility: Undergraduates, graduates, adults, teachers, professionals. Minimum age 18.
Instruction: In French. Students attend special courses for foreigners at the Sorbonne.
Highlights: Program began in 1919. Excursions and field trips.
Costs: Fr. 8,250–8,500 (1987) includes tuition.
Housing: Sponsor assists in locating housing.
Deadline: Sept. 1 for fall; Dec. 1 for spring.
Contact: Cours de Civilisation Francaise de la Sorbonne, 47 rue des Ecoles, 75005 Paris, France. *Phone:* (33-1) 40 46 22 11.

440 UNIVERSITE DE PARIS—SORBONNE
Cours d'Ete.
Location: Paris.
Dates: 4-week courses start July 4, Aug. 1. 6- and 8-week courses start July 4. Special summer session July 4–Sept. 24. Accelerated session about Sept. 1–Oct. 2. Language and culture for foreign teachers/advanced students, July 4–Aug. 12.
Subjects: French language on all levels; French culture.
Credit: None.
Eligibility: Undergraduates, adults, teachers, precollege. Minimum age 18. Foreign teacher/student session requires 2 years of college-level French.
Instruction: In French. Students attend special courses for foreigners at the Sorbonne.
Highlights: Program began in 1919.
Costs: About $300–$1,300 depending on program selected, includes tuition.
Housing: In residence halls, furnished rooms, apartments, boardinghouses.
Deadline: 2 weeks before course begins.
Contact: Directeur, Cours de Civilisation Francaise de la Sorbonne, 47 rue des Ecoles, 75005 Paris, France. *Phone:* (33-1) 43 29 12 13, Ext. 3430/3431/3859.

441 UNIVERSITY OF ILLINOIS AT CHICAGO
Illinois Program in Paris.
Location: Paris.
Dates: Sept. 15–June 10.
Subjects: Advanced French language, business French; French civilization, literature, political science. Internship teaching English in a French lycee.
Credit: Up to 54 undergraduate credits.
Eligibility: Juniors, seniors, graduates. Requires 3.75 GPA on 5.0 scale, fluency in French beyond intermediate level.
Instruction: In French. Students attend special courses for foreigners and regular classes at University of Paris III (Sorbonne Nouvelle).
Highlights: Program began in 1972. Orientation in U.S. and 2 weeks abroad.
Costs: $6,000–$8,000 includes tuition, housing, meals, round-trip transportation, excursions, fees.
Housing: In residence halls, private homes.
Deadline: March 15 for undergraduates; Jan. 1 for graduates.
Contact: Barbara Mittman, French Dept., University of Illinois at Chicago, Box 4348, Chicago, IL 60680. *Phone:* (312) 996-3222.

ROYAN

442 CENTRE AUDIO-VISUEL DE ROYAN (CAREL)
Intensive Language Courses for Adults.
Location: Royan.
Dates: Late September–late January and/or mid-February–mid-June.
Subjects: Intensive French language on all levels.
Credit: Available by special arrangement.

Eligibility: Undergraduates, graduates, adults, teachers. Minimum age 18.
Instruction: In French. Students attend special courses for foreigners at the Centre Audio-Visuel.
Highlights: Program began in 1966. Offered in cooperation with the University of Poitiers and the Royan Town Council. Excursions and field trips.
Costs: About Fr. 2,050–2,300 per month, includes tuition. Work-study available.
Housing: Sponsor assists in locating housing.
Deadline: June 15; Feb. 28 for teaching assistantships.
Contact: Monsieur Edward Brown, Centre Audio-Visuel de Royan (CAREL), Universite de Poitiers, 48 bis Bd. Franck Lamy, 17205 Royan Cedex, France. *Phone:* (33) 46 05 31 08. *Telex:* OTROYAN 790441.

VERSAILLES

443 EUROPEAN UNIVERSITY VERSAILLES
Business Administration.
Location: Versailles.
Dates: October–June; students may enroll for 1 or both semesters.
Subjects: French, German, Italian, and Spanish languages; bachelor's and master's programs in business administration. Internships available.
Credit: 5 graduate credits per term. Degree.
Eligibility: Undergraduates, graduates, adults, teachers, professionals. Minimum age 18; maximum age 55.
Instruction: In English, French. Students attend regular classes at European University.
Highlights: Program began in 1973. 1-day orientation. Excursions. Contact with previous participants available.
Costs: About $9,500–$11,200 per year, includes tuition, housing, some meals. Work-study available.
Housing: In furnished rooms, apartments, pensions.
Deadline: Aug. 31 for fall; Jan. 31 for spring.
Contact: Director of Admissions, European University Versailles, 35 rue des Chantiers, 78000 Versailles, France. *Phone:* (33-1) 30 21 11 77.

VICHY

444 NORTH CAROLINA STATE UNIVERSITY
France Summer Program.
Location: Vichy.
Dates: June 26–Aug. 1.
Subjects: French language on all levels; French culture, civilization.
Credit: Available.
Eligibility: Undergraduates, adults, elementary and secondary schoolteachers. Requires overall 2.0 GPA, 1 semester of college French or equivalent.
Instruction: In French. Students attend special courses for foreigners at Centre Audio Visuel de Langues Modernes (CAVILAM).
Highlights: Program began in 1985. Offered in cooperation with the Centre Audio Visuel de Langues Modernes. Orientation in U.S. Excursions. 5 days of program-related travel in Paris. Contact with previous participants available.
Costs: $2,200 includes tuition, housing, meals, round-trip transportation, excursions, fees, insurance, hotel and some meals in Paris.
Housing: In private homes.
Deadline: Jan. 15.
Contact: Cynthia Felbeck Chalou, North Carolina State University, 105 Alexander Hall, Box 7315, Raleigh, NC 27695-7315. *Phone:* (919) 737-2087.

GERMAN DEMOCRATIC REPUBLIC

BERLIN

445 HUMBOLDT-UNIVERSITAET ZU BERLIN
International Summer Course of German Studies.
Location: Berlin.
Dates: 3 weeks, July.
Subjects: Advanced German language, literature, and culture.

All program information is subject to change without notice and must be confirmed directly with the sponsor.

Credit: None.
Eligibility: Graduates, teachers, and professionals in the field of German studies.
Instruction: In German. Students attend special courses for foreigners at Humboldt University.
Highlights: Program began in 1964. Excursions, cultural and social events.
Costs: $325 includes tuition, housing, meals, excursions, cultural events.
Housing: In residence halls.
Deadline: May 31.
Contact: Humboldt-Universitaet zu Berlin, Sektion Fremdsprachen, Internationaler Hochschulferienkurs, Reinhardstrasse 7, DDR-1040 Berlin, German Democratic Republic. *Phone:* (37-2) 2093-2846.

DRESDEN

446 PALUCCA SCHULE DRESDEN
38th International Summer Course 1987.
Location: Dresden.
Dates: 2 weeks, June.
Subjects: Classical ballet; jazz, modern, and Spanish dance; other dance techniques.
Credit: None.
Eligibility: Professional dancers, teachers of dance, choreographers.
Instruction: In German. Students attend special courses for foreigners at the Palucca Ballet School.
Highlights: Program began in 1950.
Costs: DM 460 includes tuition, housing, meals.
Housing: In residence halls.
Deadline: April 5.
Contact: The Secretariate of the Palucca Schule, Basteiplatz 4, DDR-8020 Dresden, German Democratic Republic. *Phone:* (37-51) 239-1091.

447 TECHNISCHE UNIVERSITAET DRESDEN
International Summer Courses of German Studies.
Location: Dresden.
Dates: 3 weeks, July.
Subjects: Advanced German language, technical German; current GDR literature, culture.
Credit: None.
Eligibility: Graduates, teachers of German, interpreters, translators, philologists.
Instruction: In German. Students attend special courses for foreigners at Technical University of Dresden.
Highlights: Program began in 1966. Excursions.
Costs: $325 includes tuition, housing, meals, excursions, cultural events.
Housing: In residence halls.
Deadline: May 31.
Contact: Internationaler Hochschulferienkurs fuer Deutsche Sprache und Germanistik, Technische Universitaet Dresden, Mommsenstrasse 13, DDR-8027 Dresden, German Democratic Republic. *Phone:* (37-51) 463-6015.

ERFURT

448 PAEDAGOGISCHE HOCHSCHULE DR. THEODOR NEUBAUER
International Summer Courses.
Location: Erfurt/Muehlhausen.
Dates: 3-week courses, July–August.
Subjects: Advanced German language, phonetics; GDR education, literature, society.
Credit: None.
Eligibility: Graduates, teachers of German. Requires good knowledge of German.
Instruction: In German. Students attend special courses for foreigners at Paedagogische Hochschule Dr. Theodor Neubauer.
Highlights: Excursions and field trips.
Costs: DM 550 includes tuition, housing, meals, excursions, social activities.
Housing: In residence halls.

Deadline: March 30.
Contact: Paedagogische Hochschule Dr. Theodor Neubauer, Abteilung Auslaenderstudium, Nordhaeuser Strasse 63 PSF 848, DDR-5010 Erfurt, German Democratic Republic.

HALLE

449 MARTIN-LUTHER-UNIVERSITAET HALLE
International Summer Courses of German Studies.
Location: Halle.
Dates: July.
Subjects: Advanced German language, phonetics; GDR literature.
Credit: None.
Eligibility: Graduates, teachers, professionals in the fields of German and philology.
Instruction: In German. Students attend special courses for foreigners at Martin Luther University.
Highlights: Program began in 1968. Excursions.
Costs: $325 includes tuition, housing, meals, excursions, social events.
Housing: In residence halls.
Deadline: May 31.
Contact: Martin-Luther-Universitaet, Sektion Germanistik und Kunstwissenschaften, Internationaler Hochschulferienkurs, Universitaetsring 4, DDR-4020 Halle (Saale), German Democratic Republic. *Phone:* (37-46) 832348.

KARL-MARX-STADT

450 TECHNISCHE UNIVERSITAET KARL-MARX-STADT
International Summer Courses of German Studies.
Location: Karl-Marx-Stadt.
Dates: 3 weeks, July.
Subjects: Advanced German language; GDR literature and culture.
Credit: None.
Eligibility: Graduates, adults, teachers of German, philologists.
Instruction: In German. Students attend special courses for foreigners at Karl-Marx-Stadt Technical University.
Highlights: Program began in 1973. Excursions.
Costs: $325 includes tuition, housing, meals, excursions, social events.
Housing: In residence halls.
Deadline: May 31.
Contact: Technische Universitaet Karl-Marx-Stadt, Sektion Fremdsprachen, Internationaler Hochschulferienkurs fuer Germanistik, PSF 964, DDR-9010 Karl-Marx-Stadt, German Democratic Republic. *Phone:* (37-71) 561-4247.

LEIPZIG

451 HERDER-INSTITUT
German Language Program.
Location: Leipzig.
Dates: 5 months, beginning in September or February.
Subjects: German language; German culture, literature.
Credit: None.
Eligibility: Graduates, adults, teachers of German.
Instruction: In German. Students attend special courses for foreigners at the Herder Institute.
Highlights: Program began in 1968.
Costs: Contact sponsor for information.
Housing: In residence halls.
Deadline: May 31.
Contact: Herder-Institut der Karl-Marx-Universitaet, Kennwort: Sprachintensivkurs Deutsch, Lumumbastrasse 4, DDR-7022 Leipzig, East Germany. *Phone:* (37-41) 7 42 94/7 30 33.

452 HERDER-INSTITUT
International Summer Courses of German Language and Culture.
Location: Leipzig.
Dates: 3 weeks, July.
Subjects: Advanced German language; German culture, literature.
Credit: None.
Eligibility: Graduates, adults, teachers of German.

All program information is subject to change without notice and must be confirmed directly with the sponsor.

89

Instruction: In German. Students attend special courses for foreigners at Karl Marx University.
Highlights: Program began in 1968. Excursions to Dresden and Weimar.
Costs: $325 includes tuition, housing, meals, excursions, cultural events.
Housing: In residence halls.
Deadline: May 31.
Contact: Hochschulferienkurs fuer Germanistik am Herder-Institut der Karl-Marx-Universitaet, Lumumbastrasse 4, DDR-7022 Leipzig, German Democratic Republic. *Phone:* (37-41) 56320.

WEIMAR

453 FRIEDRICH-SCHILLER-UNIVERSITAET JENA
International Summer Courses of German Language and Culture.
Location: Weimar.
Dates: 3 weeks, July.
Subjects: Advanced German language; GDR culture, literature.
Credit: None.
Eligibility: Graduates, teachers, professionals in the field of German studies.
Instruction: In German. Students attend special courses for foreigners at Friedrich Schiller University.
Highlights: Program began in 1966. Excursions.
Costs: $325 includes tuition, housing, meals, excursions, social activities.
Housing: In hotels, private homes.
Deadline: May 31.
Contact: Friedrich-Schiller-Universitaet Jena, Universitaetshochhaus, 4 Obergeschoss, DDR-6900 Jena, German Democratic Republic. *Phone:* (37-791) 822-4121.

454 FRIEDRICH-SCHILLER-UNIVERSITAET JENA
International Summer Courses of German Language and Culture.
Location: Weimar.
Dates: 3 weeks, August.
Subjects: Advanced German language; GDR culture, literature.
Credit: None.
Eligibility: Teachers, professionals in the field of German studies.
Instruction: In German. Students attend special courses for foreigners at Friedrich Schiller University.
Highlights: Program began in 1966. Excursions.
Costs: $325 includes tuition, housing, meals, excursions, social activities.
Housing: In hotels, private homes.
Deadline: May 31.
Contact: Friedrich-Schiller-Universitaet Jena, Universitaetshochhaus, 4 Obergeschoss, DDR-6900 Jena, German Democratic Republic. *Phone:* (37-791) 822-4121.

455 HOCHSCHULE FUER MUSIK FRANZ LISZT
International Music Seminar.
Location: Weimar.
Dates: 2 weeks, July.
Subjects: Master classes for soloists (instrumental and vocal) and teachers of music.
Credit: None.
Eligibility: Graduates, professional musicians, teachers of music. Minimum age 19; maximum age 50. Requires advanced technical skills in music.
Instruction: In German (interpreter available). Students attend special courses for foreigners at the Franz Liszt College of Music.
Highlights: Program began in 1960.
Costs: $350 includes tuition, housing, meals.
Housing: In residence halls.
Deadline: April 30.
Contact: Hochschule fuer Musik Franz Liszt, Platz der Demokratie 2, DDR-5300 Weimar, German Democratic Republic. *Phone:* (37-621) 5241.

ZWICKAU

456 PAEDAGOGISCHE HOCHSCHULE ERNST SCHNELLER
International Summer Course for Teachers of German.
Location: Zwickau.
Dates: 3 weeks, July 6–26.
Subjects: Advanced German language, phonetics; GDR education, literature, society.
Credit: None.
Eligibility: Graduates, teachers of German.
Instruction: In German. Students attend special courses for foreigners at Paedagogische Hochschule Ernst Schneller.
Highlights: Program begins in 1988. Excursions to Berlin/Potsdam or Dresden/Meissen. Social and cultural activities.
Costs: DM 700 includes tuition, housing, meals, excursions, fees, social and cultural activities.
Housing: In residence halls.
Deadline: March 30.
Contact: Paedagogische Hochschule Ernst Schneller, Internationale Beziehungen, Scheffelstrasse 39, DDR-9560 Zwickau, German Democratic Republic. *Phone:* (37-71) 748248.

FEDERAL REPUBLIC OF GERMANY
MORE THAN ONE CITY

457 INSTITUTE FOR FOREIGN CULTURAL RELATIONS
Education Seminars.
Location: Berlin, Black Forest, Munich, Stuttgart.
Dates: 3 weeks, July–August.
Subjects: Contemporary German arts, educational system, history, society.
Credit: None.
Eligibility: Teachers, administrators. Minimum age 18; maximum age 65.
Instruction: In English. Students attend special courses for foreigners taught by foreign faculty.
Highlights: Program began in 1967. Offered in cooperation with European Education Institutes. 1 week of program-related travel. Program evaluations available to prospective participants.
Costs: $600 includes tuition, housing, meals, excursions, fees.
Housing: In furnished rooms.
Deadline: April 1.
Contact: U. Schweneke, North America Dept., Institute for Foreign Cultural Relations, Charlottenplatz 17, D-7000 Stuttgart 1, Federal Republic of Germany. *Phone:* (49-711) 222-5138. *Telex:* 0723772.

458 UNIVERSITY OF CONNECTICUT
Goethe Institute Credit Program.
Location: 16 cities, including Berlin.
Dates: 8-week courses year-round; students may enroll for 4 weeks.
Subjects: German language on all levels; German civilization, culture. Special courses for teachers.
Credit: Undergraduate credit. Graduate credit.
Eligibility: Undergraduates, graduates, teachers, precollege. Minimum age 18.
Instruction: In German. Students attend special courses for foreigners at Goethe-Institut.
Highlights: Program began in 1975. Program evaluations available to prospective participants.
Costs: $1,800 includes tuition.
Housing: In residence halls, furnished rooms, private homes.
Deadline: Rolling.
Contact: Goethe House New York, 1014 Fifth Ave., New York, NY 10028. *Or:* Dept. of Germanic and Slavic Languages, University of Connecticut, Box U-137, Storrs, CT 06268.

COLOGNE

459 EUROCENTRES
Learn a Language—Live a Language.
Location: Cologne.
Dates: 4-week and longer courses, July–September. 3-month terms begin in mid-January, late April, early July, late September.

All program information is subject to change without notice and must be confirmed directly with the sponsor.

90

Subjects: Intensive German on all levels, business/technical German; German culture, literature; courses for teachers of German.
Credit: None. Statement of achievement, internal and external exams available.
Eligibility: Adults. Minimum age 16; average age 25.
Instruction: In German. Students attend special courses for foreigners at Cologne Eurocentre.
Highlights: New school building. Optional excursions.
Costs: About $1,160 for 4 weeks, $2,500–$3,200 for 12 weeks, includes tuition, housing, some meals, books.
Housing: In private homes.
Deadline: Apply early.
Contact: Head Office, Eurocentres, Seestrasse 247, CH-8038 Zurich, Switzerland. *Phone:* (41-1) 482-5040. *Telex:* 815250. *Or:* Dr. W. Raatz, Principal, Eurozentrum, Sedanstrasse 31-33, D-5000 Cologne, Federal Republic of Germany. *Phone:* (49-221) 380428. *Telex:* 8882903.

HEIDELBERG

460 UNIVERSITY OF HEIDELBERG
International Vacation Course.
Location: Heidelberg.
Dates: July 17–Aug. 12.
Subjects: German language on all levels; special course for teachers of German.
Credit: None.
Eligibility: Adults, teachers. Minimum age 18.
Instruction: In German. Students attend special courses for foreigners at the University of Heidelberg.
Highlights: Program began in 1926. Weekend excursions.
Costs: DM 420 includes tuition, fees.
Housing: In residence halls, furnished rooms.
Deadline: June 1.
Contact: University of Heidelberg, Akademisches Auslandsamt, Seminarstr. 2, Postfach 105 760, D-6900 Heidelberg, Federal Republic of Germany. *Phone:* (49-6221) 542490/542338.

KASSEL

461 EUROPA-KOLLEG KASSEL
Intensive German Language Studies.
Location: Kassel.
Dates: 3–4 weeks, June 12–Sept. 26. 2-week course for teachers of German, July 3–16. Year-round courses also available.
Subjects: German language on all levels; German arts, civilization, culture, literature; courses for teachers of German.
Credit: None.
Eligibility: Undergraduates, adults, teachers, precollege. Minimum age 16; average age 19–24.
Instruction: In German. Students attend special courses for foreigners at Europa-Kolleg.
Highlights: Program began in 1967. Excursions and field trips. Contact with previous participants available.
Costs: DM 500 per week, includes tuition, housing, meals, books, excursions.
Housing: In private homes.
Deadline: 4 weeks before course begins.
Contact: Europa-Kolleg Kassel, Wilhelmshoher Allee 19, D-3500 Kassel, Federal Republic of Germany. *Phone:* (49-561) 776788. *Telex:* 99617 EUKOL D. *Or:* Prof. E. Kuhn-Osius, 230 W. 105th St., Apt. 7B, New York, NY 10025. *Phone:* (212) 865-7332.

TRIER

462 UNIVERSITY OF TRIER
German Language Summer Courses.
Location: Trier.
Dates: Aug. 8–Sept. 2.
Subjects: German language; German literature, society; special language courses for German teachers and advanced students.
Credit: None.

Eligibility: Adults, teachers. Minimum age 18; average age 25. Requires basic knowledge of German.
Instruction: In German. Students attend special courses for foreigners at the Universitaet Trier.
Highlights: Program began in 1971. 1 week of optional program-related travel to Berlin.
Costs: About DM 500 includes tuition, books, excursions, fees; DM 300 for Berlin trip.
Housing: In residence halls, furnished rooms, apartments, private homes.
Deadline: May 1.
Contact: Gretlies Haungs, Akademisches Auslandsamt, Universitaet Trier, Postfach 3825, D-5500 Trier, Tarforst, Federal Republic of Germany. *Phone:* (49-651) 2011.

463 UNIVERSITY OF TRIER
Zusatzzertifikat Deutsch als Fremdsprache.
Location: Trier.
Dates: 2–4 semesters, beginning in October.
Subjects: Teaching German as a foreign language.
Credit: Certificate.
Eligibility: Graduates, teachers, professionals. Requires MA in German or another language.
Instruction: In German. Students attend regular classes at University of Trier.
Highlights: Program began in 1981. 2-week orientation. Excursions.
Costs: DM 7,500 per academic year, includes tuition, housing, meals, books, excursions, fees, insurance. Scholarships available.
Housing: Sponsor assists in locating housing.
Deadline: Aug. 31.
Contact: Gretlies Haungs, Leiterin des Akademischen Auslandsamtes, Universitaet Trier, P.B. 3825, D-5500 Trier, West Germany. *Phone:* (49-651) 201 28 06/8. *Telex:* 472680 UNITR.

TUBINGEN

464 SPRACHINSTITUT TUBINGEN (SIT) and INTERNATIONALER BUND FUER SOZIALARBEIT
Intensive Language Courses.
Location: Tubingen.
Dates: 4–8 weeks, year-round.
Subjects: Intensive German language on all levels; technical German, teaching German; preparation for entrance into German universities.
Credit: None.
Eligibility: Undergraduates, graduates, teachers, adults. Minimum age 16.
Instruction: In German. Students attend special courses for foreigners at SIT.
Highlights: Orientation abroad. Field trips. Contact with previous participants available.
Costs: $1,550 includes tuition, housing, meals, books, excursions, cultural activities.
Housing: In furnished rooms, apartments, private homes.
Deadline: 1 month before course begins.
Contact: Dr. Otto Letze, Director, Sprachinstitut Tubingen (SIT), Eugenstrasse 71, D-7400 Tubingen, Federal Republic of Germany. *Phone:* (49-7071) 34018/19.

GREECE

MORE THAN ONE CITY

465 STATE UNIVERSITY COLLEGE AT BROCKPORT
Greek Mythology.
Location: Athens and nearby cities, Crete.
Dates: May 27–June 17, July 1–22.
Subjects: Greek literature, mythology.
Credit: 3 undergraduate credits. Graduate credit.
Eligibility: Undergraduates, graduates, teachers.
Instruction: In English. Students attend courses arranged for the group taught by U.S. faculty.
Highlights: Program began in 1972. 1-day orientation.

All program information is subject to change without notice and must be confirmed directly with the sponsor.

91

Costs: About $1,500 includes tuition, books, housing, meals, round-trip transportation, excursions, fees.
Housing: In hotels.
Deadline: May 1.
Contact: Dr. John Perry, Office of International Education, State University College at Brockport, Brockport, NY 14420. *Phone:* (716) 395-2119.

ATHENS

466 AMERICAN SCHOOL OF CLASSICAL STUDIES AT ATHENS
Summer Session.
Location: Athens and nearby cities.
Dates: 6-week sessions.
Subjects: Greek antiquities, culture, history, literature.
Credit: Available by arrangement.
Eligibility: Upperclassmen, graduates, teachers.
Instruction: In English. Students attend courses arranged for the group taught by U.S. faculty.
Highlights: Orientation abroad. Excursions and field trips.
Costs: About $1,500 includes tuition, housing, some meals, excursions, field trips, fees. Scholarships available.
Housing: In hotels.
Deadline: Feb. 1.
Contact: Dept. A-3, Summer Session, American School of Classical Studies, 41 E. 72nd St., New York, NY 10021. *Phone:* (212) 861-0302.

THESSALONIKI

467 ARISTOTLE UNIVERSITY OF THESSALONIKI, SCHOOL OF MODERN GREEK LANGUAGE
Winter Programme.
Location: Thessaloniki (Salonica), northern Greece.
Dates: October–June; students must enroll for entire period. Summer program also available.
Subjects: Greek language on all levels; Greek civilization; student teaching.
Credit: By special arrangement.
Eligibility: Undergraduates, graduates, adults, teachers, professionals. Requires high school diploma.
Instruction: In English, Greek. Students attend special courses for foreigners at the School of Modern Greek Language of the University of Thessaloniki.
Highlights: Program began in 1987.
Costs: 27,000 drachmas (1987) per year, includes tuition. Scholarships available.
Housing: Students make own arrangements.
Deadline: Sept. 10.
Contact: Secretary, School of Modern Greek Language, Aristotle University of Thessaloniki, GR-54006 Thessaloniki, Greece. *Phone:* (30-31) 981380/991381.

IRELAND

CORK

468 CORK SCHOOL OF MUSIC
Teaching Diploma Course.
Location: Cork, Ireland.
Dates: September–June; 2-year program.
Subjects: Music education: practical studies, musicianship skills, composition, history, teaching skills.
Credit: Diploma.
Eligibility: Undergraduates, adults, teachers. Requires high school diploma, audition, interview, reference.
Instruction: In English. Students attend regular classes at the Cork School of Music.
Highlights: Program began in 1878.
Costs: £350 per session, includes tuition.
Housing: Students make own arrangements.
Deadline: None.

Contact: John C. Murphy, Director, Cork School of Music, 13 Union Quay, Cork, Ireland. *Phon:* (353-21) 270076/965583.

GALWAY

469 UNIVERSITY COLLEGE GALWAY
International Seminar: Education in Ireland.
Location: Galway.
Dates: June 24–July 19.
Subjects: Irish education system, culture, history, literature.
Credit: 6 graduate credits.
Eligibility: Teachers, professionals in the field of education and related disciplines.
Instruction: In English. Students attend special courses for foreigners at University College Galway.
Highlights: Program began in 1981. Excursions and cultural events.
Costs: $1,050 includes tuition, housing, some meals, excursions, fees, theater tickets.
Housing: In private homes.
Deadline: May 6.
Contact: Administrative Director, Summer School Office, University College, Galway, Ireland. *Phone:* (353-91) 24411, Ext. 146. *Telex:* 28823.

ITALY

MORE THAN ONE CITY

470 CENTRO DI LINGUA E CULTURA ITALIANA FIORENZA
Intensive Group and Individual Courses.
Location: Elba, Florence.
Dates: 2- and 4-week courses, year-round.
Subjects: Italian language on all levels; business and medical Italian; ceramics; Italian art history, cuisine, culture, literature.
Credit: Available by arrangement.
Eligibility: Undergraduates, graduates, adults, teachers. Minimum age 18.
Instruction: In Italian. Students attend special courses for foreigners at Centro Fiorenza.
Highlights: Program began in 1983. 1-day orientation. Excursions. Contact with previous participants available.
Costs: Contact sponsor for information.
Housing: In residence halls, furnished rooms, apartments, hotels, pensions, private homes.
Deadline: 1 month before course begins.
Contact: Mrs. Merlini-Seiwald, Secretary, Centro Fiorenza, Via San Spirito 14, 50125 Firenze, Italy. *Phone:* (39-55) 298274. *Telex:* 570215 PPFI ATT: FIORENZA 27.

471 PARSONS SCHOOL OF DESIGN
Parsons in Italy.
Location: Florence, Rome, Venice.
Dates: About June 30–July 30.
Subjects: Italian architecture, contemporary Italian design.
Credit: 6 undergraduate credits. Graduate credit available.
Eligibility: Undergraduates, graduates, teachers, professionals.
Instruction: In English. Students attend courses arranged for the group taught by U.S. and foreign faculty.
Highlights: Program began in 1982. 1-day orientation abroad.
Costs: About $3,600 includes tuition, round-trip transportation, housing, excursions, fees.
Housing: In hotels.
Deadline: May 1.
Contact: Office of Special Programs, Parsons School of Design, 66 Fifth Ave., New York, NY 10011. *Phone:* (212) 741-8975.

BAGNO DI ROMAGNA

472 SCUOLA PALAZZO MALVISI
Italian as a Foreign Language/Italian Culture.
Location: Bagno di Romagna (Forlì), Italy.
Dates: 8- and 12-week courses, March–November. Shorter courses also available.

Subjects: Intensive Italian language on all levels; Italian culture, including art history, cinema, literature.
Credit: Certificate.
Eligibility: Undergraduates, graduates, adults, teachers. Minimum age 17.
Instruction: In Italian. Students attend special courses for foreigners at the Scuola Palazzo Malvisi.
Highlights: Program began in 1981. Excursions.
Costs: About Lit. 1,700,000 per month, includes tuition, books, housing, meals, fees, insurance. Scholarships available.
Housing: In hotels.
Deadline: 1 month before course begins.
Contact: Scuola Palazzo Malvisi, Via Fiorentina 36, 47021 Bagno di Romagna (Forli), Italy.

FLORENCE

473 EUROCENTRES
Italian Language and Culture Programs.
Location: Florence.
Dates: Summer courses, 4 weeks, July–September. 3-month terms begin in mid-January, late April, early July, late September.
Subjects: Intensive Italian language on all levels, business/technical Italian; Italian culture, literature; courses for teachers of Italian.
Credit: None. Certificate available.
Eligibility: Undergraduates, adults, teachers. Minimum age 16.
Instruction: In Italian. Students attend special courses for foreigners at Florence Eurocentre.
Highlights: Program began in 1959. Optional excursions.
Costs: About $1,150 for 4 weeks, $3,200–3,500 for 3 months, includes tuition, housing, some meals.
Housing: In private homes.
Deadline: Apply early.
Contact: Head Office, Eurocentres, Seestrasse 247, CH-8038 Zurich, Switzerland. *Phone:* (41-1) 482-5040. *Telex:* 815250. *Or:* Eurocentro, Piazza S. Spirito 9, Palazzo Guadagni, I-50125 Florence, Italy. *Phone:* (39-55) 29 46 05. *Telex:* 572645.

474 FAIRFIELD UNIVERSITY
Summer Campus in Florence.
Location: Florence.
Dates: June 28–July 30.
Subjects: Conversational Italian language on all levels.
Credit: 9 undergraduate credits. 9 graduate credits.
Eligibility: Undergraduates, graduates, adults, artists, teachers. Minimum age 18. Requires letters of recommendation from home school.
Instruction: In English, Italian. Students attend special courses for foreigners at Lorenzo de' Medici School of Arts and Languages.
Highlights: Program began in 1987. 1-day orientation in U.S. and 3 days abroad. Program-related travel to Assisi, Rome, Siena, Venice. Excursions. Contact with previous participants available.
Costs: About $3,350 includes tuition, housing, some meals, round-trip transportation, fees.
Housing: In hostels, hotels, pensions.
Deadline: April 15, or until program is filled; apply early.
Contact: Dr. Philip Eliasoph, Chairman, Fine Arts Dept., or Dr. Vilma Allen, Dean of Continuing Education, Fairfield University, Fairfield, CT 06430-7524. *Phone:* (203) 254-4000, Ext. 4220.

475 SCUOLA LEONARDO DA VINCI
Italian Language and Culture for Foreigners.
Location: Florence.
Dates: 2–4 weeks, summer. 12 weeks, beginning in April and late September; 16 weeks, beginning in March and late August.
Subjects: Italian language on all levels; business Italian, medical Italian, courses for teachers of Italian; art history, cooking, drawing, handicrafts, painting, politics, wine.
Credit: None.
Eligibility: Undergraduates, graduates, teachers, adults, precollege. Minimum age 16.

Instruction: In Italian. Students attend special courses for foreigners at Scuola Leonardo da Vinci.
Highlights: Program began in 1977. Excursions and field trips. Contact with previous participants available.
Costs: Vary depending on course selected and length of stay; about $370 per month, includes tuition, books. Scholarships and work-study available.
Housing: Sponsor assists in locating housing.
Deadline: 1 month before course begins.
Contact: U.S. Student Programs, Institute of International Education, 809 United Nations Plaza, New York, NY 10017. *Phone:* (212) 984-5330. *Telex:* 175977 INTERED.

LA SPEZIA

476 SOCIETA ITALIANA DI FISICA
Enrico Fermi International School of Physics.
Location: Villa Marigola, Lerici (La Spezia).
Dates: 3 weeks, June–July.
Subjects: Physics: current trends in the physics of materials.
Credit: None.
Eligibility: Physicists: teachers, professionals. Requires letter of recommendation from research group leader or professor.
Instruction: In English, Italian. Students attend regular classes at the Enrico Fermi International School of Physics.
Highlights: Offered in cooperation with the Centro Studi Sociali di La Spezia.
Costs: Lit. 2,300,000 includes tuition, housing, meals. Scholarships available.
Housing: In hotels.
Deadline: April 30.
Contact: Mario Tosi, International Centre for Theoretical Physics, P.O. Box 586, 34100 Trieste, Italy. *Phone:* (39-40) 224 02 78/22 42 41. *Telex:* 460449 APH I. *Telefax:* (39-40) 22 45 31.

RAVENNA

477 SCUOLA PALAZZO MALVISI
Italian Language and Culture.
Location: Ravenna.
Dates: 8- and 12-week courses, March–November. Shorter courses also available.
Subjects: Italian language on all levels; Italian art history, literature, mosaics.
Credit: Certificate.
Eligibility: Undergraduates, graduates, adults, teachers. Minimum age 17.
Instruction: In Italian. Students attend special courses for foreigners at the Scuola Palazzo Malvisi.
Highlights: Program began in 1986. Excursions.
Costs: About Lit. 600,000 per month, includes tuition, books, fees, insurance. Scholarships available.
Housing: Sponsor assists in locating housing.
Deadline: 4 weeks before course begins.
Contact: Scuola Palazzo Malvisi, Via Ponte Marino 10, 48100 Ravenna, Italy.

ROME

478 AMERICAN ACADEMY IN ROME
School of Classical Studies Summer Session.
Location: Rome.
Dates: 6 weeks, late June–early Aug.
Subjects: Roman civilization from the earliest times to the age of Constantine.
Credit: Graduate credit.
Eligibility: Undergraduates, graduates, professionals. Latin teachers and graduate students in the classics preferred.
Instruction: In English. Students attend regular classes at the American Academy in Rome.
Highlights: Program began in 1922. Excursions and field trips to archaeological sites and museums.

All program information is subject to change without notice and must be confirmed directly with the sponsor.

93

Costs: About $1,500 includes tuition, housing, some meals, round-trip transportation, excursions, field trips.
Housing: Sponsor assists in locating housing.
Deadline: March 1.
Contact: American Academy in Rome, 41 E. 65th St., New York, NY 10021. *Phone:* (212) 517-4200.

479 DILIT-INTERNATIONAL HOUSE
Italian Language.
Location: Rome.
Dates: 4-week courses begin alternate Mondays, year-round.
Subjects: Italian language on all levels; teacher training.
Credit: None.
Eligibility: Undergraduates, adults, teachers, precollege. Minimum age 14.
Instruction: In Italian. Students attend special courses for foreigners at DILIT.
Highlights: Program began in 1968. Excursions.
Costs: Lit. 490,000 includes tuition, fees. Scholarships available.
Housing: Sponsor assists in locating housing.
Deadline: 2 weeks before course begins.
Contact: Mr. Giorgio Piva, DILIT-International House, Via Marghera 22, 00185 Rome, Italy. *Phone:* (39-6) 49 25 92/49 25 93. *Telex:* 626678 COOP H T. For scholarships, apply to nearest Istituto di Cultura Italiana.

SIENA

480 SCUOLA DI LINGUA E CULTURA ITALIANA PER STRANIERI
Italian Language and Culture Courses in Siena.
Location: Siena.
Dates: 10-week terms, beginning in early October, mid-January, early April.
Subjects: Italian language on all levels; Italian archaeology, art history, culture, history, literature; special courses for teachers of Italian.
Credit: Certificate.
Eligibility: Undergraduates, graduates, adults, teachers. Requires high school diploma.
Instruction: In Italian. Students attend special courses for foreigners at Scuola di Lingua e Cultura Italiana per Stranieri.
Highlights: Program began in 1915. Excursions and field trips.
Costs: Lit. 309,000 per term, includes tuition, fees. Scholarships available.
Housing: Sponsor assists in locating housing.
Deadline: 20 days before term begins.
Contact: Secretariat, Scuola di Lingua e Cultura Italiana per Stranieri, Piazzetta Grassi 2, 53100 Siena, Italy. *Phone:* (39-577) 49260.

URBINO

481 UNIVERSITY OF CENTRAL FLORIDA
Summer Study Program.
Location: Urbino.
Dates: June 26–Aug. 12.
Subjects: Italian language on all levels; Italian culture, Renaissance art.
Credit: 10 undergraduate credits.
Eligibility: Undergraduates, professionals, teachers. Requires 2.0 GPA.
Instruction: In Italian, English. Students attend courses arranged for the group taught by U.S. and foreign faculty at the University of Urbino.
Highlights: Program began in 1975. Orientation in U.S. and abroad: language course placement. Program-related travel. Program evaluations available to prospective participants.
Costs: $1,975 includes meals, round-trip transportation, housing, excursions, fees.
Housing: In furnished rooms, private homes.
Deadline: April 30.
Contact: Dr. A.V. Cervone, Program Director, Dept. of Foreign Languages, University of Central Florida, Orlando, FL 32816. *Phone:* (305) 275-2466.

VARENNA

482 SOCIETA ITALIANA DI FISICA
Enrico Fermi International School of Physics.
Location: Villa Monastero, Varenna sul Lago di Como.
Dates: 10-day courses, June–August.
Subjects: Physics: (June 28–July 7) chemical physics of atomic and molecular clusters; (July 12–22) photoemission and absorption spectroscopy of solids and interfaces with synchrotron radiation; (July 26–Aug. 5) nonlinear topics in ocean physics.
Credit: None.
Eligibility: Physicists: teachers, professionals. Requires letter of recommendation from research group leader or professor.
Instruction: In English, Italian. Students attend regular classes at the Enrico Fermi International School of Physics.
Highlights: Offered in cooperation with the Ministero della Pubblica Istruzione and the Consiglio Nazionale delle Ricerche.
Costs: Lit. 1,200,000 per course, includes tuition, meals, H. Scholarships available.
Housing: In hotels.
Deadline: May 7.
Contact: Societa Italiana di Fisica, Via degli Andalo 2, 40124 Bologna, Italy. *Phone:* (39-51) 33 15 54. *Telex:* 583376 SIF I. *Telefax:* (39-51) 58 13 40.

NETHERLANDS

AMSTERDAM

483 AMSTERDAM SUMMER SCHOOL OF ART
Art History and Studio Arts.
Location: Amsterdam.
Dates: 6 weeks, June 27–Aug. 6.
Subjects: Flemish and Dutch art history; studio arts, including beginning and advanced drawing and painting.
Credit: 3 credits available per course.
Eligibility: Undergraduates, adults, teachers. Requires 2 recommendations, 1 year of previous art study.
Instruction: In English. Students attend regular classes at the Amsterdam Summer School of Art.
Highlights: Program began in 1986. Offered in cooperation with the Rijksakademie van Beeldende Kunsten (National Academy of Fine Arts). Excursions and field trips.
Costs: About $650 per course, includes tuition, E. Scholarships available.
Housing: In residence halls, apartments.
Deadline: April 1.
Contact: Ursula Neubauer, Program Director, Amsterdam Summer School of Art, Keizersgracht 822, 1017 EE Amsterdam, Netherlands. *Phone:* (31-20) 235541. ($20 application fee required.)

BARNEVELD

484 BARNEVELD COLLEGE
International Training Center for Animal Husbandry and Milling Technology.
Location: Barneveld.
Dates: Vary.
Subjects: Animal husbandry, including animal feed, milling technology; beekeeping; environmental hygiene; cattle, goat, pig, poultry, sheep husbandry; rabbit keeping, breeding.
Credit: None.
Eligibility: Teachers of agriculture, agriculture extension officers, adults, nationals from developing countries.
Instruction: In English, French, Dutch. Students attend regular classes at Barneveld College.
Highlights: Program began in 1961. Excursions.
Costs: Contact sponsor for information.
Housing: In castle, guest houses.
Deadline: May 1.
Contact: Director, International Studies and Projects, Barneveld College, P.O. Box 64, 3770 AB, Barneveld, Netherlands. *Phone:* (31-3420) 14881.

All program information is subject to change without notice and must be confirmed directly with the sponsor.

94

SPAIN

MORE THAN ONE CITY

485 MONTEREY INSTITUTE OF INTERNATIONAL STUDIES
Summer Study in Spain.
Location: Andalucia, Madrid.
Dates: July 6–Aug. 17.
Subjects: Spanish language on all levels; Hispanic culture, business, language teaching methods.
Credit: 8 undergraduate semester hours. Graduate credit.
Eligibility: Sophomores, juniors, seniors, graduates, teachers, professionals, precollege. Requires some Spanish for intermediate level, fluency in Spanish for graduate program.
Instruction: Students attend courses arranged for the group taught by U.S. and foreign faculty.
Highlights: Program began in 1979. 1-day orientation abroad. 1 week of program-related travel. Program evaluations available to prospective participants.
Costs: $2,400 includes tuition, housing, meals, E.
Housing: In residence halls.
Deadline: May 29.
Contact: Dr. Ovidio Casado-Fuente, Director, Summer Study in Spain, Monterey Institute of International Studies, 425 Van Buren St., Monterey, CA 93940. *Phone:* (408) 647-4173.

486 UNIVERSITY STUDIES IN THE BASQUE COUNTRY CONSORTIUM
Basque and Spanish Studies in Spain.
Location: Fuenterrabia, San Sebastian.
Dates: Sept. 7–May 18; students may enroll for 1 or both semesters. Summer program also available.
Subjects: Basque and Spanish languages on all levels; Basque and Spanish studies, including anthropology, art history, culture, cuisine, economics, folk dance, history, literature, music, political science, teacher education, watercolor; independent study.
Credit: 12–17 credits per semester. Graduate credit.
Eligibility: Sophomores, juniors, seniors, graduates. Requires good academic standing.
Instruction: In English, Spanish. Students attend courses arranged for the group taught by U.S. and foreign faculty and regular classes at the University of the Basque Country.
Highlights: Program began in 1982. Orientation abroad. Program-related travel in Spain.
Costs: $5,582 per year, includes tuition, books, round-trip transportation, excursions, fees, some meals, some H. Scholarships available.
Housing: In residence halls, apartments (with Spanish roommates), private homes.
Deadline: June 15 for fall; Dec. 1 for spring.
Contact: Dr. Carmelo Urza, University Studies in the Basque Country Consortium, University of Nevada Library, Reno, NV 89557. *Phone:* (702) 784-4854.

CANARY ISLANDS

487 GRAN CANARIA SCHOOL OF LANGUAGES
Intensive Spanish Courses.
Location: Las Palmas de Gran Canaria, Canary Islands.
Dates: 2 weeks or longer, year-round.
Subjects: Spanish language on all levels; business Spanish, teaching Spanish as a foreign language, Spanish civilization.
Credit: Credit and teacher certification available.
Eligibility: Undergraduates, adults, teachers, precollege. Minimum age 15.
Instruction: In Spanish. Students attend special courses for foreigners at Gran Canaria School.
Highlights: Program began in 1964. Orientation abroad. Excursions, cultural events, and sports. Program evaluations available to prospective participants.

Costs: Contact sponsor for information.
Housing: In private homes, or sponsor assists in locating housing.
Deadline: 1 month before course begins.
Contact: Louise Harber, Gran Canaria S.O.L., Programs Coordinator, Box 5409, G.C.S., New York, NY 10163. *Phone:* (212) 662-1090. *Telex:* 645646 LHARBER NYK. *Or:* Jose L. Lagartos, Director, Gran Canaria S.O.L., Tomas Morales 54, 35003 Las Palmas de Gran Canaria, Spain. *Phone:* (34-28) 371957. *Telex:* 95005 (Spain).

MADRID

488 BOWLING GREEN STATE UNIVERSITY
Academic Year Abroad in Spain.
Location: Madrid.
Dates: Sept. 6–Dec. 17 and/or Jan. 9–May 6. Summer program also available.
Subjects: Spanish language; Spanish art, art history, business, culture, history, geography, literature, philosophy, theater.
Credit: 15 credits per semester.
Eligibility: Undergraduates, graduates, precollege, teachers, professionals. Requires good academic standing, 2 years of college-level Spanish or equivalent.
Instruction: In Spanish. Students attend courses arranged for the group taught by U.S. and foreign faculty.
Highlights: Program began in 1962. Offered in cooperation with the Instituto de Cooperacion Ibero-Americano. 3-day orientation in U.S. and abroad.
Costs: About $2,600 per semester, includes tuition, housing, meals, excursions, fees. Scholarships available.
Housing: In private homes.
Deadline: Until program is filled; apply early.
Contact: Dr. Mercedes Junquera, Director, AYA Spain, Department of Romance Languages, Bowling Green State University, Bowling Green, OH 43403. *Phone:* (419) 372-0053/353-1643.

489 EUROCENTRES
Learn a Language—Live a Language.
Location: Madrid.
Dates: 3, 4, and 8 weeks, July–September. 3-month terms begin in early January, late April, late September.
Subjects: Intensive Spanish language on all levels; business/technical Spanish, Spanish culture; courses for teachers of Spanish.
Credit: None.
Eligibility: Undergraduate, adults, teachers. Minimum age 16; average age 21.
Instruction: In Spanish. Students attend special courses for foreigners at Madrid Eurocentre.
Highlights: Program began in 1960. Excursions.
Costs: About $700 for 4 weeks, $1,400 for 8 weeks, $2,300–$2,400 for 3 months, includes tuition, books, housing, fees, some meals.
Housing: In private homes.
Deadline: Apply early.
Contact: Head Office, Eurocentres, Seestrasse 247, CH-8038 Zurich, Switzerland. *Phone:* (41-1) 482-5040. *Telex:* 815250. *Or:* Eurocentro, Institutos Mangold S.A., Gran Via 32, E-28013 Madrid, Spain. *Phone:* (34-1) 231-4040. *Telex:* 22847.

490 ROLLINS COLLEGE
Verano Espanol.
Location: Madrid.
Dates: 6 weeks, mid-June–mid-July.
Subjects: Advanced Spanish language; Spanish art history, literature, society.
Credit: 10–15 undergraduate quarter hours.
Eligibility: Undergraduates, professionals, teachers, precollege. Requires 2 years of college-level Spanish or equivalent, good academic standing.
Instruction: In Spanish. Students attend courses arranged for the group taught by foreign faculty at the Center for International Studies.
Highlights: Program began in 1960. Orientation by mail. Excursions and group events in Madrid. Contact with previous participants available.

All program information is subject to change without notice
and must be confirmed directly with the sponsor.

Costs: About $2,400 includes tuition, meals, round-trip transportation, housing, excursions, fees.
Housing: In private homes.
Deadline: April 15.
Contact: Dept. of Foreign Languages, Rollins College, Box 2632, 1000 Holt Ave., Winter Park, FL 32789. *Phone:* (305) 646-2623.

SALAMANCA

491 AMERICAN INSTITUTE FOR FOREIGN STUDY (AIFS)
Spanish Language and Culture.
Location: Salamanca.
Dates: 4-, 6-, and 8-week programs starting June 25.
Subjects: Intensive Spanish language on all levels; special courses for elementary and secondary school teachers of Spanish; Spanish culture.
Credit: Up to 8 undergraduate semester hours.
Eligibility: Undergraduates, graduates, teachers.
Instruction: In Spanish. Students attend courses arranged for the group taught by foreign faculty.
Highlights: Program began in 1969. Offered in cooperation with the University of Salamanca. Program evaluations available to prospective participants.
Costs: $1,939 for 4 weeks, includes tuition, meals, round-trip transportation, housing, excursions, fees.
Housing: In residence halls.
Deadline: May 1.
Contact: Gerry Thompson, American Institute for Foreign Study (AIFS), 102 Greenwich Ave., Greenwich, CT 06830. *Phone:* (203) 869-9090.

492 NEW YORK UNIVERSITY
NYU in Spain Graduate Summer Program.
Location: Salamanca.
Dates: July 6–31.
Subjects: Spanish literature, Hispanic civilization.
Credit: 8 undergraduate credits. Graduate credit.
Eligibility: Seniors, graduates, teachers, auditors. Requires bachelor's degree or permission of program director.
Instruction: In Spanish. Students attend courses arranged for the group taught by U.S. and foreign faculty.
Highlights: Program began in 1975. Offered in cooperation with the University of Salamanca. Orientation.
Costs: About $3,300 includes tuition, housing, meals, round-trip transportation, books, fees. Scholarships available.
Housing: In residence halls.
Deadline: June 1.
Contact: Prof. Salvador Martinez, Director, NYU in Spain Program, New York University, 19 University Pl., Room 409, New York, NY 10003.

493 UNIVERSITY OF RHODE ISLAND
URI/Colegio de Espana Summer Study Program.
Location: Salamanca.
Dates: 5 weeks, late June–July.
Subjects: Spanish language on all levels; Spanish culture, history, literature.
Credit: Up to 9 undergraduate credits.
Eligibility: Undergraduates, graduates, adults, language teachers.
Instruction: In Spanish. Students attend courses arranged for the group taught by U.S. and foreign faculty.
Highlights: Program began in 1984. Offered in cooperation with the Colegio de Espana. 6-day orientation abroad. Excursions and field trips. Contact with previous participants available.
Costs: $935–$995 includes tuition, housing, meals, books, excursions, field trips, fees, insurance.
Housing: In residence halls, private homes.
Deadline: May 1.
Contact: Prof. Mario F. Trubiano, Director, Department of Languages, University of Rhode Island, Independence Hall, Room 306B, Kingston, RI 02881. *Phone:* (401) 792-4717. *Or:* Dr. Jean S. Hyland, Study Abroad Coordinator, University of Rhode Island, 112 Roosevelt Hall, Kingston, RI 02881. *Phone:* (401) 792-5165.

SORIA

494 UNIVERSITY OF NORTHERN IOWA
Summer Institute for Teachers of Spanish.
Location: Soria.
Dates: About June 22–Aug. 17.
Subjects: Intermediate and advanced Spanish language; Spanish culture, literature.
Credit: 9 graduate credits.
Eligibility: Teachers of Spanish only. Requires bachelor's degree.
Instruction: In Spanish. Students attend courses arranged for the group taught by foreign faculty at the Delegacion Provincial de Cultura de Soria.
Highlights: Program began in 1971. 1 week of program-related travel in Spain. Program evaluations available to prospective participants.
Costs: About $2,000 includes tuition, housing, meals, books, excursions, fees.
Housing: In private homes.
Deadline: Jan. 1.
Contact: Dr. Adolfo Franco, Director, Dept. of Modern Languages, University of Northern Iowa, Cedar Falls, IA 50614. *Phone:* (319) 273-2200.

VALENCIA

495 JUNIOR YEAR IN SPAIN
Junior Year in Valencia, Spain.
Location: Valencia.
Dates: Sept. 10–May 3; students may enroll for 1 or both semesters.
Subjects: Advanced Spanish language; business Spanish, composition, conversation, phonetics, translation; Spanish art history, cinema, geography, history, music, literature.
Credit: Undergraduate credit.
Eligibility: Juniors, teachers of Spanish. Requires 2 years of college-level Spanish or equivalent.
Instruction: In Spanish. Students attend courses arranged for the group taught by foreign faculty.
Highlights: Program began in 1959. Orientation abroad. Excursions and field trips. Postsession review. Contact with previous participants available.
Costs: About $3,572 includes tuition, housing, meals, round-trip transportation, excursions, fees.
Housing: In private homes.
Deadline: 2 months before course begins.
Contact: Dr. Carlos Sanchez, Director, or Secretary, Junior Year in Spain, 1315 Monterey Blvd., San Francisco, CA 94127. *Phone:* (415) 586-0180/387-6817.

VALLADOLID

496 UNIVERSIDAD DE VALLADOLID
Curso de Estudios Hispanicos.
Location: Valladolid.
Dates: Mid-January–late March and/or mid-April–late May.
Subjects: Spanish language on all levels; Spanish studies, including art history, cinema, economics, geography, history, literature, sociology.
Credit: Certificate.
Eligibility: Sophomores, juniors, seniors, graduates, adults, teachers, professionals. Minimum age 18.
Instruction: In Spanish. Students attend special courses for foreigners at the Universidad de Valladolid.
Highlights: Program began in 1962. Excursions and field trips.
Costs: About 277,400 ptas. per term, includes tuition, housing, meals, excursions, fees.
Housing: In residence halls, private homes.
Deadline: Jan. 5.
Contact: Sr. Director, Curso de Estudios Hispanicos, Facultad de Filosofia y Letras, Universidad de Valladolid, 47002 Valladolid, Spain.

All program information is subject to change without notice
and must be confirmed directly with the sponsor.

SWITZERLAND

LAUSANNE

497 EUROCENTRES
Learn a Language—Live a Language.
Location: Lausanne.
Dates: 3-month terms begin in mid-January, late April, early July, late September. Shorter courses also available.
Subjects: Intensive French language on all levels; business and technical French; French art, culture, literature; courses for teachers of French.
Credit: Certificate.
Eligibility: Undergraduates, adults, teachers. Minimum age 16.
Instruction: In French. Students attend special courses for foreigners at Lausanne Eurocentre.
Highlights: Program began in 1961. Optional excursions.
Costs: About $3,355–$4,000 per term, includes tuition, housing, some meals.
Housing: In private homes.
Deadline: Apply early.
Contact: Head Office, Eurocentres, Seestrasse 247, CH-8038 Zurich, Switzerland. *Phone:* (41-1) 482 50 40. *Telex:* 815250.

NEUCHATEL

498 STATE UNIVERSITY COLLEGE AT CORTLAND
Cortland International Program at Neuchatel.
Location: Neuchatel.
Dates: July 6–31.
Subjects: French language on all levels, including advanced courses for secondary school teachers.
Credit: 6 undergraduate credits. Graduate credit.
Eligibility: Undergraduates, graduates, teachers. Requires teaching experience for graduate-level course in language and method.
Instruction: In French. Students attend regular courses at University of Neuchatel.
Highlights: Program began in 1968. Orientation abroad. Program evaluations available to prospective participants.
Costs: About $1,200 includes overseas tuition, housing, meals, round-trip transportation, books, fees.
Housing: In student residences.
Deadline: May 1.
Contact: Dr. Willi A. Uschald, Director, Cortland International Programs, State University College at Cortland, P.O. Box 2000, Cortland, NY 13045. *Phone:* (607) 753-2209.

499 UNIVERSITE DE NEUCHATEL
Cours de Vacances.
Location: Neuchatel.
Dates: 4 weeks, July.
Subjects: French language on all levels; special course for teachers of French.
Credit: None.
Eligibility: Undergraduates, adults, teachers. Minimum age 17; average age 20–30.
Instruction: In French. Students attend special classes for foreigners at Universite de Neuchatel.
Highlights: Program began in 1893. Excursions.
Costs: About SFr. 1,400 includes tuition, housing, meals, books, excursions.
Housing: In residence halls, furnished rooms, pensions, private homes.
Deadline: July 1.
Contact: Universite de Neuchatel, Cours de Vacances, Faculte des Lettres, 26 Ave. du Premier-Mars, CH-2000 Neuchatel, Switzerland.

UNION OF SOVIET SOCIALIST REPUBLICS

MORE THAN ONE CITY

500 CITIZEN EXCHANGE COUNCIL
Newsletter: Communique.
Location: 35 cities and towns throughout the USSR.
Dates: 9-day to 3-week courses, year-round.

Subjects: Soviet culture, economics, education system, foreign policy, social services; specialization in Soviet-American relations.
Credit: None.
Eligibility: Undergraduates, adults, teachers, professionals, precollege. Minimum ages 14; maximum age 85; average age 20.
Instruction: In English. Students attend courses arranged for the group.
Highlights: Program began in 1962. Orientation in U.S. and abroad. Discussions with Soviet citizens and field trips to schools, farms, other sites. Contact with previous participants available.
Costs: $1,800–$2,400 depending on program, includes housing, meals, round-trip transportation, field trips, fees, insurance. Scholarships available.
Housing: In hotels.
Deadline: 4 months before course begins.
Contact: Citizen Exchange Council, 18 E. 41st St., Suite 10-04, New York, NY 10017. *Phone:* (212) 889-7960. *Telex:* 4900001648 CEC UI.

LENINGRAD

501 AMERICAN COUNCIL OF TEACHERS OF RUSSIAN
US/USSR Summer Exchange of High School Language Teachers.
Location: Leningrad.
Dates: 6 weeks, June 27–Aug. 9.
Subjects: Intensive advanced Russian language; teaching Russian, methodology.
Credit: Graduate credit.
Eligibility: High school teachers.
Instruction: In Russian. Students attend courses arranged for the group taught by foreign faculty at the Herzen Institute.
Highlights: Program began in 1986. 2-day orientation in U.S. Excursions and program-related travel in Russia. Contact with previous participants available.
Costs: U.S. Information Agency funding includes tuition, housing, meals, round-trip transportation, books, excursions, fees, insurance.
Housing: In residence halls.
Deadline: March 31.
Contact: ACTR: USSR Programs Group, 815 New Gulph Road, Bryn Mawr, PA 19010. *Phone:* (215) 525-6559.

MOSCOW

502 AMERICAN COUNCIL OF TEACHERS OF RUSSIAN
ACTR Ten-Month Program in Moscow.
Location: Moscow.
Dates: Sept. 1–June 30.
Subjects: Advanced Russian language; Soviet culture, literature.
Credit: Undergraduate credit equivalent to academic year. Graduate credit.
Eligibility: Juniors, seniors, graduates. Graduate students and teachers of Russian preferred. Requires 3 years of college-level Russian or equivalent.
Instruction: In Russian. Students attend special courses for foreigners at the Pushkin Institute of Russian Language.
Highlights: Program began in 1976. 2-day orientation in U.S. Excursions and field trips. 4 weeks of program-related travel. Contact with previous participants available.
Costs: $7,700 includes tuition, housing, meals, books, excursions, field trips, fees, insurance. Scholarships available.
Housing: In residence halls.
Deadline: Dec. 6.
Contact: ACTR USSR Programs Group, Russian Center, 815 New Gulph Road, Bryn Mawr, PA 19010. *Phone:* (215) 525-6559.

503 OHIO STATE UNIVERSITY
OSU Russian Language Program.
Location: Moscow.
Dates: Sept. 1–Dec. 28 and/or Feb. 1–May 13; students may enroll for 1 or both semesters.
Subjects: Intermediate and advanced Russian language; Russian and Soviet culture, history, literature, teaching methodology.
Credit: 23 undergraduate quarter hours.
Eligibility: Undergraduates, graduates. Requires 30 quarter hours or 18 semester hours of Russian language prior to departure.

All program information is subject to change without notice and must be confirmed directly with the sponsor.

97

Instruction: In Russian. Students attend special courses for foreigners at Pushkin Russian Language Institute.
Highlights: Program began in 1975. Orientation abroad. Excursions and field trips. Program-related travel in the USSR. Program evaluations available to prospective participants.
Costs: About $2,800 per semester, includes housing, meals, books, excursions, fees.
Housing: In residence halls.
Deadline: March 1 for fall; Oct. 1 for spring.
Contact: Department of Slavic and East European Languages and Literatures, Ohio State University, 1841 Millikin Rd., Columbus, OH 43210. *Phone:* (614) 292-6733.

504 OHIO STATE UNIVERSITY
Ten-Month Russian Language Program.
Location: Moscow.
Dates: Sept. 1–June 30; students must enroll for entire period.
Subjects: Teaching Russian as a foreign language; Soviet civilization, culture, literature.
Credit: 45 graduate quarter hours or 30 semester hours.
Eligibility: Graduates. Prospective Russian language teachers only. Requires previous participation in USSR program, passing score on Russian language test.
Instruction: In Russian. Students attend special courses for foreigners at Pushkin Russian Language Institute.
Highlights: Program began in 1980. 1-day orientation abroad. Excursions and field trips. 4 weeks of program-related travel in the USSR.
Costs: About $7,000 includes tuition, housing, meals, books, excursions, fees. Scholarships available.
Housing: In residence halls.
Deadline: March 1.
Contact: Department of Slavic and East European Languages and Literatures, Ohio State University, 1841 Millikin Rd., Columbus, OH 43210. *Phone:* (614) 292-6733.

UNITED KINGDOM

MORE THAN ONE CITY

505 COUNCIL OF INTERNATIONAL FELLOWSHIP and COUNCIL OF INTERNATIONAL PROGRAMS
International Exchanges of Professionals in Human Services.
Location: Cities throughout the U.K.
Dates: May 7–June 24.
Subjects: Professional placements in social and human services agencies.
Credit: None.
Eligibility: Social workers, youth leaders, teachers in special education. Requires 2 years of professional experience, relevant professional qualifications.
Instruction: In English. Students attend assignments in human services agencies.
Highlights: Program began in 1978. 1-week orientation in London. Excursions. Postsession review. Contact with previous participants available.
Costs: About $3,000 includes meals, round-trip transportation, excursions, fees.
Housing: Provided.
Deadline: Oct. 10.
Contact: Naomi Hollander, Coordinator, International Exchanges of Professionals in Human Services, Council of International Programs, 1030 Euclid Ave., Suite 410, Cleveland, OH 44115. *Phone:* (216) 861-5478. *Telex:* 241423. *Or:* Barbara Warner, Vice Chair, CIF United Kingdom, 14 Queens Court, Queens Road, High Wycombe, Bucks. HP13 6BA, England. *Phone:* (44-494) 35727.

506 WESTERN WASHINGTON UNIVERSITY
Summer Study in England.
Location: London, Oxford.
Dates: June 22–July 22.
Subjects: Full curriculum.
Credit: 12 graduate credits.

Eligibility: Graduates, teachers, professionals in education. Requires teaching or administrative contract.
Instruction: In English. Students attend courses arranged for the group taught by U.S. and foreign faculty at Oriel College, Oxford University.
Highlights: Program began in 1972. Orientation in U.S. Program-related travel to Avebury, Stratford, Warwick Castle.
Costs: About $2,850 includes tuition, housing, meals, books, fees.
Housing: In residence halls, hotels, private homes.
Deadline: March 15.
Contact: Dr. Marian J. Tonjes, Western Washington University, Dept. of Educational Curriculum and Instruction, Bellingham, WA 98225. *Phone:* (206) 676-3336/733-5580.

BRISTOL

507 TEXAS WESLEYAN COLLEGE
Summer Term in England.
Location: Bristol.
Dates: July 11–Aug. 12.
Subjects: English literature, church history, education, history, political science.
Credit: Undergraduate credit. Graduate credit.
Eligibility: Undergraduates, graduates, teachers. Requires overall 2.0 GPA.
Instruction: In English. Students attend courses arranged for the group taught by U.S. faculty.
Highlights: Program began in 1982. Offered in cooperation with Wesley College, Bristol. Excursions in England. Postsession review. Contact with previous participants available.
Costs: $1,450 includes tuition, housing, some meals, excursions, fees, cultural events, transportation to/from airport.
Housing: In residence halls.
Deadline: May 1.
Contact: Dr. Jesse J. Sowell, Jr., Director, Summer Term in England, Texas Wesleyan College, Box 50010, Fort Worth, TX 76105. *Phone:* (817) 534-0251, Ext. 4145.

CAMBRIDGE

508 CAMBRIDGESHIRE COLLEGE OF ARTS AND TECHNOLOGY
International Programmes.
Location: Cambridge.
Dates: 10-week terms, September–June; students may enroll for 1 or more terms.
Subjects: Intermediate and advanced French, German, Italian, and Spanish languages; full university curriculum, including art history, biology, business studies, economics, English literature, geography, history, music, science, sociology.
Credit: 10 undergraduate credits per term.
Eligibility: Juniors, seniors, adults, teachers. Minimum age 19. Requires 3.0 GPA.
Instruction: In English. Students attend regular classes at the Cambridgeshire College of Arts and Technology.
Highlights: Program begins in 1988. 1-week orientation. Field trips. Postsession review.
Costs: About £4,500 includes tuition, fees.
Housing: In hostels, private homes.
Deadline: March 31.
Contact: Dr. J.C. Simmonds, Coordinator of International Programmes, Cambridgeshire College of Arts and Technology, East Road, Cambridge CB3 0NL, U.K. *Phone:* (44-223) 63271, Ext. 2075. *Or:* Sally Jackson, Assistant Registrar, Degree Admissions Office, CCAT, East Road, Cambridge CB1 1PT, U.K. *Phone:* (44-223) 276535.

CAPEL CURIG

509 PLAS Y BRENIN (NATIONAL CENTRE FOR MOUNTAIN ACTIVITIES)
Mountain and Outdoor Activities.
Location: Capel Curig, Gwynedd county, North Wales.
Dates: Weekend to 10-week courses.

All program information is subject to change without notice and must be confirmed directly with the sponsor.

98

Subjects: Canoeing, mountaineering, orienteering, training and assessment courses; special programs for youth and community leaders, teachers, instructors and families.
Credit: None. Certificate program available.
Eligibility: Adults, teachers, sports instructors. Minimum age 16.
Instruction: In English. Students attend regular classes at Plas y Brenin, the National Centre for Mountain Activities.
Highlights: Program began in 1955. Offered in cooperation with the relevant governing bodies of the Sports Council.
Costs: Vary depending on course selected.
Housing: In residence halls.
Deadline: 8 weeks before course begins.
Contact: Plas y Brenin, The National Centre for Mountain Activities, Capel Curig, Gwynedd, North Wales LL24 0ET, U.K. *Phone:* (44-6904) 214/280.

510 PLAS Y BRENIN, PLAS MENAI, and UNIVERSITY COLLEGE OF NORTH WALES
Outdoor Education.
Location: Capel Curig, Gwynedd, North Wales.
Dates: 10 weeks, April 13–June 19 or Sept. 14–Nov. 20.
Subjects: Outdoor education, with emphasis on mountain and water-based activities; in-service training course for teachers and youth and community workers.
Credit: Certificate.
Eligibility: Teachers, professionals in the fields of youth and community work.
Instruction: In English. Students attend regular classes at Plas y Brenin and Plas Menai.
Highlights: Program began in 1955. Offered in cooperation with the relevant governing bodies of the Sports Council.
Costs: About £1800 includes tuition, housing, meals, local transportation, equipment.
Housing: In residence halls.
Deadline: 8 weeks before course begins.
Contact: Plas y Brenin, The National Centre for Mountain Activities, Capel Curig, Gwynedd, North Wales LL24 0ET, U.K. *Phone:* (44-6904) 214/280.

EAST GRINSTEAD

511 TOBIAS SCHOOL OF ART
Visual Arts Programme.
Location: East Grinstead.
Dates: 1–3 years.
Subjects: Visual arts, including drawing, painting, modeling; art education, artistic therapy, sculpture therapy.
Credit: None.
Eligibility: Undergraduates, graduates, artists, teachers. Requires basic knowledge of anthroposophy.
Instruction: In English. Students attend regular classes at Tobias School of Art and Emerson College.
Highlights: Program began in 1979. Offered in cooperation with Emerson College (England).
Costs: About £3,300–£3,500 per year, includes tuition, housing, meals.
Housing: In hostels.
Deadline: None.
Contact: Tobias School of Art, Coombe Hill Road, East Grinstead, Sussex, England. *Phone:* (44-342) 313655.

512 TOBIAS SCHOOL OF ART
Teacher Training in the Arts.
Location: East Grinstead.
Dates: 1 year.
Subjects: Art education, including child development, curriculum, drawing, modeling, painting; student teaching placements.
Credit: None.
Eligibility: Advanced art students, artists, teachers, eurythmists. Requires basic knowledge of anthroposophy.
Instruction: In English. Students attend regular classes at Tobias School of Art and Emerson College.
Highlights: Program began in 1979. Offered in cooperation with Emerson College (England).
Costs: About £3,300–£3,500 per year, includes tuition, housing, meals.

Housing: In hostels.
Deadline: None.
Contact: Tobias School of Art, Coombe Hill Road, East Grinstead, Sussex, England. *Phone:* (44-342) 313655.

HULL

513 UNIVERSITY OF HULL, SCHOOL OF ADULT AND CONTINUING EDUCATION
Bachelor of Arts in Adult and Continuing Education.
Location: Hull.
Dates: 10 months, October–July.
Subjects: Adult and continuing education, including specializations in teaching/training/curriculum and policy/organization/management.
Credit: Degree.
Eligibility: Teachers, educational organizers/administrators with interest in adult education. Minimum age 21. Requires bachelor's degree, 3 years of experience in adult education.
Instruction: In English. Students attend regular classes at the University of Hull.
Highlights: Program began in 1977. 1-week orientation. Excursions. Contact with previous participants available.
Costs: £3,690 (1987) includes tuition.
Housing: In residence halls, furnished rooms.
Deadline: April.
Contact: Dr. G. Harries-Jenkins, Director, or Judi Irving, Administrative Assistant, School of Adult & Continuing Education, University of Hull, 49 Salmon Grove, Hull HU6 7SZ, U.K. *Phone:* (44-482) 465435/465530. *Telex:* 592530 UNIHUL G.

514 UNIVERSITY OF HULL, SCHOOL OF ADULT AND CONTINUING EDUCATION
Master of Arts in Adult and Continuing Education.
Location: Hull.
Dates: 1 year, October–September.
Subjects: Adult and continuing education, with specializations in teaching/learning, curriculum studies, organization/management, or policy studies.
Credit: Degree.
Eligibility: Graduates, teachers, adult educators. Requires bachelor's degree, experience in adult education.
Instruction: In English. Students attend regular classes at the University of Hull.
Highlights: Program began in 1977. 1-week orientation. Excursions. Contact with previous participants available.
Costs: £3,690 (1987) includes tuition.
Housing: In residence halls, furnished rooms.
Deadline: April.
Contact: Dr. G. Harries-Jenkins, Director, or Judi Irving, Administrative Assistant, School of Adult & Continuing Education, University of Hull, 49 Salmon Grove, Hull HU6 7SZ, U.K. *Phone:* (44-482) 465435/465530. *Telex:* 592530 UNIHUL G.

515 UNIVERSITY OF HULL, SCHOOL OF ADULT AND CONTINUING EDUCATION
Master of Education in Adult and Continuing Education.
Location: Hull.
Dates: 1 year, October–September.
Subjects: Adult and continuing education, including comparative adult education, curriculum theory, psychology, social change, social commitment, staff development.
Credit: Degree.
Eligibility: Graduates, teachers, adult educators. Requires bachelor's degree, experience in adult education.
Instruction: In English. Students attend regular classes at the University of Hull.
Highlights: Program began in 1977. 1-week orientation. Excursions. Contact with previous participants available.
Costs: £3,690 (1987) includes tuition.
Housing: In residence halls, furnished rooms.
Deadline: April.
Contact: Dr. G. Harries-Jenkins, Director, or Judi Irving, Administrative Assistant, School of Adult & Continuing Education, University of Hull, 49 Salmon Grove, Hull HU6 7SZ, U.K. *Phone:* (44-482) 465435/465530. *Telex:* 592530 UNIHUL G.

LINCOLN

516 MANSFIELD UNIVERSITY
An Introduction to British Education.
Location: Lincoln, Lincolnshire.
Dates: Late June–mid-July; students may enroll for 3 weeks.
Subjects: British education, reading in British schools.
Credit: Available.
Eligibility: Graduates. Requires teaching certification.
Instruction: In English. Students attend regular classes at Lincoln schools.
Highlights: Program began in 1974. 1-day orientation in U.S. Program includes observation and working with children in British schools. Program-related travel in Europe. Postsession review. Contact with previous participants available.
Costs: $1,500 includes housing, some meals, round-trip transportation, books, excursions, fees.
Housing: In residence halls, hotels.
Deadline: April 1.
Contact: Dr. John Heaps or Dr. Craig Cleland, Mansfield University, Mansfield, PA 16933. *Phone:* (717) 662-4372.

LONDON

517 CITY COLLEGE
Summer Institute in England.
Location: London.
Dates: July 4–Aug. 2.
Subjects: Education: contemporary educational issues and methods in England, special education in the U.S. and U.K.
Credit: 6 graduate credits in education.
Eligibility: Teachers, graduates.
Instruction: In English. Students attend courses arranged for the group taught by U.S. and foreign faculty at the Polytechnic of North London and the Polytechnic of the South Bank.
Highlights: Program began in 1984.
Costs: $1,695 includes tuition, housing, some meals, round-trip transportation, fees.
Housing: In residence halls.
Deadline: Jan. 24.
Contact: Dean Alfred S. Posamentier, The City College, NAC-6207, Convent Avenue at 138th St., New York, NY 10031. *Phone:* (212) 690-5471.

518 CITY COLLEGE
Summer Study in London for Mathematics Teachers.
Location: London.
Dates: July 4–Aug. 2.
Subjects: Mathematics courses for teachers: history of mathematics, recreational mathematics, current issues in mathematics education.
Credit: 3 graduate credits in education and 3 in mathematics.
Eligibility: Mathematics teachers, graduates.
Instruction: In English. Students attend courses arranged for the group taught by U.S. and foreign faculty at the Polytechnic of the South Bank.
Highlights: Program began in 1986.
Costs: $1,695 includes tuition, housing, some meals, round-trip transportation, fees.
Housing: In residence halls.
Deadline: Jan. 24.
Contact: Dean Alfred S. Posamentier, The City College, NAC-6207, Convent Avenue at 138th St., New York, NY 10031. *Phone:* (212) 690-5471.

519 MIDDLESEX POLYTECHNIC
Postgraduate Certificate in Education.
Location: London.
Dates: 1-year programs, September–June.
Subjects: Secondary education, with specializations in art/design, craft/design/technology, drama, music. 1-year in-service diploma programs in craft/design/technology and home economics also available.
Credit: Certificate/diploma.
Eligibility: Graduates, teachers. Requires bachelor's degree in related field, qualified teacher status.

Instruction: In English. Students attend regular classes at Middlesex Polytechnic.
Highlights: Program began in 1983. Orientation.
Costs: Contact sponsor for information.
Housing: In residence halls, apartments, furnished rooms, private homes.
Deadline: Apply early.
Contact: Mrs. Roberta de Joia, Coordinator of Overseas Students' Programmes, Middlesex Polytechnic, 114 Chase Side, London N14 5PN, U.K. *Phone:* (44-1) 886-6599. *Telex:* 8954762.

520 UNIVERSITY OF LONDON
English Theatre, Literature and Culture of the 20th Century.
Location: London.
Dates: About July 6–Aug. 14.
Subjects: English culture, literature.
Credit: None.
Eligibility: Seniors, graduates, teachers.
Instruction: In English. Students attend regular classes at the University of London summer school.
Highlights: Program began in 1948.
Costs: About £1,230 for residential students, includes tuition, housing, meals; £600 includes tuition. Scholarships available.
Housing: In residence halls.
Deadline: March 15.
Contact: U.S. Student Programs, Institute of International Education, 809 United Nations Plaza, New York, NY 10017. *Phone:* (212) 984-5330.

521 UNIVERSITY OF LONDON, INSTITUTE OF EDUCATION
International Centre for Advanced Study of Education and the Arts (CEDAR)—Summer Programme.
Location: London.
Dates: July.
Subjects: Current drama productions, contemporary British literature, continuing education, assessment in education, multiculturalism and antiracism, education and tourism, children's literature, museums and education, gender in education, cultural studies in Britain and Europe, curriculum policies and practices, film and television media, early childhood education.
Credit: 3 graduate credits per course.
Eligibility: Graduates, teachers, professionals, and exceptional seniors in the field of education.
Instruction: In English. Students attend regular classes at the University of London.
Highlights: Program began in 1987. 1-day orientation abroad. Excursions and cultural events.
Costs: About $2,300 includes tuition, housing, some meals, fees.
Housing: In residence halls.
Deadline: Jan. 29.
Contact: CEDAR International, University of London Institute of Education, 20 Bedford Way, Bloomsbury, London WC1H 0AL, England. *Phone:* (44-1) 636-1500, Ext. 225.

522 UNIVERSITY OF LONDON, INSTITUTE OF EDUCATION
Master's Programs in Education.
Location: London.
Dates: October–September; students must enroll for entire period.
Subjects: Education, including administration, art/design, child development, comparative education, curriculum studies, developing countries, music, philosophy of education, psychology, statistics, other topics. 1-year MA, MSc, and MEd programs available.
Credit: Degree.
Eligibility: Graduates, teachers. Requires bachelor's degree in education or equivalent.
Instruction: In English. Students attend regular classes at the Institute of Education, University of London.
Highlights: Program began in 1965.
Costs: $3,690 (1987) per year, includes tuition, fees.
Housing: In residence halls.
Deadline: Apply early.
Contact: Academic Registrar, Institute of Education, University of London, 20 Bedford Way, London WC1H 0AL, England. *Phone:* (44-1) 636-1500.

OXFORD

523 OXFORD INTERNATIONAL SUMMER SCHOOL
Summer Program at Lady Spencer-Churchill College.
Location: Oxford.
Dates: 5 weeks, July 10–Aug. 13.
Subjects: The arts, British and European history, British education, British politics, English literature, management.
Credit: 4–6 credits.
Eligibility: Sophomores, juniors, seniors, graduates, adults, teachers. Requires 2.5 GPA.
Instruction: In English. Students attend regular courses at Lady Spencer-Churchill College summer session.
Highlights: Program begins in 1988. Orientation. Excursions and field trips.
Costs: $2,500 includes tuition, housing, meals, excursions, fees.
Housing: In residence halls.
Deadline: June 1.
Contact: Overseas Liaison Office, Oxford International Summer School, Hanover House, Marine Court, St. Leonards-on-Sea, East Sussex TN38 0DX, England. *Phone:* (44-424) 720282. *Telex:* 957391 Embassy G. *Fax:* (44-424) 444204. *Or:* Richard Dixon, The Travel Spot, 109 South Ave. West, Cranford, NJ 07016. *Phone:* (800) 843-1489.

524 SUSQUEHANNA UNIVERSITY
Susquehanna at Oxford.
Location: Oxford.
Dates: June 13–Aug. 24.
Subjects: British archaeology, architectural history, business, economic history, education, history, literature, politics, theater.
Credit: 7–8 credits.
Eligibility: Undergraduates, teachers, adults. Requires at least 2 years of college with 2.5 GPA.
Instruction: In English. Students attend regular classes at Oxford University summer session.
Highlights: Program began in 1966. Program-related travel to Edinburgh, London, Paris, Stratford, York; optional 2-week tours of Germany, Austria, and Switzerland or Italy. Program evaluations available to prospective participants.
Costs: About $2,650 includes tuition, housing, meals, round-trip transportation, excursions, fees; $900 for continental tour.
Housing: In residence halls.
Deadline: March 30.
Contact: Dr. Robert Bradford, Director, Susquehanna at Oxford Program, 114 Bogar Hall, Box 1830, Susquehanna University, Selinsgrove, PA 17870. *Phone:* (717) 374-0101, Ext. 4254.

525 UNIVERSITY OF OXFORD
Britain: Literature, History, and Society from 1870 to Present Day.
Location: Oxford.
Dates: July 6–Aug. 14.
Subjects: British history, literature, social history.
Credit: Available.
Eligibility: Juniors, seniors, graduates, teachers.
Instruction: In English. Students attend regular classes at Exeter College.
Highlights: Program began in 1947.
Costs: About £1,180 for residential students, includes tuition, housing, meals; £590 for nonresidential students, includes tuition. Scholarships available.
Housing: In residence halls.
Deadline: March 15.
Contact: U.S. Student Programs, Institute of International Education, 809 United Nations Plaza, New York, NY 10017. *Phone:* (212) 984-5330.

READING

526 BRITISH COUNCIL
Teaching Agriculture in Universities.
Location: Reading.
Dates: March 20–31.
Subjects: Education: methods of teaching agriculture, role of the university agriculture faculty in national development.
Credit: None.
Eligibility: Professors of agriculture.
Instruction: In English. Students attend courses arranged for the group at the University of Reading.
Highlights: Program begins in 1988. Offered in cooperation with the Faculty of Agriculture and Food and the AERDC, University of Reading. Visits to agricultural facilities of Reading University and neighboring institutions.
Costs: £845 includes tuition, housing, meals, fees.
Housing: In residence halls.
Deadline: Nov. 20.
Contact: Director, Courses Department, The British Council, 65 Davies St., London W1Y 2AA, England. *Phone:* (44-1) 499-8011. *Telex:* 8952201 BRICON G.

STRATFORD-UPON-AVON

527 UNIVERSITY OF BIRMINGHAM
Drama and Theater in the Age of Shakespeare.
Location: Stratford-upon-Avon.
Dates: About July 6–Aug. 14.
Subjects: Shakespearean drama, English theater.
Credit: Available.
Eligibility: Juniors, seniors, graduates, teachers.
Instruction: In English. Students attend regular classes at the University of Birmingham.
Highlights: Program began in 1947.
Costs: About £1,160 for residential students, includes tuition, housing; £790 for nonresidential students, includes tuition. Scholarships available.
Housing: Provided.
Deadline: March 15.
Contact: U.S. Student Programs, Institute of International Education, 809 United Nations Plaza, New York, NY 10017. *Phone:* (212) 984-5330.

SOUTHAMPTON

528 LA SAINTE UNION COLLEGE OF HIGHER EDUCATION and UNIVERSITY OF SOUTHAMPTON
Postgraduate Certificate in Education.
Location: Southampton.
Dates: 1 year, September–June.
Subjects: Advanced French language; education, curriculum subjects in elementary schools; student teaching.
Credit: Certificate.
Eligibility: Graduates, adults, teachers.
Instruction: In English. Students attend regular classes at La Sainte Union College of Higher Education.
Highlights: Program began in 1967. Field trips.
Costs: About $6,300 per year, includes tuition, meals, field trips, fees.
Housing: In residence halls.
Deadline: December.
Contact: Mrs. Pauline Wilson, Registrar, LSU College of Higher Education, The Avenue, Southampton SO9 5HB, U.K. *Phone:* (44-703) 228761.

WORCESTER

529 WORCESTER COLLEGE OF HIGHER EDUCATION
Advanced Diploma in Children's Literature.
Location: Worcester.
Dates: September–May; students must enroll for entire period.
Subjects: Children's literature.
Credit: Diploma.
Eligibility: Graduates, teachers, librarians, adults. Minimum age 21.
Instruction: In English. Students attend regular classes at Worcester College.
Highlights: Program began in 1980. Excursions to Oxford, Stratford, Lake District. Contact with previous participants available.
Costs: $9,950 includes tuition, housing, some meals, excursions, fees.
Housing: In private homes.

Deadline: May.
Contact: Admissions Tutor, Worcester College of Higher Education, Henwick Grove, Worcester WR2 6AJ, England. *Phone:* (44-905) 428080.

530 WORCESTER COLLEGE OF HIGHER EDUCATION
Bachelor of Education (Honours) In-Service.
Location: Worcester.
Dates: 1 year, beginning in July.
Subjects: Primary and secondary education, with specializations in English language and literature, reading and language arts, or special education.
Credit: Degree.
Eligibility: Teachers. Requires bachelor's degree, teacher certification, 2 years of experience.
Instruction: In English. Students attend regular classes at Worcester College of Higher Education.
Highlights: Program began in 1970. Offered in cooperation with the CNAA (Council for National Academic Awards). Contact with previous participants available.
Costs: About £3,500 per year, includes tuition, fees.
Housing: In residence halls, furnished rooms.
Deadline: March.

Contact: A.V. Venables, Senior Tutor, Worcester College of Higher Education, Henwick Grove, Worcester WR2 6AJ, England. *Phone:* (44-905) 428080.

531 WORCESTER COLLEGE OF HIGHER EDUCATION
Postgraduate Certificate in Education.
Location: Worcester.
Dates: September–July.
Subjects: Primary and secondary education, including preparation for teaching economics and commerce, English, home economics, mathematics, physical science; student teaching.
Credit: Certificate.
Eligibility: Graduates. Requires bachelor's degree.
Instruction: In English. Students attend regular classes at Worcester College of Higher Education.
Highlights: Program began in 1970. Offered in cooperation with the CNAA (Council for National Academic Awards). Contact with previous participants available.
Costs: About £3,500 per year, includes tuition, fees.
Housing: In residence halls, furnished rooms.
Deadline: March.
Contact: A.V. Venables, Senior Tutor, Worcester College of Higher Education, Henwick Grove, Worcester WR2 6AJ, England. *Phone:* (44-905) 428080.

All program information is subject to change without notice
and must be confirmed directly with the sponsor.
102

MIDDLE EAST AND NORTH AFRICA

EGYPT
CAIRO

532 CENTER FOR ARABIC STUDY ABROAD (CASA)
Full Year Program.
Location: Cairo.
Dates: Early June–May; students must enroll for entire period. Summer program also available.
Subjects: Intermediate and advanced colloquial and literary Arabic.
Credit: Available.
Eligibility: Graduates, teachers. Requires U.S. citizenship, 2 years of Arabic study, passing score on Arabic language examination.
Instruction: In Arabic. Students attend courses arranged for the group taught by foreign faculty at the American University in Cairo.
Highlights: Program began in 1967. Offered in cooperation with the American University in Cairo and funded by the U.S. Dept. of Education. Orientation abroad. Optional excursions. Cultural activities.
Costs: $1,250 program fee. Participants receive fellowship for tuition, housing, meals, round-trip transportation.
Housing: In residence halls, apartments.
Deadline: Jan. 1.
Contact: Farhat J. Ziadeh, Director, Center for Arabic Study Abroad (CASA), University of Washington, 229B Denny Hall, DH-20, Seattle, WA 98195. *Phone:* (206) 543-8982.

533 CENTER FOR ARABIC STUDY ABROAD (CASA)
Summer Institute.
Location: Cairo.
Dates: Early June–early August.
Subjects: Advanced colloquial and literary Arabic language.
Credit: Available.
Eligibility: Undergraduates, graduates, teachers. Requires U.S. citizenship, 2 years of Arabic study, and passing score on examination in Arabic.
Instruction: In Arabic. Students attend courses arranged for the group taught by foreign faculty at American University in Cairo.
Highlights: Program began in 1967. Offered in cooperation with the American University in Cairo and funded by the U.S. Dept. of Education. Orientation abroad. Optional excursions.
Costs: $500 program fee. Participants receive fellowship for tuition, housing, meals, round-trip transportation.
Housing: In residence halls, apartments.
Deadline: Jan. 1.
Contact: Farhat J. Ziadeh, Director, Center for Arabic Study Abroad (CASA), University of Washington, 229B Denny Hall, DH 20, Seattle, WA 98195. *Phone:* (206) 543-8982.

ISRAEL
JERUSALEM

534 YAD VASHEM
Teaching the Holocaust.
Location: Jerusalem.
Dates: July 6–29.
Subjects: The Holocaust: antisemitism, European Jewry, National Socialism, the war, the aftermath.
Credit: None.
Eligibility: Graduates, teachers. Requires college degree and teaching qualifications or education experience.
Instruction: In English. Students attend special classes for foreigners and regular classes at Yad Vashem.
Highlights: Program began in 1980.
Costs: $325 includes tuition, books, excursions, fees.
Housing: Students make own arrangements.
Deadline: March 31.
Contact: Elly Dlin, Education Department, Yad Vashem, Har Hazikaron, P.O. Box 3477, Jerusalem 91034, Israel. *Phone:* (972-2) 531202, Ext. 50.

TEL AVIV

535 BOSTON UNIVERSITY
Professional International Linkage Program.
Location: Tel Aviv.
Dates: Aug. 30–Dec. 19, Jan. 5–May 8; students may enroll for 1 or both semesters.
Subjects: Hebrew language on all levels; student teaching and coursework; community education, Israeli culture and society.
Credit: 16 semester hours.
Eligibility: Sophomores, juniors, seniors, professionals in the field of education. Requires 3.0 GPA.
Instruction: In English. Students attend courses arranged for the group taught by foreign faculty.
Highlights: Program began in 1986. Offered in cooperation with the American International School in Israel. Orientation in U.S. and abroad. Excursions and field trips. Postsession review.
Costs: $8,350 includes tuition, housing, meals, excursions, fees.
Housing: In residence halls.
Deadline: April 1 for fall/academic year; Nov. 1 for spring.
Contact: Margaret J. Bannister, Director of Study Abroad Programs, Boston University, 143 Bay State Rd., Boston, MA 02215. *Phone:* (617) 353-3316.

TUNISIA
TUNIS

536 BOURGUIBA INSTITUTE OF MODERN LANGUAGES
Adult Language Courses.
Location: Tunis.
Dates: October–June; students must enroll for entire period.
Subjects: Arabic, French, German, Italian, and Spanish languages on all levels.
Credit: Available by special arrangement.
Eligibility: Undergraduates, graduates, adults, teachers, professionals. Minimum age 17.
Instruction: In language of study. Students attend special courses for foreigners at Bourguiba Institute of Modern Languages.
Highlights: Program began in 1963. Offered in cooperation with the Tunisian Ministry of Education. Excursions.
Costs: Contact sponsor for information. Scholarships available.
Housing: Students make own arrangements.
Deadline: September.
Contact: Dr. Mohamed Maamouri, Director, or Saadi Ben Bechir, Secretary General, Bourguiba Institute of Modern Languages, 47 Avenue de la Liberte, 1002 Tunis Belvedere, Tunisia. *Phone:* (216-1) 282-418/282-923.

WESTERN HEMISPHERE

MORE THAN ONE COUNTRY

537 SCHOOL FOR INTERNATIONAL TRAINING
Master of Arts in Teaching.
Location: Vermont and Mexico, Puerto Rico, or Martinique.
Dates: September–June (September–December in Vermont, January–March abroad, April–June in Vermont); students must enroll for entire period.
Subjects: Advanced French and Spanish languages; anthrolinguistics, bilingual education, cross-cultural communications, education, English, French and Hispanic cultures, linguistics, sociolinguistics, teaching languages, testing and evaluation. Teaching internships.
Credit: 32–38 graduate credits.
Eligibility: Graduates. Requires major in teaching English, French, or Spanish as a second language, foreign service rating of 3 or better in major language(s).
Instruction: In English, Spanish, or French. Students attend regular classes at the School for International Training.
Highlights: Program began in 1969. Optional 3-week homestay.
Costs: $11,385 includes tuition, housing, meals, fees, insurance.
Housing: In residence halls, apartments, furnished rooms.
Deadline: July 31.
Contact: Admissions Office, School for International Training, Brattleboro, VT 05301. *Phone:* (800) 451-4465/(802) 257-7751. *Telex:* 6817462 EXPER UW.

BAHAMAS
MORE THAN ONE CITY

538 MIAMI UNIVERSITY
Modern Carbonate Deposition.
Location: San Salvador and Andros islands.
Dates: 2 weeks, June 18–July 2.
Subjects: Geology and biology of carbonate deposition.
Credit: 5 graduate credits.
Eligibility: Graduates, teachers, scientists. Minimum age 20. Requires science background.
Instruction: In English. Students attend courses arranged for the group taught by U.S. faculty.
Highlights: Program began in 1983. Excursions and field trips. Contact with previous participants available.
Costs: About $900 includes tuition, housing, meals, books, round-trip transportation, excursions, fees, insurance. Scholarships available.
Housing: Provided.
Deadline: March 1; Feb. 1 for scholarships.
Contact: Mark R. Boardman, Geology Dept., Miami University, Oxford, OH 45056. *Phone:* (513) 529-3216.

CANADA
MORE THAN ONE CITY

539 ARKANSAS TECH UNIVERSITY
Arkansas Tech University/Universite du Quebec Student Exchange.
Location: Chicoutimi, Trois-Rivieres.
Dates: August–May; students may enroll for 1 semester

Subjects: French language on all levels; French Canadian civilization, literature.
Credit: Available.
Eligibility: Sophomores, juniors, seniors, graduates, high school teachers.
Instruction: In French. Students attend special courses for foreigners and regular classes at the Universite du Quebec.
Highlights: Program began in 1985. Field trips.
Costs: $440 per semester for state residents, $880 for nonresidents, includes tuition.
Housing: In residence halls, private homes.
Deadline: None.
Contact: James Hassell, Dept. of English and Foreign Languages, or Travis Adams, Vice President for Student Affairs, Arkansas Tech University, Russellville, AR 72801. *Phone:* (501) 968-0268.

540 NORTHERN ILLINOIS UNIVERSITY
Educator's Wilderness Course in Canada.
Location: Wilderness areas of Ontario.
Dates: July 31–Aug. 23.
Subjects: Outdoor teacher education: camping, canoeing, climbing.
Credit: 3 graduate semester hours.
Eligibility: Graduates.
Instruction: In English. Students attend courses arranged for the group.
Highlights: Offered in cooperation with the Canadian Outward Bound Wilderness School of Ontario.
Costs: About $1,063 includes tuition, housing, meals, excursions, fees, insurance.
Housing: At campsites.
Deadline: May 1, or until program is filled.
Contact: Dr. Orville E. Jones, International and Special Programs, Northern Illinois University, Lowden 203, DeKalb, IL 60115. *Phone:* (815) 753-9528.

HALIFAX

541 SAINT MARY'S UNIVERSITY
Graduate Studies in Arts, Science, Commerce, and Education.
Location: Halifax.
Dates: September–May; students may enroll for 1 or both semesters.
Subjects: Master's and diploma programs in astronomy, Atlantic Canada studies, business administration, education, engineering, history, philosophy, applied psychology.
Credit: Diploma/degree. 12–18 graduate credits.
Eligibility: Graduates, teachers.
Instruction: In English. Students attend regular classes at Saint Mary's University.
Highlights: Orientation abroad. Contact with previous participants available.
Costs: CN $3,200 (1987) per year, includes tuition, fees.
Housing: Students make own arrangements.
Deadline: April 1.
Contact: E.H. Chard, Registrar, Saint Mary's University, Halifax, Nova Scotia B3H 3C3, Canada. *Phone:* (902) 420-5581. **Or:** Keith Hotchkiss, Director of Student Services, Saint Mary's University, Halifax, Nova Scotia B3H 3C3, Canada. *Phone:* (902) 420-5608.

MONTREAL

542 ECOLE DE LANGUES DE MONTREAL (MONTREAL LANGUAGE SCHOOL)
French Language Courses.
Location: Montreal, Quebec.
Dates: 4–36 weeks, year-round.
Subjects: French language on all levels, business French; teaching French as a foreign language; French-Canadian civilization.
Credit: Available by arrangement.
Eligibility: Undergraduates, adults, teachers, precollege.
Instruction: In French. Students attend special courses for foreigners at the Montreal Language School.
Highlights: Program began in 1962. Orientation. Excursions in Montreal area. Program evaluations available to prospective participants.
Costs: Depend on course selected and length of stay.
Housing: In private homes.
Deadline: 1 month before course begins.
Contact: Dennis St. John, Director, Montreal Language School, 606 rue Cathcart #330, Montreal, Que. H3B 1K9, Canada. *Phone:* (514) 875-6440. *Telex:* 055-60494 MLS MTL. *Or:* Louise Harber, Programs Coordinator, Box 5409, G.C.S., New York, NY 10163. *Phone:* (212) 662-1090. *Telex:* 645646 LHARBER NYK.

543 STATE UNIVERSITY COLLEGE AT PLATTSBURGH, CENTER FOR THE STUDY OF CANADA
Canada in the Summer—Montreal.
Location: Montreal, Quebec.
Dates: 3–6 weeks, June–August.
Subjects: Intensive French language on all levels.
Credit: Available.
Eligibility: Undergraduates, graduates, adults, teachers of French. Minimum age 18. Requires 2.5 GPA.
Instruction: In French. Students attend regular classes at the French Summer School, Concordia University.
Highlights: Program began in 1986. Offered in cooperation with Concordia University. Field trips.
Costs: $700 includes tuition, housing. Scholarships available for SUNY students only.
Housing: In residence halls or off-campus.
Deadline: April 15.
Contact: Mrs. Dodie Giltz, Study Abroad Advisor, Center for the Study of Canada, State University College at Plattsburgh, Plattsburgh, NY 12901. *Phone:* (518) 564-2086.

544 UNIVERSITE DE MONTREAL, ECOLE FRANCAISE
Didactique des Langues Secondes.
Location: Montreal, Quebec.
Dates: Session C, July 4–22, and/or session D, July 25–Aug. 12.
Subjects: Teaching French as a second language: methodology (session C); workshop (session D).
Credit: 3 credits.
Eligibility: Teachers of French. Requires fluency in French, teaching experience.
Instruction: In French. Students attend special courses for foreigners at the Ecole Francaise of the Universite de Montreal.
Highlights: Program began in 1948. Excursions.
Costs: Contact sponsor for information.
Housing: Sponsor assists in locating housing.
Deadline: June 3.
Contact: Secretariat des Inscriptions, Ecole Francaise, Faculte de l'Education Permanente, Universite de Montreal, C.P. 6128, succursale A, Montreal (Quebec) H3C 3J7, Canada. *Phone:* (514) 343-6990.

545 UNIVERSITE DE MONTREAL, ECOLE FRANCAISE
Francais Ecrit: Grammaire et Redaction Francaises.
Location: Montreal, Quebec.
Dates: July 4–22.
Subjects: Advanced written French: grammar and editing for nonfrancophone students.
Credit: 3 credits.
Eligibility: Undergraduates, graduates, adults, teachers. Requires advanced knowledge of French.
Instruction: In French. Students attend special courses for foreigners at the Ecole Francaise of the Universite de Montreal.
Highlights: Program began in 1948. Excursions.
Costs: Contact sponsor for information.
Housing: Sponsor assists in locating housing.
Deadline: June 3.
Contact: Secretariat des Inscriptions, Ecole Francaise, Faculte de l'Education Permanente, Universite de Montreal, C.P. 6128, succursale A, Montreal (Quebec) H3C 3J7, Canada. *Phone:* (514) 343-6990.

QUEBEC

546 UNIVERSITY SYSTEM OF GEORGIA, INTERNATIONAL INTERCULTURAL STUDIES PROGRAM
French Language in Quebec.
Location: Quebec City, Quebec.
Dates: Early July–mid-August; students must enroll for entire period.
Subjects: French language on all levels; Quebecois culture, literature.
Credit: 10–15 undergraduate quarter hours. 10 graduate quarter hours.
Eligibility: Undergraduates, graduates, teachers.
Instruction: In French. Students attend special courses for foreigners at Laval University.
Highlights: Program began in 1982. 1-day orientation in U.S. Program evaluations available to prospective participants.
Costs: About $1,700 includes tuition, housing, meals, round-trip transportation, excursions, fees.
Housing: In private homes.
Deadline: March 15.
Contact: Dr. Ernest Pick, International Intercultural Studies Program, Georgia State University, Box 653, Atlanta, GA 30303. *Phone:* (404) 658-2450.

VANCOUVER

547 UNIVERSITY OF BRITISH COLUMBIA, CENTRE FOR CONTINUING EDUCATION
Intensive French Programs.
Location: Vancouver, British Columbia.
Dates: June 7–24, July 11–28, Aug. 2–19.
Subjects: Intensive French language on all levels, emphasizing conversational French; business French; teaching French; French Canadian culture, literature. Intensive Chinese (Cantonese and Mandarin), Japanese, and Spanish languages also available.
Credit: None.
Eligibility: Adults, teachers. Minimum age 18; average age over 30.
Instruction: In French, language of study. Students attend special courses for foreigners and regular classes at the Centre for Continuing Education.
Highlights: Program began in 1964. Program evaluations available to prospective participants.
Costs: CN $600–$800 per session, includes tuition, housing, meals.
Housing: In student residences.
Deadline: June 1 for June session; July 1 for July; July 26 for August.
Contact: Centre for Continuing Education, Language Programs and Services, University of British Columbia, 5997 Iona Drive, Vancouver, B.C. V6T 2A4, Canada. *Phone:* (604) 222-5227.

CHILE

SANTIAGO

548 UNIVERSITY OF CHILE
Specialist in Teaching Music.
Location: Santiago.
Dates: March–December; students must enroll for entire period.
Subjects: Music education: general and specific pedagogical training.
Credit: Certificate.
Eligibility: Graduates, teachers, professionals. Requires fluency in Spanish.
Instruction: In Spanish. Students attend regular classes at the University of Chile.

Highlights: Offered in cooperation with the Organization of American States.
Costs: About $1,000 includes tuition.
Housing: Sponsor assists in locating housing.
Deadline: Apply early.
Contact: Instituto Interamericano de Educacion Musical, Facultad de Artes, Universidad de Chile, Compania 1264, Santiago, Chile.

COLOMBIA

BOGOTA

549 GREAT LAKES COLLEGES ASSOCIATION and KENYON COLLEGE
Latin America Program.
Location: Bogota.
Dates: June 9–Aug. 8. 4-week workshop for in-service teachers in July. Spring, fall terms also available.
Subjects: Spanish language on all levels; Latin American history, literature, social sciences; special course for teachers.
Credit: Up to 12 undergraduate semester hours. Graduate credit.
Eligibility: Sophomores, juniors, seniors, graduate students, teachers.
Instruction: In Spanish. Students attend special classes for foreigners.
Highlights: Program began in 1964. Orientation abroad. About 1 week of program-related travel. Program evaluations available to prospective participants.
Costs: About $1,890 for full term, includes tuition, housing, meals, fees, insurance, excursions (transportation only).
Housing: In private homes.
Deadline: April 15.
Contact: Diane K. Snell, Director, GLCA Latin America Program, Kenyon College, Gambier, OH 43022. *Phone:* (614) 427-4733.

DOMINICAN REPUBLIC

SANTIAGO DE LOS CABALLEROS

550 PONTIFICIA UNIVERSIDAD CATOLICA MADRE Y MAESTRA
Intensive Program on Language and Culture.
Location: Santiago de los Caballeros, Dominican Republic.
Dates: 8 weeks, Oct. 10–Dec. 2.
Subjects: Intensive Spanish language on all levels; Dominican and Latin American studies, including art, architecture, Afro-West Indian culture, history, literature, music, social geography.
Credit: 12 undergraduate credits.
Eligibility: Undergraduates, graduates, adults, teachers, professionals.
Instruction: In Spanish. Students attend special courses for foreigners at the Universidad Catolica.
Highlights: Program began in 1962. 3-day orientation. Excursions and field trips.
Costs: $1,650 includes tuition, housing, meals, books, excursions, fees.
Housing: In private homes.
Deadline: Aug. 15.
Contact: Liliana de Montenegro, Coordinadora Espanol para Extranjeros, Pontificia Universidad Catolica Madre y Maestra, Santiago, Republica Dominicana. *Phone:* (809) 583-0441, Ext. 347. *Telex:* ITT 346 (1032).

551 PONTIFICIA UNIVERSIDAD CATOLICA MADRE Y MAESTRA
The Study-Research Program.
Location: Santiago de los Caballeros, Dominican Republic.
Dates: 16 weeks, August–December or January–May.
Subjects: Spanish language on all levels; full university curriculum, plus research in Spanish literature or linguistics.
Credit: 6–12 undergraduate credits. 6–12 graduate credits.
Eligibility: Juniors, seniors, graduates, teachers.
Instruction: In Spanish. Students attend regular classes at the Universidad Catolica.

Highlights: Program began in 1962. 3-day orientation. Excursions and field trips.
Costs: $900–$1,200 includes tuition, fees.
Housing: In private homes.
Deadline: June 15 for fall; Nov. 15 for spring.
Contact: Liliana de Montenegro, Coordinadora Espanol Para Extranjeros, Pontificia Universidad Catolica Madre y Maestra, Santiago, Republica Dominicana. *Phone:* (809) 583-0441, Ext. 347. *Telex:* ITT 346 (1032).

ECUADOR

QUITO

552 ACADEMIA DE ESPANOL QUITO
Individualized Spanish Language Training.
Location: Quito.
Dates: 8–10 weeks, year-round. Shorter programs available.
Subjects: Intensive Spanish language on all levels.
Credit: None.
Eligibility: Undergraduates, graduates, adults, teachers, professionals, precollege. Minimum age 7.
Instruction: In Spanish. Students attend special courses for foreigners at the Academia de Espanol Quito.
Highlights: Program began in 1982. Individual instruction. Optional excursions. Contact with previous participants available.
Costs: $1,436 for 8 weeks, includes tuition, housing, meals, fees, airport transfer.
Housing: In private homes.
Deadline: Rolling.
Contact: Edgar J. Alvarez, Director, Academia de Espanol Quito, P.O. Box 39-C, Quito, Ecuador. *Phone:* (593-2) 553-647. *Telex:* 21281 ED-ACAZA.

553 OREGON STATE UNIVERSITY
Summer in Latin America.
Location: Quito.
Dates: June 20–Aug. 2.
Subjects: Intermediate and advanced Spanish language; teaching English as a second language; Spanish-American culture, literature.
Credit: Available.
Eligibility: Undergraduates, graduates, teachers, adults.
Instruction: In Spanish. Students attend courses arranged for the group taught by foreign faculty at Pontificia Universidad Catolica del Ecuador.
Highlights: Program began in 1971. Orientation in U.S. Optional program-related travel to Cuzco, Mexico City. Program evaluations available to prospective participants.
Costs: $1,950 includes tuition, housing, some meals, round-trip transportation from Los Angeles, books, excursions, fees.
Housing: In private homes.
Deadline: April 15.
Contact: Dr. Robert D. Kiekel, Director, Summer in Latin America, Dept. of Foreign Languages, Oregon State University, Corvallis, OR 97311. *Phone:* (503) 754-2289.

MEXICO

MEXICO CITY

554 INSTITUTO MEXICANO NORTEAMERICANO DE RELACIONES CULTURALES
Spanish Classes.
Location: Mexico City.
Dates: 12 3-week sessions per year. Longer terms available.
Subjects: Intensive and semi-intensive Spanish language on all levels; teaching Spanish as a second language; Mexican history.
Credit: None.
Eligibility: Undergraduates, graduates, adults, teachers. Minimum age 16; average age 25.
Instruction: In Spanish. Students attend special courses for foreigners.
Highlights: Program began in 1960. Excursions.

All program information is subject to change without notice
and must be confirmed directly with the sponsor.

Costs: About $125 per session, includes tuition, fees.
Housing: Sponsor assists in locating housing.
Deadline: First day of class.
Contact: Coordinator, Spanish Division, Instituto Mexicano Norteamericano de Relaciones Culturales, Hamburgo 115 C.P. 06600, Mexico, D.F., Mexico. *Phone:* (905) 525-3357/511-4720/525-2611.

555 NATIONAL AUTONOMOUS UNIVERSITY OF MEXICO
Special Summer Workshop for Spanish Language Teachers.
Location: Mexico City.
Dates: July 11–Aug. 9.
Subjects: Teaching Spanish language, including class observation and design, grammatical aspects, linguistic theories, methodological techniques, sociolinguistics.
Credit: Available.
Eligibility: Teachers of Spanish. Requires teaching certification, B average.
Instruction: In Spanish. Students attend courses arranged for the group taught by foreign faculty.
Highlights: Program began in 1984. Orientation abroad. Contact with previous participants available.
Costs: $325 includes tuition, fees.
Housing: In furnished rooms, private homes.
Deadline: June 8.
Contact: School for Foreign Students, National Autonomous University of Mexico, Apartado Postal 70-391, C.U. Delegacion Coyoacan, 04510 Mexico, D.F., Mexico. *Phone:* (52-5) 550-51-72. *Telex:* 1774523 UNAMME.

556 STATE UNIVERSITY COLLEGE AT PURCHASE
Purchase Language Quarter in Mexico.
Location: Mexico City.
Dates: 4–6 weeks, June–July.
Subjects: Spanish language on all levels; anthropology, art history, history, language teaching, literature, philosophy, political science, sociology. Internships in social work.
Credit: 6 undergraduate credits. 6 graduate credits.
Eligibility: Undergraduates, graduates, adults, precollege. Requires one year of college-level Spanish or equivalent.
Instruction: In English, Spanish. Students attend courses arranged for the group taught by foreign faculty and special courses for foreigners at Universidad Iberoamericana.
Highlights: Program began in 1972. Offered in cooperation with Universidad Iberoamericana. Excursions. Postsession review. Contact with previous participants available.
Costs: About $1,300 includes tuition, housing, meals, round-trip transportation, books, excursions, fees.
Housing: In private homes.
Deadline: April 1.
Contact: Dr. David A. Villecco, or Director of International Education, State University College at Purchase, Purchase, NY 10577. *Phone:* (914) 253-5573.

MORELIA

557 NORTH CAROLINA STATE UNIVERSITY
Mexico Summer Program.
Location: Morelia.
Dates: 4 weeks, July.
Subjects: Spanish language on all levels; Hispanic studies, civilization, culture.
Credit: 6 undergraduate credits. No graduate credit.
Eligibility: Undergraduates, graduates, precollege, teachers. Requires 1 semester of high school Spanish or equivalent.
Instruction: In Spanish. Students attend courses arranged for the group taught by foreign faculty and special courses for foreigners.
Highlights: Program began in 1981. 1-day orientation in U.S. Excursions. Program-related travel to Ixtapa. Contact with previous participants available.
Costs: $1,800 includes tuition, housing, meals, round-trip transportation, excursions, fees, insurance.
Housing: In private homes.
Deadline: Feb. 15.

Contact: Cynthia Felbeck Chalou, Study Abroad Adviser, North Carolina State University, 105 Alexander Hall, Box 7315, Raleigh, NC 27695-7315. *Phone:* (919) 737-2087. *Or:* Dept. of Foreign Languages and Literatures, North Carolina State University, P.O. Box 8106, Raleigh, NC 27695-8106. *Phone:* (919) 737-2475. *Telex:* 4996937 NCSTATE.

PUEBLA

558 OREGON INTERNATIONAL COUNCIL
Graduate Seminar for Teachers: Mexico and Latin America.
Location: Puebla.
Dates: 1 month, June–July.
Subjects: Spanish language on all levels; Latin American culture, current affairs, education, history.
Credit: 6 graduate credits.
Eligibility: Teachers preferred; graduates, adults.
Instruction: In English. Students attend courses arranged for the group taught by U.S. and foreign faculty and special courses for foreigners at the University of the Americas.
Highlights: Program began in 1986. Offered in cooperation with the University of the Americas. 1-day orientation in U.S. Excursions to Mexico City, Oaxaca, and local sites. Postsession review. Contact with previous participants available.
Costs: About $1,315 includes tuition, housing, round-trip transportation, excursions, fees, insurance.
Housing: In residence halls.
Deadline: April 1.
Contact: Robert Willner, Executive Director, Oregon International Council, 999 Locust St. NE, Salem, OR 97303. *Phone:* (503) 378-4960.

559 UNIVERSIDAD DE LAS AMERICAS—PUEBLA
Academic Year Abroad Program.
Location: Puebla.
Dates: August–May; student may enroll for 1 or both semesters. Summer session also available.
Subjects: French, German, Japanese, and Spanish language on all levels; full university curriculum for students fluent in Spanish.
Credit: 12–15 undergraduate credits. 12–15 graduate credits.
Eligibility: Undergraduates, graduates, adults, teachers. Minimum age 18. Requires good academic standing.
Instruction: In Spanish, English. Students attend special courses for foreigners and regular classes at the Universidad de las Americas.
Highlights: Program began in 1968. Orientation. Excursions and field trips.
Costs: $1,000 (1987) per semester, includes tuition, housing, meals, books, excursions, fees, insurance.
Housing: Sponsor assists in locating housing.
Deadline: 1 month before term begins.
Contact: Bertha Martinez, Coordinator of International Programs, or Margaret Hough, Director of International Programs, Universidad de las Americas—Puebla, Apartado Postal 100, Santa Catarina Martir, 72820 Puebla, Mexico. *Phone:* (52-22) 47-06-33.

SALTILLO

560 INSTITUTO DE FILOLOGIA HISPANICA
Programs for International Students.
Location: Saltillo.
Dates: 3, 6, or 12 weeks, year-round.
Subjects: Spanish language on all levels; Latin American studies, including art, folklore, history, literature, music, sociology; student teaching; courses for teachers of Spanish. Certificate, diploma, and master's programs available.
Credit: Available by special arrangement. Certificate/diploma.
Eligibility: Undergraduates, graduates, teachers, professionals, precollege.
Instruction: In Spanish. Students attend regular classes at the Instituto de Filologia Hispanica.
Highlights: Program began in 1968. Orientation. Excursions and field trips. Contact with previous participants available.
Costs: $598 for 3 weeks, $1,130 for 6 weeks, $1,400 for 12 weeks, includes tuition, housing, meals.
Housing: In private homes.

All program information is subject to change without notice and must be confirmed directly with the sponsor.

Deadline: 1 month before course begins.
Contact: Admissions, Instituto de Filologia Hispanica, Apdo. 144, 25000 Saltillo, Coah., Mexico. *Phone:* (52-841) 2-15-11. ($25 application fee required.) *Or:* National Registration Center for Study Abroad, 823 N. Second St., Milwaukee, WI 53202. *Phone:* (800) 558-9988/(414) 278-7070.

SAN MIGUEL DE ALLENDE

561 **ACADEMIA HISPANO AMERICANA**
Intensive Spanish Language Courses.
Location: San Miguel de Allende, Guanajuato.
Dates: 4-, 8-, and 12-week sessions, Jan. 4–Dec. 9.
Subjects: Intensive Spanish language on all levels; Mexican studies, including culture, folklore, folk music, history, literature. Internships, teaching English as a foreign language.

Credit: 14 undergraduate credits for 8 weeks, available by arrangement.
Eligibility: Undergraduates, graduates, adults, teachers, precollege. Minimum age 16.
Instruction: In Spanish. Students attend special courses for foreigners at Academia Hispano Americana.
Highlights: Program began in 1960. 1-day orientation. Excursions and cultural events. Contact with previous participants available.
Costs: About $1,020 for 8 weeks, includes tuition, housing, meals, books. Scholarships available.
Housing: In apartments, pensions, hotels, private homes.
Deadline: Until program is filled.
Contact: Gary De Mirjyn, Director, or Ann Levine, Registrar, Academia Hispano Americana, Mesones 4, San Miguel de Allende, 37700 Guanajuato, Mexico. *Phone:* (52-465) 2-03-49/2-23-33.

APPENDIX A

SOURCES OF ADDITIONAL INFORMATION

RECRUITING FAIRS

European Council of International Schools
ECIS' February recruiting fair attracts administrators from about 50 international schools, who interview candidates for teaching and administrative positions at their schools. Candidates attend by invitation only, but it is not necessary to be an ECIS member to attend.

Contact: Deborah Jordan, Staffing Services Officer, European Council of International Schools, 21B Lavant St., Petersfield, Hants. GU32 3EL, England; (44-730) 68244.

International Schools Services
ISS holds two recruiting fairs each February: one on the East Coast and the second following the annual conference of the American Association of International Education (AAIE). Each fair is attended by 50–100 representatives of overseas schools and by 300–400 primary and secondary school teachers and administrators who are registered with ISS.

Teaching candidates must have two years of current teaching experience, unless they are fully certified in mathematics, science, or business subjects.

Contact: Educational Staffing, International Schools Services, 13 Roszel Rd., Box 5910, Princeton, NJ 08543; (609) 452-0990.

Overseas Placement Service for Educators
The annual Midwest Overseas Recruiting Fair, sponsored by this University of Northern Iowa service, helps primary and secondary school teachers and administrators connect with representatives of more than 60 overseas schools. Most positions require teaching certification and experience.

Registered candidates also receive the "Vacancy Newsletter."

Contact: Overseas Placement Service for Educators, University of Northern Iowa, Cedar Falls, IA 50614-0390.

STARTING AN EXCHANGE PROGRAM

USIA University Affiliations Program
Through this program, which began in 1982, USIA provides seed money for the development of linkages between U.S. and foreign postsecondary institutions for a period of two to three years. Participating institutions exchange faculty and staff for teaching, lecturing, or research assignments of one month or longer in the fields of humanities, social sciences, education, and communications. Each institution maintains its faculty and staff on full salary and benefits during the exchange period, using the USIA grant to defray international travel and per diem expenses of exchangees.

About 20–30 grants in amounts of $50,000–$60,000 are awarded annually through a fall competition announced in the Federal Register. The U.S. institution submits a formal proposal to USIA. Each year the competition is limited to certain countries or geographic regions and to specific fields of study.

Contact: University Affiliations Program (E/AS), U.S. Information Agency, 301 Fourth St. SW, Washington, DC 20547; (202) 485-8489.

Guidelines for College and University Linkages Abroad. Washington, DC: American Council on Education. $2.00.
General information on developing formal contacts with an institution in another country.
Available from: American Council on Education, Division of International Education, One Dupont Circle NW, Suite 800, Washington, DC 20036.

PERIODICALS

Association of African Universities (AAU) Newsletter. Accra-North, Ghana: Documentation and Information Centre, Association of African Universities. Monthly.
Lists teaching and educational administration vacancies in African universities.
Available from: Documentation and Information Centre, Association of African Universities, P.O. Box 5744, Accra-North, Ghana.

The Chronicle of Higher Education. Washington, DC: The Chronicle of Higher Education. Weekly. $1.95 per issue; $50 per year.
The "Bulletin Board" classified section of this weekly newspaper regularly contains announcements of foreign college and university openings.
Available from: The Chronicle of Higher Education, 1255 23rd St. NW, Washington, DC 20037.

Current Opportunities in the ESL/EFL/Bilingual Field. Washington, DC: TESOL. Bimonthly.
This bulletin, distributed to member subscribers of Teachers of English to Speakers of Other Languages (TESOL), includes descriptions of job openings worldwide for teachers, lecturers, administrators, guidance counselors, curriculum developers, and researchers involved in English as a second/foreign language training.
Available from: TESOL, 1118 22nd St. NW, Suite 205, Washington, DC 20037; (202) 872-1271.

The Economist. London: The Economist Newspaper, Ltd. Weekly. $3 per issue; $98 per year ($60 for students).
The classified section of this magazine include listings of foreign college and university openings.
Available from: The Economist, Subscription Department, P.O. Box 904, Farmingdale, NY 11737-9804; (800) 227-7585. Also available at newsstands.

Job Information List. New York: Modern Language Association. Quarterly. $30 per year.
Subscribers choose from two lists: one for English language teachers, the other for teachers of foreign languages. Both cover openings in language teaching and related fields mainly in the U.S., but with a few listings in Canada, Israel, and other countries.
Available from: Modern Language Association, 10 Astor Place, New York, NY 10003; (212) 614-6378.

The Times Higher Education Supplement. London: The Times. Weekly. 70 p. per issue in the U.K.; $75 per year.

This weekly supplement to the London *Times* includes several pages of classified advertisements and announcements of postsecondary faculty positions available, primarily at British and Commonwealth colleges, universities, and polytechnics.

Available from: The Times Higher Education Supplement, Priory House, St. John's Lane, London EC1M 4BX, England.

GENERAL REFERENCE BOOKS

American Elementary & Secondary Community Schools Abroad. Paul T. Luebke. 2nd ed. Arlington, VA: American Association of School Administrators, 1976. $2.50.

Discusses the characteristics and distribution of U.S. citizens abroad and describes the American-sponsored overseas schools.

Available from: American Association of School Administrators, 1801 N. Moore St., Arlington, VA 22209; (703) 528-0700.

China Bound: A guide to academic life and work in the PRC. Karen Turner-Gottschang with Linda A. Reed. Washington, DC: National Academy Press, 1987. $14.95.

Specific information for teachers, researchers, and students who plan to reside in China.

Available from: National Academy Press, 2101 Constitution Ave. NW, Washington, DC 20418; (202) 334-3313.

The Directory of Work & Study in Developing Countries. David Leppard. Oxford: Vacation Work, 1986. £6.95.

A resource guide of opportunities for working or studying in developing countries, including teaching opportunities. General information and listings of possible sources of employment.

Available from: Vacation Work, 9 Park End St., Oxford, United Kingdom.

Educators' Passport to International Jobs: How to find and enjoy employment abroad. Rebecca Anthony and Gerald Roe. Princeton, NJ: Peterson's Guides, 1984. $9.95.

Provides positive, straightforward advice on every aspect of overseas employment.

Available from: Peterson's Guides Inc., Box 2123, Princeton, NJ 08543-2123; (800) 225-0261.

Faculty Handbook for Sabbaticals Abroad. Sally Innis Klitz. Storrs, CT: Office for International Education and Development, University of Connecticut, 1980.

Funding sources, writing proposals, educational exchanges, adjusting to life overseas.

Available from: Office for International Education and Development, 213 Nathan E. Whetten Graduate Center, U-6, The University of Connecticut, Storrs, CT 06268; (203) 486-3855.

Foreign Jobs: The most popular countries. Curtis W. Casewit. New York: Monarch Press, 1984. $8.95.

Extensive general information on working overseas, including teaching, and more specific information on working in some of the most popular destinations for Americans.

Available from: Monarch Press, Simon & Schuster Inc., Simon & Schuster Bldg., 1230 Avenue of the Americas, New York, NY 10020; (212) 245-6400.

A Guide to Teaching English in Japan. Charles B. Wordell, ed. Tokyo: The Japan Times, Ltd., 1985. 2,500 yen.

How to get and keep a job teaching English in Japan at all levels.

Available from: The Japan Times, Ltd., 5-4 Shibaura 4-chome, Minato-ku, Tokyo 108, Japan.

How To Find Jobs Teaching Overseas. Jim Muckle. Jim Muckle, 1988. $5.

A guide to getting teaching jobs overseas, based on the author's personal experiences of teaching abroad; also lists 150 schools and agencies.

Available from: Jim Muckle, 7021 Fellers Lane, Sebastopol, CA 95472.

International Jobs: Where they are, how to get them. Eric Kocher. Reading, MA: Addison-Wesley Publishing Co., 1984. $8.95.

General information on jobs overseas, and a listing of schools abroad and organizations that recruit teachers for overseas positions.

Available from: Addison-Wesley Publishing Co., 1 Jacob Way, Reading, MA 01867; (800) 447-2226.

A Librarian's Directory of Exchange Programs, Study Tours, Funding Sources, and Job Opportunities outside the United States. Diane Stine. Chicago: American Library Association, 1982.

Listing of permanent and temporary job exchange situations, as well as study tours abroad designed specifically for librarians.

Available from: American Library Association, Office for Library Personnel Resources, 50 E. Huron, Chicago, IL 60611; (800) 545-2433.

Looking for Employment in Foreign Countries. 7th ed. New York: World Trade Academy Press Inc., 1985. $16.50.

Includes a section of listings for teachers.

Available from: World Trade Academy Press, Inc., 50 E. 42nd St., Suite 509, New York, NY 10017; (212) 697-4999.

Opportunities Abroad for Educators: Fulbright Teacher Exchange Program. Washington, DC: U.S. Information Agency. Annual. Free.

Describes positions available worldwide under the Fulbright Teacher Exchange Program.

Available from: Teacher Exchange Branch, E/ASX, United States Information Agency, Washington, DC 20547; (202) 485-2555/6.

Overseas Employment Opportunities for Educators. Alexandria, VA: Department of Defense Dependents Schools, 1986/87. Annual. Free.

Contains complete information on U.S. Department of Defense dependents schools, including eligibility requirements; position categories; application procedures; basic program information; salaries and benefits; and housing, living, and working conditions. An application form and forms for supporting documents are attached.

Available from: Department of Defense Dependents Schools, 2461 Eisenhower Ave., Alexandria, VA 22331-1100.

The Overseas List: Opportunities for living and working in developing countries. David M. Beckmann, Timothy J. Mitchell, and Linda L. Powers. Minneapolis: Augsburg Publishing House, 1985. $11.95.

Contains information about church missions, development agencies, volunteer-sending agencies, foundations, the U.N. system, and the U.S. government; a separate chapter discusses teaching abroad. Also included is a section on living in the Third World.

Available from: Augsburg Publishing House, 57 E. Main St., Columbus, OH 43215; (800) 848-2738.

Teach in Great Britain. Gordon E. Speed. London: G.E. Speed, 1971.

Explains the British method of education and lists schools and education authorities throughout the U.K.

Available from: G.E. Speed, Publishers, 1207 Seminole Rd., Atlantic Beach, FL 32233.

Teach Overseas: The educator's world-wide handbook and directory to international teaching in overseas schools, colleges, and universities. Steve Webster. New York: Maple Tree Publishing Co., 1984. $12.95.

A comprehensive manual of educational opportunities in schools at all levels for teachers, librarians, administrators, and university professors.

Available from: Maple Tree Publishing Co., G.P.O. Box 479, New York, NY 10116; (516) 536-6280.

Teaching Opportunities in the Middle East and North Africa. Washington, DC: AMIDEAST. $14.95.

Describes jobs, requirements, and benefits at over 140 institutions on all educational levels, including positions for teachers, technical/vocational trainers, and educational administrators.

Available from: AMIDEAST, 1100 17th St. NW, Washington, DC 20036; (202) 785-0022.

Teaching Overseas: The Caribbean and Latin American area. 3rd ed. Carlton H. Bowyer and Burton B. Fox, eds. Kingston, Jamaica: Inter-Regional Center for Curriculum and Materials Development, 1984.

Information about American-sponsored primary and secondary schools in these areas.

Available from: Inter-Regional Center for Curriculum and Materials Development, Kingston, Jamaica.

Teaching Tactics for Japan's English Classrooms. John Wharton. Jobs in Japan Teaching Supplement, 1986. $6.95.

Information on teaching English in Japan and a listing of private English schools.

Available from: The Global Press, 1510 York St., Suite 204, Denver, CO 80206; (800) 227-1516.

A World of Options: Guide to international educational exchange, community service and travel for persons with disabilities. Susan Sygall. Eugene, OR: Mobility International USA, 1985.

Describes organizations offering educational exchange and international community service programs open to participants with disabilities.

Available from: Mobility International USA, P.O. Box 3551, Eugene, OR 97403; (503) 343-1284.

DIRECTORIES

Commonwealth Universities Yearbook. Anastasios Christodolou and Tom Craig, eds. London: Association of Commonwealth Universities. Annual. $185.

Information on teaching staff, courses, facilities, activities, and organizations of several hundred institituions in the British Commonwealth.

Available from: Gale Research Co., Book Tower, Detroit, MI 48226; (800) 223-4253.

Guide to Summer Camps and Summer Schools, 1987/88. 25th ed. Boston: Porter Sargent Publishers. Biennial. $21 (paperback).

Lists over 1,100 summer camps and schools by type, specialty, and individual features. Descriptions include location and enrollment, director's winter address, fees, length of camping period, and other pertinent information.

Available from: Porter Sargent Publishers, Inc., 11 Beacon St., Boston, MA 02108; (617) 523-1670.

International Handbook of Universities. 10th ed. D.J. Aitken and A. Taylor, eds. New York: Stockton Press, 1986. Biennial. $140.

A comprehensive directory of universities and other institutes of higher education presented alphabetically, country by country. Includes information on technical and professional education, as well as teacher training and general education.

Available from: Stockton Press, 15 E. 26th St., New York, NY 10010; (212) 481-1334.

ISS Directory of Overseas Schools, 1986/87. Mea Johnston, ed. Princeton, NJ: International Schools Services, 1986. $25.

Listing of international schools and educational programs for English-speaking students by country and by city. Includes background information on schools, countries, ISS, and other aspects of education.

Available from: International Schools Services, Inc., P.O. Box 5910, Princeton, NJ 08543; (609) 452-0990.

Overseas American-Sponsored Elementary and Secondary Schools Assisted by the U.S. Department of State. Washington, DC: U.S. Department of State. Annual. Free.

Complete list of U.S.-affiliated elementary and secondary schools overseas.

Available from: Office of Overseas Schools (A/OS), Room 234, SA-6, U.S. Department of State, Washington, DC 20520; (703) 235-9600.

The Prentice Hall Global Employment Guide. James N. Powell. Englewood Cliffs, NJ: Prentice-Hall, Inc., 1983. $8.95.

Listing of organizations and associations that recruit teachers for overseas assignments.

Available from: Prentice-Hall, Inc., 200 Old Tappan Rd., Old Tappan, NJ 07675; (201) 767-5054.

Schools Abroad of Interest to Americans, 1985/86. 6th ed. Boston: Porter Sargent Publishers, 1985. $29.

Listing of schools abroad. Provides brief descriptions of size, grade levels, costs, and curriculum. Special section on educational systems of other nations.

Available from: Porter Sargent Publishers, 11 Beacon St., Boston, MA 02108; (617) 523-1670.

Teachers' Guide to Overseas Teaching. 3rd ed. Louis A. Bajkai, ed. San Diego: Friends of World Teaching, 1983. $19.95.

A comprehensive listing of English-language schools and colleges overseas.

Available from: Friends of World Teaching, P.O. Box 1049, San Diego, CA 92112-1049; (619) 274-5282.

World List of Universities. 16th ed. D.J. Aitken, ed. New York: Stockton Press, 1985. $70.

A directory of universities and other institutes of higher education, presented country by country.

Available from: Stockton Press, 15 E. 26th St., New York, NY 10010; (212) 481-1334.

The World of Learning 1988. 38th ed. London: Europa Publications. $190.

Information on more than 400 international, educational, scientific, and cultural organizations, as well as full descriptions of universities and colleges in 164 countries and territories around the world.

Available from: Europa Publications Ltd., 18 Bedford Square, London WC1B 3JN, England.

IIE PUBLICATIONS

Prices of IIE publications change annually. Please write for current price list: Publications Service, Institute of International Education, 809 United Nations Plaza, New York, NY 10017.

Academic Year Abroad. E. Marguerite Howard, ed. Annual.

Describes over 1650 semester, term, and academic-year study programs overseas. Part 1 lists programs offered by accredited U.S. colleges and universities. Part 2 describes courses of study at foreign universities, language schools, nonaccredited U.S. schools, and other organizations.

Available from: Publications Service, Institute of International Education, 809 United Nations Plaza, New York, NY 10017.

Basic Facts on Study Abroad. 1987. Free.

Essential information for U.S. students planning study abroad.

Available from: Publications Service, Institute of International Education, 809 United Nations Plaza, New York, NY 10017.

British Universities Summer Schools. Annual.

Information on a joint program conducted by the universities of Birmingham (at Stratford-upon-Avon), London, and Oxford in literature, drama, and history.

Available from: U.S. Student Programs, Institute of International Education, 809 United Nations Plaza, New York, NY 10017.

Fulbright and Other Grants for Graduate Study Abroad. Annual.

This booklet describes IIE-administered fellowships available to U.S. graduate students for study abroad. It also includes information on U.S. Information Agency (USIA) Fulbright fellowships.

Available from: U.S. Student Programs, Institute of International Education, 809 United Nations Plaza, New York, NY 10017.

Fulbright Collaborative Research. Annual.

This booklet describes joint research scholarships available to U.S. citizens through this U.S. Information Agency program administered by IIE.

Available from: U.S. Student Programs, Institute of International Education, 809 United Nations Plaza, New York, NY 10017.

Study in the United Kingdom and Ireland. E. Marguerite Howard, ed. Biennial.

A guide to more than 800 programs offered throughout the year in the United Kingdom and the Republic of Ireland.

Available from: Publications Service, Institute of International Education, 809 United Nations Plaza, New York, NY 10017.

Vacation Study Abroad. E. Marguerite Howard, ed. Annual.

Provides information on over 1,000 summer and short-term postsecondary study-abroad programs around the world offered by U.S. and foreign educational institutions and other organizations.

Available from: Publications Service, Institute of International Education, 809 United Nations Plaza, New York, NY 10017.

APPENDIX B

FOREIGN EMBASSIES IN THE U.S.A.

AFGHANISTAN
Embassy of the Democratic Republic of Afghanistan
2341 Wyoming Ave. NW
Washington, DC 20008

ALGERIA
Embassy of the Democratic and Popular Republic of Algeria
2118 Kalorama Rd. NW
Washington, DC 20008

ANTIGUA AND BARBUDA
Embassy of Antigua and Barbuda
3400 International Dr. NW, Suite 2H
Washington, DC 20008

ARGENTINA
Embassy of the Argentine Republic
1600 New Hampshire Ave. NW
Washington, DC 20009

AUSTRALIA
Embassy of Australia
1601 Massachusetts Ave. NW
Washington, DC 20036

AUSTRIA
Embassy of Austria
2343 Massachusetts Ave. NW
Washington, DC 20008

BAHAMAS
Embassy of The Commonwealth of The Bahamas
600 New Hampshire Ave. NW, Suite 865
Washington, DC 20037

BAHRAIN
Embassy of the State of Bahrain
3502 International Dr. NW
Washington, DC 20008

BANGLADESH
Embassy of the People's Republic of Bangladesh
2201 Wisconsin Ave. NW
Washington, DC 20007

BARBADOS
Embassy of Barbados
2144 Wyoming Ave. NW
Washington, DC 20008

BELGIUM
Embassy of Belgium
3330 Garfield St. NW
Washington, DC 20008

BELIZE
Embassy of Belize
3400 International Dr. NW, Suite 2J
Washington, DC 20008

BENIN
Embassy of the People's Republic of Benin
2737 Cathedral Ave. NW
Washington, DC 20008

BOLIVIA
Embassy of Bolivia
3014 Massachusetts Ave. NW
Washington, DC 20008

BOTSWANA
Embassy of the Republic of Botswana
4301 Connecticut Ave. NW, Suite 404
Washington, DC 20008

BRAZIL
Embassy of Brazil
3006 Massachusetts Ave. NW
Washington, DC 20008

BRUNEI
Embassy of the State of Brunei Darussalam
2600 Virginia Ave. NW, Suite 300
Washington, DC 20037

BULGARIA
Embassy of the People's Republic of Bulgaria
1621 22nd St. NW
Washington, DC 20008

BURKINA FASO
Embassy of Burkina Faso
2340 Massachusetts Ave. NW
Washington, DC 20008

BURMA
Embassy of the Socialist Republic of the Union of Burma
2300 S St. NW
Washington, DC 20008

BURUNDI
Embassy of the Republic of Burundi
2233 Wisconsin Ave. NW, Suite 212
Washington, DC 20007

CAMEROON
Embassy of the Republic of Cameroon
2349 Massachusetts Ave. NW
Washington, DC 20008

CANADA
Embassy of Canada
1746 Massachusetts Ave. NW
Washington, DC 20036

CAPE VERDE
Embassy of the Republic of Cape Verde
3415 Massachusetts Ave. NW
Washington, DC 20007

CENTRAL AFRICAN REPUBLIC
Embassy of Central African Republic
1618 22nd St. NW
Washington, DC 20008

CHAD
Embassy of the Republic of Chad
2002 R St. NW
Washington, DC 20009

CHILE
Embassy of Chile
1732 Massachusetts Ave. NW
Washington, DC 20036

CHINA
Embassy of the People's Republic of China
2300 Connecticut Ave. NW
Washington, DC 20008

COLOMBIA
Embassy of Colombia
2118 Leroy Place NW
Washington, DC 20008

COMOROS
Embassy of the Federal and Islamic Republic of the Comoros
c/o Permanent Mission of the Federal and Islamic Republic of the
Comoros to the United Nations
336 E. 45th St., 2nd Floor
New York, NY 10017

CONGO (PEOPLE'S REPUBLIC)
Embassy of the People's Republic of the Congo
4891 Colorado Ave. NW
Washington, DC 20011

COSTA RICA
Embassy of Costa Rica
1825 Connecticut Ave. NW, Suite 211
Washington, DC 20009

CUBA
Cuban Interests Section
2630 and 2639 16th St. NW
Washington, DC 20009

CYPRUS
Embassy of the Republic of Cyprus
2211 R St. NW
Washington, DC 20008

CZECHOSLOVAKIA
Embassy of the Czechoslovak Socialist Republic
3900 Linnean Ave. NW
Washington, DC 20008

DENMARK
Royal Danish Embassy
3200 Whitehaven St. NW
Washington, DC 20008

DJIBOUTI
Embassy of the Republic of Djibouti
c/o the Permanent Mission of the Republic of Djibouti to the United
Nations
866 United Nations Plaza, Suite 4011
New York, NY 10017

DOMINICAN REPUBLIC
Embassy of the Dominican Republic
1715 22nd St. NW
Washington, DC 20008

ECUADOR
Embassy of Ecuador
2535 15th St. NW
Washington, DC 20009

EGYPT
Embassy of the Arab Republic of Egypt
2310 Decatur Place NW
Washington, DC 20008

EL SALVADOR
Embassy of El Salvador
2308 California St. NW
Washington, DC 20008

EQUATORIAL GUINEA
Embassy of Equatorial Guinea
801 Second Ave., Suite 1403
New York, NY 10017

ESTONIA
Legation of Estonia Office of Consulate General
9 Rockefeller Plaza
New York, NY 10017

ETHIOPIA
Embassy of Ethiopia
2134 Kalorama Rd. NW
Washington, DC 20008

FIJI
Embassy of Fiji
2233 Wisconsin Ave. NW
Washington, DC 20007

FINLAND
Embassy of Finland
3216 New Mexico Ave. NW
Washington, DC 20016

FRANCE
Embassy of France
4101 Reservoir Rd. NW
Washington, DC 20007

GABON
Embassy of the Gabonese Republic
2034 20th St. NW
Washington, DC 20009

GAMBIA
Embassy of The Gambia
1030 15th St. NW, Suite 720
Washington, DC 20005

GERMANY (DEMOCRATIC REPUBLIC)
Embassy of the German Democratic Republic
1717 Massachusetts Ave. NW
Washington, DC 20036

GERMANY (FEDERAL REPUBLIC)
Embassy of the Federal Republic of Germany
4645 Reservoir Rd. NW
Washington, DC 20007

GHANA
Embassy of Ghana
2460 16th St. NW
Washington, DC 20009

GREECE
Embassy of Greece
2221 Massachusetts Ave. NW
Washington, DC 20008

GRENADA
Embassy of Grenada
1701 New Hampshire Ave. NW
Washington, DC 20009

GUATEMALA
Embassy of Guatemala
2220 R St. NW
Washington, DC 20008

GUINEA
Embassy of the Republic of Guinea
2112 Leroy Place NW
Washington, DC 20008

GUINEA-BISSAU
Embassy of the Republic of Guinea-Bissau
c/o the Permanent Mission of Guinea-Bissau
211 E. 43rd St., Suite 604
New York, NY 10017

GUYANA
Embassy of Guyana
2490 Tracy Place NW
Washington, DC 20008

HAITI
Embassy of Haiti
2311 Massachusetts Ave. NW
Washington, DC 20008

HONDURAS
Embassy of Honduras
4301 Connecticut Ave. NW, Suite 100
Washington, DC 20008

HUNGARY
Embassy of the Hungarian People's Republic
3910 Shoemaker St. NW
Washington, DC 20008

ICELAND
Embassy of Iceland
2022 Connecticut Ave. NW
Washington, DC 20008

INDIA
Embassy of India
2107 Massachusetts Ave. NW
Washington, DC 20008

INDONESIA
Embassy of the Republic of Indonesia
2020 Massachusetts Ave. NW
Washington, DC 20036

IRAQ
Embassy of the Republic of Iraq
1801 P St. NW
Washington, DC 20036

IRELAND
Embassy of Ireland
2234 Massachusetts Ave. NW
Washington, DC 20008

ISRAEL
Embassy of Israel
3514 International Dr. NW
Washington, DC 20008

ITALY
Embassy of Italy
1601 Fuller St. NW
Washington, DC 20009

IVORY COAST
Embassy of the Republic of Cote d'Ivoire
2424 Massachusetts Ave. NW
Washington, DC 20008

JAMAICA
Embassy of Jamaica
1850 K St. NW, Suite 355
Washington, DC 20006

JAPAN
Embassy of Japan
2520 Massachusetts Ave. NW
Washington, DC 20008

JORDAN
Embassy of the Hashemite Kingdom of Jordan
3504 International Dr. NW
Washington, DC 20008

KENYA
Embassy of Kenya
2249 R St. NW
Washington, DC 20008

KOREA
Embassy of the Republic of Korea
2370 Massachusetts Ave. NW
Washington, DC 20008

KUWAIT
Embassy of the State of Kuwait
2940 Tilden St. NW
Washington, DC 20008

LAOS
Embassy of the Lao People's Democratic Republic
2222 S St. NW
Washington, DC 20008

LATVIA
Legation of Latvia
4325 17th St. NW
Washington, DC 20011

LEBANON
Embassy of Lebanon
2560 28th St. NW
Washington, DC 20008

LESOTHO
Embassy of the Kingdom of Lesotho
1430 K St. NW, 6th Floor
Washington, DC 20005

LIBERIA
Embassy of the Republic of Liberia
5201 16th St. NW
Washington, DC 20011

LITHUANIA
Legation of Lithuania
2622 16th St. NW
Washington, DC 20009

LUXEMBOURG
Embassy of Luxembourg
2200 Massachusetts Ave. NW
Washington, DC 20008

MADAGASCAR
Embassy of the Democratic Republic of Madagascar
2374 Massachusetts Ave. NW
Washington, DC 20008

MALAWI
Malawi Embassy
2408 Massachusetts Ave. NW
Washington, DC 20008

MALAYSIA
Embassy of Malaysia
2401 Massachusetts Ave. NW
Washington, DC 20008

MALI
Embassy of the Republic of Mali
2130 R St. NW
Washington, DC 20008

MALTA
Embassy of Malta
2017 Connecticut Ave. NW
Washington, DC 20008

MARSHALL ISLANDS
Representative Office of the Republic of the Marshall Islands
1901 Pennsylvania Ave. NW, Suite 1004
Washington, DC 20006

MAURITANIA
Embassy of the Islamic Republic of Mauritania
2129 Leroy Place NW
Washington, DC 20008

MAURITIUS
Embassy of Mauritius
4301 Connecticut Ave. NW
Washington, DC 20008

MEXICO
Embassy of Mexico
2829 16th St. NW
Washington, DC 20009

MICRONESIA
Representative Office of the Federated States of Micronesia
706 G St. SE
Washington, DC 20003

MOROCCO
Embassy of Morocco
1601 21st St. NW
Washington, DC 20009

MOZAMBIQUE
Embassy of the People's Republic of Mozambique
1990 M St. NW, Suite 570
Washington, DC 20036

NEPAL
Royal Nepalese Embassy
2131 Leroy Place NW
Washington, DC 20008

NETHERLANDS
Embassy of the Netherlands
4200 Linnean Ave. NW
Washington, DC 20008

NEW ZEALAND
Embassy of New Zealand
37 Observatory Circle NW
Washington, DC 20008

NICARAGUA
Embassy of Nicaragua
1627 New Hampshire Ave. NW
Washington, DC 20009

NIGER
Embassy of the Republic of Niger
2204 R St. NW
Washington, DC 20008

NIGERIA
Embassy of the Federal Republic of Nigeria
2201 M St. NW
Washington, DC 20037

NORWAY
Royal Norwegian Embassy
2720 34th St. NW
Washington, DC

OMAN
Embassy of the Sultanate of Oman
2342 Massachusetts Ave. NW
Washington, DC 20008

PAKISTAN
Embassy of Pakistan
2315 Massachusetts Ave. NW
Washington, DC 20008

PANAMA
Embassy of Panama
2862 McGill Terrace NW
Washington, DC 20008

PAPUA NEW GUINEA
Embassy of Papua New Guinea
1330 Connecticut Ave. NW, Suite 350
Washington, DC 20036

PARAGUAY
Embassy of Paraguay
2400 Massachusetts Ave. NW
Washington, DC 20008

PERU
Embassy of Peru
1700 Massachusetts Ave. NW
Washington, DC 20036

PHILIPPINES
Embassy of Philippines
1617 Massachusetts Ave. NW
Washington, DC 20036

POLAND
Embassy of the Polish People's Republic
2640 16th St. NW
Washington, DC 20009

PORTUGAL
Embassy of Portugal
2125 Kalorama Rd. NW
Washington, DC 20008

QATAR
Embassy of the State of Qatar
600 New Hampshire Ave. NW, Suite 1180
Washington, DC 20037

ROMANIA
Embassy of the Socialist Republic of Romania
1607 23rd St. NW
Washington, DC 20008

RWANDA
Embassy of the Republic of Rwanda
1714 New Hampshire Ave. NW
Washington, DC 20009

SAINT KITTS AND NEVIS
Embassy of St. Kitts and Nevis
2501 M St. NW, Suite 540
Washington, DC 20037

SAINT LUCIA
Embassy of Saint Lucia
2100 M St. NW, Suite 309
Washington, DC 20037

SAO TOME AND PRINCIPE
Embassy of Sao Tome and Principe
801 Second Ave., Suite 1504
New York, NY 10017

SAUDI ARABIA
Embassy of Saudi Arabia
601 New Hampshire Ave. NW
Washington, DC 20037

SENEGAL
Embassy of the Republic of Senegal
2112 Wyoming Ave. NW
Washington, DC 20008

SEYCHELLES
Embassy of the Republic of Seychelles
c/o the Permanent Mission of Seychelles to the United Nations
820 Second Ave., Suite 203
New York, NY 10017

SIERRA LEONE
Embassy of Sierra Leone
1701 19th St. NW
Washington, DC 20009

SINGAPORE
Embassy of Singapore
1824 R St. NW
Washington, DC 20009

SOMALIA
Embassy of the Somali Democratic Republic
600 New Hampshire Ave. NW, Suite 710
Washington, DC 20037

SOUTH AFRICA
Embassy of the Republic of South Africa
3051 Massachusetts Ave. NW
Washington, DC 20008

SPAIN
Embassy of Spain
2700 15th St. NW
Washington, DC 20009

SRI LANKA
Embassy of the Democratic Socialist Republic of Sri Lanka
2148 Wyoming Ave. NW
Washington, DC 20008

SUDAN
Embassy of the Republic of the Sudan
2210 Massachusetts Ave. NW
Washington, DC 20008

SURINAME
Embassy of the Republic of Suriname
4301 Connecticut Ave. NW, Suite 108
Washington, DC 20008

SWAZILAND
Embassy of the Kingdom of Swaziland
4301 Connecticut Ave. NW
Washington, DC 20008

SWEDEN
Embassy of Sweden
600 New Hampshire Ave. NW, Suite 1200
Washington, DC 20037

SWITZERLAND
Embassy of Switzerland
2900 Cathedral Ave. NW
Washington, DC 20008

SYRIA
Embassy of the Syrian Arab Republic
2215 Wyoming Ave. NW
Washington, DC 20008

TANZANIA
Embassy of the United Republic of Tanzania
2139 R St. NW
Washington, DC 20008

THAILAND
Embassy of Thailand
2300 Kalorama Rd. NW
Washington, DC 20008

TOGO
Embassy of the Republic of Togo
2208 Massachusetts Ave. NW
Washington, DC 20008

TRINIDAD AND TOBAGO
Embassy of Trinidad and Tobago
1708 Massachusetts Ave. NW
Washington, DC 20036

TUNISIA
Embassy of Tunisia
1515 Massachusetts Ave. NW
Washington, DC 20005

TURKEY
Embassy of the Republic of Turkey
1606 23rd St. NW
New York, NY 20008

UGANDA
Embassy of the Republic of Uganda
5909 16th NW
Washington, DC 20011

UNION OF SOVIET SOCIALIST REPUBLICS
Embassy of the Union of Soviet Socialist Republics
1125 16th St. NW
Washington, DC 20036

UNITED ARAB EMIRATES
Embassy of the United Arab Emirates
600 New Hampshire Ave. NW, Suite 740
Washington, DC 20037

UNITED KINGDOM
Embassy of the United Kingdom
3100 Massachusetts Ave. NW
Washington, DC 20008

URUGUAY
Embassy of Uruguay
1918 F St. NW
Washington, DC 20006

VATICAN
Embassy of the Vatican City (Apostolic Nunciature)
3339 Massachusetts Ave. NW
Washington, DC 20008

VENEZUELA
Embassy of Venezuela
2445 Massachusetts Ave. NW
Washington, DC 20008

WESTERN SAMOA
Embassy of Western Samoa
c/o the Permanent Mission of Samoa to the United Nations
820 2nd Ave.
New York, NY 10017

YEMEN
Embassy of the Yemen Arab Republic
600 New Hampshire Ave. NW, Suite 840
Washington, DC 20037

YUGOSLAVIA
Embassy of the Socialist Federal Republic of Yugoslavia
2410 California St. NW
Washington, DC 20008

ZAIRE
Embassy of the Republic of Zaire
1800 New Hampshire Ave. NW
Washington, DC 20009

ZAMBIA
Embassy of the Republic of Zambia
2419 Massachusetts Ave. NW
Washington, DC 20008

ZIMBABWE
Embassy of Zimbabwe
2852 McGill Terrace NW
Washington, DC 20008

INDEX

SCHOOLS AND ORGANIZATIONS

References are to entry numbers.

COMPLETE THIS ORDER FORM AND MAIL TO:
Publications Service, IIE
809 United Nations Plaza
New York, N. Y. 10017

All orders must be prepaid. Check/money order should be made payable to **Institute of International Education.** IIE pays domestic postage. **Overseas add $7.00.**

For more information about IIE books, call (212) 984-5412.

Quantity	Title	Price	Total
	ACADEMIC YEAR ABROAD	$19.95	
	VACATION STUDY ABROAD	$19.95	
	STUDY IN THE U.K.	$14.95	
	TEACHING ABROAD	$21.95	
		Total Books	$

Name _____

Address _____

City/State/Country _____

Zip _____ Telephone _____

TA 88

COMPLETE THIS ORDER FORM AND MAIL TO:
Publications Service, IIE
809 United Nations Plaza
New York, N. Y. 10017

All orders must be prepaid. Check/money order should be made payable to **Institute of International Education.** IIE pays domestic postage. **Overseas add $7.00.**

For more information about IIE books, call (212) 984-5412.

Quantity	Title	Price	Total
	ACADEMIC YEAR ABROAD	$19.95	
	VACATION STUDY ABROAD	$19.95	
	STUDY IN THE U.K.	$14.95	
	TEACHING ABROAD	$21.95	
		Total Books	$

Name _____

Address _____

City/State/Country _____

Zip _____ Telephone _____

TA 88

The Institute of International Education (IIE) is the largest U.S. higher educational exchange agency. A nonprofit organization with over 550 U.S. college and university members, IIE has provided information on educational exchange to higher education and the public for over 65 years. The Institute administers grants and fellowships that aid 9,000 individuals from the United States and 120 other nations annually.

USIA Fulbright Program. IIE assists the U.S. Information Agency (USIA) in the administration of the Fulbright Program of grants for graduate study abroad for U.S. students. Enrolled students who want to apply for Fulbright and other IIE-related graduate awards tenable in 1989/90 can request information and applications from their campus Fulbright Program Adviser after May 1 and before October 15, 1988. Students not currently enrolled may contact IIE's U.S. Student Programs Office for applicant information.

Information Center. Students and educators visiting New York City are encouraged to make use of the IIE International Education Information Center in planning study abroad. The center is open from 10 a.m.–4 p.m. Monday, Tuesday, Thursday, and Friday, 10 a.m.–7 p.m. Wednesday, extended hours underwritten by the Reader's Digest Foundation, each weekday except holidays. The center cannot provide research assistance by phone or letter.

IIE Offices. IIE services are offered through U.S. offices located in New York; Washington, D.C.; Atlanta; Chicago; Denver; Houston; and San Francisco. Overseas educational information centers are maintained in Bangkok, Thailand; Guangzhou, China; Hong Kong; and Mexico City. Program management offices are located in Bridgetown, Barbados; Harare, Zimbabwe; and Jakarta, Indonesia. For further information, contact the Communications Division at IIE's central office in New York City.

**INSTITUTE OF INTERNATIONAL EDUCATION
809 UNITED NATIONS PLAZA, NEW YORK, N.Y. 10017**